DANIEL ROSE, PH.D

AN EDUCATOR'S COMPANION

A GUIDE TO THE KOREN YOUTH SIDDUR

SEPHARADIM

KOREN PUBLISHERS JERUSALEM

An Educator's Companion
A Guide to the Koren Youth Siddur
Nusaḥ Sepharadim

POB 4044, Jerusalem 91040, Israel
POB 8531, New Milford, CT 06776, USA
www.korenpub.com

Large size, paperback, ISBN 978 965 301 757 3

Introduction to the Koren Magerman Educational Siddur Series

"Prayer is the language of the soul in conversation with God. It is the most intimate gesture of the religious life, and the most transformative." (Rabbi Jonathan Sacks)

These are the words with which Rabbi Sacks begins his introduction to the Koren Sacks Siddur. The act of praying can be transformative intellectually as well as spiritually and emotionally. To engage in the act of praying is to testify to the fundamentals of our faith: That the world was created by a benevolent God who participates in the history of the universe He created. There is purpose to our existence and destiny to our lives. But prayer can also be a crying out from deep within the soul. It is the aim of this siddur series to serve as a tool to encourage and facilitate our children's engagement in *tefilla* both cognitively and emotionally, leading to an overall spiritual development.

This Koren Magerman Educational Siddur Series is an exciting new project that signals a refreshing and innovative approach to *tefilla* education in the school, home and synagogue. Each siddur in the series is appropriately designed for its developmental stage of the day-school journey, and beyond. With emphasis placed firmly on the critical foundations of Reflection, Connection, and Learning, this series of siddurim creates an impactful prayer experience that places God and the user at its center.

This second siddur in the series, the Koren Youth Siddur, has been designed to be developmentally appropriate for use in school, shul, and the home, for children in grades 3–5 (8–11 years old). This siddur is a bridge between the Koren Children's Siddur for grades K–2, and the Koren middle school siddur for grades 6–8, which then transitions into the Koren Ani Tefilla Siddur (aimed at grades 9–12). The Koren Youth Siddur combines stimulating and beautiful illustrations with thought-provoking educational components on each page, to provide teachers and parents with an educational resource as much as a conventional siddur. The siddur is also accompanied by this Educator's Companion, a comprehensive guide for teachers and parents, to maximize the educational potential of this siddur.

The Educator's Companion complements the siddur as an educational resource, to provide support to the educator and parent in the form of a thorough explanation of every page of the siddur, and suggestions of how to use the siddur in a day-school or congregational context. While the language of the companion may often be more appropriate for the teacher in a classroom context, the parent in the synagogue or in the home is also at the forefront of the design of the siddur and the writing of the companion, and our hope is that the companion will be as useful to the parent as to the teacher.

Acknowledgments

Many people contributed to both the siddur itself, and to this Educator's Companion and we would like to take this opportunity to express our thanks here. First and biggest acknowledgments must go to Rinat Gilboa and Tani Bayer for the way the siddur looks. Both its beauty and visual educational utility are down to them. The siddur was extensively reviewed by the members of the Educational Editorial Board, namely Rabbi Boruch Sufrin, Rabbi Adam Englander, Rabbi Benji Levy and Rabbi Dr. Jay Goldmintz. Their feedback was invaluable to the development of the siddur. The following Tefilla Education specialists also provided invaluable input and deserve much thanks: Eli Broner, Chayim Dimont, Sharon Richter, David Saltzman, and Hadassah Smolarcik. Special thanks to Rabbi Dr. Jay Goldmintz, Rachel Meghnagi, Aryeh Grossman and Rabbi David Fuchs for reviewing this Educator's Companion, and sharing their insightful feedback and comments.

The Educational Vision

When we consider the paths toward a relationship with God, we need not only consider the knowledge that will help us understand God but the skills that will help us interact with and access God too. We recognize that prophecy is a skill beyond most so we settle for the ability to read the siddur and to perform the mechanics of *tefilla*. We assume that regular performance of these actions will lead to emotional and spiritual connections with God. After all, "אחרי הפעולות נמשכים הלבבות – The heart is drawn after action" (*Sefer HaḤinukh* mitzva 16). We expect that a child who reads his or her prayers regularly will have a meaningful spiritual experience as a result. Of course, many educators, parents, and children know this not to be entirely true. Indeed, even those who are adept at reading the *tefillot* and navigating the choreography throughout the siddur, still do not necessarily experience God with any greater sense of spirituality than those who struggle through the siddur. Thus, we are left with the question, if we accept the concept of אחרי הפעולות נמשכים הלבבות, then what are those actions that will lead to inspiration and connection?

An encounter with God requires preparation that amounts to building a relationship with Him. Without such a relationship, how can one expect to have deep meaningful conversations, sharing the most intimate details of one's life? How can one expect to experience God in prayer without preparing for such an encounter by building a relationship with God in other ways? We transact all the time with strangers – the checkout person at the store, for example. We want *tefilla,* though, to be more than a transactional experience for our children and thus aspire for them to have a relationship with God as a Father, as a King, and as something greater, in order for them to experience God in meaningful ways during *tefilla*. Engaging children in conversations about God, sharing with children the connectors and disconnectors that you experience related to God, bringing God into the mundane as well as the lofty will help children appreciate that which is transcendent and prepare them for encounters with God. Then, built on that relationship, prayer can become a heavenly experience. These are the types of actions that will lead to the emotional connection before and during *tefilla* – אחרי הפעולות נמשכים הלבבות.

So what, then, of the siddur itself? How can the siddur support this heavenly experience? The underlying assumption of this series of siddurim is that *tefilla* is more than a reading exercise, and the object of *tefilla* is not simply mastery of the *tefillot* themselves. Rather, God and the *mitpallel* are partners in the act of *tefilla,* together with the family, community, and others that comprise the world of the *mitpallel.*

Unfortunately, too often in our schools, homes, and synagogues, the words of the siddur are the focus of *tefilla* as we pray. We focus on keeping our students' exactly on the right word, pronouncing the words perfectly, and following the mechanics and choreography of prayer. No doubt, these are important and we are not suggesting that reading is not a component of prayer education worthy of time in the curriculum. We would, in fact, urge schools to find ways outside of *tefilla* to have students practice reading the words of the siddur. That is, preparation for accuracy in reading the *tefillot* is important. However, this should not be the focus during *tefilla*. And, as we said earlier, such accuracy alone will likely not lead to experiencing God during *tefilla*.

The Koren Children's Siddur, and the series of siddurim that follow, highlight the child as an actor in prayer, asking questions and making statements that urge the child to think and engage with the world and the God that created it, directs it, and supports it daily.

It is important to note that we have purposefully chosen particular *tefillot*, guided by the centrality of those *tefillot* objectively, and also by their relevance to the daily lives of children. We have followed the guiding principle of "less is more" with regard to quantity of prayers, as the goal is to give the children a developmentally appropriate amount of text and keep the focus on the making of meaning. We appreciate those who question the omission of certain *tefillot* that their class currently recites or that a parent recalls fondly from their own upbringing. But we encourage you to consider whether the additional prayers you would include would detract from the focus we have articulated. With the goal of strengthening the spiritual connection in mind, we, along with our practitioner colleagues on the Educational Editorial Board of this series have concluded that a recalibration of *tefilla* education and the role of the siddur is necessary.

We all aspire for a relationship with God for ourselves and for our children. Rather than counting solely on the words of prayer to build a relationship with God, we believe a strengthened relationship can prepare us for and support us through prayer. This series of siddurim is a requisite tool for enabling this shift, as it empowers the student to go beyond the words to build on his or her relationship with God.

Dr. Scott Goldberg
Chairman, Koren Educational Editorial Board
Dr. Daniel Rose
Director of Educational Projects, Koren Publishers Jerusalem
Adar 5775 (March 2015)

The Koren Youth Siddur Explained

The Liturgical Text

One of the central educational goals of the Koren Magerman Educational Siddur Series is that the student, by progressing through the four developmentally appropriate siddurim, will graduate the program of *tefilla* education with the breadth and depth of *tefilla* skills and emotional and cognitive relationship to the liturgy necessary to feel total comfort and engagement with the adult siddur. Motivated by this goal, we have tried at every possible appropriate opportunity to create bridges between each of the siddurim, from the Koren Children's Siddur, to the adult Koren Siddur.

As much as possible, the structure of the adult Koren Siddur has been retained, with the Hebrew text of the *tefillot* on the left-hand page, and educational resources (see below) on the facing page (where the translation is found in the adult siddur). This aesthetic, together with the use of the Koren font and paragraph formatting, will allow the student to be immediately familiar and at ease with the adult siddur whenever they encounter it. The dimensions of all the siddurim in the series also match those of the adult Koren Siddur for the same reason.

The font size varies depending on the amount of text on the page. In principle, the font size chosen is as large as possible without unduly compromising the other elements of the page such as the illustration and rubric (instructional sentence), and while at the same time maintaining the feel that this siddur is not a first-stage siddur, but rather for children who already have basic Hebrew literacy and *tefilla* literacy skills.

Line numbering has been used once again, as in the Koren Children's Siddur, as an educational tool to help the child and teacher alike. When it is obvious that a single unit *tefilla* has been split on to one or more pages, the line numbers have continued from the first page onto subsequent pages. This is so the child gets a sense of this *tefilla* as a single unit. Examples of this are *Ashrei* on p.41–43 and *Aleinu*, on p.143–145.

Educational Components And Resources On The Page

On each page of the siddur several educational elements have been built into the page, either for teachers to reference in the classroom as they would a textbook, or simply for the student to find engaging should their mind wander during the *tefilla*. If the student does find themselves losing focus, these resources function as a constructive distraction for them. Better they should still be engaged in the siddur page than with other external distractions. Great thought has been put into each and every page to maximize the educational potential of the siddur as a resource in school. No element of this siddur has been inserted for merely aesthetic purposes alone, but rather each is designed to be used as a resource for the educator.

The Illustrations

For each page of the siddur the illustrator was given a choice of several educational themes inspired by the text of the *tefilla* found on that page; these were based on the general meaning behind the prayer, or a specific line from the text, or a related educational objective. A guide to understanding each illustration and its educational potential is found in this Educator's Companion. If the illustration was inspired by or relates to a specific line of text from the liturgy, that line of the text appears in a color taken from the illustration, making a clear link in an aesthetically pleasing yet subtle way. This is not to overemphasize this line of the text or suggest it is more important or prominent in any way, but merely to draw attention to the thematic link between the illustration and the text of the *tefilla*.

The Navigation Bar

The Navigation Bar appears at the bottom of every left-hand page. This is a subtle navigational tool designed to familiarize the student with the structure of *Tefillat Shaḥarit*, enabling their awareness of where in the process of *tefilla* they are at any given point. The Navigation Bar illustrates the concept of ascent to the presence of God (while saying the *Shema* and *Amida*) and then descent back to the routine of everyday life.

The aesthetic of the Navigation Bar has been inspired by this idea of ascent/descent in *tefilla* as expressed by Rabbi Jonathan Sacks in his Introduction to the Koren Siddur.[1] Rabbi Sacks sees the structure of *tefilla* through the metaphor of Yaakov's ladder. Prayer is the ladder, and we are the angels, ascending to heaven and then descending back to earth. This reflects the structure of *tefilla* as creation-revelation-redemption. *Birkhot HaShaḥar* and *Pesukei DeZimra*, with the theme of creation, allow us to ascend to the summit of the ladder, and stand in the presence of God while we say the *Amida*. From here prayer begins its descent as we turn to the theme of redemption with *Keriat HaTorah*, *Ashrei* and *Aleinu*, allowing us to redeem our everyday lives by bringing the emotional-spiritual experience of *tefilla* (as experienced in the presence of God while at the summit of the ladder) into the routine of our everyday lives. We are now ready to reenter life and its challenges.

Each of the icons found on the Navigation Bar represents one of the nine identified sections of *Tefillat Shaḥarit*. The icon representing the current section of *tefilla* will be indicated by a stronger shade, while the other seven icons will be dimmed. This will encourage the child to see and be aware of exactly where they are in the structure of the *tefilla*.

The icons and meaning behind them are found here:

הכנה לתפילה – Preparation for Tefilla (pre-*Birkhot HaShaḥar tefillot*) is represented by a character praying before getting out of bed.

ברכות השחר – Morning Blessings are represented by the morning sun.

פסוקי דזמרה – Verses of Praise (or Verses of Song) are represented by a musical note.

קריאת שמע – The *Shema* is represented by a character lifting the hand to cover the eyes.

עמידה – The *Amida* is represented by a character standing during this *tefilla*.

קריאת התורה – The Reading of the Torah (or verses said when removing the *Sefer Torah* from the *Aron Kodesh*) is represented by a *Sefer Torah*.

אשרי – the second appearance of *Ashrei* is represented by a happy character with hands up rejoicing.

1. This is a well-known idea which was developed by the early kabbalists, and also succinctly expressed in the siddur of Rabbi Yaakov Emden.

שיר של יום – The Daily Psalm that concludes the *tefilla* is represented by the page of a calendar with a musical note on it.

עלינו – *Aleinu* is represented by a bowing character.

The second section of the siddur that contains non-weekday prayers, such as Shabbat and Ḥagim *tefillot*, will have a different navigation bar containing the following five icons:

ליל שבת – The Shabbat Evening *tefillot* are represented by an icon containing Shabbat candles.

יום שבת – The remaining *tefillot* for Shabbat day are represented by an icon containing the traditional Shabbat items of a *Kiddush* cup and *ḥallot* (despite these also being relevant for Shabbat Evening).

חגים – *Tefillot* for Ḥagim (including Rosh Ḥodesh) is represented by an icon containing a *ḥanukkia* and a moon.

ברכת המזון – *Birkat HaMazon* is represented by a cup for the ritual washing of hands.

קריאת שמע על המיטה – The final page of our siddur is the bedtime *Shema*, which has its own icon that represents nighttime with a moon and stars.

Kavanot

Every page of the siddur (where space allows) has one or two thought elements to encourage the child to engage in the *tefilla* emotionally and cognitively. We have termed these "*Kavanot*," as they are designed to "direct" the child toward a particular idea from the *tefilla*, or line of thought, encouraging them toward a process of reflection, connection and learning.

There are three kinds of *kavanot* on any given page. Each has its own icon and font color and style to make it clear to the reader the type of educational element they are reading. When appropriate, the *kavana* is anchored to a specific phrase or line of the *tefilla* text through its highlighting in the appropriate color.

Wherever possible the page has been structured consistently so the child can become familiar with the elements on the page and is aware of what to expect even before they begin reading. For example, the Conceptual translation is found on the top right-hand corner of the facing page to the *tefilla* text (except in the Shabbat section where it appears alongside the *tefilla* text), and the other *kavanot* (stories and thought questions) are always found in the lower half of the page, much in the same way as the commentary is always found "below the line" in the Koren Ani Tefilla Siddur for high-school age students and beyond. Each of the three *kavanot* has its own icon, making it immediately recognizable to the reader.

The three kinds of *kavanot* are:

Conceptual Translation: This is a non-literal Conceptual translation that focuses on capturing the essence of the meaning of each *tefilla*, or one or two of the core concepts of the *tefilla*. The goal of this siddur is that the focus of the *tefilla* experience should be the child's relationship with Hashem rather than the text of the *tefilla* itself. Therefore a conceptual translation rather than a literal word-by-word translation was chosen, as a more powerful tool for advancing the student's relationship beyond the text of the *tefilla* itself. For this reason, developmentally appropriate words have often been chosen at the expense of more literal words available. While these words may be less faithful to the Hebrew text, they are better at achieving the goal of meaning-making for this age group. A Conceptual translation is not found on every page or for every *tefilla* in the siddur. The aim is to provide translation at strategic locations in the siddur, in order to provide the child with an understanding of the essence of the *tefilla*, and encourage connection to the *tefilla* and to Hashem through the *tefilla*. The Conceptual Translation is always color coded in brown.

Thought Questions: Building on the *kavanot* in the Koren Children's Siddur, and toward the high- school Koren Ani Tefilla Siddur, thought questions are also a critical part of the

Koren Youth Siddur. These encourage children to be reflective and to relate in a personal way to the *tefillot*. Often, but not always, a quote will precede the thought questions, in order to stimulate the thought in a specific direction, and to provide another educational resource on the page. These quotes are often verses from Tanakh, Talmudic and midrashic sources, or quotes from contemporary thinkers. The educational thinking behind the quotes and the thought questions, as well as creative ideas for how they can be used in the classroom is found in the page-by-page guide to the siddur below. The quote and thought questions will often complement each other and lead the reader in the same direction of thought. However, on occasion, the quote, while relevant to an aspect of the *tefilla* considered in the thought question, will stand alone as a resource for the teacher to use, while the thought question will not explore the idea in the quote, but rather relate only to the *tefilla* text itself. Thought Questions are always color coded in olive green.

Stories: The narrative is an ancient and effective method to encourage the reader to relate experientially to the themes contained in the siddur in a personal and direct way. Each story found in the siddur explores one or more educational themes that are contained in the *tefilla* text on that page. The educational thinking behind the choice of the story, as well as creative ideas for how they can be used in the classroom is found in the page-by-page guide to the siddur below. Stories are always color coded in rust.

Many primary and secondary sources are quoted as both stories, and in the Thought Questions. The type of source can be detected by the format in which it is presented. The following guide will help the reader understand the source of the quote:

- **Verses from Tanakh** are always quoted in their original Hebrew and are followed by the source.
- **Mishna** is quoted in English translation, in quotation marks, and is immediately followed by the source.
- **Talmudic sources**, including Midrash (but not including Mishna) is found in italics and quotation marks. The source is not quoted on the page but can be found in this Educator's Companion.
- Direct and Conceptual **secondary quotes** (both modern and medieval) are found in quotation marks. The source is not quoted on the page but can be found in this Educator's Companion.
- **Retold stories** from non-classical texts are presented in italics without quotation marks. The source is not quoted on the page but can be found in this Educator's Companion.
- **Imagination exercises** are presented on the page without quotation marks and in roman type.

Rubrics

On many pages a green rubric (instructional sentence) is provided, aimed at aiding the student (or helping the teacher to aid the student) to understand the choreography of the *tefilla* service, and in some cases a little of the background behind the *tefilla*. In several instances in the siddur, visual icons are used to illustrate the instructions found in the rubric. These can be found here:

Boys say

Girls say

Amida (and *Aleinu*) bowing icons

Conclusion of the *Amida* bowing (bowing forward, left and right)

Bridges to the other siddurim in the *Koren Magerman Educational Siddur Series*

The Koren Youth Siddur is the second stage of a four-stage, developmentally designed program of *tefilla* education. There are several themes and elements that provide concurrent themes that appear in all four of the siddurim, and others that form bridges between each siddur and the next.

The format and presentation of the adult Koren Siddur is present in all four of these siddurim in the series. The Hebrew text of the *tefillot* is almost always found only on the left-hand page, and the educational resources are generally found on the facing page (where the translation appears in the adult siddur). This aesthetic, together with the use of the Koren font and paragraph formatting, will allow the student to be immediately familiar and at ease with the adult siddur whenever they encounter it. The size and dimensions of all the siddurim in the series also match those of the adult Koren Siddur for the same reason. New to the Koren Youth Siddur (KYS) that was not a feature of the Koren Children's Siddur (KCS), is the familiar Table of Contents format, and the "*Sha'ar*" page for each of the four sections of the siddur. These are all features that are taken from adult Koren siddurim.

The illustrations, both in style, and often content, create a bridge between the KYS and the KCS. The illustrator, Rinat Gilboa, worked hard to create more mature and developmentally appropriate illustrations, while replicating the beauty and meaning found in the illustrations of the KCS. The same two characters from the Children's Siddur, the boy and girl, are also found in many of the illustrations in the KYS but are obviously more mature in their appearance. There are also some examples of matching illustrations in both siddurim, such as the boy and girl walking to synagogue on Shabbat, found on p.79 of the KCS and p.193 of the KYS. The navigation bar found in the KCS is also found in the same place on the page of the KYS. These examples of bridges between the KCS and the KYS eases the transition for those children that have graduated to the KYS from the KCS. Finally, the thought questions and stories found as *kavanot* in the KYS are also found in all four of the siddurim on the series, using developmentally appropriate language and concepts, all created with Reflection, Connection, and Learning in mind.

Page-by-Page Guide

This remainder of this Educator's Companion will explore and explain each page spread from the siddur in detail, and provide ideas and strategies for the educator to best maximize the educational potential of each page. Each page of this guide will present the following resources in order to do this:

- The text of the *tefilla* translated (translation by Rabbi Jonathan Sacks taken from the Koren Sacks Siddur)
- Possible educational themes from the text listed (for exploration independently from the other elements found on the page of the siddur)
- Highlighting of the text explained
- The illustration fully explained, together with suggested discussions that could emanate from it
- The Conceptual Translation reproduced alongside the corresponding *tefilla* text, with a short educational rationale
- An explanation and exploration of the *kavanot* (Thought Questions and Stories) including ideas for ensuing discussion from the *kavanot*, and possible classroom activities for teachers to further explore the educational potential of the *kavanot*
- Additional *Kavanot*: *kavanot* that could be used in the classroom, but were not included in the siddur, usually due to spatial constraints.

This will give the educator flexibility in how they wish to use the siddur in their own particular educational context. For example, the classroom teacher could choose to focus on a spread for a 5–10-minute period each day during the *tefilla* period over one week; one day on the meaning of the text, the next day on the illustration, a day on each *kavana*, and then a final day to summarize and reflect on everything the class has learned that week and their new understanding of the *tefilla*. Or perhaps the teacher wishes to abridge the *tefilla* one day a week, and dedicate 30 minutes to consider a *tefilla* using all the educational elements of the page at the same time. The congregational *tefilla* leader, with weekly programming opportunities, could choose to explore a different page in depth as part of the more extended time they have with the children, or may also wish to compare and contrast different spreads.

מודה אני/על נטילת ידים

pp. 8–9

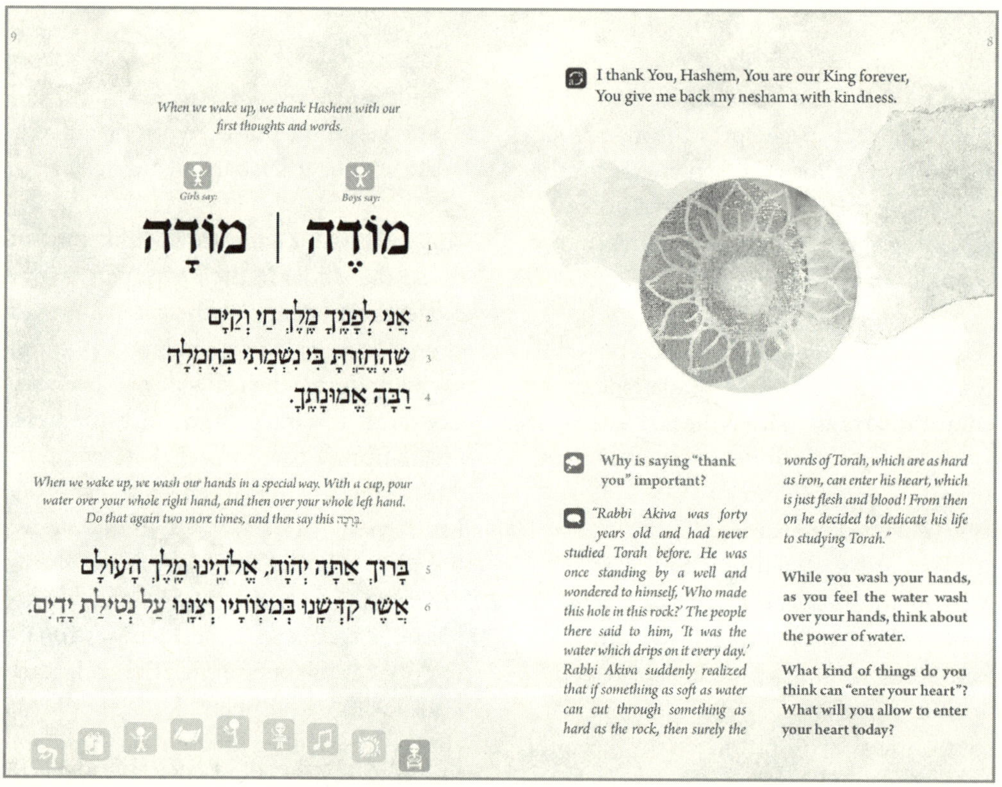

9

When we wake up, we thank Hashem with our first thoughts and words.

Girls say: | Boys say:

1 מוֹדֶה | מוֹדָה

2 אֲנִי לְפָנֶיךָ מֶלֶךְ חַי וְקַיָּם

3 שֶׁהֶחֱזַרְתָּ בִּי נִשְׁמָתִי בְּחֶמְלָה

4 רַבָּה אֱמוּנָתֶךָ.

When we wake up, we wash our hands in a special way. With a cup, pour water over your whole right hand, and then over your whole left hand. Do that again two more times, and then say this בְּרָכָה.

5 בָּרוּךְ אַתָּה יְהֹוָה, אֱלֹהֵינוּ מֶלֶךְ הָעוֹלָם

6 אֲשֶׁר קִדְּשָׁנוּ בְּמִצְוֹתָיו וְצִוָּנוּ עַל נְטִילַת יָדָיִם.

8

I thank You, Hashem, You are our King forever, You give me back my neshama with kindness.

Why is saying "thank you" important?

"Rabbi Akiva was forty years old and had never studied Torah before. He was once standing by a well and wondered to himself, 'Who made this hole in this rock?' The people there said to him, 'It was the water which drips on it every day.' Rabbi Akiva suddenly realized that if something as soft as water can cut through something as hard as the rock, then surely the words of Torah, which are as hard as iron, can enter his heart, which is just flesh and blood! From then on he decided to dedicate his life to studying Torah."

While you wash your hands, as you feel the water wash over your hands, think about the power of water.

What kind of things do you think can "enter your heart"? What will you allow to enter your heart today?

The *Tefilla* Text

Translation:

I thank You, living and eternal King, for giving me back my soul in mercy. Great is Your faithfulness.

Blessed are You, Lord our God, King of the Universe, who has made us holy through His commandments, and has commanded us about washing hands.

Highlighted Text:

The words על נטילת ידים that conclude the *berakha* on the ritual washing of the hands is highlighted in the same color as the story.

Educational Themes contained in the text:

- God as "King"/Kingship (מלכות)
- God as Creator of the world
- Gratitude
- Life is a gift from God
- Waking, renewal, creation
- Gender specific relationships with God
- Hands = action/behavior
- Water is life giving (plants, animals, humans)
- Water and ritual purity

The Illustration

Here we have the morning sun with her rays shining on the world in the early morning, heralding a new day and a fresh start. Within the full circle of the sun is the form of the moon, with its blueish light emanating from the previous night, while the first rays of the sun begin to shine on the world. This is the only time of the day when both the sun and moon are perceivable in our sky. This also gives the illustration a sense of cyclical time, and the daily cycle. After the darkness of the night, with only the moon to give us comfort and limited light, comes the new dawn, with a fresh start, the brightening light of the sunrise giving us new hope for the new day.

The *Kavanot*

Conceptual Translation of:

מודה /מודה/ אני לפניך מלך חי וקים שהחזרת בי נשמתי בחמלה רבה אמונתך.

Thought Question:
We begin our *tefillot* with the ultimate "thank you" – to Hashem for giving us renewed life each morning after we wake up. This question asks the child to consider why.

Secondary questions to consider:

- Why start the siddur this way?
- Why start our day this way?
- Why is it important for us to be grateful, and to voice that?
- When we say thank you to other people, are we doing it for them or for ourselves?
- When we say thank you to Hashem, are we doing it for Him or for ourselves?

Activity ideas:
The teacher may wish to use this opportunity to plan experiential activities in the classroom connected to saying thank you. These could include:

- Asking for volunteers to say thank you to someone in the class. Then exploring with the students what it felt like to say thank you and to be thanked.
- Asking students to make a list of people that they think they ought to thank that day and why.
- Asking students to make a list of things they ought to thank Hashem for (see the thought question on page 124).

Story:
This famous story, found in *Avot deRabbi Natan* (6:2), asks the reader to consider the properties of water, both physical and spiritual. It was chosen and placed on this page in order to encourage the child to relate to the *berakha* of the ritual washing of hands in the context of water and its role in our life. While water can be physically gentle and life giving, in this story it is seen to be powerful, and the question following the story asks the reader to consider that power. The Torah is often compared to water in both Tanakh and the Talmud, including this aggadic story, and the message is clearly that something as pleasant as the Torah has the power to penetrate the hearts and minds of man. The other follow-up question asks the child to consider what other ideas, values or experiences may penetrate their heart, in general, and specifically on this day.

Activity ideas:
The teacher may wish to bring water into the classroom, or take the class outside of the classroom to a body of water, such as a stream or lake. In both these cases experiencing water in some way will encourage the child to consider the properties of water, and the role it plays in their life. The internet could also be utilized for research on the power and role of water, as a whole class activity, or individual/small group mini-projects.

Additional *Kavanot*:
Thought questions:

- What do you want to say thank you for today?
- How do you feel when someone thanks you?
- Why do we describe Hashem as a King? What other jobs does Hashem have, and why is the job of king the one we think about here?
- What is a *neshama*? How is your *neshama* different from everyone else's?
- What else are you going to do with your hands today?

אשר יצר

pp. 10–11

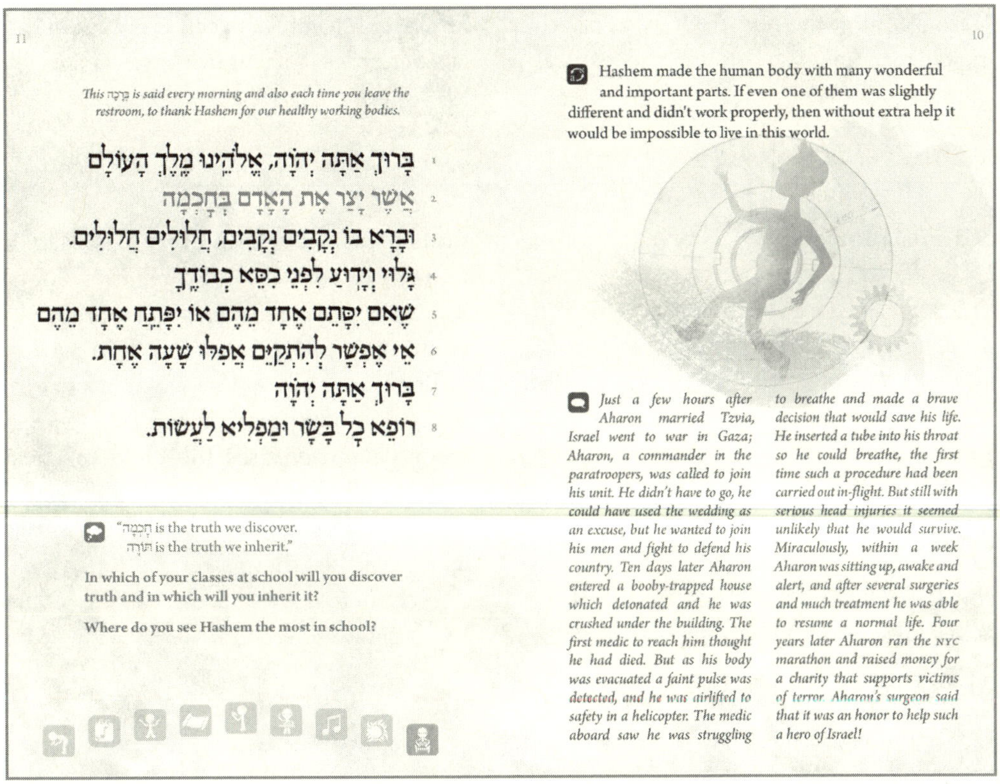

10

Hashem made the human body with many wonderful and important parts. If even one of them was slightly different and didn't work properly, then without extra help it would be impossible to live in this world.

Just a few hours after Aharon married Tzvia, Israel went to war in Gaza; Aharon, a commander in the paratroopers, was called to join his unit. He didn't have to go, he could have used the wedding as an excuse, but he wanted to join his men and fight to defend his country. Ten days later Aharon entered a booby-trapped house which detonated and he was crushed under the building. The first medic to reach him thought he had died. But as his body was evacuated a faint pulse was detected, and he was airlifted to safety in a helicopter. The medic aboard saw he was struggling to breathe and made a brave decision that would save his life. He inserted a tube into his throat so he could breathe, the first time such a procedure had been carried out in-flight. But still with serious head injuries it seemed unlikely that he would survive. Miraculously, within a week Aharon was sitting up, awake and alert, and after several surgeries and much treatment he was able to resume a normal life. Four years later Aharon ran the NYC marathon and raised money for a charity that supports victims of terror. Aharon's surgeon said that it was an honor to help such a hero of Israel!

11

This בְּרָכָה is said every morning and also each time you leave the restroom, to thank Hashem for our healthy working bodies.

בָּרוּךְ אַתָּה יְהֹוָה, אֱלֹהֵינוּ מֶלֶךְ הָעוֹלָם
אֲשֶׁר יָצַר אֶת הָאָדָם בְּחָכְמָה
וּבָרָא בוֹ נְקָבִים נְקָבִים, חֲלוּלִים חֲלוּלִים.
גָּלוּי וְיָדוּעַ לִפְנֵי כִסֵּא כְבוֹדֶךָ
שֶׁאִם יִסָּתֵם אֶחָד מֵהֶם אוֹ יִפָּתֵחַ אֶחָד מֵהֶם
אִי אֶפְשָׁר לְהִתְקַיֵּם אֲפִלּוּ שָׁעָה אֶחָת.
בָּרוּךְ אַתָּה יְהֹוָה
רוֹפֵא כָל בָּשָׂר וּמַפְלִיא לַעֲשׂוֹת.

"חָכְמָה is the truth we discover.
תּוֹרָה is the truth we inherit."

In which of your classes at school will you discover truth and in which will you inherit it?

Where do you see Hashem the most in school?

The *Tefilla* Text

Translation:

Blessed are You, Lord our God, King of the Universe, who formed man in wisdom and created in him many orifices and cavities. It is revealed and known before the throne of Your glory that were one of them to be blocked or ruptured, it would be impossible to survive even for a moment. Blessed are You, Lord, Healer of all flesh who does wondrous deeds.

Highlighted Text:

The words אשר יצר את האדם בחכמה are highlighted in an aqua color from the illustration.

Educational Themes contained in the text:

- The miracle of life/the human body
- God as the Creator of the world and of man
- The holiness of the human body as well as the soul
- Healing and God as a Healer
- The fragility of human life
- Health and personal responsibility to lead a healthy life
- The role of the physician and the role of God in healing

- The responsibility to heal others
- Not taking health for granted
- Human biology as proof of God's existence

The Illustration

This illustration was inspired by Leonardo da Vinci's famous painting, *Vitruvian Man*. The illustration, just as the *berakha* of אשר יצר, expresses the beauty of the system of the human body (as opposed to the external beauty of the human body itself). The wheels and cogs in the illustration hint at the human body as a well-oiled, remarkable machine. The coloring and textures behind the mechanisms in the illustration hint at the spiritual aspect of human existence, and although we celebrate the physical aspects of the human in this *berakha*, and the *neshama* and spiritual elements in the following *berakha* of אלוהי נשמה, this reflects Judaism's refusal to separate between the two – human existence is a perfect balance of the physical and the spiritual.

The *Kavanot*

Conceptual Translation of:

אשר יצר את האדם בחכמה וברא בו נקבים נקבים, חלולים חלולים.
גלוי וידוע לפני כסא כבודך שאם יסתם אחד מהם או יפתח אחד מהם
אי אפשר להתקים אפילו שעה אחת.

Thought Question:
"חכמה is the truth we discover. תורה is the truth we inherit."

This quote comes from Rabbi Sacks' book *Future Tense* and summarizes his approach to finding religious significance and value in secular sources. For Rabbi Sacks there are two legitimate paths to finding God and religious inspiration in this world, and they complement each other. חכמה is truth that we discover in "secular" studies, including the physical and social sciences, literature and the arts, and general culture. תורה, taken in its widest sense as a body of religious knowledge that has evolved and developed within a clear framework of truth revealed at a historical moment in time, is truth inherited by a particular people through their particular religion. Both are equally legitimate paths to truth, and to knowledge of and intimacy with God. Each provides a unique path to the same destination, and these paths complement each other, making that journey the most efficient and effective when taken together.

The questions for reflection that follow this quote ask the student to consider where in their school day they will have the opportunity to progress down each of these paths. Hopefully, every class they have will fit into one or both of these categories. For some people, it is easier to see and experience God in a Torah class or during *tefilla*, and for others a science or sports or literature class will be where they find it easier to perceive God's presence and role in the world. The second question asks the child to consider where they are most likely to feel God's presence, and it is also important to note that it asks this in a sufficiently wide sense that the answer could also include areas of the school that are outside the classroom such as the lunch hall or the school yard.

This quote and these questions are placed here because this *berakha* can be considered a meeting point between these two paths to Divine Truth. This *berakha* asks us to consider the beauty of the system of the human body (as reflected in the illustration) and its Divine Architect. This *berakha* reminds us to see God in our biology class as much as our Talmud class.

Activity ideas:
This could be a good opportunity for the teacher to demonstrate the two paths to God explored in this *kavana*, by bringing חכמה into the Judaics classroom (or the *Beit Kenesset*) in the form of physical props, or the science teacher, or taking the class out into nature. The object must be to find the footprint of God in our world, using חכמה and also תורה (finding related Torah sources to the experience of חכמה that you provide for your students).

Story:

This story provides several points of inspiration to help the reader find the imprint of God in the human body. The focus of this story in the context of this *berakha* should be the miraculous nature of the human body to heal itself, and to achieve amazing feats. The following themes in the story could be discussed and explored:

- Aharon's heroism – putting his people before his own happiness
- Healing (and health) as a partnership between man and God
- The miraculous ability of the human body to heal itself
- Is the human body miraculous? (natural miracles vs. supernatural miracles)
- The power of the human mind in overcoming illness
- Pushing one's body to the limits in order to achieve difficult feats.

Activity Ideas:

Human machines: Get your class to replicate the functions of human organs through their bodies or by using props. Divide your class into two teams. Ask each one to act out the functions of a machine that replicates the function of an internal organ in the body. You can choose which one or let them choose (for example, a kidney, a lung, the heart).

Additional *Kavanot*:

Story:

The son of Rabbi Steinsaltz was very sick with leukemia when he was a young boy of fifteen. The doctors were very worried about his condition, and recommended that he have a bone marrow transplant. Rabbi Steinsaltz traveled to New York to visit the Lubavitcher Rebbe to receive a blessing and ask his advice. The Rebbe took Rabbi Steinsaltz's hand and blessed his son with long life. He told him that he would make a full recovery. But he also warned him not to allow the doctors to proceed with the transplant. The doctors were not happy when the family informed them that they would only allow their son to be treated with other methods, and not have the transplant. The Rebbe's prediction came true, and the boy made a full recovery.

אלהי נשמה

pp. 12–13

12

Hashem, You created my soul and breathed it into me. And You look after it while it is in me.

"Whoever destroys a single soul, it is as if he destroyed an entire world. And whoever saves a single soul, it is as if he has saved an entire world." (Mishna Sanhedrin, 4:5)

Why do you think the Mishna uses the word "soul" to describe a life?
Why do you think a single soul is equal to an entire world?

"Man creates a hundred coins from one press and each coin is exactly the same. But Hashem, the King of kings, creates all mankind from one man (Adam), and each person is totally unique!" (Mishna Sanhedrin, 4:5)

Look around at all your friends right now.
What is unique about you?

13

אֱלֹהַי
נְשָׁמָה שֶׁנָּתַתָּ בִּי טְהוֹרָה.
אַתָּה בְרָאתָהּ, אַתָּה יְצַרְתָּהּ, אַתָּה נְפַחְתָּהּ בִּי
וְאַתָּה מְשַׁמְּרָהּ בְּקִרְבִּי, וְאַתָּה עָתִיד לִטְּלָהּ מִמֶּנִּי
וּלְהַחֲזִירָהּ בִּי לֶעָתִיד לָבוֹא.
כָּל זְמַן שֶׁהַנְּשָׁמָה בְקִרְבִּי
מוֹדֶה | מוֹדָה
אֲנִי לְפָנֶיךָ
יְהוָה אֱלֹהַי וֵאלֹהֵי אֲבוֹתַי
רִבּוֹן כָּל הַמַּעֲשִׂים
אֲדוֹן כָּל הַנְּשָׁמוֹת.
בָּרוּךְ אַתָּה יְהוָה
הַמַּחֲזִיר נְשָׁמוֹת לִפְגָרִים מֵתִים.

The *Tefilla* Text

Translation:
My God, the soul You placed within me is pure. You created it, You formed it, You breathed it into me, and You guard it while it is within me. One day You will take it from me, and restore it to me in the time to come. As long as the soul is within me, I will thank You, Lord my God and God of my ancestors, Master of all works, Lord of all souls. Blessed are You, Lord, who restores souls to lifeless bodies.

Blessed are You, Lord our God, King of the Universe, who has made us holy through His commandments, and has commanded us about the command of tasseled garments.

Highlighted Text:
The words נשמה and נשמות are highlighted in the color of the Thought Questions.

Educational Themes contained in the text:

- The soul and its divine source

- The duality of man as both a physical and spiritual being (mutual dependency)
- השגחה פרטית (Divine Providence)
- Gratitude
- God as Creator of the world, both physical and spiritual
- Our soul is pure and we have free choice to lead it to good or bad
- Man is inherently good (implied by the fact that the soul Hashem has given us is "pure")
- The soul cannot be felt physically, only sensed spiritually (like other incorporeal concepts)
- The soul as what is unique in each human

The Illustration

Here we meet the character from the Koren Children's Siddur for the first time in our siddur, and of course he is more mature looking, now that he has reached fourth grade. We find him slowly waking to meet the new day that awaits him outside the open window as the sun rises on the new day.

There is a strong breeze blowing through the open window, and this represents the returning of his soul to his body as described in מודה אני, the first *tefilla* of the morning said before this one. This is a concrete representation of the abstract concept of the *neshama*, as described in this *tefilla*, helping the student to connect to the themes of the *tefilla*, which include God blowing the soul into our bodies.

The *Kavanot*

Conceptual Translation of:

אלֹהי נשמה שנתת בי טהורה היא. אתה בראתה, אתה יצרתה, אתה נפחתה בי ואתה משמרה בקרבי

Thought Questions:
Both quotes in the thought question *kavanot* are from the same mishna in *Sanhedrin* (4:5), and while they are clearly related, each section delivers a distinct and important educational message. The text of the *tefilla* focuses our attention on the soul. The incorporeal soul is a difficult abstract concept for any adult to consider, let alone a third- to fifth-grade student. We have chosen, with the help of this mishna and these thought questions, to focus the child on the soul as each person's unique spiritual personality and unique worth in the eyes of God and hopefully the world.

> "Whoever destroys a single soul, it is as if he destroyed an entire world. And whoever saves a single soul, it is as if he has saved an entire world."

> "Man creates a hundred coins from one press and each coin is exactly the same. But Hashem, the King of kings, creates all mankind from one man [Adam], and each person is totally unique!" (Mishna *Sanhedrin*, 4:5)

The mishna uses the word soul to draw our attention to the infinite value of each unique human being. This point is driven home by the juxtaposition of this statement with the *reisha* of the mishna. The child is being asked to realize that the soul they are thanking God for in this *tefilla* is what makes them unique, and what gives them infinite spiritual value in the world. Their soul is worth an entire world. This is both a statement of spiritual worth, as well as a conceptual statement about the infinite souls that can come from each soul if allowed to procreate.

The value of each individual soul as a unique being in the world created by God is also found in the verse from Bereshit (1:27), where God described man as created "in His image":

ויברא אלהים את-האדם בצלמו, בצלם אלהים ברא אתו: זכר ונקבה, ברא אתם.

Using this verse to explore the concepts found in this *tefilla* and in the mishna helps us to understand that while each soul is unique, each soul is created by the same Creator, and in its Creator's image, and is therefore of infinite value and worth. The fact that every human being is similar (created in God's image), and also unique (each has their own unique soul), leads us to believe in the dignity of human life, and the value of human rights. These are core Jewish values.

Activity ideas:

- The final thought question – "What is unique about you?" – could be the basis of a class activity, where everyone in the class volunteers a unique character trait they possess. Variations on this theme could be: each child writes a trait on a piece of paper, and the papers are collected in a box. Everyone then picks one out and has to guess who that trait belongs to. Or, a piece of paper is passed around the class, and folded each time someone writes their trait on the paper. By the end, the teacher can read out all the traits written on the paper, as an expression of the unique qualities of the class as a whole, made up of many unique personalities.
- To illustrate how many souls can come from one, a family tree could be brought into class, or the class could be asked to create their own family trees, and understand how many generations can come from one soul. This could also be an arts and crafts project.
- The final scene in the film *Schindler's List* is a moving expression of this same theme, when the descendants of the thousand souls that Schindler saved visit his grave on the Mount of Olives. While the film itself may not be appropriate to show this age group, the last scene is not inappropriate, and the message is powerfully expressed in it.
- An activity using finger prints (or a demonstration of how DNA works) would be a creative way to explore how unique we are physically from one another. The discussion of whether this is true spiritually could come from there.
- A creative art project involving snowflakes is also a fun way to consider millions of unique creations.
- Two-minute biographies: Ask students to find a partner and give them two minutes to tell them what they would especially like them to know about themselves and their lives: past, present, hopes, plans, facts, etc. After each has a turn, they join another pair to make a foursome, and introduce the partner to the new pair, by relating what they remember about the partner's autobiography. When each of the four has had a turn, they join the whole group and introduce their partners to the class.

ברכות השחר 1

pp. 14–15

15

The following בְּרָכוֹת help you to think about and thank Hashem for all the things we are and have. They were originally said at home after each stage of waking up and getting ready for the day, as we realize how much we have to be thankful to Hashem for. Now we say them as part of our תְּפִלָּה.

בָּרוּךְ אַתָּה יְהֹוָה, אֱלֹהֵינוּ מֶלֶךְ הָעוֹלָם
אֲשֶׁר נָתַן לַשֶּׂכְוִי בִינָה
לְהַבְחִין בֵּין יוֹם וּבֵין לָיְלָה.

בָּרוּךְ אַתָּה יְהֹוָה, אֱלֹהֵינוּ מֶלֶךְ הָעוֹלָם
פּוֹקֵחַ עִוְרִים.

בָּרוּךְ אַתָּה יְהֹוָה, אֱלֹהֵינוּ מֶלֶךְ הָעוֹלָם
מַתִּיר אֲסוּרִים.

בָּרוּךְ אַתָּה יְהֹוָה, אֱלֹהֵינוּ מֶלֶךְ הָעוֹלָם
זוֹקֵף כְּפוּפִים.

בָּרוּךְ אַתָּה יְהֹוָה, אֱלֹהֵינוּ מֶלֶךְ הָעוֹלָם
מַלְבִּישׁ עֲרֻמִּים.

14

"The eyes are the window to your soul."

What can you use your eyes for?

What do you plan to use your sight for today?

The people of Chelm were not a bright bunch. Once, when a rabbi and his student from Chelm were staying at an inn, the student asked the innkeeper to wake him up early to catch a train. When he awoke he didn't want to disturb the rabbi, so he dressed himself in the dark. But by mistake he put on the rabbi's long black coat instead of his own clothes. When he arrived at the train station he caught a glimpse of his reflection in a window. When he saw the rabbi's long black coat he shouted aloud "Oh no... The inn keeper woke the Rabbi up instead of me!"

The *Tefilla* Text

Translation:
Blessed are You, Lord our God, King of the Universe, who gives the heart understanding to distinguish day from night.
Blessed are You, Lord our God, King of the Universe, who gives sight to the blind.
Blessed are You, Lord our God, King of the Universe, who sets captives free.
Blessed are You, Lord our God, King of the Universe, who raises those bowed down.
Blessed are You, Lord our God, King of the Universe, who clothes the naked.

Highlighted Text:
The conclusion to the *berakha* פוקח עורים is highlighted in the same color as the thought question and the conclusion to the *berakha* מתיר אסורים is highlighted in the green of the bird of the illustration.

Educational Themes contained in the text:

- What are your needs?
- What do we need to thank Hashem for on a daily basis?
- גם זו לטובה (seeing the good retroactively in the "bad") – Hashem provides us with everything we need
- Sub-themes:
  - gift of sight
  - dignity of clothing
  - appreciation of physical abilities/functioning
  - freedom (physical/spiritual)

The Illustration

The character in the illustration sets a bird free. The bird is a symbol of freedom, unrestricted in movement, flying free above the world. Here the boy releases the bird, and gives us a visual metaphor for the *berakha* מתיר אסורים, thanking Hashem for our freedom, both physical and spiritual, and also within our own bodies (this *berakha* was originally said upon waking up and taking one's first stretch, thanking Hashem for the use of all our limbs). Notice the boy's eyes are also closed. This is a subtle hint towards the first *berakha* on the page – פוֹקֵחַ עוורים – thanking Hashem for our sight. Perhaps we can say that his closed eyes tell us that just as freedom is not always physical, and sometimes the key to freedom is within our own hearts, so sight is not always about our eyes, but it can also be enlightenment and openness.

The *Kavanot*

Thought Question:
This thought question explores the eyes that we thank God for opening each morning in the *berakha* פוֹקֵחַ עוורים. The quote "The eyes are the window to the soul" is often attributed to Shakespeare, but there is some debate about this. Its source is not important to us, but the concept that you can see the essence of someone through their eyes is a powerful one. Whether this is an abstract mystical idea, or a more scientific statement that through physical cues one can perceive emotional information about another person, either way it encourages us to really look at the people around us, and to "see them" rather than look through them.

The thought questions following the quote ask the child to consider what else their eyes and sight can be used for, and in a more practical personal way, ask them to consider what they will use their sight for today. This takes the child from the gratitude they have for their sight, as expressed in the *berakha,* to the next stage – how they will use their sight for good.

Activity games:
Disability obstacle course. Ask for volunteers to traverse an obstacle course arranged in the classroom (or outside). For each volunteer take away a sense or ability. One is blindfolded. One has his hands tied behind his back. One has to hop on one leg only. Or you could divide the class into teams and have every student do the obstacle course, each time having one disability.

Story:
The story, a classic from the Chelm genre, has an important message as well as an entertaining punch line. Linked to the *berakha* of מלביש ערמים, it asks the child to consider the role of clothes in our life. While there are many general directions a discussion on clothing could take, such as the dignity of clothing, and modesty, and the pitfalls of fashion, the story explores identity and clothing issues, and what messages our clothes can send, both about and to us and the outside world. These questions are also asked later on in the siddur, in the context of *tzitzit* on page 80, and more indirectly in the story of "Mashiaḥ's Hat,"

on page 118. In this story, the boy from Chelm saw his image in the mirror wearing the rabbi's clothes, and confused himself for the rabbi, because he was unable to see the person behind the clothes. This is a case of judging a book by its cover, and obviously a pitfall to be avoided. One must judge a person on more substantial evidence other than the superficial statement their clothes make, or better still, avoid judging them at all. However, clothes do make a statement, and we believe in the importance of clothes as a chance to make value statements, such as wearing special clothing on Shabbat to sanctify and elevate the status of the day. The statement one's clothes make on Shabbat are as much to oneself as they are to others. The same can be said when it comes to *tzeniut* as expressed in one's clothing. A message is sent both to the outside world and to oneself.

Additional *Kavanot*:

Story (for מלביש ערומים):

A poor man once entered a wedding feast but was turned away by the bride's father because his clothes were worn and scruffy. The man went to his rich friend and borrowed fine clothes befitting a prince. When he returned to the wedding the bride's father didn't even recognize him as he gracefully strode into the banquet hall wearing his elegant clothes. The father welcomed him to the wedding, and the man begins to stuff his pockets with the food from the lavish feast. All the guests stop and stare at the man in the nice suit who is behaving in such a strange manner. The father of the bride angrily asks him what he thinks he is doing. The man calmly explains that he is feeding his clothes, because they are the ones really welcome at the wedding, more than he was.

Story (for מתיר אסורים):

Reb Zusya used to travel cross-country to raise funds to ransom Jewish prisoners that had been taken captive. He once came to an inn when the inn-keeper was not at home. He noticed there a large cage with all sorts of beautiful birds. As he admired the beauty of the birds he noticed how they longed to fly free in the sky. Zusya said to himself, "You walk for miles and miles to fulfill the mitzva of *pidyon shevu'im* (setting prisoners free). What better way to fulfill this mitzva than to set these birds free from their prison?" And so he did.

ברכות השחר 2

pp. 16–17

17

16

בָּרוּךְ אַתָּה יְהוָה, אֱלֹהֵינוּ מֶלֶךְ הָעוֹלָם
הַנּוֹתֵן לַיָּעֵף כֹּחַ.

בָּרוּךְ אַתָּה יְהוָה, אֱלֹהֵינוּ מֶלֶךְ הָעוֹלָם
רוֹקַע הָאָרֶץ עַל הַמָּיִם.

בָּרוּךְ אַתָּה יְהוָה, אֱלֹהֵינוּ מֶלֶךְ הָעוֹלָם
הַמֵּכִין מִצְעֲדֵי גָבֶר.

בָּרוּךְ אַתָּה יְהוָה, אֱלֹהֵינוּ מֶלֶךְ הָעוֹלָם
שֶׁעָשָׂה לִי כָּל צָרְכִּי.

בָּרוּךְ אַתָּה יְהוָה, אֱלֹהֵינוּ מֶלֶךְ הָעוֹלָם
אוֹזֵר יִשְׂרָאֵל בִּגְבוּרָה.

בָּרוּךְ אַתָּה יְהוָה, אֱלֹהֵינוּ מֶלֶךְ הָעוֹלָם
עוֹטֵר יִשְׂרָאֵל בְּתִפְאָרָה.

The Beren Academy Stars were having their most successful basketball season ever. In fact, they were the first Jewish day school to ever reach the Texas state semi-final. But they couldn't play in it. The game was scheduled for the evening of Shabbat, and the state tournament refused to move it. It wasn't even a question for the team. The decision was made. To give up their dream and to stand up for what they believed in. But as their story spread reaching the national and international news across the globe, the tournament relented and allowed the game to be moved. The Stars' prayers were answered, and they got their chance to achieve their dreams. And they took it, convincingly beating their semi-final opponents 58–46 and making history, reaching the championship game. Unfortunately they narrowly lost in the final (46–42), but won hearts and inspired people across the world with their commitment to their values and to Shabbat.

The *Tefilla* Text

Translation:

Blessed are You, Lord our God, King of the Universe, who gives strength to the weary.
Blessed are You, Lord our God, King of the Universe, who spreads the earth above the waters.
Blessed are You, Lord our God, King of the Universe, who makes firm the steps of man.
Blessed are You, Lord our God, King of the Universe, who has provided me with all I need.
Blessed are You, Lord our God, King of the Universe, who girds Israel with strength.
Blessed are You, Lord our God, King of the Universe, who crowns Israel with glory.

Highlighted Text:

The words אוזר ישראל בגבורה are highlighted in the same green as the soldier in the illustration.

Educational Themes contained in the text:

- What are your needs?
- What do we need to thank Hashem for on a daily basis?

- Sub-themes:
  - physical abilities/functioning
  - strength (physical/spiritual)
  - nature
  - national glory (achievements/talents of Israel)
  - heroism

The Illustration

This illustration could be an expression of each *berakha* on this page of the siddur, but it is primarily exploring the *berakha* of אוֹזֵר יִשְׂרָאֵל בִּגְבוּרָה. Here we have an Israeli *ḥayal* (soldier), wrapped in his *tallit*, praying with a siddur open in his hands, and his rifle over his shoulder. This *berakha* thanks Hashem for "girding Israel with strength." Here we thank Hashem for our spiritual and physical national strength. This can be represented by every single IDF soldier, fighting to defend his land (seen in the background of the illustration) and his people.

Rabbi J.B. Soloveitchik[2] says that this *berakha* does not speak of physical strength (which is covered in the *berakha* of הַנּוֹתֵן לַיָּעֵף כֹּחַ), but rather the heroism of spiritual strength. As a nation, the IDF and its brave Jewish soldiers represent both these types of strength.

The *tallit,* siddur, and act of praying, next to the rifle, express the combination of faith in Hashem and strength and courage to stand and fight and risk and sacrifice. Rabbi Soloveitchik's definition of heroism is sacrifice, and these soldiers are prepared to, and sadly often do, make the ultimate sacrifice for their nation.

The *ḥayal* praying reminds us of Yaakov on his way to meet Eisav after many years apart (Bereshit, chapter 33). Yaakov hoped for peace with his brother but feared war. So he sent gifts and peace offerings, but also divided the camp in two and prepared for war, and most importantly prayed to Hashem. This is our approach to conflict in our land – we hope for peace, prepare for war and self-defense, and pray to Hashem to deliver us.

The *Kavanot*

Thought Question:
The entire mishna (*Avot* 4:1) in the original is:

בן זומא אומר, איזה הוא חכם–הלמד מכל אדם, שנאמר "מכל מלמדיי, השכלתי" (תהילים קיט, צט). **איזה הוא גיבור - הכובש את יצרו**, שנאמר "טוב ארך אפיים, מגיבור" (משלי טז, לב). איזה הוא עשיר - השמח בחלקו, שנאמר "יגיע כפיך, כי תאכל; אשריך, וטוב לך" (תהילים קכח, ב): "אשריך", בעולם הזה; "וטוב לך", לעולם הבא. איזה הוא מכובד - המכבד את הברייות, שנאמר "כי מכבדיי אכבד ובוזיי ייקלו" (שמואל א׳ ב, ל).

The first three clauses of the mishna are quoted in the siddur, on pages 19, 96 and 124.

The word strength, mentioned in the second *berakha* on this page and in the mishna, can be interpreted in many varied ways (see the explanation of the illustration). Physical, emotional and spiritual strength are all virtues to strive for. While the word in common usage is probably more often used to refer to physical strength, the mishna believes that quintessential strength is spiritual-emotional strength, and one who has this virtue is one who can overcome their natural urges that we would term the *Yetzer HaRa* (evil inclination). Everyone without exception has temptation for bad, and a strong person is someone who can surmount these desires.

2. In the Mesorat HaRav Siddur

While it should be acceptable for a child to answer these questions in terms of physical strength, the mishna clearly wants us to understand that ultimate strength is spiritual-emotional, and the child should be guided to explore this form of strength. Just as the illustration suggests that Israel's strength is physical as well as spiritual-emotional, so we can interpret the *berakha* in that way too, but the child should be encouraged to consider the non-physical forms of strength, especially when answering the final question.

Activity idea:
Place a candy on the desk in front of every child in the class. Tell them if they resist the temptation to eat it until the end of the class they will get another one.

Story:
This true story that took place in March 2012[3] is a great example of regular Jewish kids showing unity and non-physical spiritual strength in the face of adversity (as well as some physical strength on the basketball court!). This story could just as easily have been placed in the Shabbat section of this siddur, but more important than serving as an example of commitment to Shabbat, it is an example of courage and strength, performed by regular Jewish day-school kids, and should be considered an example of the strength that we are thanking God for in this *berakha*.

Activity ideas:
Role-playing scenarios of situations that take strength can be fun as well as experientially and educationally rewarding. Examples of this could be finding a $50 bill in the classroom, being served food of questionable *kashrut* at a friend's house, and being invited to watch the ball game on Shabbat at a friend's house.

Additional *Kavanot*:
Thought questions:

- You just said many ברכות. What else are you thankful for? What else did God give you?
- Close your eyes and picture all the things Hashem has blessed you with. Now say thank you to Hashem for each of them.

Story (הנותן ליעף כח)*:*
Tony Cavallo was crushed by the car he was fixing as it slipped off the jacks that were supporting it. When his mother Angela heard the screams of her teenage son as the car fell on top of him, she came running to help, and somehow managed to lift the car high enough and for long enough for neighbors to replace the jacks that had fallen, saving her son's life.

3. http://www.nytimes.com/2013/03/02/sports/jewish-academy-competes-in-texas-after-winning-the-right-to-play.html
http://www.huffingtonpost.com/edwin-black/the-texas-sabbath-showdow-tapps-and-beren-academy_b_1377057.html

ברכות השחר 3

pp. 18–19

19

1 בָּרוּךְ אַתָּה יְהֹוָה, אֱלֹהֵינוּ מֶלֶךְ הָעוֹלָם

2 שֶׁלֹּא עָשַׂנִי גּוֹי | שֶׁלֹּא עָשַׂנִי גּוֹיָה

3 בָּרוּךְ אַתָּה יְהֹוָה, אֱלֹהֵינוּ מֶלֶךְ הָעוֹלָם

4 שֶׁלֹּא עָשַׂנִי עֶבֶד | שֶׁלֹּא עָשַׂנִי שִׁפְחָה.

5 בָּרוּךְ אַתָּה יְהֹוָה | בָּרוּךְ שֶׁעָשַׂנִי כִּרְצוֹנוֹ.

6 אֱלֹהֵינוּ מֶלֶךְ הָעוֹלָם

7 שֶׁלֹּא עָשַׂנִי אִשָּׁה

"Who is a strong person? Someone who controls their bad wishes." (Pirkei Avot 4:1)

What does it mean to be strong and where does strength come from?

Who do you know that is really strong?

How will you be strong today?

18

When you look in the mirror what do you see? Who are you? Who would you like to be?

The great Hasidic leader Reb Zusia once began crying in front of his followers, pale faced and with red eyes. "What's the matter Rebbe?" his Hasidim inquired. "I had a dream," he explained, "and the question the angels will ask me when I pass on to the World to Come was revealed to me," he said, trembling. His followers were puzzled. "But Rebbe, you are pious and holy and scholarly and humble. What question could they possibly ask of you that you should fear so much?" Zusia turned to heaven and replied with his eyes closed tightly, "I have learned that the angels will not ask me why I wasn't more like Avraham our father or Moses our teacher. But they will ask me why I wasn't more like Zusia!"

The *Tefilla* Text

Translation:

Blessed are You, Lord our God, King of the Universe, who has not made me a heathen.
Blessed are You, Lord our God, King of the Universe, who has not made me a slave.
Blessed are You, Lord our God, King of the Universe, who has not made me a woman/who has made me according to His will.

Educational Themes contained in the text:

- Who am I? (Personal identity exploration.)
- Who would I like to be (what will I do with what I have been given)?
- The ability to distinguish (between good and evil, light and dark, myself and others) is God-given
- What are your unique talents and where did they come from?
- Is intelligence nature or nurture?
- What are your needs and who fulfills them?
- Starting a new day with new appreciation

The Illustration

In this illustration we see the character looking intently in the mirror. The mirror is a metaphor for inner reflection and identity questioning. He is asking himself, "Who am I?" just as the questions of *Birkhot HaShaḥar* do the same, encouraging us to consider our own identities and to thank Hashem for the opportunities to be who we are. The illustration compliments the Thought Question which asks for the child to do this process themselves. What does it mean to be a Jewish boy or girl and why are we thanking Hashem for that?

The *Kavanot*

Thought Question:
Berakhot 2–5 of *Birkhot Hashaḥar* focus on personal identity. They ask us to consider who we are and encourage us to be thankful for that. The thought question on this page does the same. The question is phrased in a way that asks the reader to take a moment to literally and metaphorically look at themselves in the mirror (as seen in the illustration), and see who they are. Using the *berakhot* as cues, hopefully this will encourage them to explore their personal and national identities. But more than that, it also asks them to go a step further and to refuse to stand still and admire this, but rather dream of who they wish to be and what they hope to achieve.

Activity ideas:
Identity games:

- Ask the class to line up in order of age; shoe size; height; alphabetical order of first name and then last name.
- Concentric circles: Have half the class sit in a circle sitting facing outwards, and the other half in a circle outside them facing inwards (each child face-to-face with another). Ask them to discuss a list of questions about themselves, such as where they were born, siblings, pets, likes and dislikes, etc. After each question ask one of the circles to move up a chair, so that each question is discussed with a different partner. The questions should get increasingly personal, and end with hopes for the future.
- Two-minute biographies: Ask students to find a partner and give them two minutes to tell them what they would especially like them to know about themselves and their lives: past, present, hopes, plans, facts, etc. After each has a turn, they join another pair to make a foursome, and introduce the partner to the new pair, by relating what they remember about the partner's autobiography. When each of the four has had a turn, they join the whole group and introduce their partners to the class.
- "A strong wind blows": Ask students to sit in a very tight circle with one person standing in the middle. The person in the middle says, "A strong wind blows on anyone who _____," and then fills in the blank with something true about them. This can be appearance (e.g., anyone wearing pink socks) or personality-based (e.g., anyone who likes math; anyone who has a sister, etc.). Upon finishing the sentence, everyone to whom the statement applies is "blown" out of their seat and everyone, including the person in the middle, must find new seats. The one left standing in the end must come up with a new statement.
- Ask the class to stand by the person that is most likely to:
  - Become a millionaire
  - Become a rabbi
  - Be the first to get married
  - Make *aliya*
  - Go to jail
  - Become president

Story:
This often quoted story validates our self-identity (and removes the pressure of becoming a Moshe Rabbeinu, something only Moshe Rabbeinu could do) while at the same time encouraging us to be the best we can be. It has been placed here with these *berakhot* that ask us to consider who we are and who we might become.

Additional *Kavanot*:

Story:

Close your eyes. Imagine one day you woke up and you had lost all your memories. You couldn't remember your name, where you lived, who your family was or what food you like to eat. How would you go about finding out who you were? What questions would you ask and to whom would you ask them? What things would you try to discover about who you really were? What do you think you would discover about yourself? What would you discover that you have to be thankful to Hashem for?

Thought question:

- *"Hashem gave each of His creatures special gifts."*[4] What special gifts has Hashem given you?

4. Rabbi S.R. Hirsch on the siddur

המעביר

pp. 20–21

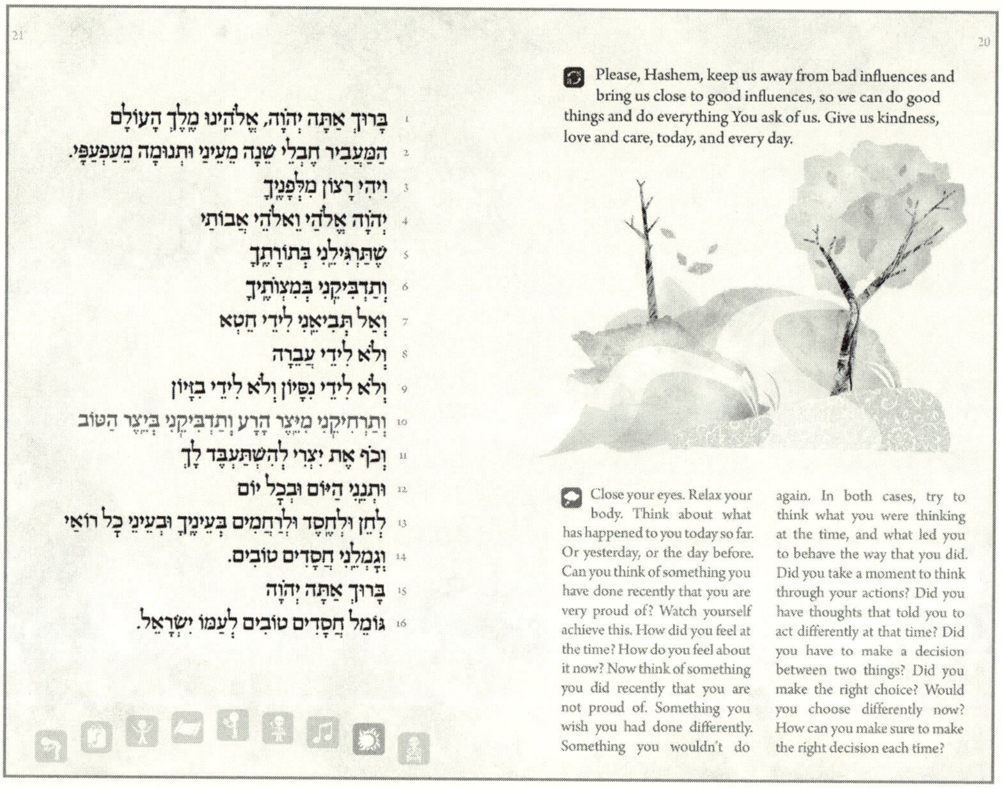
21

בָּרוּךְ אַתָּה יְהֹוָה, אֱלֹהֵינוּ מֶלֶךְ הָעוֹלָם
הַמַּעֲבִיר חֶבְלֵי שֵׁנָה מֵעֵינַי וּתְנוּמָה מֵעַפְעַפָּי.
וִיהִי רָצוֹן מִלְּפָנֶיךָ
יְהֹוָה אֱלֹהַי וֵאלֹהֵי אֲבוֹתַי
שֶׁתַּרְגִּילֵנִי בְּתוֹרָתֶךָ
וְתַדְבִּיקֵנִי בְּמִצְוֹתֶיךָ
וְאַל תְּבִיאֵנִי לִידֵי חֵטְא
וְלֹא לִידֵי עֲבֵרָה
וְלֹא לִידֵי נִסָּיוֹן וְלֹא לִידֵי בִזָּיוֹן
וְתַרְחִיקֵנִי מִיֵּצֶר הָרָע וְתַדְבִּיקֵנִי בְּיֵצֶר הַטּוֹב
וְכֹף אֶת יִצְרִי לְהִשְׁתַּעְבֶּד לָךְ
וּתְנֵנִי הַיּוֹם וּבְכָל יוֹם
לְחֵן וּלְחֶסֶד וּלְרַחֲמִים בְּעֵינֶיךָ וּבְעֵינֵי כָל רוֹאַי
וְגָמְלֵנִי חֲסָדִים טוֹבִים.
בָּרוּךְ אַתָּה יְהֹוָה
גּוֹמֵל חֲסָדִים טוֹבִים לְעַמּוֹ יִשְׂרָאֵל.

20

Please, Hashem, keep us away from bad influences and bring us close to good influences, so we can do good things and do everything You ask of us. Give us kindness, love and care, today, and every day.

Close your eyes. Relax your body. Think about what has happened to you today so far. Or yesterday, or the day before. Can you think of something you have done recently that you are very proud of? Watch yourself achieve this. How did you feel at the time? How do you feel about it now? Now think of something you did recently that you are not proud of. Something you wish you had done differently. Something you wouldn't do again. In both cases, try to think what you were thinking at the time, and what led you to behave the way that you did. Did you take a moment to think through your actions? Did you have thoughts that told you to act differently at that time? Did you have to make a decision between two things? Did you make the right choice? Would you choose differently now? How can you make sure to make the right decision each time?

The *Tefilla* Text

Translation:

Blessed are You, Lord our God, King of the Universe, who removes sleep from my eyes and slumber from my eyelids. And may it be Your will, Lord my God and God of my ancestors, to accustom me to Your Torah, and make me attached to Your commandments. Lead me not into error, transgression, temptation or disgrace. Help me to distance myself from the evil instinct and to attach myself to the good instinct, and bend my instinct to be subservient to You. Grant us, this day and every day, grace, loving-kindness and compassion in Your eyes and in the eyes of all who see me, and bestow loving-kindness upon me. Blessed are You, Lord, who bestows loving-kindness on His people Israel.

Highlighted Text:

The words ותרחיקני מיצר הרע are highlighted in the color from the illustration that represents the path to evil and desolation. The words ותדביקני ביצר הטוב are highlighted in the color from the illustration that represents the path to goodness and life.

Educational Themes contained in the text:

- What does it mean to be a Jew in our everyday lives? (Torah and mitzvot)
- *Yetzer HaRa* vs. *Yetzer HaTov*
- Hashem helps protect us from sin and temptation
- Distancing from bad neighbors/friends
- Using our blessings to serve Hashem and to be a good person

The Illustration

The illustration is a metaphor for the choice between the *Yetzer HaRa* and the *Yetzer HaTov*. There are two paths in the forest, representing the choice between two directions, two lifestyles, two different ways of behaving in any given situation. One path leads to the light and beauty of healthy growth and fertile vegetation. The other leads to the dark barren wilderness of destruction. Which path will you take? This *tefilla* asks Hashem to help guide us to the path of light and life and *Yetzer HaTov*.

Activity ideas:
Divide the class into two teams. Each team provides a volunteer to traverse an obstacle course blindfolded. Their team must shout out instructions while the other team shouts out incorrect instructions, and the volunteer must choose which direction to follow.

The *Kavanot*

Conceptual Translation of:

ותרחיקנו מאדם רע ומחבר רע ודבקנו ביצר הטוב ובמעשים טובים
וכֹף את יצרנו להשתעבד לך ותננו היום ובכל יום לחן ולחסד ולרחמים
בעיניך ובעיני כל רואינו ותגמלנו חסדים טובים.

Story:
This imagination simulation aims to ask the child to use their imagination to revisit and reexperience events that took place in their lives where they have made correct decisions and listened to positive influences; and also where they have made decisions they regret (perhaps because they listened to negative influences) and would do differently if given the chance. The simulation asks them to understand what led them to the decisions they made, and whether being more aware of these factors and influences would perhaps lead them to choose differently next time. It also asks them to be more aware of these influences generally in their lives, where they may normally be less aware of them.

The activity is best performed when the children are quiet with their eyes closed, and the script is read to them aloud. This should be followed by a discussion, with some participants sharing their experiences with the class.

Additional *Kavanot*:
Thought questions:

- What can you do today to keep yourself away from bad influences?
- Who is a good influence on you in your life? How can you be a good influence on your friends today?

Story:
In the world to come, Hashem will bring the *Yetzer HaRa* to all the people and kill it in front of them. When the righteous people look at it, it will appear as something huge like a mountain, but it will appear to the evil people as something tiny like a strand of hair. The righteous will cry tears of emotion that they managed to fight something so large and powerful, and the evil will also cry, that they could not manage to fight something as small and weak as a strand of hair.[5]

5. *Sukka* 52a

על דברי תורה

pp. 22–23

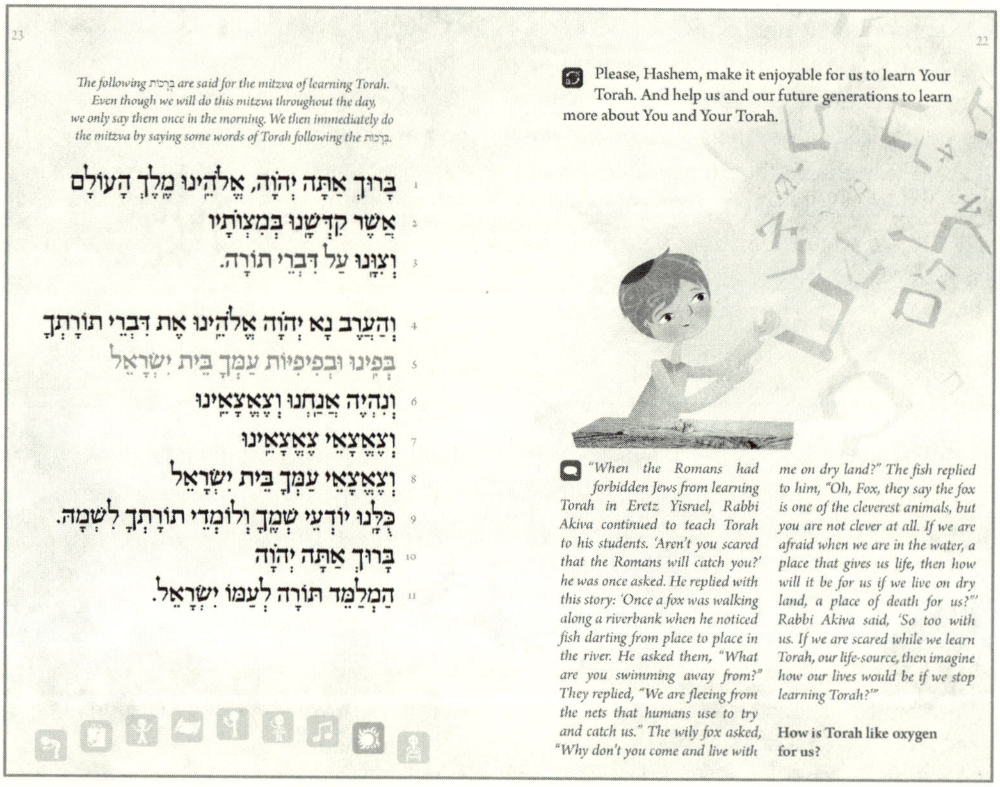

23

The following בְּרָכוֹת *are said for the mitzva of learning Torah. Even though we will do this mitzva throughout the day, we only say them once in the morning. We then immediately do the mitzva by saying some words of Torah following the* בְּרָכוֹת.

בָּרוּךְ אַתָּה יְהֹוָה, אֱלֹהֵינוּ מֶלֶךְ הָעוֹלָם
אֲשֶׁר קִדְּשָׁנוּ בְּמִצְוֹתָיו
וְצִוָּנוּ עַל דִּבְרֵי תוֹרָה.

וְהַעֲרֶב נָא יְהֹוָה אֱלֹהֵינוּ אֶת דִּבְרֵי תוֹרָתְךָ
בְּפִינוּ וּבְפִיפִיּוֹת עַמְּךָ בֵּית יִשְׂרָאֵל
וְנִהְיֶה אֲנַחְנוּ וְצֶאֱצָאֵינוּ
וְצֶאֱצָאֵי צֶאֱצָאֵינוּ
וְצֶאֱצָאֵי עַמְּךָ בֵּית יִשְׂרָאֵל
כֻּלָּנוּ יוֹדְעֵי שְׁמֶךָ וְלוֹמְדֵי תוֹרָתְךָ לִשְׁמָהּ.
בָּרוּךְ אַתָּה יְהֹוָה
הַמְלַמֵּד תּוֹרָה לְעַמּוֹ יִשְׂרָאֵל.

22

Please, Hashem, make it enjoyable for us to learn Your Torah. And help us and our future generations to learn more about You and Your Torah.

"When the Romans had forbidden Jews from learning Torah in Eretz Yisrael, Rabbi Akiva continued to teach Torah to his students. 'Aren't you scared that the Romans will catch you?' he was once asked. He replied with this story: 'Once a fox was walking along a riverbank when he noticed fish darting from place to place in the river. He asked them, "What are you swimming away from?" They replied, "We are fleeing from the nets that humans use to try and catch us." The wily fox asked, "Why don't you come and live with me on dry land?" The fish replied to him, "Oh, Fox, they say the fox is one of the cleverest animals, but you are not clever at all. If we are afraid when we are in the water, a place that gives us life, then how will it be for us if we live on dry land, a place of death for us?"' Rabbi Akiva said, 'So too with us. If we are scared while we learn Torah, our life-source, then imagine how our lives would be if we stop learning Torah?'"

How is Torah like oxygen for us?

The *Tefilla* Text

Translation:

Blessed are You, Lord our God, King of the Universe, who has made us holy through His commandments, and has commanded us about the words of Torah.

Please, Lord our God, make the words of Your Torah sweet in our mouths and in the mouths of Your people, the house of Israel, so that we, our descendants and their descendants, and the descendants of Your people, the house of Israel, may all know Your name and study Your Torah for its own sake. Blessed are You, Lord, who teaches Torah to His people Israel.

Highlighted Text:

The words על דברי תורה are highlighted in the same color as the story, and the words בפינו ובפיפיות עמך בית ישראל are highlighted in olive green connecting it to the illustration.

Educational Themes contained in the text:

- A *berakha* for *Limmud Torah* means it is a mitzva – divine command/spiritual experience (and not just intellectual/educational act)
- We are "chosen" to be the only People with the Torah, and with this the responsibility of being an "*Am Segula*"
- We pray that the Torah will be "sweet" in our mouths (as spiritual nourishment, just like sweet food is physical nourishment)
- We pray that we will be successful at educating (and passing our enthusiasm) to our children
- *Limmud Torah* is our gateway to understanding the ways of God
- The Torah that Moshe received, the same one we learn today, represents an unbroken tradition/heritage throughout the generations and our history
- The text of the blessing is to "engage in the words of the Torah" rather than merely "study" them
- Hashem is the source of the Torah, and He teaches it to us personally
- Learning Torah "for its own sake/לשמה"

The Illustration

Here our friend is learning Torah in his school classroom, as we say the *berakha* on this mitzva. The words roll out of his mouth, hinting at the highlighted words בפִינו ובפיפיות עמך בית ישראל – (*make the words of Your Torah sweet) in our mouths and in the mouths of Your people.* Notice the words he is learning – בראשית ברא אלֹהים – the very first words of the Torah.

The *Kavanot*

Conceptual Translation of:

והערב נא ה׳ אלֹהינו את דברי תוֹרתך בפינו ובפיפיות עמך בית ישראל
ונהיה אנחנו וצאצאינו וצאצאי צאצאינו וצאצאי עמך בית ישראל
כלנו יודעי שמך ולומדי תורתך לשמה.

Story:
This famous story from the Talmud (*Berakhot* 61b) has Rabbi Akiva explaining with a parable why it is not possible for Jews to live without the constant presence of *Limmud Torah* in their lives. Just as a fish would die on dry land because the water is the source of its oxygen, its lifeline, so the Jew could not live without Torah. Perhaps that is intimated in the language of this, the first of the *berakhot* for *Limmud Torah* – לַעסֹק בדברי תורה – which implies a constant engagement in the mitzva.

The question for further thought asks the child to consider why we relate to Torah in that way. Why do we think that we could not live a life without constant Torah learning? What do we gain from learning Torah that we could not live without?

Activity ideas:
It could be a fun activity to go around the class asking everyone to volunteer something they don't think they could live life without. Then as a class, discuss what these things have in common, and how the Torah fits in to that picture.

Additional *Kavanot*:
Thought questions:

- What important lessons have your parents taught you? What do you think is important to teach your children?
- Why do we make a ברכה on learning Torah?
- *If praying is talking to Hashem, then learning Torah is listening to Hashem!*[6] What are you going to say to Hashem today and what will you hear from Him?

6. Based on a comment made by Rabbi Jonathan Sacks in his commentary on the *Shema* in the Koren Sacks Siddur

אשר בחר בנו

pp. 24–25

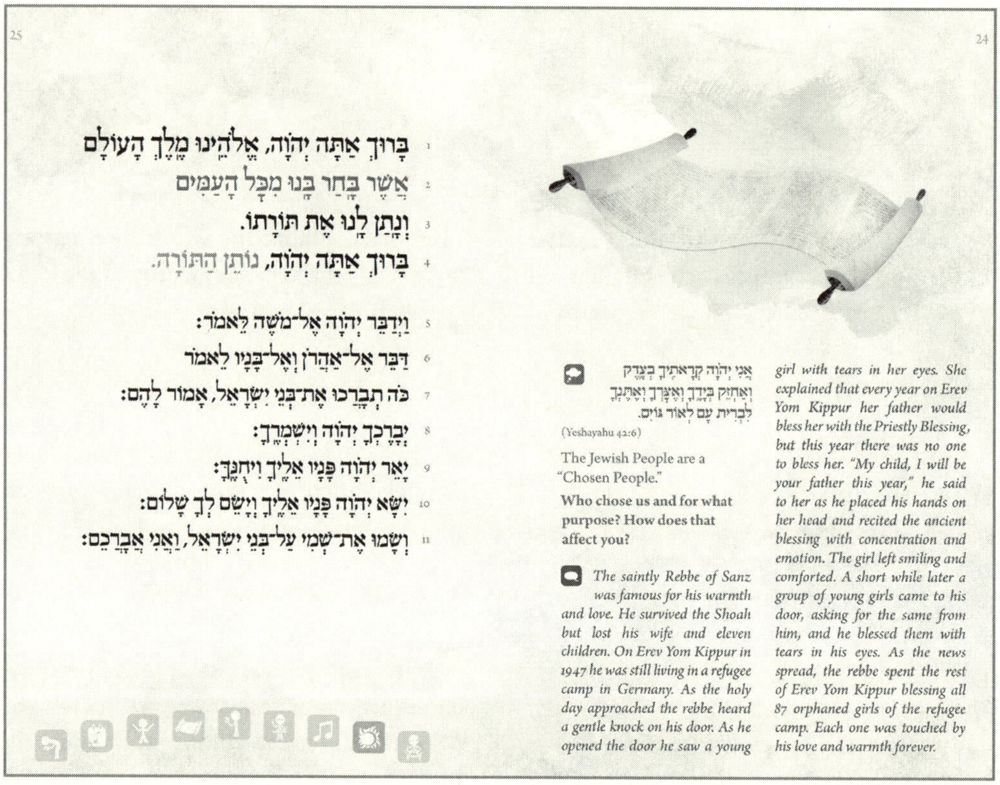

25

24

1 בָּרוּךְ אַתָּה יְהֹוָה, אֱלֹהֵינוּ מֶלֶךְ הָעוֹלָם
2 אֲשֶׁר בָּחַר בָּנוּ מִכָּל הָעַמִּים
3 וְנָתַן לָנוּ אֶת תּוֹרָתוֹ.
4 בָּרוּךְ אַתָּה יְהֹוָה, נוֹתֵן הַתּוֹרָה.

5 וַיְדַבֵּר יְהֹוָה אֶל־מֹשֶׁה לֵּאמֹר:
6 דַּבֵּר אֶל־אַהֲרֹן וְאֶל־בָּנָיו לֵאמֹר
7 כֹּה תְבָרְכוּ אֶת־בְּנֵי יִשְׂרָאֵל, אָמוֹר לָהֶם:
8 יְבָרֶכְךָ יְהֹוָה וְיִשְׁמְרֶךָ:
9 יָאֵר יְהֹוָה פָּנָיו אֵלֶיךָ וִיחֻנֶּךָּ:
10 יִשָּׂא יְהֹוָה פָּנָיו אֵלֶיךָ וְיָשֵׂם לְךָ שָׁלוֹם:
11 וְשָׂמוּ אֶת־שְׁמִי עַל־בְּנֵי יִשְׂרָאֵל, וַאֲנִי אֲבָרְכֵם:

אֲנִי יְהֹוָה קְרָאתִיךָ בְצֶדֶק וְאַחְזֵק בְּיָדֶךָ וְאֶצָּרְךָ וְאֶתֶּנְךָ לִבְרִית עָם לְאוֹר גּוֹיִם.
(Yeshayahu 42:6)

The Jewish People are a "Chosen People."

Who chose us and for what purpose? How does that affect you?

The saintly Rebbe of Sanz was famous for his warmth and love. He survived the Shoah but lost his wife and eleven children. On Erev Yom Kippur in 1947 he was still living in a refugee camp in Germany. As the holy day approached the rebbe heard a gentle knock on his door. As he opened the door he saw a young girl with tears in her eyes. She explained that every year on Erev Yom Kippur her father would bless her with the Priestly Blessing, but this year there was no one to bless her. "My child, I will be your father this year," he said to her as he placed his hands on her head and recited the ancient blessing with concentration and emotion. The girl left smiling and comforted. A short while later a group of young girls came to his door, asking for the same from him, and he blessed them with tears in his eyes. As the news spread, the rebbe spent the rest of Erev Yom Kippur blessing all 87 orphaned girls of the refugee camp. Each one was touched by his love and warmth forever.

The *Tefilla* Text

Translation:
Blessed are You, Lord our God, King of the Universe, who has chosen us from all the peoples and given us His Torah. Blessed are You, Lord, Giver of the Torah.

The Lord spoke to Moses, saying, "Speak to Aaron and his sons, saying: Thus you shall bless the sons of Israel. You shall say to them: "May the Lord bless you and protect you. May the Lord make His face shine on you and be gracious to you. May the Lord turn His face toward you and grant you peace. They shall place my name on the children of Israel, and I will bless them".

Highlighted Text:
The words אשר בָחר בָנו מכל העמים are highlighted in the color of the thought question which deals with the concept of chosenness, and the words נוֹתן התוֹרה are colored in a light brown to match the illustration of the *Sefer Torah*.

Educational Themes contained in the text:

- We are "chosen" to be the only People with the Torah, and with this the responsibility of being an *"Am Segula"*

- We pray that the Torah will be "sweet" in our mouths (as spiritual nourishment just like sweet food is physical nourishment)
- The mitzva of educating our children/next generation
- *Limmud Torah* is our gateway to understanding the ways of God
- The Torah that Moshe received, the same one we learn today, represents an unbroken tradition/heritage throughout the generations and our history
- Torah is "commanded" by Hashem (i.e., it is an imperative/instruction)

The Illustration

The illustration is of a *Sefer Torah*, floating with an ethereal textured background behind it. While *Birkhot HaTorah* is for the mitzva of learning Torah in its widest sense, the illustration reminds us that the basis for the whole belief system of Torah lifestyle and learning is the original Torah text. The spiritual ethereal feel behind the illustration reminds us of the spiritual aspects of Torah learning, as well as the more obvious cognitive and legal elements of Torah learning.

The *Kavanot*

Thought Question:

אני הי קראתיך בצדק ואחזק בידך ואצרך ואתנך לברית עם לאור גוים
(Yeshayahu 42:6)

I the LORD *have called you in righteousness, and have taken hold of your hand, and kept you, and set you for a covenant of the people, for a light of the nations;*

This thought question is anchored to the words in the *berakha* אשר בְחר בְנו מכל העמים and asks the student to begin to think about what it means to be a member of a chosen people. The verse from Yeshayahu is one possible answer – being chosen means having the responsibility to be a "light unto the nations." However, the thought question is open ended and students may arrive at many varied conclusions on what chosenness means, including special love from God, special relationship of responsibility to protect, chosen to keep the Torah, chosen to be successful etc. To link being a Chosen People to being a "light unto the nations" is to suggest that God has chosen the Jewish People to spread His word to the world in order to improve it.

There is an example of a story about the Jewish People being a "light unto the nations" on page 74, which is linked to the mention of chosenness in the *tefilla* (אהבה רבה) on that page, and the two thought questions on page 142 explore the concept of *Am Segula* (in the context of the *Tikkun Olam* referred to in the עלינו there).

Story:
The story found on this page about the Rebbe of Sanz is about the priestly blessing that is found on this page of the siddur. There is a widespread custom to give this *berakha* to one's children on Erev Yom Kippur, and this is the central point of the story. Many people also give their children this *berakha* every Friday night, and it can be found on page 172 with an illustration of a father giving his daughter the *berakha*. The story explores the notion that this *berakha* expresses the love and care that a parent, and the rebbe, and God, have for Jewish children. While the verses of this *berakha* are included at this point of the siddur as a way to fulfill the mitzva of learning Torah (for which we have just made the *berakha*), perhaps the choice of these verses specifically suggest a quid-pro-quo relationship between us and God. If we keep and learn the Torah (for which we have just made the *berakha*), then God will look after us (as written in these verses).

אדון עולם

pp. 26–27

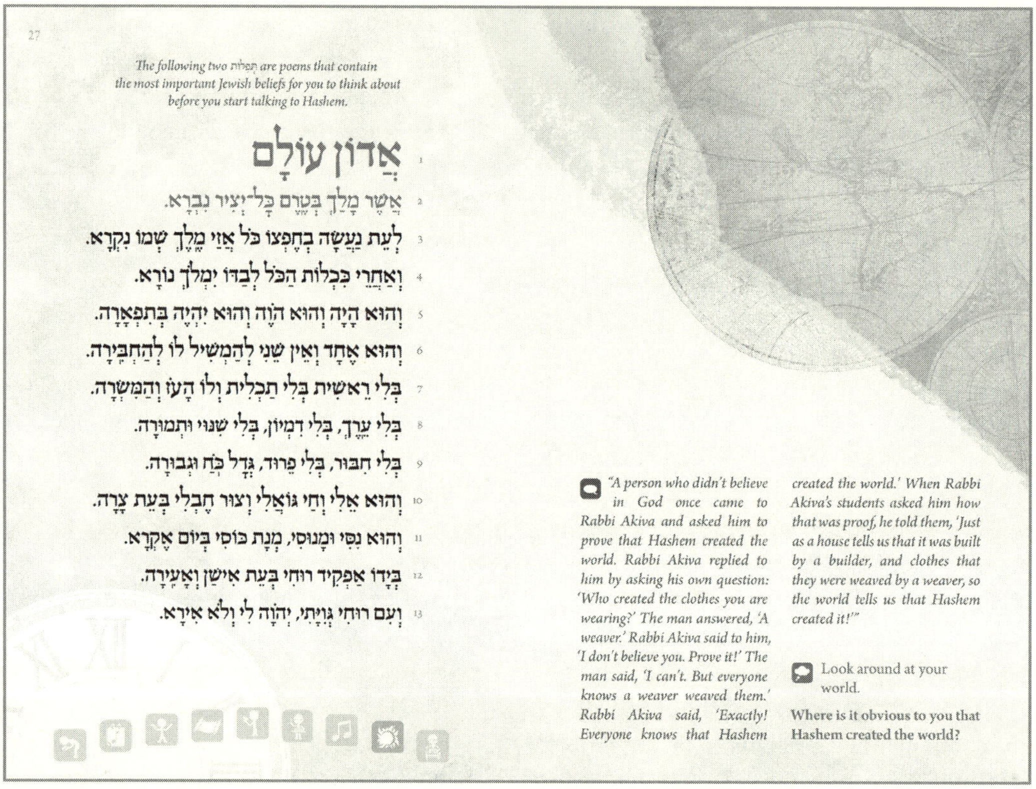

27

The following two תְּפִלּוֹת are poems that contain the most important Jewish beliefs for you to think about before you start talking to Hashem.

אֲדוֹן עוֹלָם
אֲשֶׁר מָלַךְ בְּטֶרֶם כָּל־יְצִיר נִבְרָא.
לְעֵת נַעֲשָׂה בְחֶפְצוֹ כֹּל אֲזַי מֶלֶךְ שְׁמוֹ נִקְרָא.
וְאַחֲרֵי כִּכְלוֹת הַכֹּל לְבַדּוֹ יִמְלֹךְ נוֹרָא.
וְהוּא הָיָה וְהוּא הֹוֶה וְהוּא יִהְיֶה בְּתִפְאָרָה.
וְהוּא אֶחָד וְאֵין שֵׁנִי לְהַמְשִׁיל לוֹ לְהַחְבִּירָה.
בְּלִי רֵאשִׁית בְּלִי תַכְלִית וְלוֹ הָעֹז וְהַמִּשְׂרָה.
בְּלִי עֵרֶךְ, בְּלִי דִמְיוֹן, בְּלִי שִׁנּוּי וּתְמוּרָה.
בְּלִי חִבּוּר, בְּלִי פֵרוּד, גְּדָל כֹּחַ וּגְבוּרָה.
וְהוּא אֵלִי וְחַי גּוֹאֲלִי וְצוּר חֶבְלִי בְּעֵת צָרָה.
וְהוּא נִסִּי וּמָנוּסִי, מְנָת כּוֹסִי בְּיוֹם אֶקְרָא.
בְּיָדוֹ אַפְקִיד רוּחִי בְּעֵת אִישַׁן וְאָעִירָה.
וְעִם רוּחִי גְּוִיָּתִי, יְהֹוָה לִי וְלֹא אִירָא.

"A person who didn't believe in God once came to Rabbi Akiva and asked him to prove that Hashem created the world. Rabbi Akiva replied to him by asking his own question: 'Who created the clothes you are wearing?' The man answered, 'A weaver.' Rabbi Akiva said to him, 'I don't believe you. Prove it!' The man said, 'I can't. But everyone knows a weaver weaved them.' Rabbi Akiva said, 'Exactly! Everyone knows that Hashem created the world.' When Rabbi Akiva's students asked him how that was proof, he told them, 'Just as a house tells us that it was built by a builder, and clothes that they were weaved by a weaver, so the world tells us that Hashem created it!'"

Look around at your world.

Where is it obvious to you that Hashem created the world?

The *Tefilla* Text

Translation:
Lord of the universe, who reigned before the birth of any thing –
When by His will all things were made, then was His name proclaimed King.
And when all things shall cease to be, He alone will reign in awe.
He was, He is, and He shall be glorious for evermore.
He is One, there is none else, alone, unique, beyond compare;
Without beginning, without end, His might, His rule are everywhere.
He is my God; my Redeemer lives. He is the Rock on whom I rely –
My banner and my safe retreat, my cup, my portion when I cry.
Into His hand my soul I place, when I awake and when I sleep.
The Lord is with me, I shall not fear; body and soul from harm will He keep.

Highlighted Text:
The words אדון עולם אשר מלך בטרם כל־יציר נברא are highlighted in a light brown taken from the illustration.

Educational Themes contained in the text:

- God as "King"
- God as Creator of the world
- God of the universe (transcendent) vs. Personal God (immanent)
- God of history – God is infinite, eternal (pre-dates history), but is involved in the history of the universe, world, Jewish people, and our own history
- God protects me (my body and soul) when I sleep and when I wake up

The Illustration

The illustration here expresses some of the core themes of this *tefilla*, through representing the world, and time (bottom left-hand corner). These are:

- God created the world
- God rules the world (interventionist/God of history)
- God is eternal – He existed before the world and will exist after the world ceases to exist

The *Kavanot*

Story:
This Talmudic story (*Temura* 3) presents the classic "intelligent design" argument for God's existence. While the existence of God is a complex and challenging topic to embark on with students of any age, students from third grade and up will be able to relate to this simple argument. This story is brought here next to the *tefilla* which starts with the simple statement of faith that God created the universe.

Activity ideas:
Using props such as an article of clothing (as in the story) or a watch (another classic example of "intelligent design") or something more contemporary from the lives of modern-day children like a cell phone or a personal computer, ask the child to tell the story of the creation of the object based on what they can know of it. They should be able to identify various people that contributed to the computers creation, such as a designer, an electrical engineer, a software programmer, etc. Ask them how they can see and know these things. Then ask them to look at the world around them to see if they can make the same statement – is there an obvious system to the world and to nature that suggests someone designed it? This can lead on nicely to the thought question below.

Thought Question:
To follow on from the story ask your students where they see proof from nature and the world around them that God exists, created the world, and plays an active part in it today. Their "world" should include their school, their homes, their neighborhood and their wider world.

Activity ideas:
Take the class outside into nature to ask them to do this. This could be rural nature or urban nature, or better still both, and see how their answers differ. God should be detectable in both contexts.

יגדל

pp. 28–29

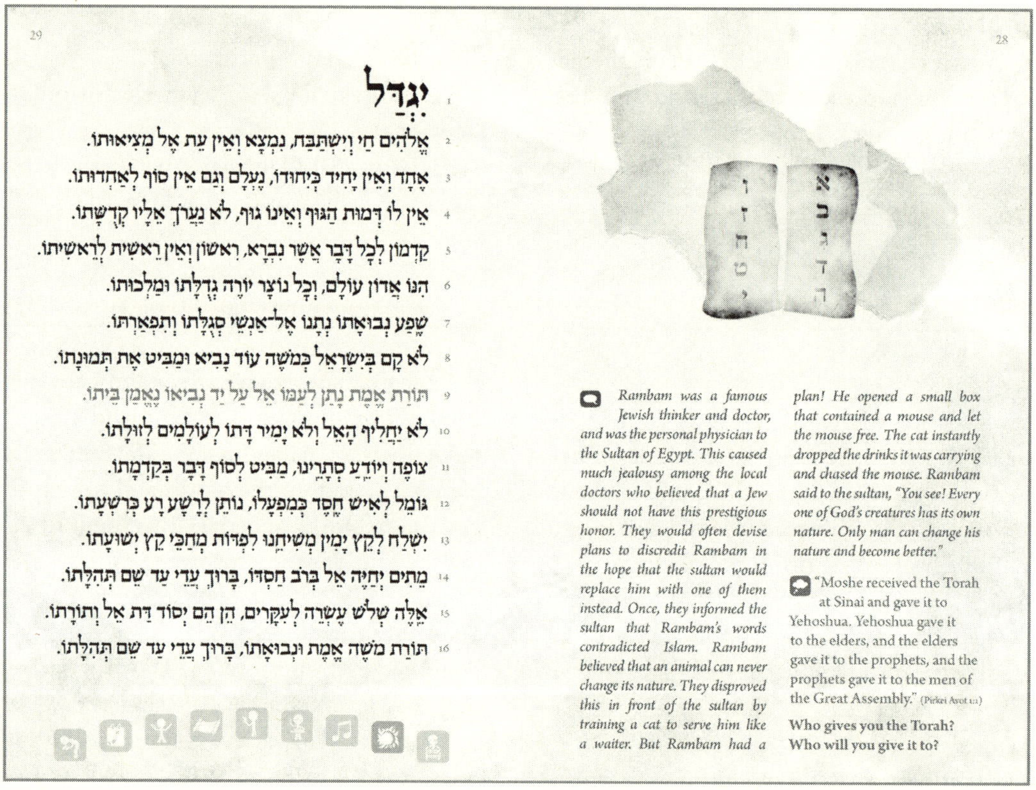
29

28

יִגְדַּל

אֱלֹהִים חַי וְיִשְׁתַּבַּח, נִמְצָא וְאֵין עֵת אֶל מְצִיאוּתוֹ.
אֶחָד וְאֵין יָחִיד כְּיִחוּדוֹ, נֶעְלָם וְגַם אֵין סוֹף לְאַחְדּוּתוֹ.
אֵין לוֹ דְּמוּת הַגּוּף וְאֵינוֹ גוּף, לֹא נַעֲרֹךְ אֵלָיו קְדֻשָּׁתוֹ.
קַדְמוֹן לְכָל דָּבָר אֲשֶׁר נִבְרָא, רִאשׁוֹן וְאֵין רֵאשִׁית לְרֵאשִׁיתוֹ.
הִנּוֹ אֲדוֹן עוֹלָם, וְכָל נוֹצָר יוֹרֶה גְדֻלָּתוֹ וּמַלְכוּתוֹ.
שֶׁפַע נְבוּאָתוֹ נְתָנוֹ אֶל־אַנְשֵׁי סְגֻלָּתוֹ וְתִפְאַרְתּוֹ.
לֹא קָם בְּיִשְׂרָאֵל כְּמֹשֶׁה עוֹד נָבִיא וּמַבִּיט אֶת תְּמוּנָתוֹ.
תּוֹרַת אֱמֶת נָתַן לְעַמּוֹ אֵל עַל יַד נְבִיאוֹ נֶאֱמַן בֵּיתוֹ.
לֹא יַחֲלִיף הָאֵל וְלֹא יָמִיר דָּתוֹ לְעוֹלָמִים לְזוּלָתוֹ.
צוֹפֶה וְיוֹדֵעַ סְתָרֵינוּ, מַבִּיט לְסוֹף דָּבָר בְּקַדְמָתוֹ.
גּוֹמֵל לְאִישׁ חֶסֶד כְּמִפְעָלוֹ, נוֹתֵן לְרָשָׁע רָע כְּרִשְׁעָתוֹ.
יִשְׁלַח לְקֵץ יָמִין מְשִׁיחֵנוּ לִפְדּוֹת מְחַכֵּי קֵץ יְשׁוּעָתוֹ.
מֵתִים יְחַיֶּה אֵל בְּרֹב חַסְדּוֹ, בָּרוּךְ עֲדֵי עַד שֵׁם תְּהִלָּתוֹ.
אֵלֶּה שְׁלֹשׁ עֶשְׂרֵה לְעִקָּרִים, הֵן הֵם יְסוֹד דַּת אֵל וְתוֹרָתוֹ.
תּוֹרַת מֹשֶׁה אֱמֶת וּנְבוּאָתוֹ, בָּרוּךְ עֲדֵי עַד שֵׁם תְּהִלָּתוֹ.

Rambam was a famous Jewish thinker and doctor, and was the personal physician to the Sultan of Egypt. This caused much jealousy among the local doctors who believed that a Jew should not have this prestigious honor. They would often devise plans to discredit Rambam in the hope that the sultan would replace him with one of them instead. Once, they informed the sultan that Rambam's words contradicted Islam. Rambam believed that an animal can never change its nature. They disproved this in front of the sultan by training a cat to serve him like a waiter. But Rambam had a plan! He opened a small box that contained a mouse and let the mouse free. The cat instantly dropped the drinks it was carrying and chased the mouse. Rambam said to the sultan, "You see! Every one of God's creatures has its own nature. Only man can change his nature and become better."

"Moshe received the Torah at Sinai and gave it to Yehoshua. Yehoshua gave it to the elders, and the elders gave it to the prophets, and the prophets gave it to the men of the Great Assembly." (Pirkei Avot 1:1)

**Who gives you the Torah?
Who will you give it to?**

The *Tefilla* Text

Translation:
Great is the living God and praised. He exists, and His existence is beyond time.
He is One, and there is no unity like His. Unfathomable, His Oneness is infinite.
He has neither bodily form nor substance; His holiness is beyond compare.
He preceded all that was created. He was first: there was no beginning to His beginning.
Behold He is Master of the Universe; and every creature shows His greatness and majesty.
The rich flow of His prophecy He gave to His treasured people in whom He gloried.
Never in Israel has there arisen another like Moses, a prophet who beheld God's image.
God gave His people a Torah of truth by the hand of His prophet, most faithful of His House.
God will not alter or change His law for any other, for eternity.
He sees and knows our secret thoughts; as soon as something is begun, He foresees its end.

He rewards people with loving-kindness according to their deeds; He punishes the wicked according to his wickedness.
At the end of days He will send our Messiah to redeem those who await His final salvation.
God will revive the dead in His great loving-kindness.
Blessed for evermore is His glorious name!

Highlighted Text:
The line תורת אמת נתן לעמו אל על יד נביאו נאמן ביתו is highlighted in the aqua from the illustration.

Educational Themes contained in the text:

- Rambam's Thirteen Principles of Faith
  1. Belief in the existence of God
  2. Belief in God's unity
  3. Belief in God's incorporeality
  4. Belief in God's eternity
  5. The imperative to pray to God
  6. Belief that God communicates with man through prophecy
  7. Belief in the primacy of the prophecy of Moses
  8. Belief in the divine origin of the Torah
  9. Belief in the immutability of the Torah
  10. Belief in God's omniscience
  11. Belief in divine reward and punishment
  12. Belief in the arrival of the Messiah
  13. Belief in the resurrection of the dead
- God = Creator, and the God of history (*Hashgaḥa*)
- Revelation through prophecy
- Moshe = archetypal prophet
- *Torah min HaShamayim* (The divine origin of the Torah)

The Illustration

This illustration depicts the following line from the *tefilla*: *God gave His people a Torah of truth by the hand of His prophet, most faithful of His House.* Here we have the *Luḥot HaBerit* (Tablets of Law) which represent the Torah Moshe received on Mount Sinai, with the light of truth emanating from behind the *luḥot.*

The *Kavanot*

Story:
Yigdal is a poetic summary of Rambam's Thirteen Principles of Faith. So we chose a story about the Rambam here that introduces the students to him as a historical figure, and from it the following facts and concepts can be explored:

- Rambam was a famous Jewish philosopher (the term thinker was used but what a philosopher is could be a useful discussion to have in class).
- Rambam was also a famous and accomplished doctor. He didn't rely on money from his rabbinic career, but rather had another profession that involved him knowing a lot about science and medicine.
- Rambam lived in Egypt (although he was born and lived first in Spain).
- Rambam believed in God, and that God created the world and all of God's creatures, that man has free-will, and that he should try to improve himself.
- Rambam was very smart.

Thought Question:

משה קבל תורה מסיני, ומסרה ליהושע, ויהושע לזקנים, וזקנים לנביאים, ונביאים מסרוה לאנשי כנסת הגדולה
(*Avot* 1:1)

The sentence that is highlighted and linked to the *luḥot* illustration could also have been linked to this thought question. Mishna *Avot* begins with the transmission of Torah, from God to Moshe, and then to Yehoshua, and ultimately all the way down to us, and to your students. This is a statement of faith in the context of *Yigdal*, and a historical-legal fact in the mishna. The follow-up thought question asks the child to relate to it in a personal way – where are they in the line of transmission? The answer hopefully will be that they received their Torah from their parents and teachers, and will pass it on to their children, and perhaps their friends and others that they are in a position to influence.

Activity ideas:

- Games that have a transmission aspect to them, like "Broken Telephone" where a message is whispered round the circle. Every child is only allowed to whisper it once into their neighbor's ear. At the end we see how close to the original message it was. And then we can discuss how the Torah is exactly word-for-word the same as the original (according to *Yigdal* and Rambam's *ikarim*) and how that came about.
- Broken Telephone in actions: Four volunteers go out of the room. A fifth volunteer who is inside the classroom acts out an activity decided on by the rest of the class (like making breakfast or ironing or something equally mundane). Then the first volunteer returns to the room and watches the action and then performs it for the second volunteer, who then performs it for the third volunteer, who performs it for the fourth, who then needs to tell the class what they think it is.

Additional *Kavanot*:
Thought questions:

- The mishna says that Moshe received the Torah from Sinai. Why doesn't it say that he received it from God?
- Why is it important to know where the Torah came from?
- When you think of Hashem what comes to mind?

ציצית

pp. 30–31

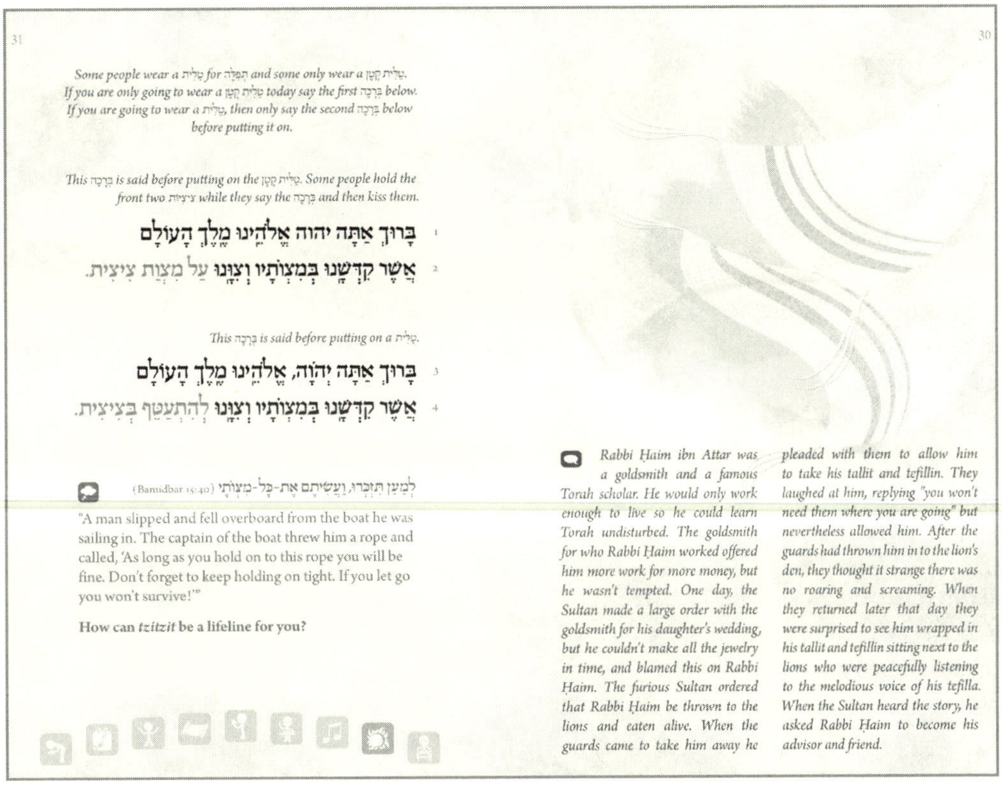

30

Rabbi Ḥaim ibn Attar was a goldsmith and a famous Torah scholar. He would only work enough to live so he could learn Torah undisturbed. The goldsmith for who Rabbi Ḥaim worked offered him more work for more money, but he wasn't tempted. One day, the Sultan made a large order with the goldsmith for his daughter's wedding, but he couldn't make all the jewelry in time, and blamed this on Rabbi Ḥaim. The furious Sultan ordered that Rabbi Ḥaim be thrown to the lions and eaten alive. When the guards came to take him away he pleaded with them to allow him to take his tallit and tefillin. They laughed at him, replying "you won't need them where you are going" but nevertheless allowed him. After the guards had thrown him in to the lion's den, they thought it strange there was no roaring and screaming. When they returned later that day they were surprised to see him wrapped in his tallit and tefillin sitting next to the lions who were peacefully listening to the melodious voice of his tefilla. When the Sultan heard the story, he asked Rabbi Ḥaim to become his advisor and friend.

31

Some people wear a טַלִּית for תְּפִלָּה and some only wear a טַלִּית קָטָן. If you are only going to wear a טַלִּית קָטָן today say the first בְּרָכָה below. If you are going to wear a טַלִּית, then only say the second בְּרָכָה below before putting it on.

This בְּרָכָה is said before putting on the טַלִּית קָטָן. Some people hold the front two צִיצִית while they say the בְּרָכָה and then kiss them.

1 בָּרוּךְ אַתָּה יהוה אֱלֹהֵינוּ מֶלֶךְ הָעוֹלָם

2 אֲשֶׁר קִדְּשָׁנוּ בְּמִצְוֹתָיו וְצִוָּנוּ עַל מִצְוַת צִיצִית.

This בְּרָכָה is said before putting on a טַלִּית.

3 בָּרוּךְ אַתָּה יְהֹוָה, אֱלֹהֵינוּ מֶלֶךְ הָעוֹלָם

4 אֲשֶׁר קִדְּשָׁנוּ בְּמִצְוֹתָיו וְצִוָּנוּ לְהִתְעַטֵּף בְּצִיצִית.

לְמַעַן תִּזְכְּרוּ, וַעֲשִׂיתֶם אֶת-כָּל-מִצְוֹתָי (Bamidbar 15:40)

"A man slipped and fell overboard from the boat he was sailing in. The captain of the boat threw him a rope and called, 'As long as you hold on to this rope you will be fine. Don't forget to keep holding on tight. If you let go you won't survive!'"

How can *tzitzit* be a lifeline for you?

The *Tefilla* Text

Translation:

Blessed are You, Lord our God, King of the Universe, who has made us holy through His commandments, and has commanded us about the command of tasseled garments.

Blessed are You, Lord our God, King of the Universe, who has made us holy through His commandments, and has commanded us to wrap ourselves in the tasseled garment.

Highlighted Text:

The words על מצות ציצית and להתעטף בציצית are highlighted in the blue of the *tallit* in the illustration.

Educational Themes contained in the text:

- *Tzitzit* as a visual reminder/signpost
- The values of Jewish clothing

The Illustration

The illustration shows us a *tallit katan* The feel of the illustration as a whole is very spiritual as the *tallit katan* gently blows in the wind.

The *tzitzit katan* here has the stripes of *tekhelet* (turquoise) associated with the mitzva of *tzitzit*. This is explained more fully on page 80 with the third paragraph of the *Shema*, where a *tallit gadol* features in the illustration, and the link between these stripes and the Israeli national flag is explored. On that page a story relevant to *tzitzit* is also found.

The *Kavanot*

Thought Question:
This midrash, from *Bemidbar Raba* 17:6, begins with the verse from the shema (Bamidbar 15:40) that makes a connection between the mitzva of *tzitzit*, and remembering all other mitzvot. The midrash tells a story of a man who fell overboard and was saved by holding on to the rope that the captain of the boat threw him. The midrash presents this as a metaphor for the strings of *tzitzit*. If one is to "hold on to them", i.e. wear them fastidiously, and focus on them continuously, then you too will be "saved". Perhaps, in the knowledge that the mitzva of *tzitzit* represents the rest of the other mitzvot, focusing on this mitzva will ensure that one leads a life of Torah and mitzvot.

The well-known idea, that the mitzva of *tzitzit* should be considered a visual reminder of all the other mitzvot, comes from a Rashi on Bemidbar 15:39, where the numerical value of the word ציצית comes to 600. Add to this the 8 strings (4 strings doubled over to form 8) and the 5 knots required to tie them all together, and it comes to 613, the number of mitzvot in the Torah.

Story:
This wonderful story, with the mitzvot of tzitzit and tefillin central to Rabbi Haim's rescue from the imminent danger of being eaten alive, presents the students with a narrative of values clarification, where mitzvot are more important than money, as well as the important philosophical ideas of reward for mitzvot observance, and the value behind mitzva observance.

Activity ideas:
The question to be considered here is what is Hashem asking us to remember while we wear *tzitzit*? Answers could include "the Torah," "being good," "Hashem," or the classic understanding of Rashi, the 613 mitzvot. The children can be asked what they think of when they see or wear *tzitzit*, and the discussion can emanate from there. An interesting but more abstract line of discussion could also be why we need signs and reminders in our life in general. The educator could introduce other signs from the world of the student(either by mentioning them or, more creatively, by bringing them into class, asking the children to create signs, or playing a game with them), including signs in school, traffic signs, advertising signs, warning signs in various contexts, etc., and follow up by exploring with the children why Hashem may want to provide us with a sign to remind us of His mitzvot/Torah.

מה טבו

pp. 32–33

33

Many people say this תְּפִלָּה when they first enter the בֵּית כְּנֶסֶת in the morning.

1 וַאֲנִי בְּרֹב חַסְדְּךָ אָבוֹא בֵיתֶךָ

2 אֶשְׁתַּחֲוֶה אֶל־הֵיכַל־קָדְשְׁךָ בְּיִרְאָתֶךָ:

1 מַה־טֹּבוּ

2 אֹהָלֶיךָ יַעֲקֹב, מִשְׁכְּנֹתֶיךָ יִשְׂרָאֵל:

3 בְּבֵית אֱלֹהִים נְהַלֵּךְ בְּרָגֶשׁ:

4 יְהוָה צְבָאוֹת עִמָּנוּ

5 מִשְׂגָּב לָנוּ אֱלֹהֵי יַעֲקֹב סֶלָה:

6 יְהוָה צְבָאוֹת, אַשְׁרֵי אָדָם בֹּטֵחַ בָּךְ:

7 יְהוָה הוֹשִׁיעָה, הַמֶּלֶךְ יַעֲנֵנוּ בְיוֹם־קָרְאֵנוּ:

32

Why do you think a synagogue is called a בֵּית כְּנֶסֶת and not a בֵּית תְּפִלָּה?

When the great Hasidic rebbe Menaḥem Mendel of Kotzk was a small boy of just five years old, he asked his father, "Where is God?" His father replied, "God is everywhere, my son." Young Menaḥem Mendel said to him, "I think God is only where you let Him in!"

How can you let Hashem in today?

The *Tefilla* Text

Translation:
As for Me, in Your great loving-kindness, I will come into Your House. I will bow down to Your holy Temple in awe of You. How goodly are your tents, Jacob, your dwelling places, Israel. We will come into the House of God with fervor. The Lord of hosts is with us; the God of Jacob is our stronghold, Selah. Lord of hosts, happy is the one who trusts in You. Lord, save! May the King answer us on the day we call.

Highlighted Text:
The words מַה־טֹּבוּ אֹהָלֶיךָ יַעֲקֹב, מִשְׁכְּנֹתֶיךָ יִשְׂרָאֵל are highlighted in the same brown as the tent from the illustration.

Educational Themes contained in the text:

- Tent = tent of learning (*Beit Midrash*)
- Tent = the Jewish home (which should also function as a *Beit Midrash* and *Beit Kenesset*)
- Parallel to our tent is God's tent = *Beit HaMikdash*

The Illustration

In the Koren Children's Siddur the illustrator explored what a Jewish building would be (an "*Ohel Tov*," so to speak) and depicted a tent as a metaphor for the home and the synagogue with its accompanying values of *ḥesed* (loving-kindness) and *hakhnasat orḥim* (welcoming guests, reminiscent of Avraham's hospitality and his four-doored tent). Here we have a development of the theme, with the "Jewish Building," the tent (home/synagogue), linked to the mitzva and meta-value of *Limmud Torah*. The biblical character is learning Torah in front of his tent, and the path behind him represents a Torah scroll stretching through the generations connecting them on the basis of this value, and expressing the article of faith that the *Sefer Torah* we read today contains the very same words as the original Torah that Moshe wrote.

The *Kavanot*

Thought Question:
The Hebrew for synagogue literally means a house of gathering, implying that there is more to the synagogue than just a house of prayer. It is a community center, and the focus of the community. Activities and services for the community are provided through the synagogue including social, charitable, and educational services. The synagogue is an example of a Jewish building/tent referred to in the *tefilla* מה טבו.

Story:
This famous story[7] challenges the child to think about where we can find God, and if we need specific buildings such as synagogues and study halls to find God, or whether God can be found wherever we are. These themes are also explored in the story on page 54 and the thought question on page 55 in the context of Yerushalayim as a focus for God's presence.

Activity idea:
A scavenger hunt for God: as a class, search throughout your school for Hashem. In each place you choose (such as the lunch hall, the synagogue, the art studio, the principal's office, the gym, etc.) an argument could be made for why God can be found in this place. At the end of the hunt, the class can vote for where they most felt God in their school.

Additional *Kavanot*:
Thought questions:

- How often do you visit Hashem's House? How often does Hashem visit your house?
- What makes a tent or building "good"? What makes it Jewish?

7. There are other versions of how this story happened exactly. This one was based on the version found in Rabbi Aryeh Kaplan's book *Innerspace*.

קרבן תמיד

pp. 34–35

35

Since the בֵּית הַמִּקְדָּשׁ was destroyed it has not been possible to offer sacrifices to Hashem. The rabbis decided that instead we should learn the laws of the sacrifices every day as the next best thing. The following passage contains the laws of the Daily Sacrifice, the קָרְבַּן תָּמִיד, as found in the Torah (Bemidbar 28).

וַיְדַבֵּר יְהֹוָה אֶל־מֹשֶׁה לֵּאמֹר: צַו אֶת־בְּנֵי יִשְׂרָאֵל וְאָמַרְתָּ אֲלֵהֶם אֶת־קָרְבָּנִי לַחְמִי לְאִשַּׁי רֵיחַ נִיחֹחִי תִּשְׁמְרוּ לְהַקְרִיב לִי בְּמוֹעֲדוֹ: וְאָמַרְתָּ לָהֶם זֶה הָאִשֶּׁה אֲשֶׁר תַּקְרִיבוּ לַיהֹוָה כְּבָשִׂים בְּנֵי־שָׁנָה תְמִימִם שְׁנַיִם לַיּוֹם עֹלָה תָמִיד: אֶת־הַכֶּבֶשׂ אֶחָד תַּעֲשֶׂה בַבֹּקֶר וְאֵת הַכֶּבֶשׂ הַשֵּׁנִי תַּעֲשֶׂה בֵּין הָעַרְבָּיִם: וַעֲשִׂירִית הָאֵיפָה סֹלֶת לְמִנְחָה בְּלוּלָה בְּשֶׁמֶן כָּתִית רְבִיעִת הַהִין: עֹלַת תָּמִיד הָעֲשֻׂיָה בְּהַר סִינַי לְרֵיחַ נִיחֹחַ אִשֶּׁה לַיהֹוָה: וְנִסְכּוֹ רְבִיעִת הַהִין לַכֶּבֶשׂ הָאֶחָד בַּקֹּדֶשׁ הַסֵּךְ נֶסֶךְ שֵׁכָר לַיהֹוָה: וְאֵת הַכֶּבֶשׂ הַשֵּׁנִי תַּעֲשֶׂה בֵּין הָעַרְבָּיִם כְּמִנְחַת הַבֹּקֶר וּכְנִסְכּוֹ תַּעֲשֶׂה אִשֵּׁה רֵיחַ נִיחֹחַ לַיהֹוָה:

34

Ariella was five when her one-year-old cousin was diagnosed with cancer. He was a brave little boy, and fought the disease, and beat it, and was an inspiration to all the family. When Ariella was a little older she decided she wanted to help other children who had cancer like her cousin. She raised money for the hospital that had treated her cousin by running in a race that was a mile long. But she wanted to do even more for children with cancer. So she grew her beautiful hair long enough so that she could donate it to a charity that made wigs for children who had lost their hair because of the cancer treatment. She loved her long blond hair, but didn't think twice about donating it to this very important cause. When Ariella turned ten she also became ill with cancer, and became a patient in the very same hospital as her cousin. She also beat the disease and became an inspiration to everyone that met her. This only made her want to give more and more to the children she saw fighting alongside her, and she continues to do so to this day.

The *Tefilla* Text

Translation:

The Lord said to Moses, "Command the Israelites and tell them: 'Be careful to offer to Me at the appointed time My food-offering consumed by fire, as an aroma pleasing to Me.' Tell them: 'This is the fire-offering you shall offer to the Lord – two lambs a year old without blemish, as a regular burnt-offering each day. Prepare one lamb in the morning and the other toward evening, together with a meal-offering of a tenth of an ephah of fine flour mixed with a quarter of a hin of oil from pressed olives. This is the regular burnt-offering instituted at Mount Sinai as a pleasing aroma, a fire-offering made to the Lord. Its libation is to be a quarter of a hin [of wine] with each lamb, poured in the Sanctuary as a libation of strong drink to the Lord. Prepare the second lamb in the afternoon, along with the same meal-offering and libation as in the morning. This is a fire-offering, an aroma pleasing to the Lord.'

Highlighted Text:

The following words are highlighted in the gold of the *mizbe'aḥ* in the illustration: את־הכבש אחד תעשה בבֹּקר, ואת הכֶּבש השני תעשה בין הערבִים

These verses were chosen to be highlighted because they are the subject of the following midrash that explores what the most all-encompassing concept in the Torah is – the "*kelal gadol baTorah*": Ben Azzai says it is the verse, "This is the book of the chronicles of man: On the day that God created man, He made him in the likeness of God" (Bereshit 5:1). Ben Zoma says that there is a more embracing principle: "Listen, Israel: the Lord our God, the Lord is One." Ben Nannas says there is a yet more embracing principle: "Love your neighbor as yourself." Ben Pazzi says we find a more embracing principle still: "The first sheep shall be offered in the morning, and the second sheep in the afternoon" (Shemot 29:39) – or, as we might say today, *Shaḥarit, Minḥa* and *Arvit*. In a word: "routine." The passage concludes: The law follows Ben Pazzi. [8]

Ben Pazzi is in effect saying that the most important concept found in the Torah, learned from the *Korban Tamid*, is bringing sanctity into our everyday lives by creating the routine of religious ritual.

Educational Themes contained in the text:

- Personal sacrifice in our day-to-day lives
- The *Beit HaMikdash*
- The morality of animal sacrifice (for older grades)
- Communal offering brought by the community as a show of collective commitment to God
- What are the continual themes in our life that are important to us? This is making God one of them.
- The link between *tefilla* and *korbanot*
- Making ritual Judaism a routine theme in our lives

The Illustration

This illustration represents the *mizbe'aḥ* in the *Beit HaMikdash*, where the *Korban Tamid* would be offered. Notice the golden texture of the *mizbe'aḥ* matches the other articles from the *Beit HaMikdash* that feature in the siddur – the *Aron* on page 68 and the *Menora* on page 140.

The *Kavanot*

Story:
This true story shows us how a regular young girl with a slightly irregular personal story can demonstrate the values of sacrifice in her everyday life. Animal sacrifice is a difficult concept for young and old alike to relate to, but the very same values are found in the lives of everyday people when they sacrifice their time and energy and money to do good. With this story as a trigger, your students can be encouraged to think about when they have sacrificed these things (and others) in their lives, and when they can create the opportunity to do it again.

Additional *Kavanot*:
Thought questions:

- What have you given Hashem today? What else could you give?
- *Tamid* means regular or recurring. Why do the same thing over and over again?
- What do you give Hashem every day?
- What do you do in your life instead of giving *korbanot* in the *Beit HaMikdash*?

Story:
Yeriḥo lies 30 miles away from Yerushalayim, but the sweet smell of the *korbanot* from the *Beit HaMikdash* could be smelled there. So much so, that the goats of Yeriḥo used to sneeze from the smell, and the women would have no need for perfume![9]

8. Cited in the Introduction to the commentary *HaKotev* to *Ein Yaakov*, and quoted by Maharal in *Netivot Olam, Ahavat HaRe'a* 1.
9. *Yoma* 39b

ברוך שאמר 1

pp. 36–37

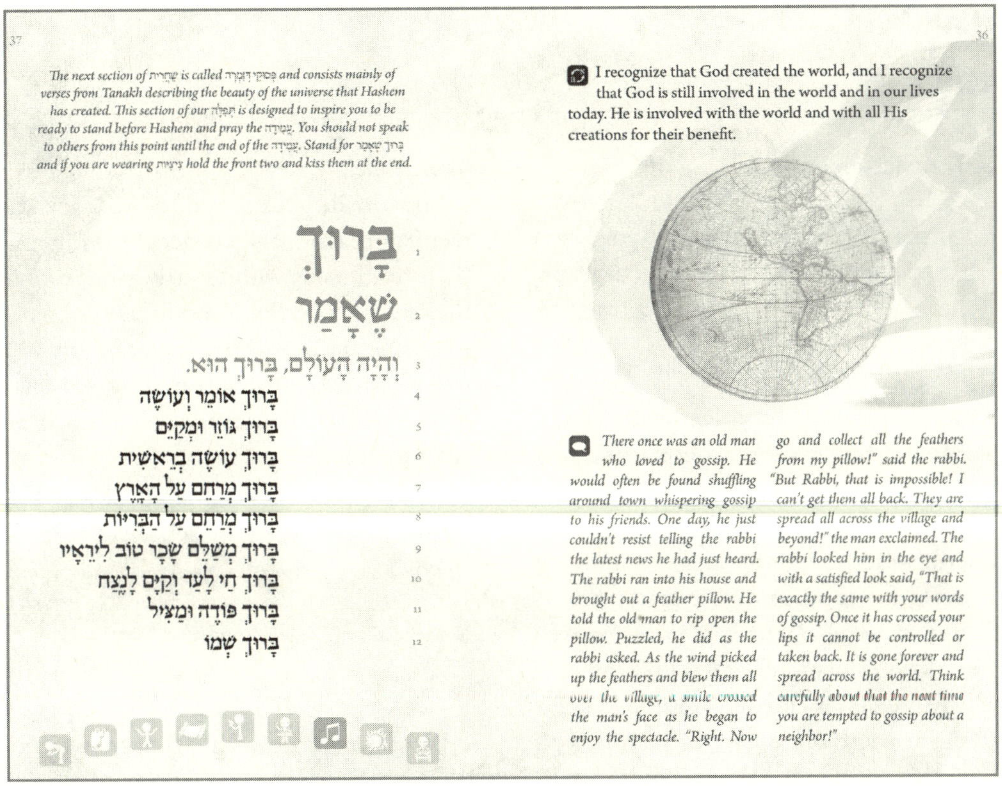

37

The next section of שַׁחֲרִית is called פְּסוּקֵי דְזִמְרָה and consists mainly of verses from Tanakh describing the beauty of the universe that Hashem has created. This section of our תְּפִלָּה is designed to inspire you to be ready to stand before Hashem and pray the עֲמִידָה. You should not speak to others from this point until the end of the עֲמִידָה. Stand for בָּרוּךְ שֶׁאָמַר and if you are wearing צִיצִית hold the front two and kiss them at the end.

בָּרוּךְ
שֶׁאָמַר
וְהָיָה הָעוֹלָם, בָּרוּךְ הוּא.
בָּרוּךְ אוֹמֵר וְעוֹשֶׂה
בָּרוּךְ גּוֹזֵר וּמְקַיֵּם
בָּרוּךְ עוֹשֶׂה בְרֵאשִׁית
בָּרוּךְ מְרַחֵם עַל הָאָרֶץ
בָּרוּךְ מְרַחֵם עַל הַבְּרִיּוֹת
בָּרוּךְ מְשַׁלֵּם שָׂכָר טוֹב לִירֵאָיו
בָּרוּךְ חַי לָעַד וְקַיָּם לָנֶצַח
בָּרוּךְ פּוֹדֶה וּמַצִּיל
בָּרוּךְ שְׁמוֹ

36

I recognize that God created the world, and I recognize that God is still involved in the world and in our lives today. He is involved with the world and with all His creations for their benefit.

There once was an old man who loved to gossip. He would often be found shuffling around town whispering gossip to his friends. One day, he just couldn't resist telling the rabbi the latest news he had just heard. The rabbi ran into his house and brought out a feather pillow. He told the old man to rip open the pillow. Puzzled, he did as the rabbi asked. As the wind picked up the feathers and blew them all over the village, a smile crossed the man's face as he began to enjoy the spectacle. "Right. Now go and collect all the feathers from my pillow!" said the rabbi. "But Rabbi, that is impossible! I can't get them all back. They are spread all across the village and beyond!" the man exclaimed. The rabbi looked him in the eye and with a satisfied look said, "That is exactly the same with your words of gossip. Once it has crossed your lips it cannot be controlled or taken back. It is gone forever and spread across the world. Think carefully about that the next time you are tempted to gossip about a neighbor!"

The *Tefilla* Text

Translation:
Blessed is He who spoke and the world came into being, blessed is He.
Blessed is He who speaks and acts.
Blessed is He who decrees and fulfills.
Blessed is He who creates the universe.
Blessed is He who shows compassion to the earth.
Blessed is He who shows compassion to all creatures.
Blessed is He who gives a good reward to those who fear Him.
Blessed is He who lives for ever and exists to eternity.
Blessed is He who redeems and saves.
Blessed is His name.

Highlighted Text:
The first words of the *tefilla* – ברוך שאמר והיה העולם, ברוך הוא – are highlighted in gold from the illustration.

Educational Themes contained in the text:

- Praising God – what would you praise God for?
- *Zimra* = song/poetry

- God as Creator of the universe
- God as the God of history (השגחה כללית ופרטית)
- The power of words
- Know before whom you stand – דע לפני מי אתה עומד
- Reward and punishment

The Illustration

The continued use of the words ויאמר אלוהים in the creation story (in the first chapter of Bereshit) led to a tradition that God created the world with words (*Pirkei Avot* 5:1 – בעשרה מאמרות נברא העולם – the world was created with ten utterances). That is reflected in this *tefilla* and expressed in this illustration, with the *Alef-Beit* emanating from infinite space towards the globe.

The *Kavanot*

Conceptual Translation of:

ברוך שאמר והיה העולם, ברוך הוא. ברוך עושה בראשית, ברוך אומר ועושה, ברוך גוזר ומקים, ברוך מרחם על הארץ, ברוך מרחם על הבריות

Story:
This classic and well-known story demonstrates the power of words – in this case in a destructive way. Once gossip is set free its impact can never be reversed or controlled. This is a lesson all children can relate to. The *tefilla* describes God as Creator and a continuous force in the world for good, and describes creation through the use of words (referring to the use of speech in the creation story – for example, "God said, 'Let there be light'"). This is clearly an example of the power of words for good. But that power can also be used destructively, and this story asks the reader to consider this idea, and how they will use their words in their lives.

Activity idea:
Taboo: divide your class into two teams. Give a volunteer from each team a concept they must describe to their teammates without using four or five keywords that are "taboo." For example, describe baseball without using the words ball, bat, hit, mitt and pitch. As well as challenging the team to discover the concept, this activity challenges the volunteer to carefully consider their words.

Additional *Kavanot*:
Thought questions:

מות וחיים, ביד-לשון; ואהביה, יאכל פריה
(Mishlei 18:21)

- Words can be powerful. What powerful words have you used recently? Did you use them for positive or negative results?
- Hashem created the world with words. What can you create with your words?
- How many examples of Hashem having an influence in the world can you find in this *tefilla*? How many examples can you find in your life?

ברוך שאמר 2

pp. 38–39

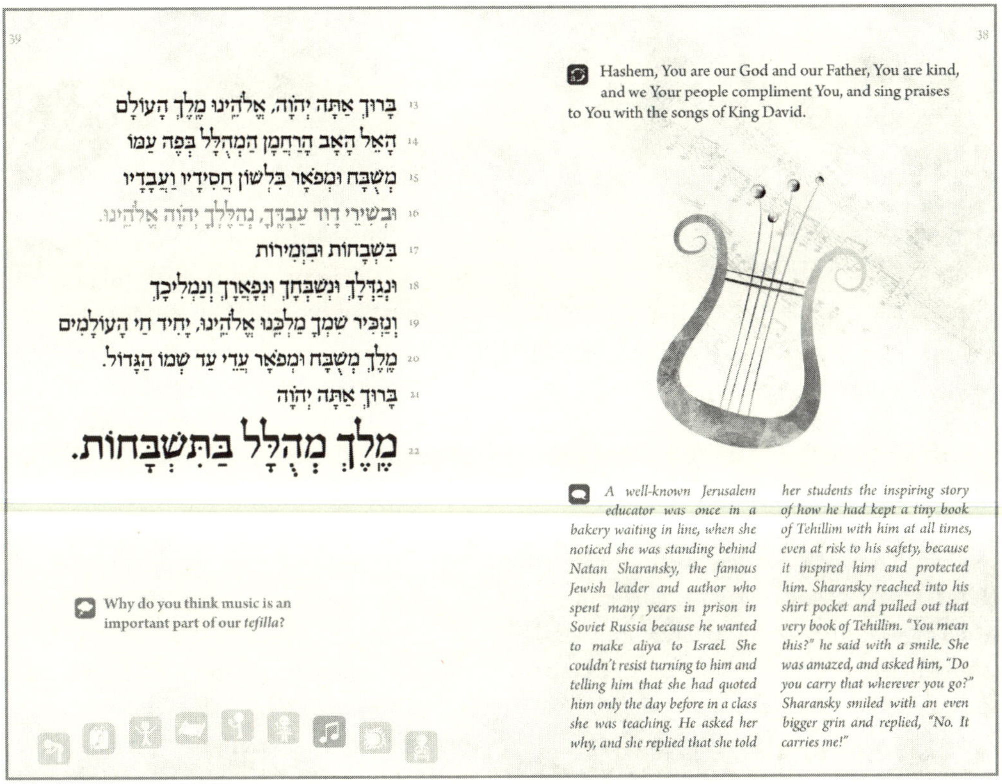

38

Hashem, You are our God and our Father, You are kind, and we Your people compliment You, and sing praises to You with the songs of King David.

A well-known Jerusalem educator was once in a bakery waiting in line, when she noticed she was standing behind Natan Sharansky, the famous Jewish leader and author who spent many years in prison in Soviet Russia because he wanted to make aliya to Israel. She couldn't resist turning to him and telling him that she had quoted him only the day before in a class she was teaching. He asked her why, and she replied that she told her students the inspiring story of how he had kept a tiny book of Tehillim with him at all times, even at risk to his safety, because it inspired him and protected him. Sharansky reached into his shirt pocket and pulled out that very book of Tehillim. "You mean this?" he said with a smile. She was amazed, and asked him, "Do you carry that wherever you go?" Sharansky smiled with an even bigger grin and replied, "No. It carries me!"

39

בָּרוּךְ אַתָּה יְהֹוָה, אֱלֹהֵינוּ מֶלֶךְ הָעוֹלָם
הָאֵל הָאָב הָרַחֲמָן הַמְהֻלָּל בְּפֶה עַמּוֹ
מְשֻׁבָּח וּמְפֹאָר בִּלְשׁוֹן חֲסִידָיו וַעֲבָדָיו
וּבְשִׁירֵי דָוִד עַבְדֶּךָ, נְהַלֶּלְךָ יְהֹוָה אֱלֹהֵינוּ.
בִּשְׁבָחוֹת וּבִזְמִירוֹת
וּנְגַדֶּלְךָ וּנְשַׁבֵּחֲךָ וּנְפָאֶרְךָ וְנַמְלִיכָךְ
וְנַזְכִּיר שִׁמְךָ מַלְכֵּנוּ אֱלֹהֵינוּ, יָחִיד חַי הָעוֹלָמִים
מֶלֶךְ מְשֻׁבָּח וּמְפֹאָר עֲדֵי עַד שְׁמוֹ הַגָּדוֹל.
בָּרוּךְ אַתָּה יְהֹוָה
מֶלֶךְ מְהֻלָּל בַּתִּשְׁבָּחוֹת.

Why do you think music is an important part of our *tefilla*?

The *Tefilla* Text

Translation:

Blessed are You, Lord our God, King of the Universe, God, compassionate Father, extolled by the mouth of His people, praised and glorified by the tongue of His devoted ones and those who serve Him. With the songs of Your servant David we will praise You, O Lord our God. With praises and psalms we will magnify and praise You, glorify You, proclaim Your kingship and speak Your name, our King, our God, the only One, Giver of life to the worlds, the King whose great name is praised and glorified to all eternity. Blessed are You, Lord, the King extolled with songs of praise.

Highlighted Text:

The words ובשירי דוד עבדך, נהללך ה׳ אלהינו are highlighted in the gold of the harp and musical notes of the illustration.

Educational Themes contained in the text:

- Praising God – what would you praise God for?
- The songs of David HaMelekh
- Know before whom you stand – דע לפני מי אתה עומד

The Illustration

The highlighted line of the *tefilla* proclaims our use of the songs of David HaMelekh for our own usage – to praise Hashem with. The harp (כינור in Hebrew) is synonymous with David HaMelekh, who was a talented poet and musician. In Shmuel I 16:23, we see a young David playing his harp to sooth Shaul HaMelekh (והיה, בהיות רוח-אלהים אל-שאול, ולקח דוד את-הכנור, ונגן בידו; ורוח לשאול וטוב לו, וסרה מעליו רוח הרעה), and the influence of David's harp throughout his life is also referenced in the Gemara (*Berakhot* 3b) – *"Rabbi Shimon Ḥasida said: 'David hung his harp above his bed and when midnight would arrive the north wind would blow upon the harp (vibrating the strings) causing music to emanate. David would immediately rise and begin studying Torah. He would continue his studies even as the first light of dawn appeared in the sky.'"*

In our illustration we have a representation of David's harp, with musical notes in the background, representing the words of Tehillim that we sing in *Pesukei DeZimra* in order to prepare to stand before Hashem in prayer.

The *Kavanot*

Conceptual Translation of:

האל האב הרחמן המהלל בפי עמו משבח ומפאר בלשון חסידיו ועבדיו ובשירי דוד עבדך

Story:
This story, which happened and was heard first-hand just before the siddur went to press, illustrates Natan Sharansky's relationship to *Sefer Tehillim*. However, it should be seen as an example of a Jew and his relationship to this book of Tanakh (just as the educator in the story used the original story of his incarceration and inspiration from the *Sefer Tehillim*). Jews for thousands of years have drawn inspiration and comfort from the poems of David HaMelekh, and this is one of the very reasons why the compilers of the siddur used them so prominently in *Shaharit* as a way to prepare us for the climax of our *tefilla* – the *Amida*.

Thought Question:
This question draws our attention to the fact that this whole section of *tefilla* is called *Pesukei DeZimra*, and consists of poems and songs from *Sefer Tehillim*. The text describes *Pesukei DeZimra* as "the Songs of David." Once we recognize that fact, we can explore why the compilers of *Tefillat Shaharit* felt that song and music was so central to the goals of *Pesukei DeZimra*. The goals, of course, are to take us on a journey of preparation, so we become ready to stand before God and say the most intimate and important of our *tefillot* before Him. Music, and the subject of the words in *Pesukei DeZimra* (God's kindness and role in the world, especially in terms of nature and creation) were deemed to achieve this goal. The question asks the child why they think that is.

Perhaps music is an example of human art, and its beauty can inspire us just as the world around us does. Perhaps music alters our mood, helps us to ignore the dreariness and pressures of the everyday, and transcend our world to a spiritual plain where we can stand before God. Perhaps music is in fact food for the soul and takes us directly on that journey itself.

There are other music related questions and stories in the siddur found on pages 50, 52, 148, 184, and 229.

Activity ideas:
Explore how music can alter one's mood and spiritual-emotional state of mind by playing various chosen songs based on the mood they engender. Ask the students to share their own favorite songs and how they feel when they hear them.

אשרי 1

pp. 40–41

40

Those people who are connected to You, Hashem, and pray to You, are happy that they know You are their God!

"It once happened that Ḥoni the Circle Drawer was walking along the way and he saw an old man planting a young fruit tree. Ḥoni asked the man how long it would take until the tree would produce fruit. 'Seventy years,' the old man answered him. 'Do you really think you will be alive for another seventy years so you can enjoy the fruit from this tree?' Ḥoni asked the man with wonder. The man replied, 'Just as I was born into a world with fully grown fruit trees that were planted by my ancestors, so I plant a tree for my children.'"

"מִצְוָה גְּדוֹלָה לִהְיוֹת בְּשִׂמְחָה"

What makes you happy? How can having Hashem in your life make you happy?

41

1 אַשְׁרֵי יוֹשְׁבֵי בֵיתֶךָ, עוֹד יְהַלְלוּךָ סֶּלָה:

2 אַשְׁרֵי הָעָם שֶׁכָּכָה לּוֹ, אַשְׁרֵי הָעָם שֶׁיְהֹוָה אֱלֹהָיו:

3 תְּהִלָּה לְדָוִד

4 אֲרוֹמִמְךָ אֱלוֹהַי הַמֶּלֶךְ, וַאֲבָרְכָה שִׁמְךָ לְעוֹלָם וָעֶד:

5 בְּכָל־יוֹם אֲבָרְכֶךָּ, וַאֲהַלְלָה שִׁמְךָ לְעוֹלָם וָעֶד:

6 גָּדוֹל יְהֹוָה וּמְהֻלָּל מְאֹד, וְלִגְדֻלָּתוֹ אֵין חֵקֶר:

7 דּוֹר לְדוֹר יְשַׁבַּח מַעֲשֶׂיךָ, וּגְבוּרֹתֶיךָ יַגִּידוּ:

8 הֲדַר כְּבוֹד הוֹדֶךָ, וְדִבְרֵי נִפְלְאֹתֶיךָ אָשִׂיחָה:

9 וֶעֱזוּז נוֹרְאֹתֶיךָ יֹאמֵרוּ, וּגְדוּלָּתְךָ אֲסַפְּרֶנָּה:

10 זֵכֶר רַב־טוּבְךָ יַבִּיעוּ, וְצִדְקָתְךָ יְרַנֵּנוּ:

11 חַנּוּן וְרַחוּם יְהֹוָה, אֶרֶךְ אַפַּיִם וּגְדָל־חָסֶד:

12 טוֹב־יְהֹוָה לַכֹּל, וְרַחֲמָיו עַל־כָּל־מַעֲשָׂיו:

The *Tefilla* Text

Translation:

Happy are those who dwell in Your House; they shall continue to praise You, Selah!
Happy are the people for whom this is so; happy are the people whose God is the Lord.
A song of praise by David.
I will exalt You, my God, the King, and bless Your name for ever and all time.
Every day I will bless You, and praise Your name for ever and all time.
God is great and greatly to be praised; His greatness is unfathomable.
One generation will praise Your works to the next, and tell of Your mighty deeds.
On the glorious splendor of Your majesty I will meditate, and on the acts of Your wonders.
They shall talk of the power of Your awesome deeds, and I will tell of Your greatness.
They shall recite the record of Your great goodness, and sing with joy of Your righteousness.

The Lord is gracious and compassionate, slow to anger and great in loving-kindness.
The Lord is good to all, and His compassion extends to all His works.

Highlighted Text:
Every time the word אשרי appears it is highlighted in the same color as the thought question. The verse דור לדור ישבח מעשיך, וגבורתיך יגידו is highlighted in the brown of the bench and table of the illustration. The first letter of each of the verses of chapter 145 of Tehillim is also highlighted in brown, to draw attention to the alphabetic acrostic found there.

Educational Themes contained in the text:

- First verse = quiet meditation
- "Your House" = Temple/*Beit Kenesset*
- God is source of all blessing in the world and in our lives
- Happiness = closeness/serving/relationship with God
- First verse = the individual; second verse = nation
- *Alef-Beit*
- Chain of generations
- Animal welfare/environmentalism

The Illustration

The illustration here has a *savta* learning with her granddaughter. This is linked to the verse that refers to generation after generation praising Hashem together. The scene, generations learning Torah together, is the basis of the generational relationship with Hashem. One generation inspires and teaches the next, and gives them the language of praise and of prayer.

The *Kavanot*

Conceptual Translation of:

אשרי יושבי ביתך, עוד יהללוך סלה:
אשרי העם שככה לו, אשרי העם שיהוה אלהיו:

Thought Question:
Happiness is a wonderful concept to reflect on and explore. It is an important theme of this *tefilla*, and the one with which the *tefilla* begins. The first two verses tell us that an intimate relationship with God leads to happiness in the life of a human. This is reflected in the conceptual translation of those verses. The well-known Rabbi Naḥman quote goes further and actually prescribes happiness as a mitzva itself. This suggests that happiness is central to being a Jew who wishes to fulfill the word of God and live a Torah lifestyle. The follow-up questions ask the child to consider what leads to his or her happiness, and perhaps suggest that these things (provided they are compatible with a Torah lifestyle) be considered a religious obligation. However, a deeper message is implied by the second follow-up question which asks how having a relationship with God and His Torah can also lead to happiness and mental health.

Story:
As well as the illustration, this story from the Talmud (*Ta'anit* 23a) explores the concept of inter-generational relationship and responsibility. Going beyond the message of the highlighted verse, to praise God in each generation, the story suggests that the strength of this generational chain lies in the way previous generations take their responsibility to future generations seriously, whether that be through education or a more physical provision for future generations.

The first half of the story of Ḥoni the Circle Drawer from *Ta'anit* 23a is found in the siddur on page 92. While the story there describes God's responsibility to the world to provide rain, this postscript describes our responsibility to the world to preserve and protect it.

אשרי 2

pp. 42–43

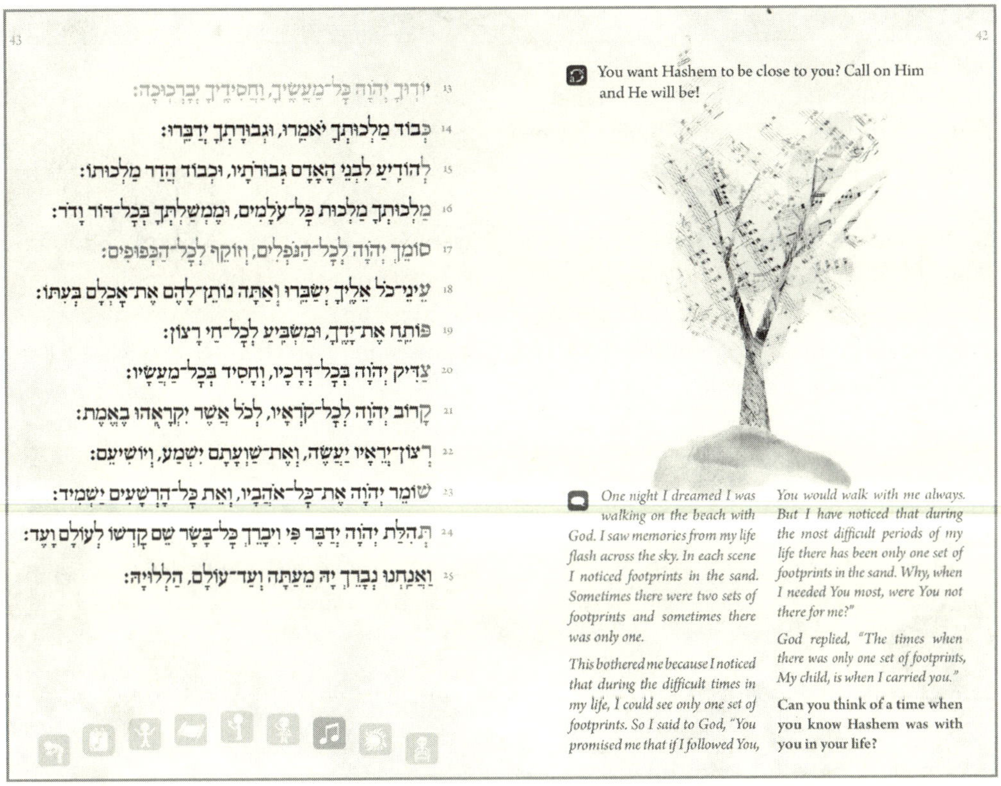

43

13 יוֹדוּךָ יְהוָה כָּל־מַעֲשֶׂיךָ, וַחֲסִידֶיךָ יְבָרְכוּכָה:
14 כְּבוֹד מַלְכוּתְךָ יֹאמֵרוּ, וּגְבוּרָתְךָ יְדַבֵּרוּ:
15 לְהוֹדִיעַ לִבְנֵי הָאָדָם גְּבוּרֹתָיו, וּכְבוֹד הֲדַר מַלְכוּתוֹ:
16 מַלְכוּתְךָ מַלְכוּת כָּל־עֹלָמִים, וּמֶמְשַׁלְתְּךָ בְּכָל־דּוֹר וָדֹר:
17 סוֹמֵךְ יְהוָה לְכָל־הַנֹּפְלִים, וְזוֹקֵף לְכָל־הַכְּפוּפִים:
18 עֵינֵי־כֹל אֵלֶיךָ יְשַׂבֵּרוּ, וְאַתָּה נוֹתֵן־לָהֶם אֶת־אָכְלָם בְּעִתּוֹ:
19 פּוֹתֵחַ אֶת־יָדֶךָ, וּמַשְׂבִּיעַ לְכָל־חַי רָצוֹן:
20 צַדִּיק יְהוָה בְּכָל־דְּרָכָיו, וְחָסִיד בְּכָל־מַעֲשָׂיו:
21 קָרוֹב יְהוָה לְכָל־קֹרְאָיו, לְכֹל אֲשֶׁר יִקְרָאֻהוּ בֶאֱמֶת:
22 רְצוֹן־יְרֵאָיו יַעֲשֶׂה, וְאֶת־שַׁוְעָתָם יִשְׁמַע, וְיוֹשִׁיעֵם:
23 שׁוֹמֵר יְהוָה אֶת־כָּל־אֹהֲבָיו, וְאֵת כָּל־הָרְשָׁעִים יַשְׁמִיד:
24 תְּהִלַּת יְהוָה יְדַבֶּר פִּי, וִיבָרֵךְ כָּל־בָּשָׂר שֵׁם קָדְשׁוֹ לְעוֹלָם וָעֶד:
25 וַאֲנַחְנוּ נְבָרֵךְ יָהּ מֵעַתָּה וְעַד־עוֹלָם, הַלְלוּיָהּ:

42

You want Hashem to be close to you? Call on Him and He will be!

One night I dreamed I was walking on the beach with God. I saw memories from my life flash across the sky. In each scene I noticed footprints in the sand. Sometimes there were two sets of footprints and sometimes there was only one.

This bothered me because I noticed that during the difficult times in my life, I could see only one set of footprints. So I said to God, "You promised me that if I followed You, You would walk with me always. But I have noticed that during the most difficult periods of my life there has been only one set of footprints in the sand. Why, when I needed You most, were You not there for me?"

God replied, "The times when there was only one set of footprints, My child, is when I carried you."

Can you think of a time when you know Hashem was with you in your life?

The *Tefilla* Text

Translation:

All Your works shall thank You, Lord, and Your devoted ones shall bless You.
They shall talk of the glory of Your kingship, and speak of Your might.
To make known to mankind His mighty deeds and the glorious majesty of His kingship.
Your kingdom is an everlasting kingdom, and Your reign is for all generations.
The Lord supports all who fall, and raises all who are bowed down.
All raise their eyes to You in hope, and You give them their food in due season.
You open Your hand, and satisfy every living thing with Your favor.
The Lord is righteous in all His ways, and kind in all He does.
The Lord is close to all who call on Him, to all who call on Him in truth.
He fulfills the will of those who revere Him; He hears their cry and saves them.

The Lord guards all who love Him, but all the wicked He will destroy.
My mouth shall speak the praise of the Lord, and all creatures shall bless His holy name for ever and all time. We will bless the Lord now and for ever. Halleluya!

Highlighted Text:
The verse יוֹדוּךָ ה׳ כׇּל־מַעֲשֶׂיךָ, וַחֲסִידֶיךָ יְבָרְכוּכָה is highlighted in the green of the tree in the illustration, and the verse סוֹמֵךְ ה׳ לְכׇל־הַנֹּפְלִים, וְזוֹקֵף לְכׇל־הַכְּפוּפִים is highlighted to match the story.

Educational Themes contained in the text:

- The glory of nature created by Hashem
- God's kingship
- Hashem sustains us/is the source of all goodness
- *Gam zu letova*

The Illustration

The tree itself in this illustration is praising Hashem with song and perhaps the words of Tehillim from *Pesukei DeZimra*. The verse יוֹדוּךָ ה׳ כׇּל־מַעֲשֶׂיךָ, וַחֲסִידֶיךָ יְבָרְכוּכָה tells of creation itself being a song of praise to Hashem, and this tree is a representation of that.

The *Tehillot Hashem* explains this verse by referencing chapter 148 of *Sefer Tehillim* (page 49 of our siddur) as an explanation of what it means that all of God's creations praise Him. He takes the words from this chapter and says that a song to God emanates from them. The moon and stars, the sea creatures, the deserts, the mountains and valleys, the vegetation and trees and animals and insects and birds – all sing a song of praise to Hashem just through their existence. This tree image recurs on page 48 of the siddur as an expression of this theme.

The *Kavanot*

Conceptual Translation of:

קָרוֹב ה׳ לְכׇל־קֹרְאָיו, לְכֹל אֲשֶׁר יִקְרָאֻהוּ בֶאֱמֶת:

Story:
This version of this well-known poem (author unknown) is adapted from the original, which is widely available on the Internet. It tells a beautiful tale of a troubled life where the subject of the story feels that during the worst periods of his life God had abandoned him. God replies that if he tries hard enough he will sense that it was at these times when God was closest. We often see in life that people are drawn closer to God when they experience challenging times. The verse beginning סוֹמֵךְ captures this belief – that God supports and strengthens those that need it the most.

Additional *Kavanot*:
Story (for the verse beginning with פּוֹתֵחַ*):*
Rabbi Yeḥiel Mikhel was very, very poor, but was always very happy. Someone once asked him how he could pray every day "וּמַשְׂבִּיעַ לְכׇל חַי רָצוֹן" – that Hashem provides every creature with his need? He replied, "Most likely my need is poverty. And that is what I have been provided with!"

תהלים 146

pp. 44–45

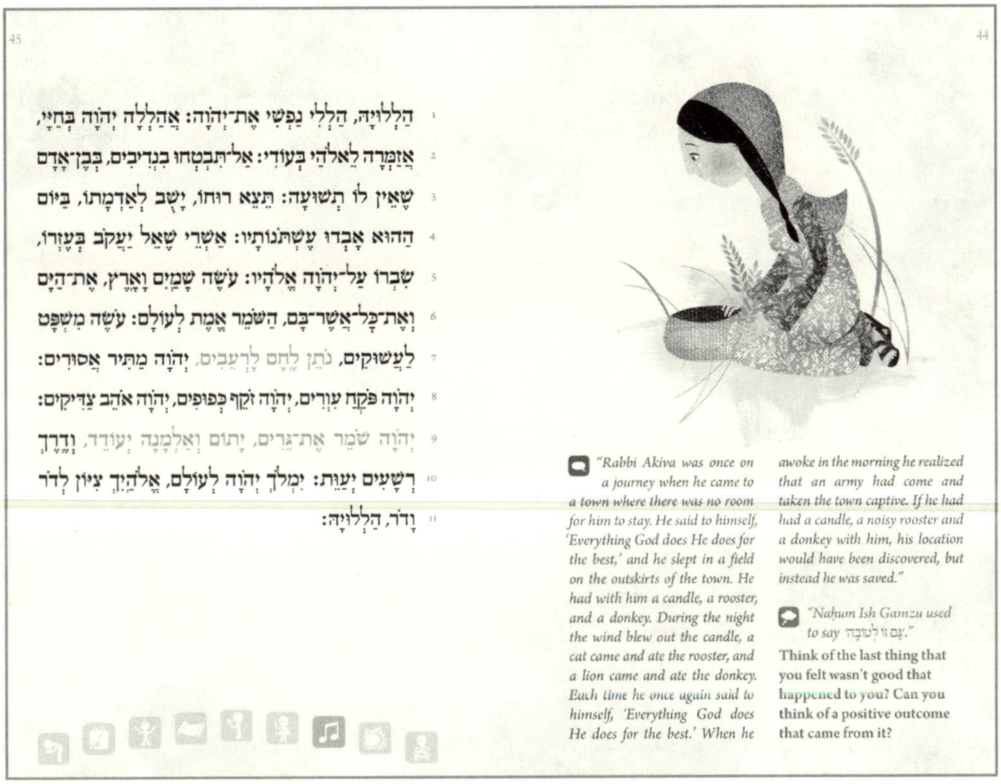
45

1 הַלְלוּיָהּ, הַלְלִי נַפְשִׁי אֶת־יְהוָה: אֲהַלְלָה יְהוָה בְּחַיָּי,
2 אֲזַמְּרָה לֵאלֹהַי בְּעוֹדִי: אַל־תִּבְטְחוּ בִנְדִיבִים, בְּבֶן־אָדָם
3 שֶׁאֵין לוֹ תְשׁוּעָה: תֵּצֵא רוּחוֹ, יָשֻׁב לְאַדְמָתוֹ, בַּיּוֹם
4 הַהוּא אָבְדוּ עֶשְׁתֹּנֹתָיו: אַשְׁרֵי שֶׁאֵל יַעֲקֹב בְּעֶזְרוֹ,
5 שִׂבְרוֹ עַל־יְהוָה אֱלֹהָיו: עֹשֶׂה שָׁמַיִם וָאָרֶץ, אֶת־הַיָּם
6 וְאֶת־כָּל־אֲשֶׁר־בָּם, הַשֹּׁמֵר אֱמֶת לְעוֹלָם: עֹשֶׂה מִשְׁפָּט
7 לַעֲשׁוּקִים, נֹתֵן לֶחֶם לָרְעֵבִים, יְהוָה מַתִּיר אֲסוּרִים:
8 יְהוָה פֹּקֵחַ עִוְרִים, יְהוָה זֹקֵף כְּפוּפִים, יְהוָה אֹהֵב צַדִּיקִים:
9 יְהוָה שֹׁמֵר אֶת־גֵּרִים, יָתוֹם וְאַלְמָנָה יְעוֹדֵד, וְדֶרֶךְ
10 רְשָׁעִים יְעַוֵּת: יִמְלֹךְ יְהוָה לְעוֹלָם, אֱלֹהַיִךְ צִיּוֹן לְדֹר
11 וָדֹר, הַלְלוּיָהּ:

44

"Rabbi Akiva was once on a journey when he came to a town where there was no room for him to stay. He said to himself, 'Everything God does He does for the best,' and he slept in a field on the outskirts of the town. He had with him a candle, a rooster, and a donkey. During the night the wind blew out the candle, a cat came and ate the rooster, and a lion came and ate the donkey. Each time he once again said to himself, 'Everything God does He does for the best.' When he awoke in the morning he realized that an army had come and taken the town captive. If he had had a candle, a noisy rooster and a donkey with him, his location would have been discovered, but instead he was saved."

"Nahum Ish Gamzu used to say גַּם זוּ לְטוֹבָה."

Think of the last thing that you felt wasn't good that happened to you? Can you think of a positive outcome that came from it?

The *Tefilla* Text

Translation:
Halleluya! Praise the Lord, my soul. I will praise the Lord all my life; I will sing to my God as long as I live. Put not your trust in princes, or in mortal man who cannot save. His breath expires, he returns to the earth; on that day his plans come to an end. Happy is he whose help is the God of Jacob, whose hope is in the Lord his God who made heaven and earth, the sea and all they contain; He who keeps faith for ever. He secures justice for the oppressed. He gives food to the hungry. The Lord sets captives free. The Lord gives sight to the blind. The Lord raises those bowed down. The Lord loves the righteous. The Lord protects the stranger. He gives courage to the orphan and widow. He thwarts the way of the wicked. The Lord shall reign for ever. He is your God, Zion, for all generations. Halleluya!

Highlighted Text:
The words נֹתֵן לֶחֶם לרעבים, and ה׳ שֹׁמֵר את־גרים, יתום ואלמנה יעודד, are highlighted in the blue of the woman's dress in the illustration.

Educational Themes contained in the text:

- God as the God of history (השגחה כללית ופרטית)
- Serving God through song
- God in nature/God as Creator of the universe
- God of justice – protecting the weak
- God provides our physical and spiritual needs
- The human soul's connection to God (ability to recognize His presence)

The Illustration

In this illustration we have Ruth the Moabite gathering *leket* in the field of Boaz. The words that are highlighted in this chapter of Tehillim refer to Hashem providing bread for the hungry, and protecting the weakest members of society, such as the strangers, widows and orphans. One of the ways Hashem does this is to encourage us to create a society based on these values by forming a body of laws that look after these people. These include the agricultural laws that look after the poor, such as *ma'aser ani* (tithes to the poor), *pe'a* (the farmer must leave the corner of each field unharvested), *shikheḥa* (forgotten sheaves of crops must be left for the poor to gather) and *leket* (dropped ears of grain that were left during the harvesting process must be left for the poor).

The *Kavanot*

Story:
This story from the Talmud (*Berakhot* 60b) is an example of seeing God's hand in history. In this case it is the personal history of Rabbi Akiva, who believed that each calamity that happened to him was divinely ordained and for the good. He demonstrates his perennially positive outlook on life (הכל לטובה) in other aggadic stories including that from *Makkot* 24a (found on page 116 of the siddur) and *Berakhot* 61b (found on page 22 of the siddur). This chapter of *Sefer Tehillim* (146) has many examples of God playing a direct role in the world and in history. Rabbi Akiva shows us how to perceive it. The thought question that follows develops the idea of seeing God's role in events in one's life, even if they seem negative at first sight.

Thought Question:

נחום איש גם זו אמר: "גם זו לטובה"

This famous phrase found in the Gemara (*Ta'anit* 21a), from which Naḥum received his appellation and very identity, is much in the same vein as Rabbi Akiva's "הכל לטובה." Despite an event appearing outwardly to be negative in nature, Naḥum Ish Gamzu always saw the good in it, or at least tried to, and had faith that everything happened for a reason. The thought questions that follow, which just as easily could have followed the story, ask the children to see their lives in the same way as Rabbi Akiva and Naḥum Ish Gamzu. Everyone can find negative things that happen to them. The trick here is to see the positive in them, and to see God's role in their lives.

Activity idea:
Show an excerpt of a picture heavily zoomed in and ask your students to describe it. Then show the full zoomed-out complete picture and only then can you see the order and beauty of the full scene.

Additional *Kavanot*:
Thought questions:

- Open up today's newspaper. Can you see Hashem interacting with the world there? Where?

Story (the full Naḥum Ish Gamzu story):
Once it happened that the Jews wished to send a gift to the Emperor in Rome. They asked Naḥum Ish Gamzu to go there and present the emperor with a box full of precious jewels. On his journey he spent the night at an inn, and the innkeepers stole the jewels and replaced them with earth. The next morning, when he saw what had happened, Naḥum said גם זו לטובה. When

he arrived in Rome and they saw the gift of earth, the emperor thought that the Jews were mocking him and he wished to put Naḥum to death. Naḥum said again גם זו לטובה. Eliyahu the Prophet then appeared to the emperor as one of his ministers, and suggested that the earth may be from the time of Avraham, and therefore miraculous. Just as Avraham threw earth at his enemies it turned to swords and arrows, so this earth would help the Romans defeat their enemies. As a reward, the emperor filled Naḥum's box with precious jewels and sent him on his way.[10]

10. *Ta'anit* 21a

תהלים 147

pp. 46–47

47

הַלְלוּיָהּ, כִּי־טוֹב זַמְּרָה אֱלֹהֵינוּ, כִּי־נָעִים נָאוָה תְהִלָּה: בּוֹנֵה יְרוּשָׁלַםִ יְהוָה, נִדְחֵי יִשְׂרָאֵל יְכַנֵּס: הָרוֹפֵא לִשְׁבוּרֵי לֵב, וּמְחַבֵּשׁ לְעַצְּבוֹתָם: מוֹנֶה מִסְפָּר לַכּוֹכָבִים, לְכֻלָּם שֵׁמוֹת יִקְרָא: גָּדוֹל אֲדוֹנֵינוּ וְרַב־כֹּחַ, לִתְבוּנָתוֹ אֵין מִסְפָּר: מְעוֹדֵד עֲנָוִים יְהוָה, מַשְׁפִּיל רְשָׁעִים עֲדֵי־אָרֶץ: עֱנוּ לַיהוָה בְּתוֹדָה, זַמְּרוּ לֵאלֹהֵינוּ בְכִנּוֹר: הַמְכַסֶּה שָׁמַיִם בְּעָבִים, הַמֵּכִין לָאָרֶץ מָטָר, הַמַּצְמִיחַ הָרִים חָצִיר: נוֹתֵן לִבְהֵמָה לַחְמָהּ, לִבְנֵי עֹרֵב אֲשֶׁר יִקְרָאוּ: לֹא בִגְבוּרַת הַסּוּס יֶחְפָּץ, לֹא־בְשׁוֹקֵי הָאִישׁ יִרְצֶה: רוֹצֶה יְהוָה אֶת־יְרֵאָיו, אֶת־הַמְיַחֲלִים לְחַסְדּוֹ: שַׁבְּחִי יְרוּשָׁלַםִ אֶת־יְהוָה, הַלְלִי אֱלֹהַיִךְ צִיּוֹן: כִּי־חִזַּק בְּרִיחֵי שְׁעָרָיִךְ, בֵּרַךְ בָּנַיִךְ בְּקִרְבֵּךְ: הַשָּׂם־גְּבוּלֵךְ שָׁלוֹם, חֵלֶב חִטִּים יַשְׂבִּיעֵךְ: הַשֹּׁלֵחַ אִמְרָתוֹ אָרֶץ, עַד־מְהֵרָה יָרוּץ דְּבָרוֹ: הַנֹּתֵן שֶׁלֶג כַּצָּמֶר, כְּפוֹר כָּאֵפֶר יְפַזֵּר: מַשְׁלִיךְ קַרְחוֹ כְפִתִּים, לִפְנֵי קָרָתוֹ מִי יַעֲמֹד: יִשְׁלַח דְּבָרוֹ וְיַמְסֵם, יַשֵּׁב רוּחוֹ יִזְּלוּ־מָיִם: מַגִּיד דְּבָרָו לְיַעֲקֹב, חֻקָּיו וּמִשְׁפָּטָיו לְיִשְׂרָאֵל: לֹא עָשָׂה כֵן לְכָל־גּוֹי, וּמִשְׁפָּטִים בַּל־יְדָעוּם, הַלְלוּיָהּ:

46

The brave Jewish soldiers fighting to conquer the holy city of Tzefat during Israel's War of Independence in 1948 found themselves greatly outnumbered and severely lacking in supplies to fight the Arab army they faced. The Jews had a secret weapon though. The Davidka! Named after its inventor, David Leibowitch, it was a homemade cannon that fired homemade bombs that were inaccurate and largely ineffective. However they made a tremendous noise when they exploded. There were rumors that because many of the inventors of the atomic bomb used by America in World War II were Jewish, the Jews fighting in Israel also had the atomic bomb, which made a very loud noise as well. It was also believed that it would "rain" after an atomic explosion. Miraculously it rained as soon as the Davidka was fired in Tzefat. Fearing for their lives, the Arabs retreated, allowing the Jews to take full control of the city of Tzefat!

"Each blade of grass has an angel pushing it and telling it to grow."

Hashem cares for everything in creation, including you.

How is Hashem caring for you today? Where in your life do you feel it?

The *Tefilla* Text

Translation:
Halleluya! How good it is to sing songs to our God; how pleasant and fitting to praise Him. The Lord rebuilds Jerusalem. He gathers the scattered exiles of Israel. He heals the brokenhearted and binds up their wounds. He counts the number of the stars, calling each by name. Great is our Lord and mighty in power; His understanding has no limit. The Lord gives courage to the humble, but casts the wicked to the ground. Sing to the Lord in thanks; make music to our God on the harp. He covers the sky with clouds. He provides the earth with rain and makes grass grow on the hills. He gives food to the cattle and to the ravens when they cry. He does not take delight in the strength of horses nor pleasure in the fleetness of man. The Lord takes pleasure in those who fear Him, who put their hope in His loving care. Praise the Lord, Jerusalem; sing to your God, Zion, for He has strengthened the bars of your gates and blessed your children in your midst. He has brought peace to your borders, and satisfied you with the finest wheat. He sends His commandment to earth; swiftly runs His word. He spreads snow like fleece, sprinkles frost like ashes, scatters hail like crumbs. Who can stand His cold? He sends

His word and melts them; He makes the wind blow and the waters flow. He has declared His words to Jacob, His statutes and laws to Israel. He has done this for no other nation; such laws they do not know. Halleluya!

Highlighted Text:
The verses בּוֹנֵה יְרוּשָׁלִַם ה׳, נִדְחֵי יִשְׂרָאֵל יְכַנֵּס: and הַנֹּתֵן שֶׁלֶג כַּצָּמֶר, כְּפוֹר כָּאֵפֶר יְפַזֵּר: are highlighted in a color from the illustration.

Educational Themes contained in the text:

- God is with us even in times of national oppression/danger (*Galut*)
- Yerushalayim
- Zionism
- God as the God of history (השגחה כללית ופרטית)
- God of Israel/God of the *Avot*
- God cares for each of His creations
- God acting in the world through the weather (nature)

The Illustration

This is a pictorial representation of the Tower of David, part of the Old City of Yerushalayim, near to the Jaffa Gate. The first words highlighted in the text are a reference to the rebuilding of Yerushalayim so the exiles can return. Then further on in the text references to Hashem intervening in the world through the weather are found, and the words that refer to snow are highlighted. The illustration paints a snowy winter scene, capturing both of these concepts. They are inherently related as examples of God's role in history and intervention in the world (*hashgaḥa*). Rebuilding Yerushalayim is a reference to modern Zionism and the weather, especially any form of precipitation in Israel, is an example of God acting in history.

The *Kavanot*

Story:
The next chapter (147) of *Sefer Tehillim* in *Pesukei DeZimra* continues to develop the role of God in our world, describing His impact and role both in terms of nature (for example, the weather) and more direct ways (for example, rebuilding Yerushalayim and gathering in the exiles to Eretz Yisrael). The story, from Israel's War of Independence in 1948, also contains God's role in history through nature (the rain) and in direct ways (the Religious Zionist approach to seeing God's role in Israel's history, especially during its wars). There is nothing more miraculous than Jewish ingenuity, and the winning of a war against all odds, sometimes just with plain and simple *ḥutzpa*!

Thought Question:

"אמר רבי סימון, אין לך כל עשב ועשב, שאין לו מזל ברקיע, שמכה אותו, ואומר לו גדל"

This midrash (*Bereshit Raba* 10:6) takes the concept of *Hashgaḥa Peratit* (Divine Providence) to an extreme degree, suggesting that God shows concern for every blade of grass, one of the smallest units of nature perceptible to the human eye. The thought question asks the child to accept this principle, that God cares for every one of His creations, including themselves, and asks them to look for evidence for that in their lives, on this very day.

Activity ideas:
Playing God: Blindfold a volunteer and tie a rope to each arm and leg. Have four volunteers play God and lead the volunteer wherever they wish.

תהלים 148

pp. 48–49

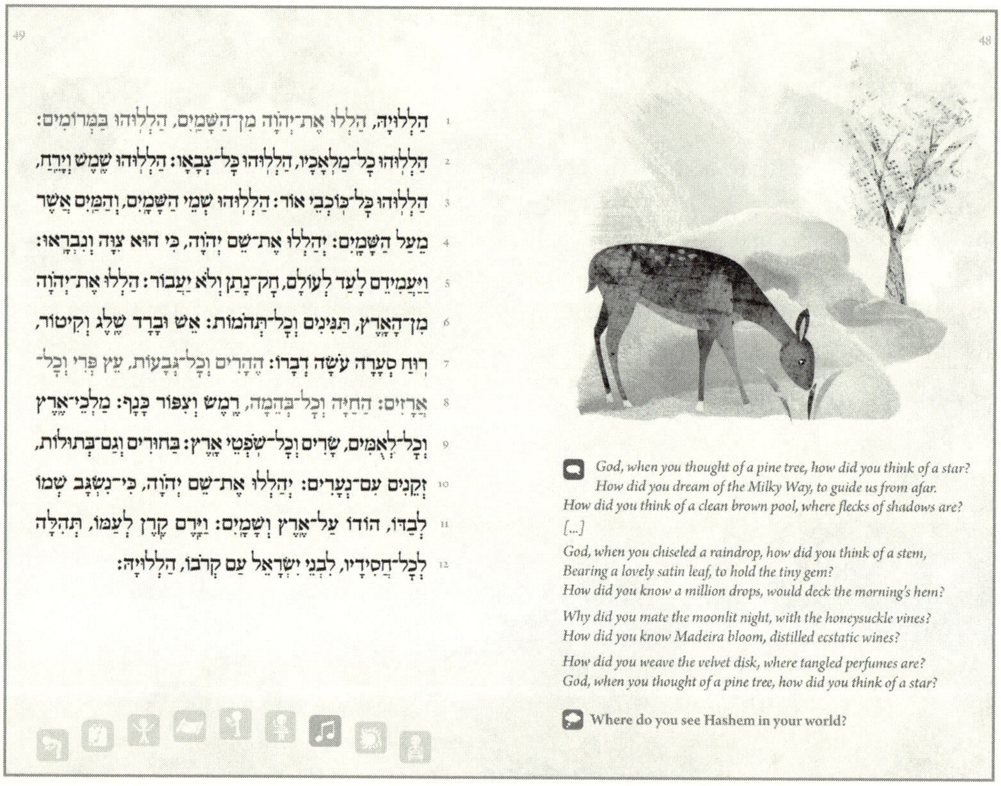

49

1 הַלְלוּיָהּ, הַלְלוּ אֶת־יְהוָה מִן־הַשָּׁמַיִם, הַלְלוּהוּ בַּמְּרוֹמִים:
2 הַלְלוּהוּ כָל־מַלְאָכָיו, הַלְלוּהוּ כָּל־צְבָאָו: הַלְלוּהוּ שֶׁמֶשׁ וְיָרֵחַ,
3 הַלְלוּהוּ כָּל־כּוֹכְבֵי אוֹר: הַלְלוּהוּ שְׁמֵי הַשָּׁמָיִם, וְהַמַּיִם אֲשֶׁר
4 מֵעַל הַשָּׁמָיִם: יְהַלְלוּ אֶת־שֵׁם יְהוָה, כִּי הוּא צִוָּה וְנִבְרָאוּ:
5 וַיַּעֲמִידֵם לָעַד לְעוֹלָם, חָק־נָתַן וְלֹא יַעֲבוֹר: הַלְלוּ אֶת־יְהוָה
6 מִן־הָאָרֶץ, תַּנִּינִים וְכָל־תְּהֹמוֹת: אֵשׁ וּבָרָד שֶׁלֶג וְקִיטוֹר,
7 רוּחַ סְעָרָה עֹשָׂה דְבָרוֹ: הֶהָרִים וְכָל־גְּבָעוֹת, עֵץ פְּרִי וְכָל־
8 אֲרָזִים: הַחַיָּה וְכָל־בְּהֵמָה, רֶמֶשׂ וְצִפּוֹר כָּנָף: מַלְכֵי־אֶרֶץ
9 וְכָל־לְאֻמִּים, שָׂרִים וְכָל־שֹׁפְטֵי אָרֶץ: בַּחוּרִים וְגַם־בְּתוּלוֹת,
10 זְקֵנִים עִם־נְעָרִים: יְהַלְלוּ אֶת־שֵׁם יְהוָה, כִּי־נִשְׂגָּב שְׁמוֹ
11 לְבַדּוֹ, הוֹדוֹ עַל־אֶרֶץ וְשָׁמָיִם: וַיָּרֶם קֶרֶן לְעַמּוֹ, תְּהִלָּה
12 לְכָל־חֲסִידָיו, לִבְנֵי יִשְׂרָאֵל עַם קְרֹבוֹ, הַלְלוּיָהּ:

48

God, when you thought of a pine tree, how did you think of a star?
How did you dream of the Milky Way, to guide us from afar.
How did you think of a clean brown pool, where flecks of shadows are?
[...]
God, when you chiseled a raindrop, how did you think of a stem,
Bearing a lovely satin leaf, to hold the tiny gem?
How did you know a million drops, would deck the morning's hem?
Why did you mate the moonlit night, with the honeysuckle vines?
How did you know Madeira bloom, distilled ecstatic wines?
How did you weave the velvet disk, where tangled perfumes are?
God, when you thought of a pine tree, how did you think of a star?

Where do you see Hashem in your world?

The *Tefilla* Text

Translation:
Halleluya! Praise the Lord from the heavens, praise Him in the heights. Praise Him, all His angels; praise Him, all His hosts. Praise Him, sun and moon; praise Him, all shining stars. Praise Him, highest heavens and the waters above the heavens. Let them praise the name of the Lord, for He commanded and they were created. He established them for ever and all time, issuing a decree that will never change. Praise the Lord from the earth: sea monsters and all the deep seas; fire and hail, snow and mist, storm winds that obey His word; mountains and all hills, fruit trees and all cedars; wild animals and all cattle, creeping things and winged birds; kings of the earth and all nations, princes and all judges on earth; youths and maidens, old and young. Let them praise the name of the Lord, for His name alone is sublime; His majesty is above earth and heaven. He has raised the pride of His people, for the glory of all His devoted ones, the children of Israel, the people close to Him. Halleluya!

Highlighted Text:
The first verse of this chapter הללויה, הללו את־ה׳ מן־השמים, הללוהו במרומים: as well as the words ההרים וכל־גבעות, עץ פרי

החיה וכל־בהמה :וכל־ ארזים are highlighted in the brown of the deer in the illustration.

Educational Themes contained in the text:

- God in nature
- Nature as a testament to God's greatness
- Nature praising God
- God of Israel
- Diversity of creation (macro)
- Complexity of creation (micro)
- Creation story

The Illustration

The *Tehillot Hashem* explains that this chapter of Tehillim is an explanation of verse יוֹדוּךָ ה׳ כָּל־מַעֲשֶׂיךָ, וַחֲסִידֶיךָ יְבָרְכוּכָה in chapter 145 of *Sefer Tehillim* (*Ashrei* on page 43 of our siddur). This verse says that all of creation itself is a song of praise to Hashem. The *Tehillot Hashem* takes the words from this chapter, such as the moon and stars, the sea creatures, the deserts, the mountains and valleys, the vegetation and trees and animals and insects and birds, and has them all singing a song of praise to Hashem just through their existence. Our illustration has many of these elements, as well as the tree that is singing Hashem's praise that we first saw on the *Ashrei* page (page 42).

The *Kavanot*

Story:
This is an excerpt from the poem "God the Artist" by Angela Morgan,[11] and is a beautiful expression of seeing God in nature, in a similar way to chapter 148 of Tehillim. A scientist who is an atheist may find a way to answer through scientific theory each and every question that the poem asks. A religious person may use the same scientific theory to explain each phenomena, but not as a random evolutionary process, rather as God's tool box, or in the spirit of the poem, His paint box to create the world.

The following two stanzas follow the first in the original, and were taken out due to space restrictions.

God, when you thought of a cobweb,
How did you think of dew?
How did you know a spider's house
Had shingles bright and new?
How did you know the human folk
Would love them like they do?

God, when you patterned a bird song,
Flung on a silver string,
How did you know the ecstasy
That crystal call would bring?
How did you think of a bubbling throat
And a darling speckled wing?

Thought Question:
The thought question follows on from the poem, and the *tefilla* text, asking the child to do the same thing as the author of the poem and look around their world and see God in it. Take a look at nature, at the city, inside the classroom, and find the imprint of God.

Activity idea:
Take your class outside of the classroom to search for God's brushstrokes in their world. Ask them to be detectives to find hints of God as Creator, in the school yard, in the lunch hall, in the street outside the school campus, etc. Ask them to gather evidence and bring it back inside the classroom, so they can present it to the rest of the class. This could also be in the form of a scavenger hunt for God: as a class, search throughout your school for Hashem. In each place you visit your students should collect evidence for God and bring it back to the classroom to share with the class.

11. http://www.familyfriendpoems.com/poem/god-the-artist-by-angela-morgan#ixzz3G6RTnLAn

תהלים 149

pp. 50–51

51

50

1 הללויה, שירו ליהוה שיר חדש, תהלתו בקהל חסידים:
2 ישמח ישראל בעשיו, בני־ציון יגילו במלכם: יהללו שמו
3 במחול, בתף וכנור יזמרו־לו: כי־רוצה יהוה בעמו,
4 יפאר ענוים בישועה: יעלזו חסידים בכבוד, ירננו על־
5 משכבותם: רוממות אל בגרונם, וחרב פיפיות בידם:
6 לעשות נקמה בגוים, תוכחות בלאמים: לאסר
7 מלכיהם בזקים, ונכבדיהם בכבלי ברזל: לעשות
8 בהם משפט כתוב, הדר הוא לכל־חסידיו, הללויה:

"Song is more precious than words."

"One fragment of melody can contain all the joy in the world."

How do you feel when you sing? Why do you think we sing so many of our *tefillot*?

Rebbe Leib the grandfather of Shpole was well known for making people happy, playing with children, and telling stories. He was the first Hasidic Rebbe to declare dancing a mitzva. When the Maggid of Mezeritch saw him dancing he commented, "Your dancing counts for more than my prayers!"

The *Tefilla* Text

Translation:

Halleluya! Sing to the Lord a new song, His praise in the assembly of the devoted. Let Israel rejoice in its Maker; let the children of Zion exult in their King. Let them praise His name with dancing; sing praises to Him with timbrel and harp. For the Lord delights in His people; He adorns the humble with salvation. Let the devoted revel in glory; let them sing for joy on their beds. Let high praises of God be in their throats, and a two-edged sword in their hand: to impose retribution on the nations, punishment on the peoples, binding their kings with chains, their nobles with iron fetters, carrying out the judgment written against them. This is the glory of all His devoted ones. Halleluya!

Highlighted Text:

The words שִׁירוּ לה׳ שִׁיר חדש, are highlighted in the color of the thought question and the words במחול, בתֹף וכנור יזמרו־לו: are highlighted to match the musical notes of the illustration.

Educational Themes contained in the text:

- A new song = our new generation finding God in their own way
- God of Israel
- Serving God through dance, song and music
- God of justice, punishment, and just war
- Creative ways to serve and praise Hashem

The Illustration

Here the illustration has an older man and a young boy dancing together, serving Hashem through song and dance. The man comes from a different generation and a different age (perhaps from the *shtetl* in Eastern Europe before his family came to America), and represents a link in the chain from the current generation to the biblical generations present at the genesis of our people and our religion. The young boy represents the new generation, which must find its own song, a שיר חדש, to come close to Hashem in its own way. Together they represent the evolution of Torah Judaism and its continuing development, while still staying firmly committed to authentic traditional Torah Judaism.

The *Kavanot*

Thought Question:
"Song is more precious than words."

"One fragment of melody can contain all the joy in the world."

Both these quotes are attributed to the Ba'al Shem Tov[12] and express the quintessential Hasidic idea that the everyday person can serve God through the everyday achievable activity of song and dance. The happiness and higher spiritual state that can be achieved through these activities can be a form of worship. These themes, happiness through song and dance and worshiping Hashem, should be explored with the students. How does song lead to happiness? Why is happiness a form of worship of God in Hasidic theology? How can we use song to help us connect to Hashem? What can song achieve that words would struggle to?

There are other music related questions and stories in the siddur found on pages 39, 52, 148, 184, and 229.

Activity ideas:
These questions obviously lead to practical and experiential activities in search of their answers.

- Teach your class a new song they don't yet know (perhaps a new tune to a part of *tefilla* they are not yet familiar with). Explore how it feels to sing that song (or songs they already know, or even songs from popular culture). Explore with them how they feel singing affects their mood and state of mind, and why they think song is such a central part of our *tefilla*.
- The song game: Split the class into teams (between two and four). Choose a word/topic, and give the teams two minutes to come up with as many songs as they can with this word in. Then have a song-down (like a show-down) – each team takes a turn to sing one of their songs. They can't repeat a song that has already been sung. A team that repeats a song or can't think of a new song is out. Good words/topics to choose are love; the weather; vehicles; Shabbat; Israel; Torah.

Story:
While song and music is mentioned in many of the texts that comprise *Pesukei DeZimra*, this chapter contains the word מחול – dance. This suggests that dance itself, separate from music and singing, is a method to connecting to God and drawing close to Him. This is both reflected in the illustration, and this story. The story describes a rebbe who sees dancing as a legitimate method of serving Hashem, and goes as far as codifying it as a mitzva, a means to achieve closeness to God. The famous Maggid of Mezeritch saw the

12. *Souls on Fire* by Elie Wisel

value in this: when he saw Rebbe Leib dancing he understood he was witnessing a religious act, one that he estimated was more valuable than his own prayers.

The act of swaying when one prays is widespread, and its origin is somewhat of a mystery though there are many unsubstantiated theories available. One such theory is that this is an expression of the need to involve more than just the heart and mind and lips in the act of worshiping God. It is a form of involving every limb of one's body. Dance is another way to do that, and one that energetic children will be able to relate to.

Activity ideas:
Have your class try it out – dance to find and draw close to Hashem. Teach them a *simḥa* dance, or just free-style dancing. Let them experience using their entire bodies in order to worship Hashem.

Additional *Kavanot*:
Stories:
A *ḥasid* of the Ba'al Shem Tov who couldn't walk once told a story about his rebbe. He related how the Ba'al Shem Tov used to hop and dance while he prayed. As he was telling the story he began to rise and became so swept away that he began to hop and dance as he imagined his rebbe doing so. From that time on he was cured and could walk.

There is a legend that the melody of the Maggid of Koznitz that he left behind when he died was learned from the lips of angels who sang it in honor of Hashem. But one of his *Hḥasidim* disagreed with this, and rather believed that the angels learned it from the Maggid's lips!

תהלים 150

pp. 52–53

53 52

1 הַלְלוּיָהּ, הַלְלוּ־אֵל בְּקָדְשׁוֹ

2 הַלְלוּהוּ בִּרְקִיעַ עֻזּוֹ:

3 הַלְלוּהוּ בִגְבוּרֹתָיו

4 הַלְלוּהוּ כְּרֹב גֻּדְלוֹ:

5 הַלְלוּהוּ בְּתֵקַע שׁוֹפָר

6 הַלְלוּהוּ בְּנֵבֶל וְכִנּוֹר:

7 הַלְלוּהוּ בְּתֹף וּמָחוֹל

8 הַלְלוּהוּ בְּמִנִּים וְעֻגָב:

9 הַלְלוּהוּ בְצִלְצְלֵי־שָׁמַע

10 הַלְלוּהוּ בְּצִלְצְלֵי תְרוּעָה:

11 כֹּל הַנְּשָׁמָה תְּהַלֵּל יָהּ, הַלְלוּיָהּ:

12 כֹּל הַנְּשָׁמָה תְּהַלֵּל יָהּ, הַלְלוּיָהּ:

Haile Gebrselassie was an Ethiopian long-distance runner who over the course of his career broke 27 world records. Any time Haile trains in the gym he likes to listen to fast loud music. In 1995 he smashed the 5,000-meters world record by playing his favorite song over and over in his head. The song has more than 130 beats per minute, and motivated him to keep the pace he needed and helped him to focus on what he had to do to win the race. This gave him an idea. For his next world-record attempt, the 10,000 meters, he requested the song be played over the loudspeakers in the stadium. With the help of the music, focusing his heart and mind, almost lifting him out of the stadium and on to greatness, he smashed that record too!

What music do you like to listen to? How does it make you feel?

The *Tefilla* Text

Translation:

Halleluya! Praise God in His holy place; praise Him in the heavens of His power. Praise Him for His mighty deeds; praise Him for His surpassing greatness. Praise Him with blasts of the shofar; praise Him with the harp and lyre. Praise Him with timbrel and dance; praise Him with strings and flute. Praise Him with clashing cymbals; praise Him with resounding cymbals. Let all that breathes praise the Lord. Halleluya! Let all that breathes praise the Lord. Halleluya!

Highlighted Text:

The words הללוהו בתף ומחול are highlighted to match the color of the drum in the illustration.

Educational Themes contained in the text:

- Serving God through song and music
- Praising God because of what He does
- Praising God in heaven and on earth
- Music as an expression of the soul

The Illustration

Here we have Miriam the Prophetess playing her drum in thanks to Hashem after the exodus from Egypt. After Moshe sang his song of thanks (the *Shira*) Miriam took her תוף (while we say this was a timbrel, the word תוף means a drum, although in Modern Hebrew, a timbrel is now termed תוף מרים – "drum of Miriam") and gathered the women together and sang their own song in praise of Hashem (Shemot 15:20).

In this chapter of Tehillim, music and dance, and specifically drumming, are mentioned as ways to praise Hashem, and so here we have Miriam showing us the way to do this.

The women's *shira* is also the focus of the illustration on page 58 of the siddur accompanying *Az Yashir* (the *shira* of Moshe).

The *Kavanot*

Story:
It is widely documented that music is an important part of many athletes' preparation for athletic performance. Music can be used to alter and prepare their mental state in order to achieve the total effort necessary to achieve athletic greatness. This is not the only realm where music can be used to achieve mental preparedness. Music can be utilized in this way in every area of our lives. *Pesukei DeZimra* is trying to achieve this too – the mental and spiritual preparation for *tefilla* through music and through the inspiring words of David HaMelekh. This story is an example of one such athlete who used music to help him achieve a world-class performance in his sport.

There are other music related questions and stories in the siddur found on pages 39, 50, 148, 184, and 229.

Activity ideas:
Explore how music can alter one's mood and spiritual-emotional state of mind by playing various chosen songs based on the mood they engender. Ask the students to share their own favorite songs and how they feel when they hear them. Or with the help of the music department, have the children use musical instruments as part of the *tefilla* experience of the morning.

ברוך ה׳ לעולם

pp. 54–55

בָּרוּךְ יְהֹוָה לְעוֹלָם

אָמֵן וְאָמֵן:

בָּרוּךְ יְהֹוָה מִצִּיּוֹן, שֹׁכֵן יְרוּשָׁלָםִ, הַלְלוּיָהּ:

בָּרוּךְ יְהֹוָה אֱלֹהִים אֱלֹהֵי יִשְׂרָאֵל

עֹשֵׂה נִפְלָאוֹת לְבַדּוֹ:

וּבָרוּךְ שֵׁם כְּבוֹדוֹ לְעוֹלָם

וְיִמָּלֵא כְבוֹדוֹ אֶת־כָּל־הָאָרֶץ

אָמֵן וְאָמֵן:

One day a young girl went in to the forest to pray to Hashem. When she returned her parents asked her where she had been. "I went to the forest to pray," she told them. The next day the same thing happened, and again her parents asked her where she had gone. "I went to the forest to pray," again she replied. When this happened on the third day they became disturbed and confronted her. "My daughter," her mother said, "why do you go to the forest to pray to Hashem? There is no need to search for Hashem in the forest, Hashem is everywhere. Even in our house. Hashem is no different in the forest. Why do you insist on going there to pray?" The girl looked into her parents' eyes and said, "I know that Hashem is no different in the forest. But out in the forest, I know that I am different."

Some people connect to Hashem more in Yerushalayim, or in a *Beit Kenesset*, or in a forest.

Where do you connect best to Hashem? Why?

The *Tefilla* Text

Translation:

Blessed be the Lord for ever. Amen and Amen.
Blessed from Zion be the Lord who dwells in Jerusalem. Halleluya!
Blessed be the Lord, God of Israel, who alone does wonders.
Blessed be His glorious name for ever, and may all the earth be filled with His glory.
Amen and Amen.

Highlighted Text:

The verse ברוך ה׳ מציון, שֹׁכן ירושלָם, הללויה: is highlighted in the gold of the *Beit HaMikdash* in the illustration.

Educational Themes contained in the text:

- The power of the word "Amen"
- Yerushalayim
- The *Shekhina*
- God's omnipresence
- A world full of God's glory

The Illustration

Yerushalayim here with the *Beit HaMikdash* at its center, radiates a spiritual light as Hashem takes up residence as we hope He will once again in Messianic times. The verse, highlighted and linked to the illustration, gives Yerushalayim its meaningful name of Tziyon, which for us is familiar as the source for the term Zionism. When considering a prayer for the rebuilding of Yerushalayim, and the return of the *Shekhina* to Yerushalayim, we bear in mind that we hope the process has already begun with the historical events of modern Zionism.

The *Kavanot*

Story:

This very powerful story explores the complex idea that while God is omnipresent, we are very much based in the physical world with its finite locations. Judaism places a lot of emphasis on location when it comes to holiness and worshiping God, such as the *Beit Kenesset*, Eretz Yisrael, Yerushalayim and the *Beit HaMikdash* (or the Kotel for us today). If God can be found and sensed and connected to in every location, why do we need these finite locations to connect to Him? The story gives us a possible answer. Perhaps *we* are different in these locations. *We* are the ones that need physical location to focus and transform our thoughts into the right mindset to worship Hashem.

Thought Question:

This thought question builds on the story, and asks the student to consider for themselves where they prefer to connect to God. There are advantages and disadvantages of each place, which can be explored as a class. And the students may have other locations they wish to share where they feel that they can connect to Hashem. All answers should be acceptable as long as a rationale can be verbalized.

Activity ideas:

Take your class outside for a *tefilla* experience that is different from the one they normally have in their classroom/*Beit Kenesset*. Take them on a different day to a grand *Beit Kenesset* in the neighborhood. On another day, use the "Kotel Cam"[13] to try and replicate (in a limited way, of course) the experience of being at the Kotel. Ask them to compare these experiences of *tefilla*.

13. http://english.thekotel.org/cameras.asp

שירה 1

pp. 56–57

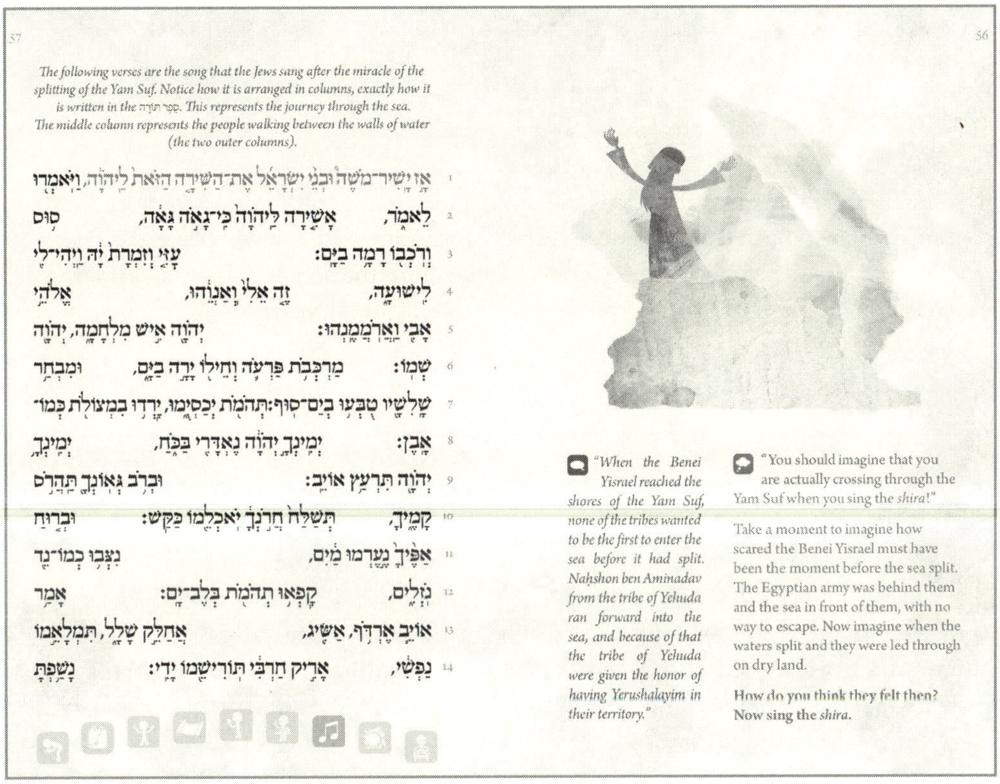

57

The following verses are the song that the Jews sang after the miracle of the splitting of the Yam Suf. Notice how it is arranged in columns, exactly how it is written in the ספר תורה. This represents the journey through the sea. The middle column represents the people walking between the walls of water (the two outer columns).

1 אז ישיר־משה ובני ישראל את־השירה הזאת ליהוה, ויאמרו
2 לאמר, אשירה ליהוה כי־גאה גאה, סוס
3 ורכבו רמה בים: עזי וזמרת יה ויהי־לי
4 לישועה, זה אלי ואנוהו, אלהי
5 אבי וארממנהו: יהוה איש מלחמה, יהוה
6 שמו: מרכבת פרעה וחילו ירה בים, ומבחר
7 שלשיו טבעו בים־סוף: תהמת יכסימו, ירדו במצולת כמו־
8 אבן: ימינך יהוה נאדרי בכח, ימינך
9 יהוה תרעץ אויב: וברב גאונך תהרס
10 קמיך, תשלח חרנך יאכלמו כקש: וברוח
11 אפיך נערמו מים, נצבו כמו־נד
12 נזלים, קפאו תהמת בלב־ים: אמר
13 אויב ארדף, אשיג, אחלק שלל, תמלאמו
14 נפשי, אריק חרבי תורישמו ידי: נשפת

56

"When the Benei Yisrael reached the shores of the Yam Suf, none of the tribes wanted to be the first to enter the sea before it had split. Naḥshon ben Aminadav from the tribe of Yehuda ran forward into the sea, and because of that the tribe of Yehuda were given the honor of having Yerushalayim in their territory."

"You should imagine that you are actually crossing through the Yam Suf when you sing the *shira*!"

Take a moment to imagine how scared the Benei Yisrael must have been the moment before the sea split. The Egyptian army was behind them and the sea in front of them, with no way to escape. Now imagine when the waters split and they were led through on dry land.

How do you think they felt then? Now sing the *shira*.

The *Tefilla* Text

Translation:

Then Moses and the Israelites sang this song to the Lord, saying:
I will sing to the Lord, for He has triumphed gloriously; horse and rider He has hurled into the sea.
The Lord is my strength and song; He has become my salvation.
This is my God, and I will beautify Him, my father's God, and I will exalt Him.
The Lord is a Master of war; Lord is His name.
Pharaoh's chariots and army He cast into the sea; the best of his officers drowned in the Sea of Reeds.
The deep waters covered them; they went down to the depths like a stone.
Your right hand, Lord, is majestic in power. Your right hand, Lord, shatters the enemy.
In the greatness of Your majesty, You overthrew those who rose against You.
You sent out Your fury; it consumed them like stubble. By the blast of Your nostrils the waters piled up.

The surging waters stood straight like a wall; the deeps congealed in the heart of the sea.
The enemy said, "I will pursue. I will overtake. I will divide the spoil. My desire shall have its fill of them.
I will draw my sword. My hand will destroy them."

Highlighted Text:
The first words of the *Shira*, אָז יָשִׁיר־מֹשֶׁה וּבְנֵי יִשְׂרָאֵל אֶת־הַשִּׁירָה הַזֹּאת לַה׳, are highlighted to match the rock on which Moshe is standing in the illustration.

Educational Themes contained in the text:

- Song as vehicle for praising Hashem
- Seeing miracles like *Keriat Yam Suf* in our everyday lives
- Just as Hashem obviously ruled over nature then, so He does today and forever.
- God's presence leads to (requires) song
- This is the climax to *Pesukei DeZimra* that sings God's praise as being present in nature – in both natural and super-natural phenomena
- Reliving Jewish history

The Illustration

The illustration here is a dramatic portrayal of Moshe's role in the splitting of the Yam Suf. His silhouette looks over the scene from a rock high above the tumult of this miraculous event, transcending the process, functioning as the messenger for God's miracle. His location, halfway between the earth and heaven, reminds the people of his role as intermediary between them and Hashem.

The *Kavanot*

Story:
This famous aggadic narrative from the Talmud (*Sota* 36b) explores the mechanics of the beginning of the splitting of the Yam Suf. The Torah text has only God and Moshe involved in the splitting, and presents the supernatural miracle as derived only from God, with Moshe as His agent in its performance. But this midrashic text returns man to the center of the miraculous experience, suggesting that the miracle only occurred once Naḥshon ben Aminadav showed his *emuna* and trust in Hashem. Once he demonstrated that in front of the entire people, the miracle occurred, and the Jews were saved. The message is clear – God wants faith and partnership from mankind, and then He will enter history and intervene.

Thought Question:
"You should imagine that you are actually crossing through the Yam Suf when you sing the *shira*!"

This *halakha*, found in the *Mishna Berura* (51:17) urges the *mitpallel* to actually reexperience the historical event of *Keriat Yam Suf*, in much the same way as we are asked to reexperience the whole historical event of the exodus on *Leil HaSeder* (see the thought question on page 61). This is an attempt to create an experiential educational activity for adult and child alike, both on *Leil HaSeder* and every single day when we say the *Shira*. This is necessary in order to experience the requisite emotions to be ready to stand before Hashem in the climax of our *tefilla*, the *Amida*, which is drawing ever closer as we reach the end of *Pesukei DeZimra*. The thought question helps to do this by asking the children to imagine the emotions of the Israelites as they felt standing at the edge of the sea with the Egyptian army bearing down on them from the rear, and then how they must have felt as the waters miraculously opened up for them and they were saved. The thought question asks them to imagine this and then to sing the *Shira*, hopefully with a strong sense of gratitude and wonder.

Activity idea:
Guided imagination exercise: Ask your students to close their eyes and describe, in much detail and with drama and excitement, the unfolding of *Keriat Yam Suf*. Then discuss the emotions that they and the ancient Israelites experienced.

Additional *Kavanot*:

Stories:

When the *Benei Yisrael* were walking through the Reed Sea on dry land, with a wall of water on the left and a wall of water on the right, one of the children was crying because he was hungry. His mother reached out into the water and plucked an apple and a pomegranate.[14]

When the *Benei Yisrael* left Egypt and saw the splitting of the Reed Sea, they all felt a strong need to sing a song of praise to Hashem. Every single person, from the oldest to the youngest started to sing together the *Shira*. Even the babies![15]

14. *Bereshit Raba* 21:10
15. *Sota* 30b–31a

שירה 2

pp. 58–59

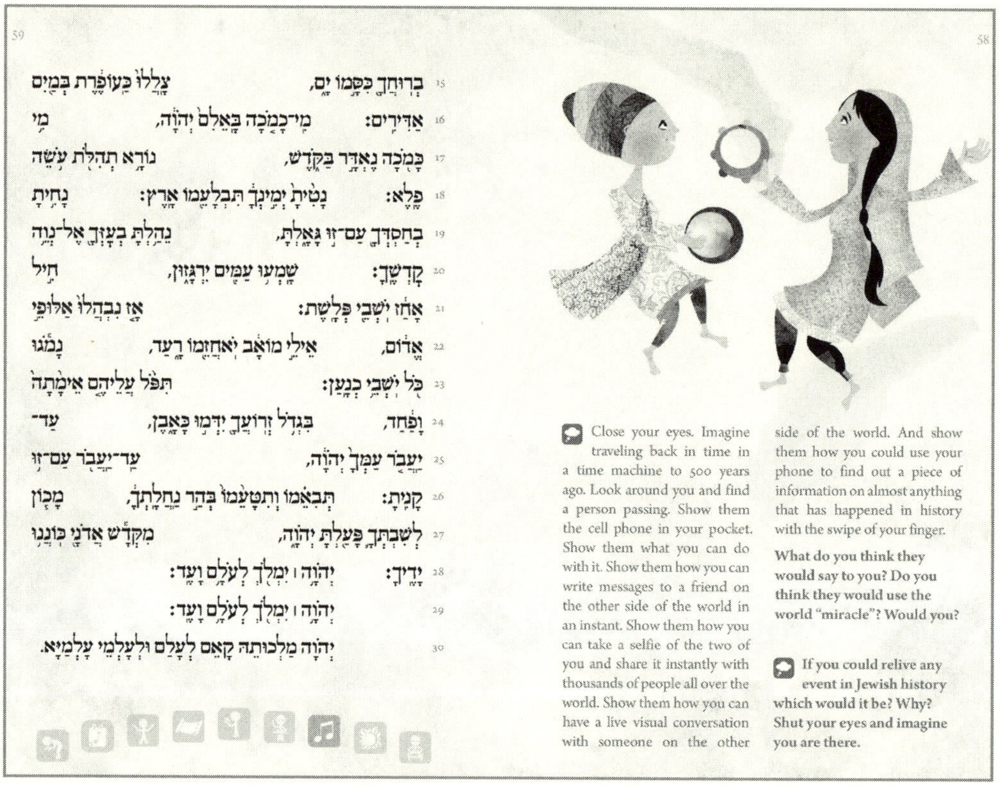

59

בְּרוּחֲךָ כִּסָּמוֹ יָם, צָלֲלוּ כַּעוֹפֶרֶת בְּמַיִם
אַדִּירִים: מִי־כָמְכָה בָּאֵלִם יְהוָה, מִי
כָּמְכָה נֶאְדָּר בַּקֹּדֶשׁ, נוֹרָא תְהִלֹּת עֹשֵׂה
פֶלֶא: נָטִיתָ יְמִינְךָ תִּבְלָעֵמוֹ אָרֶץ: נָחִיתָ
בְחַסְדְּךָ עַם־זוּ גָּאָלְתָּ, נֵהַלְתָּ בְעָזְּךָ אֶל־נְוֵה
קָדְשֶׁךָ: שָׁמְעוּ עַמִּים יִרְגָּזוּן, חִיל
אָחַז יֹשְׁבֵי פְּלָשֶׁת: אָז נִבְהֲלוּ אַלּוּפֵי
אֱדוֹם, אֵילֵי מוֹאָב יֹאחֲזֵמוֹ רָעַד, נָמֹגוּ
כֹּל יֹשְׁבֵי כְנָעַן: תִּפֹּל עֲלֵיהֶם אֵימָתָה
וָפַחַד, בִּגְדֹל זְרוֹעֲךָ יִדְּמוּ כָּאָבֶן, עַד־
יַעֲבֹר עַמְּךָ יְהוָה, עַד־יַעֲבֹר עַם־זוּ
קָנִיתָ: תְּבִאֵמוֹ וְתִטָּעֵמוֹ בְּהַר נַחֲלָתְךָ, מָכוֹן
לְשִׁבְתְּךָ פָּעַלְתָּ יְהוָה, מִקְּדָשׁ אֲדֹנָי כּוֹנְנוּ
יָדֶיךָ: יְהוָה ׀ יִמְלֹךְ לְעֹלָם וָעֶד:
יְהוָה ׀ יִמְלֹךְ לְעֹלָם וָעֶד:
יְהוָה מַלְכוּתֵהּ קָאֵם לְעָלַם וּלְעָלְמֵי עָלְמַיָּא.

58

Close your eyes. Imagine traveling back in time in a time machine to 500 years ago. Look around you and find a person passing. Show them the cell phone in your pocket. Show them what you can do with it. Show them how you can write messages to a friend on the other side of the world in an instant. Show them how you can take a selfie of the two of you and share it instantly with thousands of people all over the world. Show them how you can have a live visual conversation with someone on the other side of the world. And show them how you could use your phone to find out a piece of information on almost anything that has happened in history with the swipe of your finger.

What do you think they would say to you? Do you think they would use the world "miracle"? Would you?

If you could relive any event in Jewish history which would it be? Why? Shut your eyes and imagine you are there.

The *Tefilla* Text

Translation:

You blew with Your wind; the sea covered them. They sank in the mighty waters like lead.
Who is like You, Lord, among the mighty?
Who is like You – majestic in holiness, awesome in glory, working wonders?
You stretched out Your right hand, the earth swallowed them.
In Your loving-kindness, You led the people You redeemed.
In Your strength, You guided them to Your holy abode.
Nations heard and trembled; terror gripped Philistia's inhabitants.
The chiefs of Edom were dismayed, Moab's leaders were seized with trembling, the people of Canaan melted away.
Fear and dread fell upon them. By the power of Your arm, they were still as stone – until Your people crossed, Lord, until the people You acquired crossed over.
You will bring them and plant them on the mountain of Your heritage – the place, Lord, You made for Your dwelling; the Sanctuary, Lord, Your hands established.

The Lord will reign for ever and all time. The Lord will reign for ever and all time.

The Lord's kingship is established for ever and to all eternity.

The Illustration

Just after Moshe and the people's *Shira* following *Keriat Yam Suf*, Miriam gathered the women together with musical instruments in order to participate themselves in their own *shira* and praise of Hashem for the great miracles they had just witnessed. The women here empowering themselves to approach Hashem and praise Him and find meaning for themselves in these events, rather than relying on the men in their nation, should be role models to our female students, in their ongoing journey for meaning-making in Judaism.

The women are shown here using the timbrel, known in Hebrew as תוף מרים (Miriam's drum) after this episode. Miriam is also the focus of the illustration on page 52.

The *Kavanot*

Thought Question 1:
On the page of the siddur where the most dramatically supernatural miracles occurred in Jewish history, this first thought question asks the child to consider whether they too live in an age of miracles. The differentiation between natural and supernatural miracles needs to be made for this to be fully explored. In the *berakha* of *Hoda'a* (page 125 of the siddur) the differentiation between נסים and נפלאות is made. One approach to the difference is that this reflects supernatural (נסים) and natural (נפלאות) miracles. The thought question on the following page (page 126, the page where the Ḥanukka and Purim stories are told in the *tefilla* – על הנסים) also explores this. *Keriat Yam Suf* seems to be an example of a supernatural miracle (although there have been scientists who have found natural ways to explain it – together with the Ten Plagues – this does not disqualify them as miracles, but rather faith in God's role in the historical narrative can be maintained with the belief that He operates and intervenes through nature). Meanwhile, the Purim story is an example of God acting in history through natural means. The Ḥanukka story has both types of miracles in its narrative, and historically some tension between the two.

The imagination exercise in this thought question asks the child to look at their own lives with a sensitivity to the miracles of nature and human endeavor. The aim here is not to suggest that the technology of a cell phone is a rival to the miraculous nature of the events in the biblical narrative, but rather to encourage them to see the miraculous nature of everyday things in their lives, and the partnership between man and God that creates them. This same discussion can be explored with the story on the following page (60) describing the modern miracle of the State of Israel.

Miracles in general and specifically the difference between natural and supernatural miracles are also considered and explored on pages 60 and 126 of the siddur.

Thought Question 2:
The second thought question on the page again asks the child to use their imagination to experience an event from Jewish history of their choice. No doubt the events chosen by the students in your class will each lend themselves to this same debate – what was God's role and was it miraculous? Jewish history as a whole can also be the focus of the same debate. These discussions and debates are exactly the thoughts that we hope to be having in the lead up to standing before God when we say the core *tefillot* of the *Shema* and *Amida* on the coming pages.

שירה 3

pp. 60–61

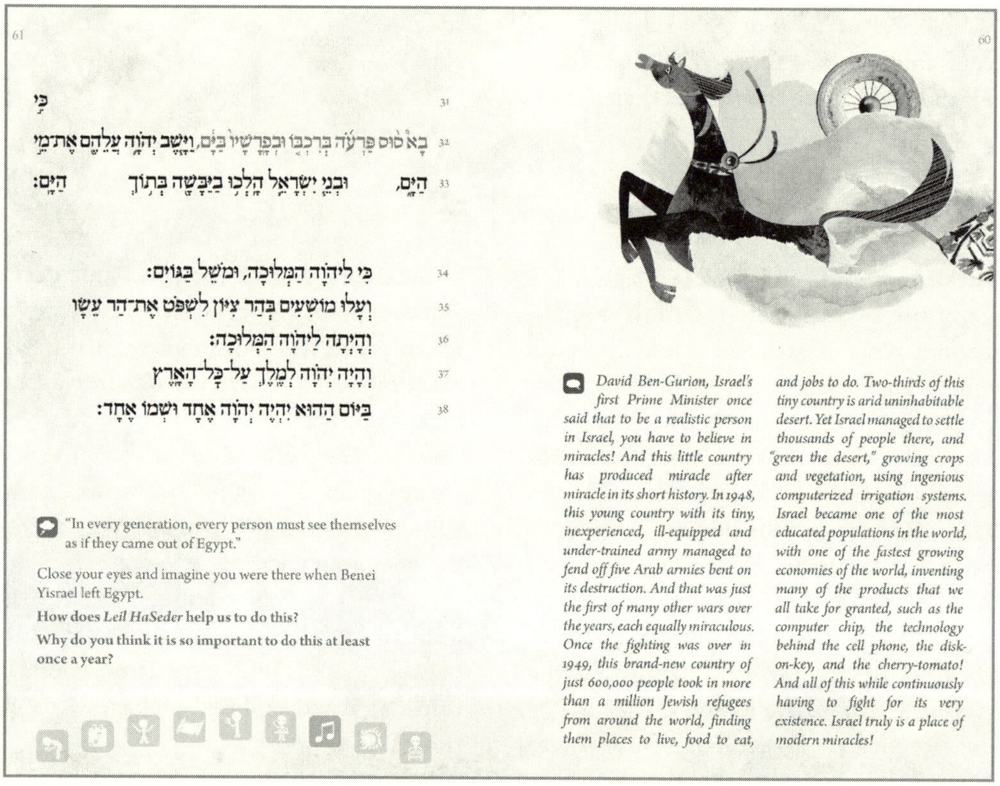
61

כִּי

בָא סוּס פַּרְעֹה בְּרִכְבּוֹ וּבְפָרָשָׁיו בַּיָּם, וַיָּשֶׁב יְהֹוָה עֲלֵהֶם אֶת־מֵי

הַיָּם, וּבְנֵי יִשְׂרָאֵל הָלְכוּ בַיַּבָּשָׁה בְּתוֹךְ הַיָּם:

כִּי לַיהֹוָה הַמְּלוּכָה, וּמֹשֵׁל בַּגּוֹיִם:

וְעָלוּ מוֹשִׁעִים בְּהַר צִיּוֹן לִשְׁפֹּט אֶת־הַר עֵשָׂו

וְהָיְתָה לַיהֹוָה הַמְּלוּכָה:

וְהָיָה יְהֹוָה לְמֶלֶךְ עַל־כָּל־הָאָרֶץ

בַּיּוֹם הַהוּא יִהְיֶה יְהֹוָה אֶחָד וּשְׁמוֹ אֶחָד:

"In every generation, every person must see themselves as if they came out of Egypt."

Close your eyes and imagine you were there when Benei Yisrael left Egypt.

How does *Leil HaSeder* help us to do this?

Why do you think it is so important to do this at least once a year?

60

David Ben-Gurion, Israel's first Prime Minister once said that to be a realistic person in Israel, you have to believe in miracles! And this little country has produced miracle after miracle in its short history. In 1948, this young country with its tiny, inexperienced, ill-equipped and under-trained army managed to fend off five Arab armies bent on its destruction. And that was just the first of many other wars over the years, each equally miraculous. Once the fighting was over in 1949, this brand-new country of just 600,000 people took in more than a million Jewish refugees from around the world, finding them places to live, food to eat, and jobs to do. Two-thirds of this tiny country is arid uninhabitable desert. Yet Israel managed to settle thousands of people there, and "green the desert," growing crops and vegetation, using ingenious computerized irrigation systems. Israel became one of the most educated populations in the world, with one of the fastest growing economies of the world, inventing many of the products that we all take for granted, such as the computer chip, the technology behind the cell phone, the disk-on-key, and the cherry-tomato! And all of this while continuously having to fight for its very existence. Israel truly is a place of modern miracles!

The *Tefilla* Text

Translation:

When Pharaoh's horses, chariots and riders went into the sea, the Lord brought the waters of the sea back over them, but the Israelites walked on dry land through the sea. For kingship is the Lord's and He rules over the nations. Saviors shall go up to Mount Zion to judge Mount Esau, and the Lord's shall be the kingdom. Then the Lord shall be King over all the earth; on that day the Lord shall be One and His name One.

Highlighted Text:

The words בא סוס פרעה ברכבו ובפרשיו בים, are highlighted in the aquamarine of the waves in the illustration.

The Illustration

This is a visual representation of the words in the *Shira* that are highlighted in our siddur – בא סוס פרעה ברכבו ובפרשיו בים. In the illustration, there are hints of the horse, the rider, and the chariot, all in a state of destruction, as Hashem orchestrates the crashing down on Pharaoh's army of the walls of water that were standing to allow Benei Yisrael to cross safely.

The *Kavanot*

Story:

This narrative describes the "miracles" that contributed to the existence and thriving of the modern State of Israel. Jews see the hand of God in history, and for a religious Jew hearing about the achievements and successes of this story, it is hard to tell the story without using the world miracle. These are miracles that are still unfolding in front of our very eyes in our generation, and it is important for our children to see it in this light. The differentiation between natural and supernatural miracles, between נסים and נפלאות that was explored on the previous page can be explored here too. It is not always clear to us when נסים end and נפלאות begin, and the history of the modern State of Israel presents us with this challenge as much as any other period of Jewish history.

Thought Question:

"In every generation, every person must see themselves as if they came out of Egypt."

This often quoted sentence from the Pesaḥ Haggada, to some extent captures the essence of the ideal *Leil HaSeder* experience each year. An experiential telling of the historical events that led to the exodus from Egypt. The fundamentals of *Leil HaSeder*, such as the culinary educational props (*matza*, *maror*, salt-water etc.), and other customs (such as dressing-up) help to contribute to the experiential nature of the evening. The question is why this needs to be reexperienced rather than cognitively understood. To really feel gratitude and wonder and connection to God, one must have had the experience on some level. These ideas have also been discussed on the previous pages relating to the *Shira*.

Activity idea:

Guided imagination exercise: Ask your students to close their eyes and describe, in much detail and with drama and excitement, the story of *Yetziat Mitzrayim*. Then discuss the emotions that they and the ancient Israelites experienced.

ישתבח

pp. 62–63

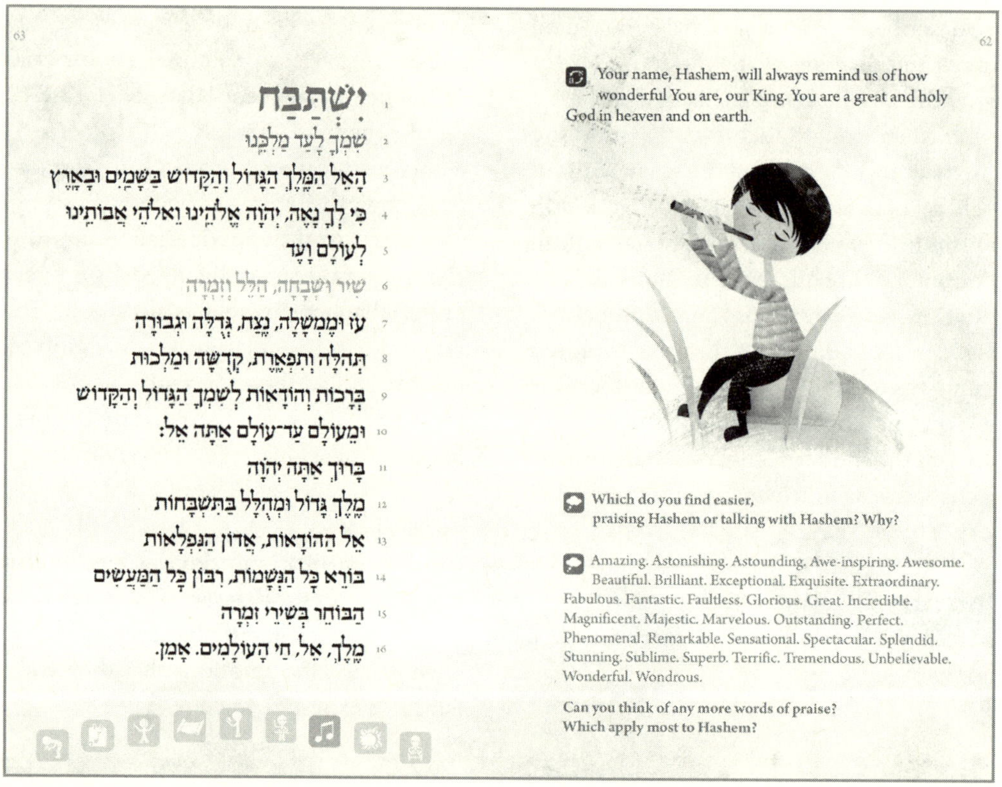

62

Your name, Hashem, will always remind us of how wonderful You are, our King. You are a great and holy God in heaven and on earth.

Which do you find easier, praising Hashem or talking with Hashem? Why?

Amazing. Astonishing. Astounding. Awe-inspiring. Awesome. Beautiful. Brilliant. Exceptional. Exquisite. Extraordinary. Fabulous. Fantastic. Faultless. Glorious. Great. Incredible. Magnificent. Majestic. Marvelous. Outstanding. Perfect. Phenomenal. Remarkable. Sensational. Spectacular. Splendid. Stunning. Sublime. Superb. Terrific. Tremendous. Unbelievable. Wonderful. Wondrous.

Can you think of any more words of praise? Which apply most to Hashem?

63

יִשְׁתַּבַּח
שִׁמְךָ לָעַד מַלְכֵּנוּ
הָאֵל הַמֶּלֶךְ הַגָּדוֹל וְהַקָּדוֹשׁ בַּשָּׁמַיִם וּבָאָרֶץ
כִּי לְךָ נָאֶה, יְהוָה אֱלֹהֵינוּ וֵאלֹהֵי אֲבוֹתֵינוּ
לְעוֹלָם וָעֶד
שִׁיר וּשְׁבָחָה, הַלֵּל וְזִמְרָה
עֹז וּמֶמְשָׁלָה, נֶצַח, גְּדֻלָּה וּגְבוּרָה
תְּהִלָּה וְתִפְאֶרֶת, קְדֻשָּׁה וּמַלְכוּת
בְּרָכוֹת וְהוֹדָאוֹת לְשִׁמְךָ הַגָּדוֹל וְהַקָּדוֹשׁ
וּמֵעוֹלָם עַד־עוֹלָם אַתָּה אֵל:
בָּרוּךְ אַתָּה יְהוָה
מֶלֶךְ גָּדוֹל וּמְהֻלָּל בַּתִּשְׁבָּחוֹת
אֵל הַהוֹדָאוֹת, אֲדוֹן הַנִּפְלָאוֹת
בּוֹרֵא כָּל הַנְּשָׁמוֹת, רִבּוֹן כָּל הַמַּעֲשִׂים
הַבּוֹחֵר בְּשִׁירֵי זִמְרָה
מֶלֶךְ, אֵל, חֵי הָעוֹלָמִים. אָמֵן.

The *Tefilla* Text

Translation:

May Your name be praised for ever, our King, the great and holy God, King in heaven and on earth.
For to You, Lord our God and God of our ancestors, for ever and ever, it is right to offer song and praise, hymn and psalm, strength and dominion, eternity, greatness and power, song of praise and glory, holiness and kingship, blessings and thanks, to Your great and holy name and for all eternities You are God. Blessed are You, Lord, God and King, exalted in praises, God of thanksgivings, Master of wonders, who delights in hymns of song, King, God, Giver of life to the worlds.

Highlighted Text:

The opening words ישתבח שמך לעד, מלכנו are highlighted in the color of the thought questions, and the words שיר ושבחה, הלל וזמרה are in the gold of the musical notes that are being played from the boy's flute in the illustration.

Educational Themes contained in the text:

- The importance of praising God
- Impossible task of praising Hashem

- Hashem's name
- God's *Malkhut*
- אדון הנפלאות
- Zimra = song/poetry – the role of song in prayer

The Illustration

Inspired by the words שיר ושבחה, הלל וזמרה, and the role of music and song in our *tefillot* in general and in *Pesukei DeZimra* in particular, here we have a young boy using his flute to praise and worship Hashem.

The illustrator drew on two sources of inspiration for this illustration. The first is a different version of the story on the following page (page 64). On that page we have a young illiterate boy who can only sing the *Alef-Beit* to serve Hashem, and asks that Hashem arrange the letters into the correct order of the prayers. There is a second version of this story where the boy, who is illiterate and cannot read from a siddur, is able to play the flute, and serves Hashem through his musical notes.

The second source of inspiration for this illustration comes from the Naomi Shemer song "שירת העשבים" ("Song of the Grasses"). The words she wrote to this song are based on words of Rebbe Naḥman of Breslov. The words to the song are:

Know that each and every shepherd has his own tune.
Know that each and every grass has its own song.
And from the song of the grasses the tune of a shepherd is made.

How beautiful, how beautiful and pleasant to hear their song.
It's very good to pray among them and to serve Hashem in joy.
And from the song of the grasses the heart is filled and yearns.

And when the heart is filled by the song yearns for the Land of Israel,
a great light is drawn forth and goes from the Land's holiness upon it.
And from the song of the grasses the tune of the heart is made.

Here we have many of the themes of *Pesukei DeZimra* coming together as a beautiful summary of the themes we have been concentrating on in order to prepare ourselves to stand before Hashem in prayer. These include music and song as a form of worship of God and creation itself praising and singing to Hashem.

The *Kavanot*

Conceptual Translation of:

ישתבח שמך לעד, מלכנו האל המלך הגדול והקדוש בשמים ובארץ.

Thought Question 1:
This thought question is subjective in nature, and there are no incorrect answers. It asks the child to find meaning in the words we use to praise Hashem, but to also consider the difficulty of that task. Talking to Hashem, having a conversation, a dialogue, is something that not every person has been encouraged to do. This question asks the child to think about what that feels like, and which they find easier and more meaningful. It could be that to praise Hashem is to relate to God in an I–It way, while talking to God is more conducive to an I–Thou relationship. Finding the right words to praise is a challenge, while dialogue is empowering. But both have their place in our *tefillot*.

Thought Question 2:
This thought question groups random words of praise in alphabetical order and asks the child to consider each word and whether it would be appropriate for them, in their understanding of the world, to use it to describe God. It also asks if there are other words they think they would be able to use for this purpose. It empowers the child to choose their own language in their mother tongue.

Activity ideas:

- Take a random object and place it in the middle of the room. Everyone takes a turn to say something praiseful about it.
- *Shevaḥ* tennis – Two opponents play back and forth saying nice things about each other. The first to hesitate or fail to think of one within five seconds, loses.
- Compliment bang-bang – Bang-bang is a game when everyone stands in a circle, and the teacher calls out the name of one student. The student must duck to avoid being shot, as the person on either side of him turns and "shoots" (with their fingers, making the sound bang-bang) the person in between. In this version, instead of shooting, they must compliment them. Whoever is out (the student whose name is called if they didn't duck in time, or the student who was second to the compliment) leaves the circle and calls the next person's name. When there are only two players left they stand back-to-back. The teacher begins to count and on each count the students take a step away from each other, until the teacher misses a number, when they must each turn and draw their guns and compliment the other. The winner is the first to do that.
- Pick and Remix – The teacher or a volunteer picks a song to sing. At some point, the volunteer calls out, "Remix…, ____ style" (fill in the blank with a style of song, e.g., opera, rap, rock, quiet, slow), and then everyone has to sing the same song in a different style showing us that there are many ways to praise Hashem.

יוצר אור

pp. 64–65

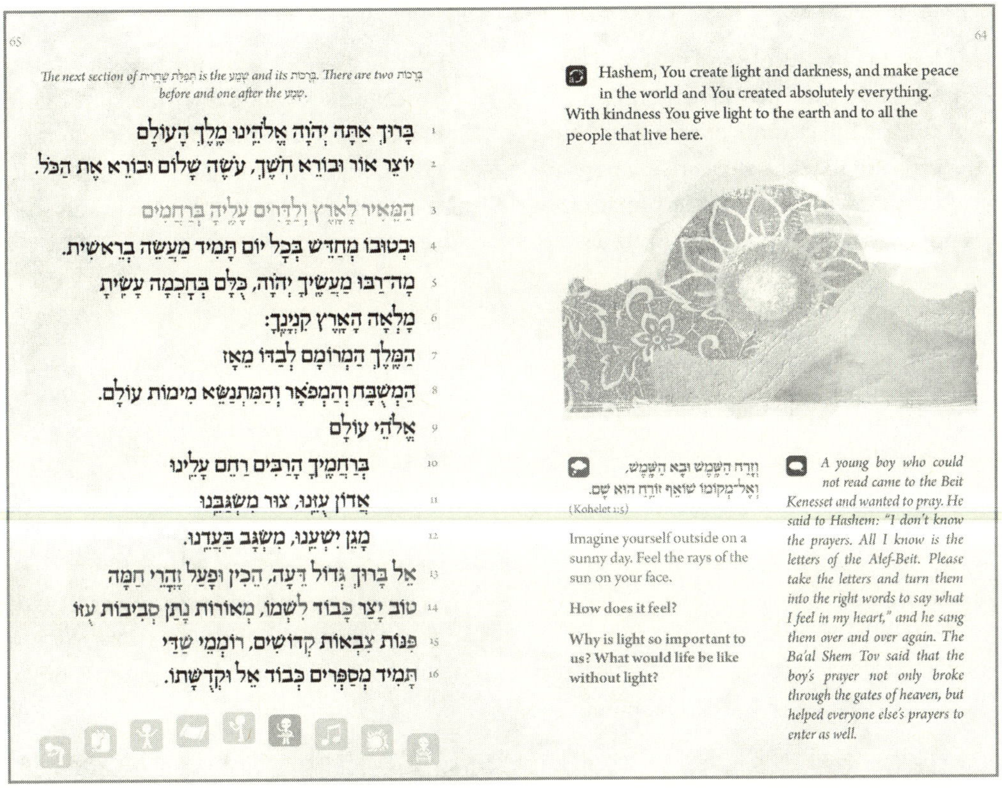

65

The next section of תפלת שחרית is the שמע and its ברכות. There are two ברכות before and one after the שמע.

ברוך אתה יהוה אלהינו מלך העולם
יוצר אור ובורא חשך, עשה שלום ובורא את הכל.
המאיר לארץ ולדרים עליה ברחמים
ובטובו מחדש בכל יום תמיד מעשה בראשית.
מה־רבו מעשיך יהוה, כלם בחכמה עשית
מלאה הארץ קנינך:
המלך המרומם לבדו מאז
המשבח והמפאר והמתנשא מימות עולם.
אלהי עולם
ברחמיך הרבים רחם עלינו
אדון עזנו, צור משגבנו
מגן ישענו, משגב בעדנו.
אל ברוך גדול דעה, הכין ופעל זהרי חמה
טוב יצר כבוד לשמו, מאורות נתן סביבות עזו
פנות צבאות קדושים, רוממי שדי
תמיד מספרים כבוד אל וקדשתו.

64

Hashem, You create light and darkness, and make peace in the world and You created absolutely everything. With kindness You give light to the earth and to all the people that live here.

וזרח השמש ובא השמש,
ואל־מקומו שואף זורח הוא שם.
(Kohelet 1:5)

Imagine yourself outside on a sunny day. Feel the rays of the sun on your face.

How does it feel?

Why is light so important to us? What would life be like without light?

A young boy who could not read came to the Beit Kenesset and wanted to pray. He said to Hashem: "I don't know the prayers. All I know is the letters of the Alef-Beit. Please take the letters and turn them into the right words to say what I feel in my heart," and he sang them over and over again. The Ba'al Shem Tov said that the boy's prayer not only broke through the gates of heaven, but helped everyone else's prayers to enter as well.

The *Tefilla* Text

Translation:
Blessed are You, Lord our God, King of the Universe, who forms light and creates darkness, makes peace and creates all.

In compassion He gives light to the earth and its inhabitants, and in His goodness continually renews the work of creation, day after day. How numerous are Your works, O Lord. You made them all in wisdom. The earth is full of Your creations. He is the King exalted alone since the beginning of time – praised, glorified and elevated since the world began. Eternal God, in Your great compassion, have compassion on us, Lord of our strength, Rock of our refuge, Shield of our salvation, You are our stronghold. The blessed God, great in knowledge, prepared and made the rays of the sun. He who is good formed glory for His name, surrounding His power with radiant stars. The leaders of His hosts, the holy ones, exalt the Almighty, constantly proclaiming God's glory and holiness.

Highlighted Text:
The words המאיר לארץ ולדרים עליה ברחמים are highlighted in the same color as the sunrise in the illustration. The

alphabetic pattern in the final paragraph is also highlighted in brown.

Educational Themes contained in the text:

- Light vs. dark (day and night) – both come from God
- God found in the rays of the morning sun
- Light = new life, wisdom, happiness (Dark = suffering, failure, death; and these also come from God)
- Light = harmony vs. Darkness = confusion (see Isaiah 45:7)
- Balance of the universe = God's *raḥamim*
- Renewal of creation (birth, spring, sunrise, etc.)
- *Alef-Beit* themes

The Illustration

The illustration here is a beautiful sunrise, with a burning sun rising and sending its rays out onto the world, providing light for the inhabitants of the world God created. The hills over which the sun is rising here are Eretz Yisrael and this gives a second interpretation of the light as a spiritual light,[16] shining on Eretz Yisrael (or Yerushalayim – Tziyon) in a redemptive way, bringing the world towards the Messianic era. This process, some believe, has begun in our modern era as the Jewish people have begun to return to Eretz Yisrael, and experience and enjoy a "new light" here with the advent of modern Zionism.[17]

The *Kavanot*

Conceptual Translation of:

ברוך אתה ה׳ אלהֵינו מֶלך העולם יוצר אור ובורא חֹשך, עֹשה שלום
ובורא את הכל. המאיר לאָרץ ולדרים עלֶיה ברחמים

Thought Question:

וזרח השמש, ובא השמש; ואל-מקומו–שואף זורח הוא שם
(Kohelet 1:5)

This quote emphasizes the cyclical nature of God's kindness when it comes to providing light and illumination in the world. Without fail we all know that the sun will rise once again in the morning, and we should never take this for granted. The thought questions themselves encourage the child to firstly experience the sensation of sunlight, and then to consider why sunlight is so important to humans living on earth. Answers to this question can include providing warmth, light to see, and photosynthesis and the production of oxygen on the planet. Sunlight is critical for life, and it is provided for us by God in mercy and kindness.

Activity ideas:
Take your class outside on a sunny day to experience and appreciate the feeling of the sun on their faces. Then have the discussion from the thought questions.

Story:
The last *tefilla* on this page, אל ברוך, is written in an alphabetic acrostic (each word begins with the next letter of the *Alef-Beit*). There are literary reasons for this, as well as mystical and spiritual. The story illustrates a spiritual approach. The *Alef-Beit* contains the spiritual building-blocks of the Torah and consequently our *tefillot* (the story [*Avoda Zara* 18a] of Rabbi Ḥananya ben Teradyon's death wrapped in a burning *Sefer Torah*, as he watched the letters of the Torah fly to heaven, is a good visual representation of this). The story here also

16. The spiritual light that the Talmud tells us was created on the first day of creation and set aside to be revealed in the Messianic future (*Ḥagiga* 12a).
17. This approach to the light mentioned in this *berakha*, that it could be either the light of the sun or a spiritual light from Hashem (or both) relies on the ruling of Rabbi Sherira Gaon, the Ḥasidei Ashkenaz, and the Rosh. Rabbi Sa'adia Gaon however, believes this blessing, יוצר המאורות, refers to "the light of the sun itself and nothing else" and this is reflected in the Sephardic text of this blessing which is therefore missing the verse אור חדש על ציון תאיר ונזכה כלנו מהרה לאורו that is found in the Ashkenazi siddur at the conclusion to the berakha.

emphasizes the spiritual power of the *Alef-Beit*, and at the same time makes the important point that even if the words are difficult for a person, as long as their heart is full of the appropriate emotions for connection towards Hashem, then the prayers can be effective.

Additional *Kavanot*:
Thought questions:

The Sun is filled with shining light,
It blazes far and wide.
The moon reflects the sunlight back
But has no light inside.

I think I'd rather be the sun,
That shines so bold and bright,
Than be the Moon, that only glows,
With someone else's light.[18]

- Who would you rather be? Is it ok sometimes to "be the moon"?

"The glory of Hashem can be felt in the rays of sunshine from the morning sun."[19]

- How are the rays of the sun like feeling God Himself?
- Can you think of what else light and dark might represent?
- Go outside. Where do you see beauty? Where do you see wisdom? Where do you see Hashem?
- Why do you think the author of this *tefilla* chose to start each word with the letters of the *Alef-Beit* in order?

18. Elaine Laron, "The Sun and the Moon," published in Marlo Thomas and friends, *Free to be… You and Me*, 1972.
19. Rabbi S.R. Hirsch's commentary on the siddur

תתברך

pp. 66–67

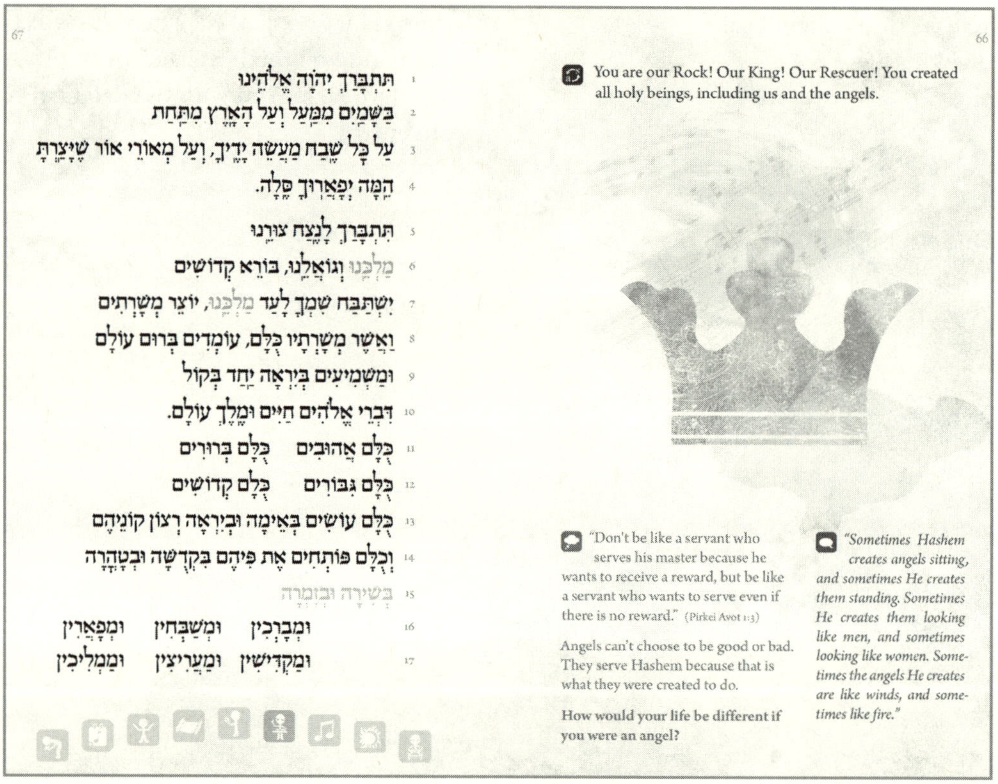

The *Tefilla* Text

Translation:
Be blessed, Lord our God, in heaven above and upon the earth below, for the magnificence of Your handiwork and for the radiant lights You have made. May they glorify You, Selah! May You be blessed eternally, our Rock, King and Redeemer, Creator of holy beings. May Your name be praised for ever, our King, Creator of the ministering angels, all of whom stand in the universe's heights, proclaiming together, in awe, aloud, the words of the living God, the eternal King. They are all beloved, all pure, all mighty, all holy, and all perform in awe and reverence the will of their Maker. All open their mouths in holiness and purity, with song and psalm, and bless, praise, glorify, revere, sanctify and declare the sovereignty of…

Highlighted Text:
The words מלכנו where they appear are highlighted in the gold of the crown in the illustration, and בשירה ובזמרה is highlighted in the turquoise of the musical notes in the illustration.

Educational Themes contained in the text:

- Angels

- *Shira* and *zimra*
- God's *Malkhut*
- God as Creator of the heavenly sphere as well as the earthly one

The Illustration

The theme of this part of the preliminary *berakhot* of the *Shema* is God's *Malkhut* and the angels modeling for us how to praise and laud God's *malkhut* and mastery over the universe. The illustration takes these highly abstract ideas and brings them down to a concrete relatable level with images of a crown representing God's kingship over the world and musical notes that dance in an ethereal spiritual manner, representing the *shira* of the angels.

The *Kavanot*

Conceptual Translation of:

צוּרֵנוּ מַלְכֵּנוּ וְגוֹאֲלֵנוּ, בּוֹרֵא קְדוֹשִׁים

Thought Question:

אל תהיו כעבדים המשמשין את הרב, על מנת לקבל פרס, אלא הוו
כעבדים המשמשין את הרב, על מנת שלא לקבל פרס (*Avot* 1:3)

Humans have free choice and the ability to choose between good and evil. They are therefore rewarded when they choose good and punished when they choose evil. Angels do not have this free choice and are therefore not good models for our own behavior. If we were like angels we would have no desire to do the wrong thing. However, the way they carry out their tasks in the service of God can be a model for us, and this is expressed in the mishna from *Pirkei Avot*. We should emulate the angels who carry out the word of God despite not receiving a reward for it.

Both the quote and the thought questions that follow it attempt to encourage the child to consider what an angel is and how it differs from us as human beings. The story on the following page (68) also explores these themes.

Story:
This midrash, from *Shemot Raba* 25:2, describes various forms that angels can take when they are sent to this world to perform the will of their Creator. It is hard for any adult to conceive of what a spiritual being could be like, let alone a child. This midrash helps us understand that these beings, when sent to earth, can take on earthly forms and that in fact we may have encountered an angel sent from heaven in the form of another human being, or in a creation in nature.

Activity ideas:
Board Games – Students play board games such as chutes and ladders, checkers, or chess, and then discuss what it feels like to be restricted by very specific rules, and only be allowed move in certain directions and spaces. This is like the angels created by God to only fulfill His word, as opposed to the creativity and freewill of human beings. These games could also take on the form of a giant board game where the students themselves are the pieces in the game.

Additional *Kavanot*:
Story:
The angel Michael is the prince of snow. The angel Gabriel is the prince of fire. But Michael never extinguishes Gabriel and Gabriel does not burn Michael. In fact, even when an angel is half fire and half snow, Hashem makes peace between the two parts.[20]

Thought questions:

וַיִּוָּתֵר יַעֲקֹב, לְבַדּוֹ; וַיֵּאָבֵק אִישׁ עִמּוֹ, עַד עֲלוֹת הַשָּׁחַר
(Bereshit 32:25)

- Hashem sends angels to earth as his messengers. Do you think you might have encountered an angel in your life?
- Yaakov wrestles an angel. Why would we need to wrestle angels? Who might the angel really be?

20. *Shir HaShirim Raba* 3:11

את שם

pp. 68–69

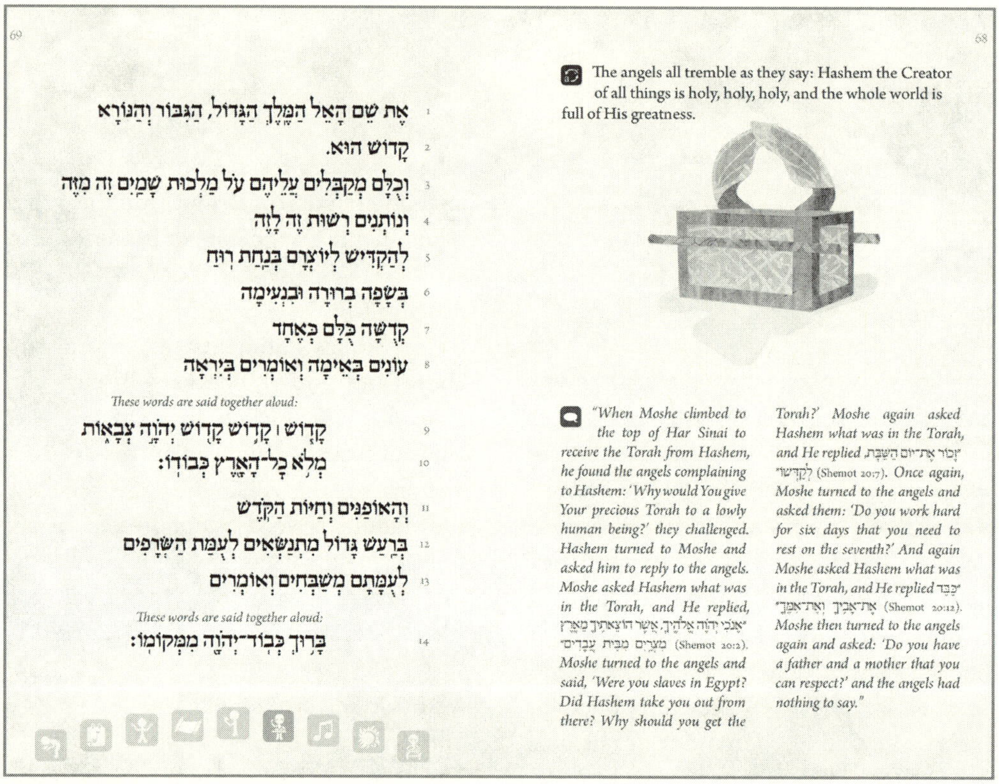

69

אֵת שֵׁם הָאֵל הַמֶּלֶךְ הַגָּדוֹל, הַגִּבּוֹר וְהַנּוֹרָא
קָדוֹשׁ הוּא.
וְכֻלָּם מְקַבְּלִים עֲלֵיהֶם עֹל מַלְכוּת שָׁמַיִם זֶה מִזֶּה
וְנוֹתְנִים רְשׁוּת זֶה לָזֶה
לְהַקְדִּישׁ לְיוֹצְרָם בְּנַחַת רוּחַ
בְּשָׂפָה בְרוּרָה וּבִנְעִימָה
קְדֻשָּׁה כֻּלָּם כְּאֶחָד
עוֹנִים בְּאֵימָה וְאוֹמְרִים בְּיִרְאָה

These words are said together aloud:

קָדוֹשׁ ׀ קָדוֹשׁ קָדוֹשׁ יְהוָה צְבָאוֹת
מְלֹא כָל־הָאָרֶץ כְּבוֹדוֹ:

וְהָאוֹפַנִּים וְחַיּוֹת הַקֹּדֶשׁ
בְּרַעַשׁ גָּדוֹל מִתְנַשְּׂאִים לְעֻמַּת הַשְּׂרָפִים
לְעֻמָּתָם מְשַׁבְּחִים וְאוֹמְרִים

These words are said together aloud:

בָּרוּךְ כְּבוֹד־יְהוָה מִמְּקוֹמוֹ:

68

The angels all tremble as they say: Hashem the Creator of all things is holy, holy, holy, and the whole world is full of His greatness.

"When Moshe climbed to the top of Har Sinai to receive the Torah from Hashem, he found the angels complaining to Hashem: 'Why would You give Your precious Torah to a lowly human being?' they challenged. Hashem turned to Moshe and asked him to reply to the angels. Moshe asked Hashem what was in the Torah, and He replied, "אָנֹכִי יְהוָה אֱלֹהֶיךָ, אֲשֶׁר הוֹצֵאתִיךָ מֵאֶרֶץ מִצְרַיִם מִבֵּית עֲבָדִים" (Shemot 20:2). *Moshe turned to the angels and said, 'Were you slaves in Egypt? Did Hashem take you out from there? Why should you get the Torah?' Moshe again asked Hashem what was in the Torah, and He replied* "זָכוֹר אֶת־יוֹם הַשַּׁבָּת לְקַדְּשׁוֹ" (Shemot 20:7). *Once again, Moshe turned to the angels and asked them: 'Do you work hard for six days that you need to rest on the seventh?' And again Moshe asked Hashem what was in the Torah, and He replied* "כַּבֵּד אֶת־אָבִיךָ וְאֶת־אִמֶּךָ" (Shemot 20:12). *Moshe then turned to the angels again and asked: 'Do you have a father and a mother that you can respect?' and the angels had nothing to say."*

The *Tefilla* Text

Translation:

…*the name of the great, mighty and awesome God and King, holy is He. All accept on themselves, one from another, the yoke of the kingdom of heaven, granting permission to one another to sanctify the One who formed them, in serene spirit, pure speech and sweet melody. All, as one, proclaim His holiness with reverence, saying in awe:*

Holy, holy, holy is the Lord of hosts; the whole world is filled with His glory.

Then the Ophanim and the Holy Ḥayyot, with a roar of noise, raise themselves toward the Seraphim and, facing them, give praise, saying:

Blessed is the Lord's glory from His place.

Educational Themes contained in the text:

- The name of God
- Angels
- The sitting *Kedusha*

The Illustration

This section of *tefilla* has a heavy focus on angels, in order to inspire us to elevate our spiritual focus from the earthly world created by Hashem (the focus of *Pesukei DeZimra*) to the spiritual creations of God that exist in the heavenly realms. While we were careful not to attempt to represent these in visual form, instead the illustration here is of the *Aron HaBerit*. The *Aron HaBerit* in the *Beit HaMikdash* had a visual representation of the *Keruvim* (Cherubim – winged angelic beings) carved from gold placed on it. The *Aron HaKadosh* is first described in Shemot 25:10–22.

Notice the golden texture of the Aron matches the other articles from the *Beit HaMikdash* that feature in the siddur – the *Mizbe'aḥ* on page 34 and the *Menora* on page 140.

The *Kavanot*

Conceptual Translation of:

כלם כאחד עוֹנים ואוֹמרים ביראה: קדוֹש, קדוֹש, קדוֹש ה׳ צבאוֹת מלא כל־הארץ כבוֹדוֹ:

Story:
Following on from the thought question of the previous page, and building on it, this story further highlights the different position of humans and angels in the eyes of God. While angels may be perfect servants of God, His written word is only addressed to humans. In this aggadic source from *Shabbat* 88b, Moshe cleverly proves to the angels themselves in the presence of God that the Torah is ours, and by implication we hold a special portion of God's love. This is an important message – despite our flaws, perhaps even because of them, God has love for us and desires a relationship with us, even above that of the angels.

Additional *Kavanot*:
Thought question:

וישא עיניו, וירא, והנה שלשה אנשים, נצבים עליו; וירא, וירץ לקראתם מפתח האהל, וישתחו, ארצה. (Bereshit 18:2)

- Hashem sends angels to earth as His messengers. Do you think you might have encountered an angel in your life?

לאל ברוך

pp. 70–71

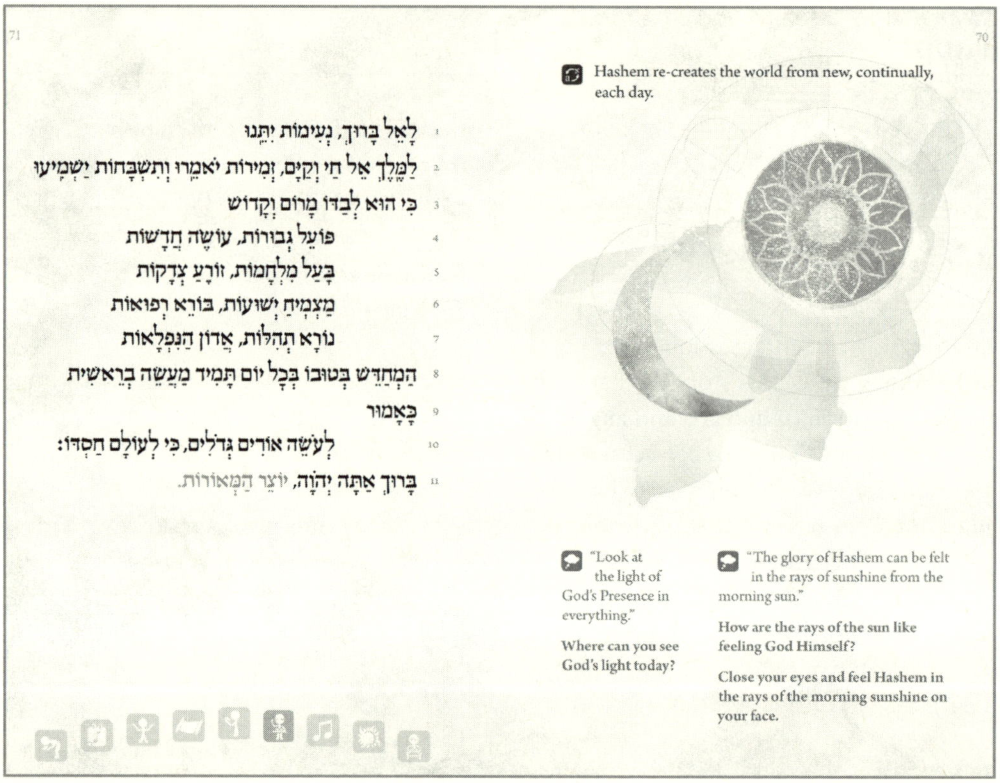
71

70

Hashem re-creates the world from new, continually, each day.

לָאֵל בָּרוּךְ, נְעִימוֹת יִתֵּנוּ
לַמֶּלֶךְ אֵל חַי וְקַיָּם, זְמִירוֹת יֹאמֵרוּ וְתִשְׁבָּחוֹת יַשְׁמִיעוּ
כִּי הוּא לְבַדּוֹ מָרוֹם וְקָדוֹשׁ
פּוֹעֵל גְּבוּרוֹת, עוֹשֶׂה חֲדָשׁוֹת
בַּעַל מִלְחָמוֹת, זוֹרֵעַ צְדָקוֹת
מַצְמִיחַ יְשׁוּעוֹת, בּוֹרֵא רְפוּאוֹת
נוֹרָא תְהִלּוֹת, אֲדוֹן הַנִּפְלָאוֹת
הַמְחַדֵּשׁ בְּטוּבוֹ בְּכָל יוֹם תָּמִיד מַעֲשֵׂה בְרֵאשִׁית
כָּאָמוּר
לְעֹשֵׂה אוֹרִים גְּדֹלִים, כִּי לְעוֹלָם חַסְדּוֹ:
בָּרוּךְ אַתָּה יְהוָה, יוֹצֵר הַמְּאוֹרוֹת.

"Look at the light of God's Presence in everything."

Where can you see God's light today?

"The glory of Hashem can be felt in the rays of sunshine from the morning sun."

How are the rays of the sun like feeling God Himself?

Close your eyes and feel Hashem in the rays of the morning sunshine on your face.

The *Tefilla* Text

Translation:
To the blessed God they offer melodies. To the King, living and eternal God, they say psalms and proclaim praises. For it is He alone who is exalted and holy, who does mighty deeds and creates new things, who is Master of battles, and sows righteousness, who makes salvation grow and creates cures, who is revered in praises, Lord of wonders, who in His goodness, continually renews the work of creation, day after day, as it is said, "[Praise] Him who made the great lights, for His love endures for ever."

Blessed are You, Lord, who forms the radiant lights.

Highlighted Text:
The words יוצר המאורות are highlighted in the golden color of the sun in the illustration.

Educational Themes contained in the text:

- Light vs. dark (day and night) – both come from God
- God found in the rays of the morning sun

- Light = new life, wisdom, happiness (Dark = suffering, failure, death; and these also come from God)
- Light = harmony vs. Darkness = confusion (see Isaiah 45:7)
- Balance of the universe = God's *raḥamim*
- Renewal of creation (birth, spring, sunrise, etc.)
- *Alef-Beit* themes

The Illustration

The illustration is a return of the recurring theme of the sun and moon, as a visual representation of the "great lights" that God created for us. As opposed to other times in the siddur, such as Modeh Ani on p.8 and Nishmat on p.81, where the moon is found within the circle of the sun, here we have them as two separate celestial entities. Each one bathing the world in its special light, as seen by the colors emanating from the sun and the moon in the illustration. In those previous illustrations where the sun and moon are inseparable, early morning sunrise is implied, when both the moon and sun can be seen in the sky. But here we wish to consider both the sun and the moon as two separate luminary creations and gifts from God, each in its own right.

The *Kavanot*

Conceptual Translation of:

המחדש בטובו בכל יום תמיד מעשה בראשית

Thought Question:
"Look at the light of God's Presence in everything"[21]

There is some disagreement among the *Geonim* whether the "lights" referred to in this *berakha* are a spiritual light or the physical light of the sun and moon. The Sephardi text of this blessing is missing the verse אור חדש על ציון תאיר ונזכה כלנו מהרה לאורו, based on the ruling of Rabbi Saadia Gaon who believes this blessing, יוצר המאורות, refers to "the light of the sun itself and nothing else." The Ashkenazi text, based on the ruling of Rabbi Sherira Gaon, the Ḥasidei Ashkenaz, and the Rosh, includes this verse, allowing for this blessing to refer to both the light from the sun, as well as the spiritual light that the Talmud tells us was created on the first day of creation and set aside to be revealed in the Messianic future (*Ḥagiga* 12a).

This quote, from Rav Kook, explores the Divine Light that fills the world, and reflects the approach of Rabbi Sherira Gaon et al. to this *berakha*. Rav Kook believed that everything in the world was holy, or "not yet holy," and that nothing in the world is devoid of divine light.

When approaching this with your students, there are many directions that can be taken, including the beauty of nature, fellow human beings (external and internal), good deeds, etc. But the link to the illustration can also be made. Seeing God's divine light in history is also a Jewish value, and as religious Zionists we see God's hand in modern Zionist history at every turn.[22]

"The glory of Hashem can be felt in the rays of sunshine from the morning sun."

This *kavana* asks the student to connect to Hashem through the world around them, especially through light, and the rays of sunshine. It is a quote from Rabbi S.R. Hirsch's commentary on the siddur. This quote brings many of the ideas intimated in the illustration together, such as the light emanating from Hashem's presence as well as from the sun. The educator could

21. Rav Kook, *Orot HaKodesh* 1, pp. 83–84 (see http://www.ravkook.net for full quote).
22. See the essay *Kol Dodi Dofek* by Rabbi J.B. Soloveitchik for a well-known example of seeing God's hand in modern Jewish history.

use this as a great opportunity to take the students outside to experience the rays of sun or nature in general, and meditate on finding and connecting to God's presence within it. Alternatively, this could be a good opportunity for a guided imagination exercise, where the students are asked to imagine and experience the rays of sun on their face (the children should have their eyes closed and be guided by the educator to a place in their imagination where they can feel the rays of the sun on their face. They can then discuss what it felt like etc.)

אהבה רבה 1

pp. 72–73

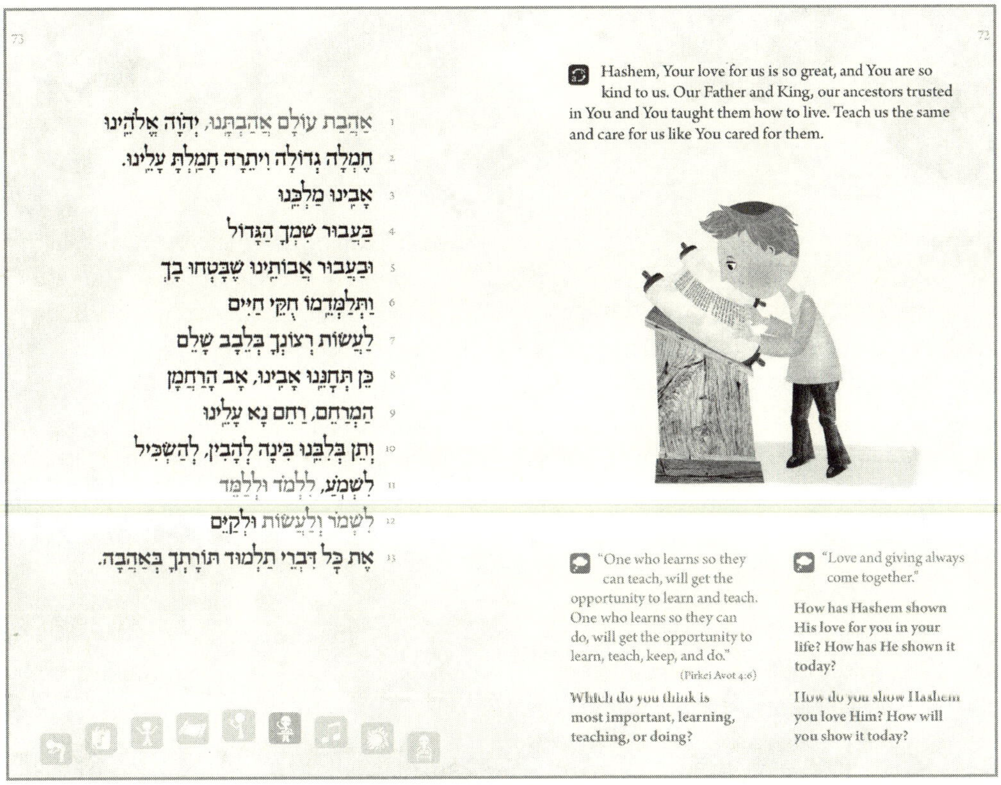

73

אַהֲבַת עוֹלָם אֲהַבְתָּנוּ, יְהֹוָה אֱלֹהֵינוּ
חֶמְלָה גְדוֹלָה וִיתֵרָה חָמַלְתָּ עָלֵינוּ.
אָבִינוּ מַלְכֵּנוּ
בַּעֲבוּר שִׁמְךָ הַגָּדוֹל
וּבַעֲבוּר אֲבוֹתֵינוּ שֶׁבָּטְחוּ בָךְ
וַתְּלַמְּדֵמוֹ חֻקֵּי חַיִּים
לַעֲשׂוֹת רְצוֹנְךָ בְּלֵבָב שָׁלֵם
כֵּן תְּחָנֵּנוּ אָבִינוּ, אָב הָרַחֲמָן
הַמְרַחֵם, רַחֵם נָא עָלֵינוּ
וְתֵן בְּלִבֵּנוּ בִינָה לְהָבִין, לְהַשְׂכִּיל
לִשְׁמֹעַ, לִלְמֹד וּלְלַמֵּד
לִשְׁמֹר וְלַעֲשׂוֹת וּלְקַיֵּם
אֶת כָּל דִּבְרֵי תַלְמוּד תּוֹרָתְךָ בְּאַהֲבָה.

72

Hashem, Your love for us is so great, and You are so kind to us. Our Father and King, our ancestors trusted in You and You taught them how to live. Teach us the same and care for us like You cared for them.

"One who learns so they can teach, will get the opportunity to learn and teach. One who learns so they can do, will get the opportunity to learn, teach, keep, and do." (Pirkei Avot 4:6)

Which do you think is most important, learning, teaching, or doing?

"Love and giving always come together."

How has Hashem shown His love for you in your life? How has He shown it today?

How do you show Hashem you love Him? How will you show it today?

The *Tefilla* Text

Translation:
With everlasting love You have loved us, Lord our God, and with surpassing compassion have You had compassion on us. Our Father, our King, for the sake of Your great name and for the sake of our ancestors who trusted in You, and to whom You taught the laws of life, to perform Your will with a complete heart, be gracious also to us and teach us. Our Father, compassionate Father, ever compassionate, please have compassion on us. Instill in our hearts the desire to understand and discern, to listen, learn and teach, to observe, perform and fulfill all the teachings of Your Torah in love.

Highlighted Text:
The first words of the *tefilla*, אהבת עולם אהבתנו are highlighted in the color of the thought question (linked to the second thought question), and the words ללמד וללמד לשמר ולעשות are also highlighted in the color of the thought question (linked to the first thought question).

Educational Themes contained in the text:

- God's love for us
- Because of His love He gave us His Torah and chose us as a nation
- Chosenness, love, and being an "*Am Segula*"
- God of *raḥamim* (parental love model)

The Illustration

Our friend here is learning from a *Sefer Torah,* the form of the Torah that is closest for us to the original Torah dictated to Moshe. The Torah is given to us as a gift from Hashem as an expression of His love for us, which is why it illustrates this *tefilla* which is about God's love for us. In the *tefilla* we ask Hashem to grant us understanding and knowledge of the Torah, and the ability and opportunity to teach Torah and observe the Torah.

The *Kavanot*

Conceptual Translation of:

אהבת עולם אהבתנו, ה׳ אלהינו חמלה גדולה ויתרה חמלת עלינו. אבינו מלכנו בעבור שמך הגדול ובעבור אבותינו שבטחו בך ותלמדם חקי חיים לעשות רצונך בלבב שלם כן תחננו ותלמדנו.

Thought Question 1:

הלמד על מנת ללמד, מספיקין בידו ללמוד וללמד; והלמד על מנת לעשות, מספיקין בידו ללמוד וללמד ולעשות. (*Avot* 4:6)

The *tefilla* asks God to grant us understanding, comprehension, to hear the words of Torah, so we can learn, teach, observe and perform. This mishna in *Pirkei Avot* asks us to consider what the focus of our Torah study should be. If our only focus of learning Torah is to teach, then Torah study will remain a theoretical academic pursuit. But if our focus is also halakhic observance, seeing the performance of God's will as the ultimate objective (rather than any other self-serving goal), then our study will lead to comprehension, knowledge to keep mitzvot, and the knowledge and ability to teach.

The thought questions that follow the quote ask the student to evaluate these values and place them into a hierarchy. While the mishna tells us that the best way to learn Torah is to focus on practical halakha, the thought question asks what is the most important value, learning Torah, teaching Torah, or keeping mitzvot? There are no incorrect answers, although one can definitely argue that the mishna believes the ultimate value here is Torah observance.

Activity ideas:
A balloon debate – three volunteers pretend they are in a sinking hot air balloon. The class vote on who should be thrown out of the balloon to save the most important of the three, based on an argument put forward by each volunteer representing one of these values.

Thought Question 2:
"Love and giving always come together."

God's love is a very abstract concept for any of us to understand. Rambam says that we can't hope to understand the essence of an infinite God, but we can understand Him through His creations and actions (*Mishneh Torah,* Laws of the Foundations of Torah 2:1–2). God's creations and gifts to us are an expression of His love for us. And understanding God's love, as expressed through His gifts, will in turn bring us to love Him.

This quote is from the essay "Discourse on Loving Kindness," written by Rabbi E.E. Dessler, which explores the relationship between love and giving. Here is a fuller version of the quote:

> *Here we come to an interesting question. We see that love and giving always come together. Is the*

giving a consequence of the love or is perhaps the reverse true: is the love a result of the giving? [...] Giving may bring about love for the same reason that a person loves what he himself has created or nurtured: he recognizes in it part of himself...

That which a person gives to another is never lost. It is an extension of his own being. He can see a part of himself in the fellow man to whom he has given. This is the attachment between one man and his fellow to which we give the name "love."

This *tefilla* has two examples of "gifts" that God has given us because of the love He has for us, that should generate love in us for Him. They are His Torah, and Eretz Yisrael mentioned in the context of the ingathering of the exiles (on the following page of the siddur).

The thought questions that follow ask the child to consider where God has shown love to them in their lives, in a general sense, and more specifically that very day, and then again where they have shown their love for God in their lives.

Additional *Kavanot*:

Story:

This is the love story of a boy called Yisrael and a girl called Tziyona. Yisrael was new in town, his family recently moved from far away. Tziyona looked after Yisrael in school and they instantly became close friends. As young children they were inseparable, played with each other all the time, cared for each other, and over the years as they grew they gradually fell in love. But then the news arrived. Yisrael was forced to leave Tziyona and move far away. They did not know when they would see each other again, if at all. But they never stopped dreaming about each other, hoping and praying that one day they could be reunited in their love. Over the years their love did not die or weaken. Each day they would think of each other and pray for the day they could be together again. This story has a happy ending. Their patience and dedication and prayers were answered. Today Yisrael and Tziyona are once again united in their love.[23]

Thought questions:

- How do you express your love to the ones you love?
- Where will you experience love today?

23. This love story is a parable for the love the Jewish people (Yisrael) have for the land of Israel (Tziyona). It connects to this *tefilla* both because it is an expression of love, parallel to God's love for us, and its focus on Eretz Yisrael, which is also found in this *tefilla*. There was some debate as to whether it was an appropriate resource to have in the siddur for these ages. We placed it in the Educator's Companion instead, allowing the educator the option.

אהבה רבה 2

pp. 74–75

75

וְהָאֵר עֵינֵינוּ בְּתוֹרָתֶךָ וְדַבֵּק לִבֵּנוּ בְּמִצְוֹתֶיךָ
וְיַחֵד לְבָבֵנוּ לְאַהֲבָה וּלְיִרְאָה אֶת שְׁמֶךָ.
לֹא נֵבוֹשׁ וְלֹא נִכָּלֵם וְלֹא נִכָּשֵׁל לְעוֹלָם וָעֶד
כִּי בְשֵׁם קָדְשְׁךָ הַגָּדוֹל הַגִּבּוֹר וְהַנּוֹרָא בָּטָחְנוּ
נָגִילָה וְנִשְׂמְחָה בִּישׁוּעָתֶךָ.
וְרַחֲמֶיךָ יְהוָה אֱלֹהֵינוּ וַחֲסָדֶיךָ הָרַבִּים
אַל יַעַזְבוּנוּ נֶצַח סֶלָה וָעֶד.

At this point if you are wearing צִיצִית or a טַלִּית you should gather the צִיצִיּוֹת together in preparation for the שְׁמַע.

מַהֵר וְהָבֵא עָלֵינוּ בְּרָכָה וְשָׁלוֹם
מְהֵרָה מֵאַרְבַּע כַּנְפוֹת כָּל הָאָרֶץ
וּשְׁבוֹר עֹל הַגּוֹיִם מֵעַל צַוָּארֵנוּ
וְהוֹלִיכֵנוּ מְהֵרָה קוֹמְמִיּוּת לְאַרְצֵנוּ.
כִּי אֵל פּוֹעֵל יְשׁוּעוֹת אָתָּה
וּבָנוּ בָחַרְתָּ מִכָּל עַם וְלָשׁוֹן
וְקֵרַבְתָּנוּ מַלְכֵּנוּ לְשִׁמְךָ הַגָּדוֹל בְּאַהֲבָה
לְהוֹדוֹת לְךָ וּלְיַחֶדְךָ, לְיִרְאָה וּלְאַהֲבָה אֶת שְׁמֶךָ.
בָּרוּךְ אַתָּה יְהוָה, הַבּוֹחֵר בְּעַמּוֹ יִשְׂרָאֵל בְּאַהֲבָה.

74

Bring us from the four corners of the earth in peace, and lead us proudly to our land.

On January 12, 2010, a massive earthquake struck the poor nation of Haiti in the Caribbean. Over 320,000 people lost their lives and a million people were left homeless. Two days later two El Al 747 jets brought a 220-strong team of volunteers, doctors, and soldiers from Israel to help care for the people of Haiti. A week later an additional team from the IDF arrived in Haiti and set up a field hospital to treat the injured. During its stay in Haiti, the Israeli team treated well over a thousand patients, performed 319 successful surgeries, and delivered 16 healthy babies. The mother of the first of the babies to be born in the hospital was so grateful to Israel, that she decided to name her newborn son "Israel."

"לִבִּי בְמִזְרָח
וְאָנֹכִי בְּסוֹף מַעֲרָב"

Why do you think we ask Hashem to bring us back to Eretz Yisrael in a *tefilla* about Hashem's love for us?

The *Tefilla* Text

Translation:
Enlighten our eyes in Your Torah and let our hearts cling to Your commandments. Unite our hearts to love and revere Your name, so that we may never be ashamed nor humiliated and so that we may never fail. And because we have trusted in Your holy, great, mighty, and revered name, may we be glad and rejoice in Your salvation. And may Your kindness and Your great mercy never abandon us, LORD our God, for all eternity, Selah. Hurry and speedily bring upon us blessing and peace from the four quarters of the earth, break the yoke of the nations from upon our necks, and speedily lead us upright to our land. For You are a God who performs acts of salvation, and You chose us from all peoples and tongues, and your brought us, our King, close to Your great name with love, that we may thank You and proclaim Your Oneness, to fear You and to love Your name. Blessed are You, Lord, who chooses His people Israel in love.

Highlighted Text:
The words והוליכנו מהרה קוממיות לארצנו are highlighted in the red of the largest suitcase in the illustration, and the words וּבָנוּ בחרת מכל עם ולשון are highlighted in the color of the story.

Educational Themes contained in the text:

- God's love for us
- Because of His love He gave us His Torah and chose us as a nation
- Chosenness, love and being an "*Am Segula*"
- God of *raḥamim* (parental love model)

The Illustration

In this *tefilla* that speaks of Hashem's love for us, it mentions the most important gifts bestowed on us as an expression of this love. On the previous page, in the first half of the *tefilla*, the Torah is mentioned, and now on this page the ingathering of the exiles is mentioned – our prayer to Hashem that He will bring us back to our land, the land He gave us as an expression of His love for us. The illustration depicts items of luggage from throughout the ages, as a metaphor for *aliya* over the generations. These range from a sack on a stick, to a parcel, an old brown suitcase, and a big red modern suitcase. Jews have always been making *aliya* to their homeland throughout history from the *Shivat Tziyon* after the destruction of the First Temple, until today. But only our own generation, the generation of our students, have merited to see mass waves of *aliya* and the reestablishment of Jewish sovereignty in our ancient homeland.

The *Kavanot*

Conceptual Translation of:

וַהֲבִיאֵנוּ לְשָׁלוֹם מֵאַרְבַּע כַּנְפוֹת הָאָרֶץ וְתוֹלִיכֵנוּ קוֹמְמִיּוּת לְאַרְצֵנוּ.

Story:
This story is one example of many incidents where the State of Israel has sent a delegation to a disaster zone somewhere in the world to share their expertise and help save lives. This *Kiddush Hashem* is one expression of what the terms *am segula* and *or lagoyim* mean in a practical sense.

The concept of the Jewish people as a chosen nation is also explored in a thought question on page 24 (in the context of the chosenness mentioned in the *berakha* for Torah study), and also in the two thought questions on page 142 (in the context of the *Tikkun Olam* referred to in the עלינו there).

Thought Question:

לִבִּי בְמִזְרָח וְאָנֹכִי בְּסוֹף מַעֲרָב

My heart is in the east, and I in the uttermost west –
How can I find savour in food? How shall it be sweet to me?
How shall I render my vows and my bonds, while yet Zion lieth beneath the fetter of Edom, and I in Arab chains?
A light thing would it seem to me to leave all the good things of Spain –
Seeing how precious in mine eyes to behold the dust of the desolate sanctuary.[24]

This title line from Yehuda HaLevi's famous poem expresses his and the Jewish people's yearning throughout the generations of exile for a return to Eretz Yisrael. The students using this siddur are lucky enough to be living in an age where this dream has been fulfilled.

The thought question asks the child to see the connection between Eretz Yisrael, the ingathering of the exiles, and God's love for us. Eretz Yisrael as an expression of God's love for us is discussed in the thought question of the previous page. God acting in history for our benefit is always considered to be an expression of His love for us, and therefore a logical choice for inclusion in this *tefilla*.

Additional *Kavanot*:
There is an imagination exercise for *Ahava Raba* on page 194 (*Shaḥarit* for Shabbat).

24. Yehuda HaLevi, "My Heart Is in the East" (c. 1141), translated from the Hebrew by Nina Salaman. This edition published in 1924 by the Jewish Publication Society of America.

שמע 1

pp. 76–77

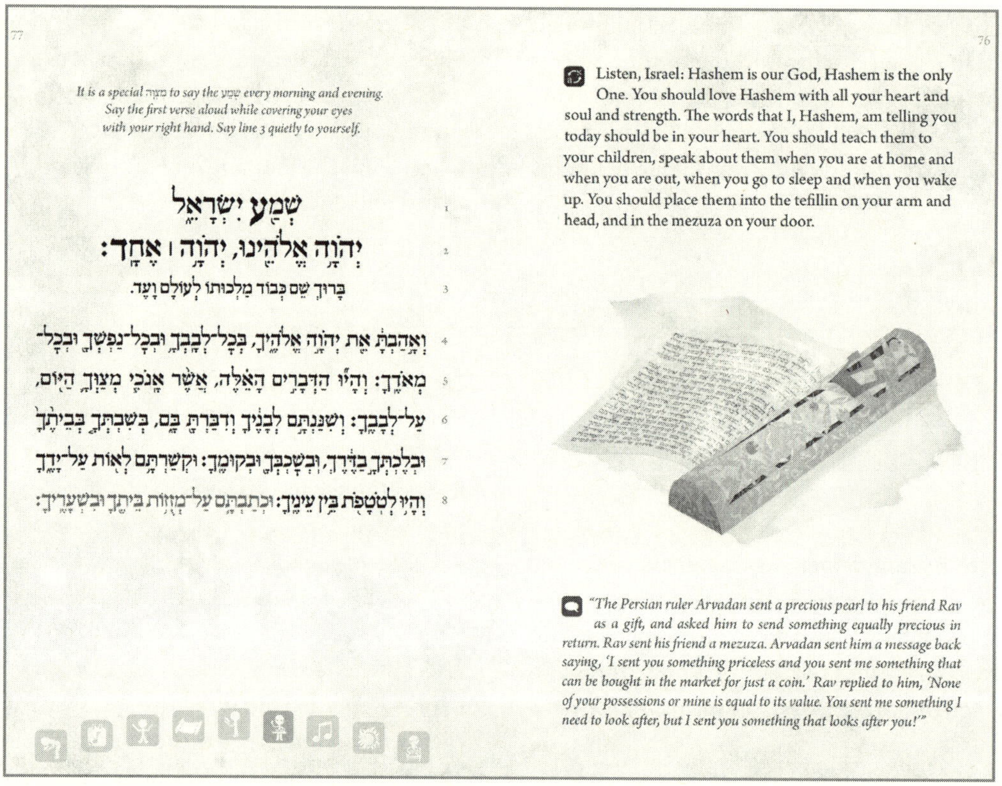
77

It is a special מִצְוָה to say the שְׁמַע every morning and evening. Say the first verse aloud while covering your eyes with your right hand. Say line 3 quietly to yourself.

1 שְׁמַע יִשְׂרָאֵל

2 יְהוָה אֱלֹהֵינוּ, יְהוָה אֶחָד:

3 בָּרוּךְ שֵׁם כְּבוֹד מַלְכוּתוֹ לְעוֹלָם וָעֶד.

4 וְאָהַבְתָּ אֵת יְהוָה אֱלֹהֶיךָ, בְּכָל־לְבָבְךָ וּבְכָל־נַפְשְׁךָ וּבְכָל־

5 מְאֹדֶךָ: וְהָיוּ הַדְּבָרִים הָאֵלֶּה, אֲשֶׁר אָנֹכִי מְצַוְּךָ הַיּוֹם,

6 עַל־לְבָבֶךָ: וְשִׁנַּנְתָּם לְבָנֶיךָ וְדִבַּרְתָּ בָּם, בְּשִׁבְתְּךָ בְּבֵיתֶךָ

7 וּבְלֶכְתְּךָ בַדֶּרֶךְ, וּבְשָׁכְבְּךָ וּבְקוּמֶךָ: וּקְשַׁרְתָּם לְאוֹת עַל־יָדֶךָ

8 וְהָיוּ לְטֹטָפֹת בֵּין עֵינֶיךָ: וּכְתַבְתָּם עַל־מְזֻזוֹת בֵּיתֶךָ וּבִשְׁעָרֶיךָ:

76

Listen, Israel: Hashem is our God, Hashem is the only One. You should love Hashem with all your heart and soul and strength. The words that I, Hashem, am telling you today should be in your heart. You should teach them to your children, speak about them when you are at home and when you are out, when you go to sleep and when you wake up. You should place them into the tefillin on your arm and head, and in the mezuza on your door.

"The Persian ruler Arvadan sent a precious pearl to his friend Rav as a gift, and asked him to send something equally precious in return. Rav sent his friend a mezuza. Arvadan sent him a message back saying, 'I sent you something priceless and you sent me something that can be bought in the market for just a coin.' Rav replied to him, 'None of your possessions or mine is equal to its value. You sent me something I need to look after, but I sent you something that looks after you!'"

The *Tefilla* Text

Translation:
God, faithful King!

Listen, Israel: the Lord is our God, the Lord is One.

Blessed be the name of His glorious kingdom for ever and ever. Love the Lord your God with all your heart, with all your soul, and with all your might. These words which I command you today shall be on your heart. Teach them repeatedly to your children, speaking of them when you sit at home and when you travel on the way, when you lie down and when you rise. Bind them as a sign on your hand, and they shall be an emblem between your eyes. Write them on the doorposts of your house and gates.

Highlighted Text:
The words וכתבתם על־מזוזות ביתך ובשעריך are highlighted in the color of the *mezuza* in the illustration.

Educational Themes contained in the text:

- עול מלכות שמים – committing to Hashem in our lives
- Hashem (Who is Hashem?)
- Kingship – God's *Malkhut*
- Love – Love of God
- Jewish education – teaching Torah to young children
- The *mezuza*

The Illustration

We chose to focus on the mitzva of *mezuza* here as the other mitzvot and themes contained in this paragraph have their place elsewhere in the siddur. Here, a beautiful *mezuza* is presented, but for aesthetic and educational reasons, the parchment is showing. This shows the students what is contained in the case of the *mezuza* (they are more than likely familiar with what a *mezuza* case looks like but many will be less familiar with the content – which is actually the *mezuza* itself). The picture demonstrates the connection between the *mezuza* and the text of the *Shema* (which can be seen on the parchment), which the children will be saying at this point in their *tefilla*.

The *Kavanot*

Conceptual Translation of:
The first paragraph of the *Shema*.

Story:
This story, taken from the Talmud (Yerushalmi, *Pesaḥim* 1:1) and the Midrash (*Bereshit Raba* 35:16), takes a spiritual approach to the power of the *mezuza* to protect those that live in a house with one on the door. It asks the reader to think about the value of precious objects and from where value is derived. Is an object's value only monetary? Or can an object have other value, such as sentimental, or in this case spiritual. The *mezuza* is an everyday object for a child who attends a Jewish day school, but this story requires the child to take a second look at this object, and give it deeper thought.

Activity idea:
Use this opportunity to take a closer look at the inside of a *mezuza* with your class. Or invite a *Sofer Stam* to demonstrate and talk about the writing of *mezuzot* (and *tefillin*).

Additional *Kavanot*:
Story (also found on page 155 of the siddur in Arvit for Shabbat):
It once happened on the battle field between two warring nations, that Jew faced Jew in mortal combat. As one of the Jewish soldiers ran for cover into a foxhole, the other called out, "Surrender, or I'll shoot." The hiding soldier covered his eyes, and crying, recited the words: "*Shema Yisrael, Hashem Eloheinu, Hashem Eḥad.*" As the other soldier heard this, he replied, "*Baruch shem kevod malkhuto le'olam va'ed,*" laid down his gun and extended a hand, and they embraced as brothers.[25]

25. This story has many incarnations, from many conflicts where Jews were pitted against each other fighting for their host country. The most famous citing is in S. Ansky's "The Enemy at His Pleasure: A Journey through the Jewish Pale of Settlement during World War I" where he reports ten different versions of the same story. However, there is reason to believe that the story may have pre-dated WWI (not that it may not have also happened during that conflict as well) and research on this can be found here: http://onthemainline.blogspot.co.il/2009/11/two-soldiers-and-shema-yisrael.html
This particular version of the story is based on a telling from the Falkland's War, Between Britain and Argentina, as reported here: http://www.thejc.com/node/67100

Additional *Kavanot*:
Thought questions:

- How do you love Hashem?
- Close your eyes. Think about what is important in your life.
- What are you going to do for Hashem today?
- If you were asked to make a very important announcement, what would it be?
- Look at the two letters in the *tefilla* that are bigger than the rest. What do they spell?
- How are we demonstrating that when we say the שמע?

שמע 2

pp. 78–79

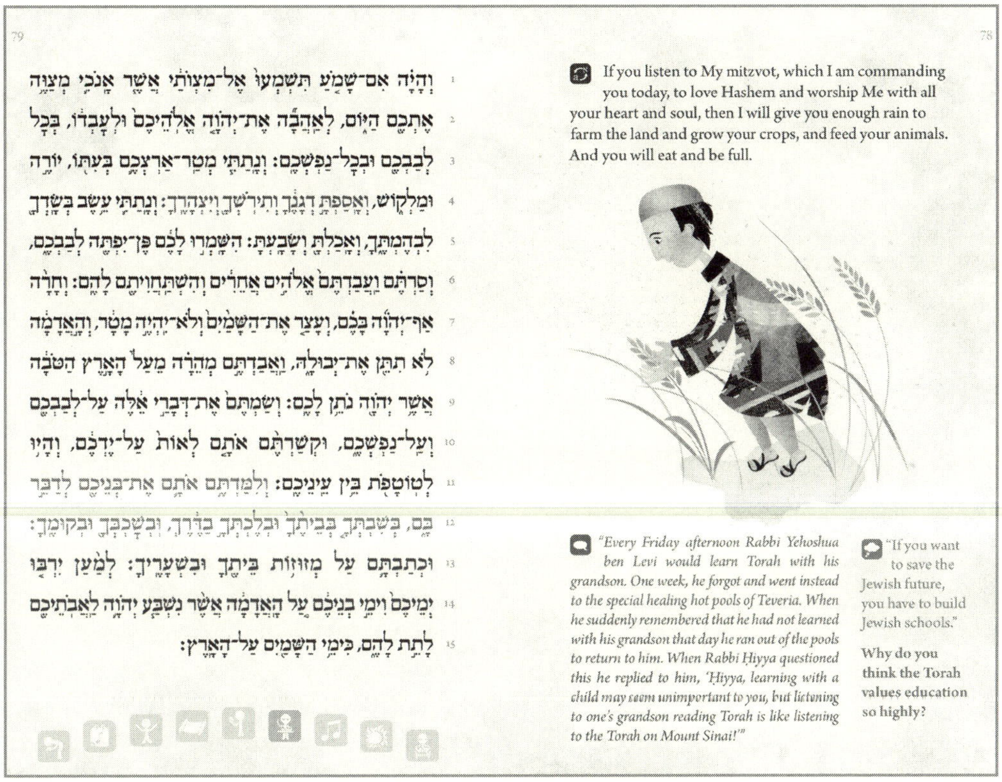
79

וְהָיָה אִם־שָׁמֹעַ תִּשְׁמְעוּ אֶל־מִצְוֺתַי אֲשֶׁר אָנֹכִי מְצַוֶּה
אֶתְכֶם הַיּוֹם, לְאַהֲבָה אֶת־יְהוָה אֱלֹהֵיכֶם וּלְעָבְדוֹ, בְּכָל
לְבַבְכֶם וּבְכָל־נַפְשְׁכֶם: וְנָתַתִּי מְטַר־אַרְצְכֶם בְּעִתּוֹ, יוֹרֶה
וּמַלְקוֹשׁ, וְאָסַפְתָּ דְגָנֶךָ וְתִירֹשְׁךָ וְיִצְהָרֶךָ: וְנָתַתִּי עֵשֶׂב בְּשָׂדְךָ
לִבְהֶמְתֶּךָ, וְאָכַלְתָּ וְשָׂבָעְתָּ: הִשָּׁמְרוּ לָכֶם פֶּן־יִפְתֶּה לְבַבְכֶם,
וְסַרְתֶּם וַעֲבַדְתֶּם אֱלֹהִים אֲחֵרִים וְהִשְׁתַּחֲוִיתֶם לָהֶם: וְחָרָה
אַף־יְהוָה בָּכֶם, וְעָצַר אֶת־הַשָּׁמַיִם וְלֹא־יִהְיֶה מָטָר, וְהָאֲדָמָה
לֹא תִתֵּן אֶת־יְבוּלָהּ, וַאֲבַדְתֶּם מְהֵרָה מֵעַל הָאָרֶץ הַטֹּבָה
אֲשֶׁר יְהוָה נֹתֵן לָכֶם: וְשַׂמְתֶּם אֶת־דְּבָרַי אֵלֶּה עַל־לְבַבְכֶם
וְעַל־נַפְשְׁכֶם, וּקְשַׁרְתֶּם אֹתָם לְאוֹת עַל־יֶדְכֶם, וְהָיוּ
לְטוֹטָפֹת בֵּין עֵינֵיכֶם: וְלִמַּדְתֶּם אֹתָם אֶת־בְּנֵיכֶם לְדַבֵּר
בָּם, בְּשִׁבְתְּךָ בְּבֵיתֶךָ וּבְלֶכְתְּךָ בַדֶּרֶךְ, וּבְשָׁכְבְּךָ וּבְקוּמֶךָ:
וּכְתַבְתָּם עַל מְזוּזוֹת בֵּיתֶךָ וּבִשְׁעָרֶיךָ: לְמַעַן יִרְבּוּ
יְמֵיכֶם וִימֵי בְנֵיכֶם עַל הָאֲדָמָה אֲשֶׁר נִשְׁבַּע יְהוָה לַאֲבֹתֵיכֶם
לָתֵת לָהֶם, כִּימֵי הַשָּׁמַיִם עַל־הָאָרֶץ:

78

If you listen to My mitzvot, which I am commanding you today, to love Hashem and worship Me with all your heart and soul, then I will give you enough rain to farm the land and grow your crops, and feed your animals. And you will eat and be full.

"Every Friday afternoon Rabbi Yehoshua ben Levi would learn Torah with his grandson. One week, he forgot and went instead to the special healing hot pools of Teveria. When he suddenly remembered that he had not learned with his grandson that day he ran out of the pools to return to him. When Rabbi Ḥiyya questioned this he replied to him, 'Ḥiyya, learning with a child may seem unimportant to you, but listening to one's grandson reading Torah is like listening to the Torah on Mount Sinai!'"

"If you want to save the Jewish future, you have to build Jewish schools."

Why do you think the Torah values education so highly?

The *Tefilla* Text

Translation:
If you indeed heed My commandments with which I charge you today, to love the Lord your God and worship Him with all your heart and with all your soul, I will give rain in your land in its season, the early and late rain; and you shall gather in your grain, wine and oil. I will give grass in your field for your cattle, and you shall eat and be satisfied. Be careful lest your heart be tempted and you go astray and worship other gods, bowing down to them. Then the Lord's anger will flare against you and He will close the heavens so that there will be no rain. The land will not yield its crops, and you will perish swiftly from the good land that the Lord is giving you. Therefore, set these, My words, on your heart and soul. Bind them as a sign on your hand, and they shall be an emblem between your eyes. Teach them to your children, speaking of them when you sit at home and when you travel on the way, when you lie down and when you rise. Write them on the doorposts of your house and gates, so that you and your children may live long in the land that the Lord swore to your ancestors to give them, for as long as the heavens are above the earth.

Highlighted Text:
The words ואספת דגנך ותירשך ויצהרך are highlighted in the red of the clothing of the man harvesting in the illustration, and the verse ולמדתם אתם את־בניכם לדבר בם, בשבתך בביתך, ובלכתך בדרך ובשכבך ובקומך: is highlighted in the color of the thought question.

Educational Themes contained in the text:

- עול מצות – committing to Hashem to do His mitzvot
- Love – Love of God
- Hashem as source of all *berakha* – prosperity
- *Mezuza*
- Reward for mitzvot
- Israel as a reward for doing mitzvot
- Renewing commitment to mitzvot

The Illustration

In the second paragraph of the *Shema*, focusing on accepting of the yoke of mitzvot observance, the text sets up a covenant between God and His people. If we keep his commandments, then He will ensure that the weather conditions are conducive to agricultural prosperity. Our biblical character is harvesting the ears of grain with which Hashem has blessed him.

The *Kavanot*

Conceptual Translation of:

והיה אם שמע תשמעו אל מצותי, אשר אנכי מצוה אתכם היום, לאהבה את ה׳ אלהיכם ולעבדו, בכל לבבכם, ובכל נפשכם. ונתתי מטר ארצכם בעתו, יורה ומלקוש; ואספת דגנך, ותירושך ויצהרך. ונתתי עשב בשדך לבהמתך, ואכלת ושבעת.

Story:
This story, taken from Talmud Yerushalmi (*Shabbat* 1:1, 3a), shows us the lengths to which Rabbi Yehoshua ben Levi would go in order to learn Torah with his grandson. While not everyone agrees that teaching one's grandchild is an extension of the obligation to teach one's child, it is clearly a priority for Rabbi Yehoshua. We have placed this story on this page where the source text for the obligation to teach one's child is found, in the second paragraph of the *Shema*. In Talmud Bavli (*Kiddushin* 30a) we have the following statement:

> R. Yehoshua ben Levi said: "Anyone who teaches his son's son Torah, Scripture considers it as though he accepted it from Mt. Sinai, as it says: 'And you shall make them known to your sons and your sons' sons (Devarim 4:9),' and it places next to it: 'The day you stood before Hashem your God at Ḥorev (Devarim 4:10).'"

This explains Rabbi Yehoshua's behavior in our story, and his opinion that listening to one's grandson is like listening to the Torah on Mount Sinai. It is striking that for Rabbi Yehoshua, hearing Torah from future generations is equal to hearing it from at the original experience of *Limmud Torah*. This approach is quite exceptional in Torah Judaism, which generally venerates previous generations as closer to the original experience of Sinai. This approach should be empowering for our students, validating their engagement with Torah and even teaching them that older generations can learn and experience from them.

Thought Question:
"If you want to save the Jewish future, you have to build Jewish Schools."[26]

This statement and the idea behind it is central to the thought of Rabbi Jonathan Sacks, who believes that the Jewish obsession with education is what has guaranteed Jewish continuity through two thousand

26. Rabbi J. Sacks – http://www.rabbisacks.org/news/rabbi-jonathan-sacks-want-save-jewish-future-build-jewish-day-schools-e-jewish-philanthropy

years of exile. The second paragraph of the *Shema* is the foundational text to support the mitzva of teaching Torah to the next generation.

Activity ideas:
Ask the head of school (or another important administrator) to come into your class and announce that the school has decided to cancel the Judaics program due to lack of funds. The school had to cut either Judaics or secular studies and decided that Judaics was less important. The principal should ask the students what their thoughts are, and whether they agree with the decision. This should be an opportunity to encourage the children to formulate an argument in defense of Jewish education.

Additional *Kavanot*:
Thought questions:

- What is the most important reward Hashem could give you?
- Why are these words important to have written on your doorposts in a *mezuza*?

שמע 3

pp. 80–81

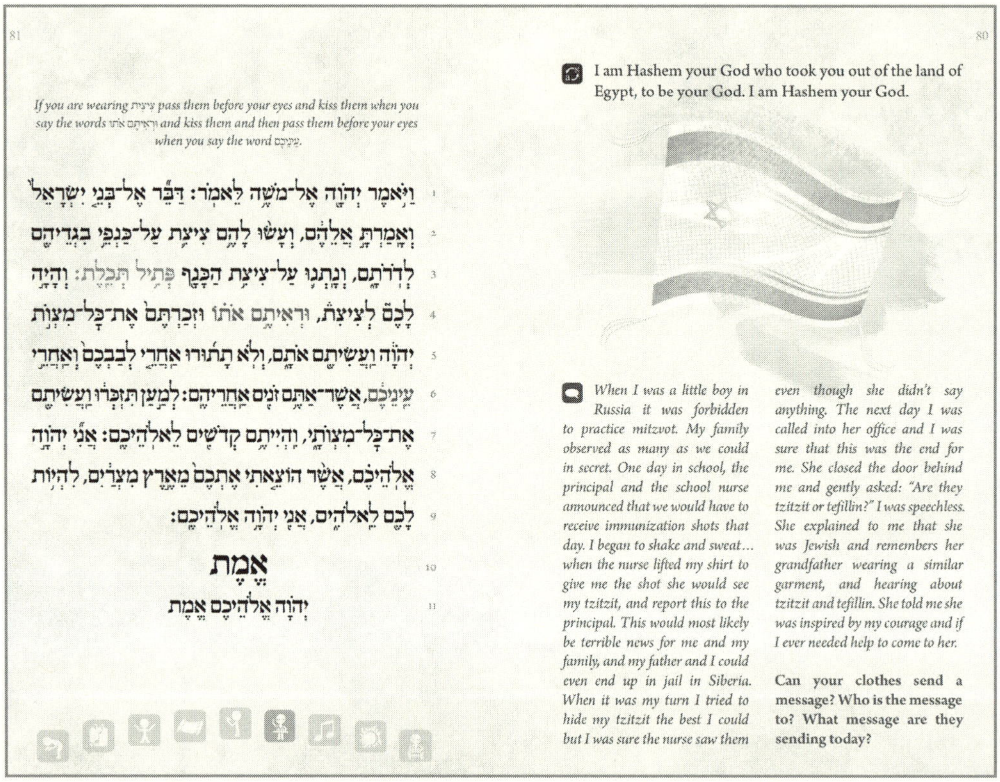
81

If you are wearing ציצית pass them before your eyes and kiss them when you say the words וראיתם אתו and kiss them and then pass them before your eyes when you say the word עיניכם.

ויאמר יהוה אל־משה לאמר: דבר אל־בני ישראל ואמרת אלהם, ועשו להם ציצת על־כנפי בגדיהם לדרתם, ונתנו על־ציצת הכנף פתיל תכלת: והיה לכם לציצת, וראיתם אתו וזכרתם את־כל־מצות יהוה ועשיתם אתם, ולא תתורו אחרי לבבכם ואחרי עיניכם, אשר־אתם זנים אחריהם: למען תזכרו ועשיתם את־כל־מצותי, והייתם קדשים לאלהיכם: אני יהוה אלהיכם, אשר הוצאתי אתכם מארץ מצרים, להיות לכם לאלהים, אני יהוה אלהיכם:

אמת

יהוה אלהיכם אמת

80

I am Hashem your God who took you out of the land of Egypt, to be your God. I am Hashem your God.

When I was a little boy in Russia it was forbidden to practice mitzvot. My family observed as many as we could in secret. One day in school, the principal and the school nurse announced that we would have to receive immunization shots that day. I began to shake and sweat… when the nurse lifted my shirt to give me the shot she would see my tzitzit, and report this to the principal. This would most likely be terrible news for me and my family, and my father and I could even end up in jail in Siberia. When it was my turn I tried to hide my tzitzit the best I could but I was sure the nurse saw them even though she didn't say anything. The next day I was called into her office and I was sure that this was the end for me. She closed the door behind me and gently asked: "Are they tzitzit or tefillin?" I was speechless. She explained to me that she was Jewish and remembers her grandfather wearing a similar garment, and hearing about tzitzit and tefillin. She told me she was inspired by my courage and if I ever needed help to come to her.

Can your clothes send a message? Who is the message to? What message are they sending today?

The *Tefilla* Text

Translation:
The Lord spoke to Moses, saying: Speak to the Israelites and tell them to make tassels on the corners of their garments for all generations. They shall attach to the tassel at each corner a thread of blue. This shall be your tassel, and you shall see it and remember all of the Lord's commandments and keep them, not straying after your heart and after your eyes, following your own sinful desires. Thus you will be reminded to keep all My commandments, and be holy to your God. I am the Lord your God, who brought you out of the land of Egypt to be your God. I am the Lord your God.

True

Highlighted Text:
The words פתיל תכלת are highlighted in the blue of the *tallit* in the illustration, and the words וראיתם אתו and עיניכם are highlighted in the green of the rubric, to indicate when the *tzitzit* should be kissed.

Educational Themes contained in the text:

- *Yetziat Mitzrayim*
- *Tzitzit* as a reminder of the mitzvot

The Illustration

The *tallit gadol* has been chosen here to represent the mitzva of *tzitzit*. There is a custom to have stripes on the *tallit gadol*, often black (and sometimes white and more recently other colors) but also frequently the color of tekhelet (sky blue). This is to remember the aspect of the mitzva, referred to in this, the third chapter of the *Shema*, that one (or some have the custom for more) of the strings of the *tzitzit* be dyed in this color with a dye that is generated from a creature called the *ḥilazon* (a type of sea snail). This is derived from the words פתיל תכלת which are highlighted in blue on our page.

On the *tallit* a *Magen David* can be seen, which together with the stripes, intimates the national flag of the State of Israel. This is a nod to the origins of the flag, which first appeared in 1891 as the flag of the Zionist movement, and whose design is based on the *tallit* with its *tekhelet* stripes.

The *Kavanot*

Conceptual Translation of:

אני ה׳ אלהיכם, אשר הוצאתי אתכם מארץ מצרים, להיות לכם לאלהים: אני ה׳ אלהיכם: אמת

Story:

This story[27] describes a period of Jewish history that this age group are most likely unfamiliar with. It would be worth giving some historical background for the story to be more powerful. Educationally, it should be used to show the power of *tzitzit* as a symbol – a symbol of Jewish identity and, as *tzitzit* is seen in halakhic literature, as a symbol of Torah and mitzvot observance. However, the questions for reflection that follow the story ask the child to consider clothes as a concept and the values that can be central to the way we dress. Clothes can send a message both to the outside world, as well as to the wearer. There are many general directions a discussion on clothing could take, such as the dignity of clothing, and modesty, and the pitfalls of fashion, and how one's clothes can transmit messages on these and other values. Uniform is also an important use of clothing to transmit a message, such as commitment to a sports team, youth movement, school, work place, or community, and therefore the values of that community. These ideas are also explored earlier during *Birkhot HaShaḥar* on page 14, as well as later on in the siddur with the story of "Mashiaḥ's Hat," on page 118.

Activity idea:

Ask for a volunteer to stand in front of the class. Tell the class they are going to play the role of anthropologist, and write research on everything they can tell about their friend from the clothes they are wearing (this will be harder but not impossible if your school has a school uniform).

Additional *Kavanot*:

Story:

למען תזכרו, ועשיתם את-כל-מצותי

A man slipped and fell overboard from the boat he was sailing in. The captain of the boat threw him a rope and called, "As long as you hold on to this rope you will be fine. Don't forget to keep holding on tight. If you let go you won't survive!"[28]

27. Adapted from a story told by Betzalel Schif – http://www.chabad.org/library/article_cdo/aid/536533/jewish/Fringes-of-Fright.htm
28. *Bemidbar Raba* 17:6 – This *kavana* is found on page 31 of the siddur where the *berakha* for *tzitzit* is found.

Thought question:

A translation of the third paragraph of the *Shema* using icons:

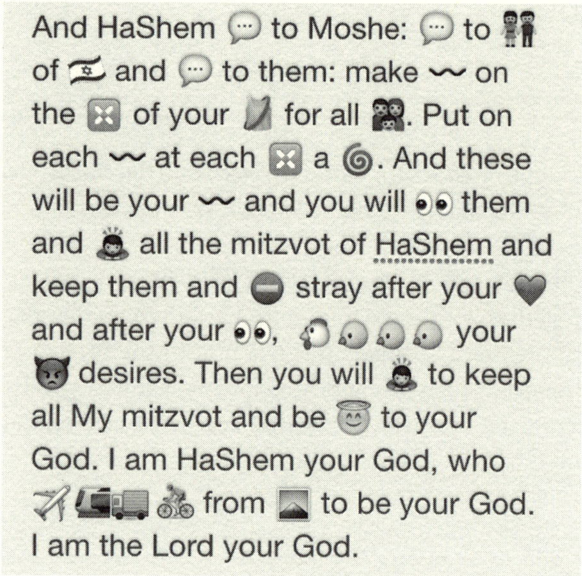

Why are signs and symbols important in your life?

ויציב

pp. 82–83

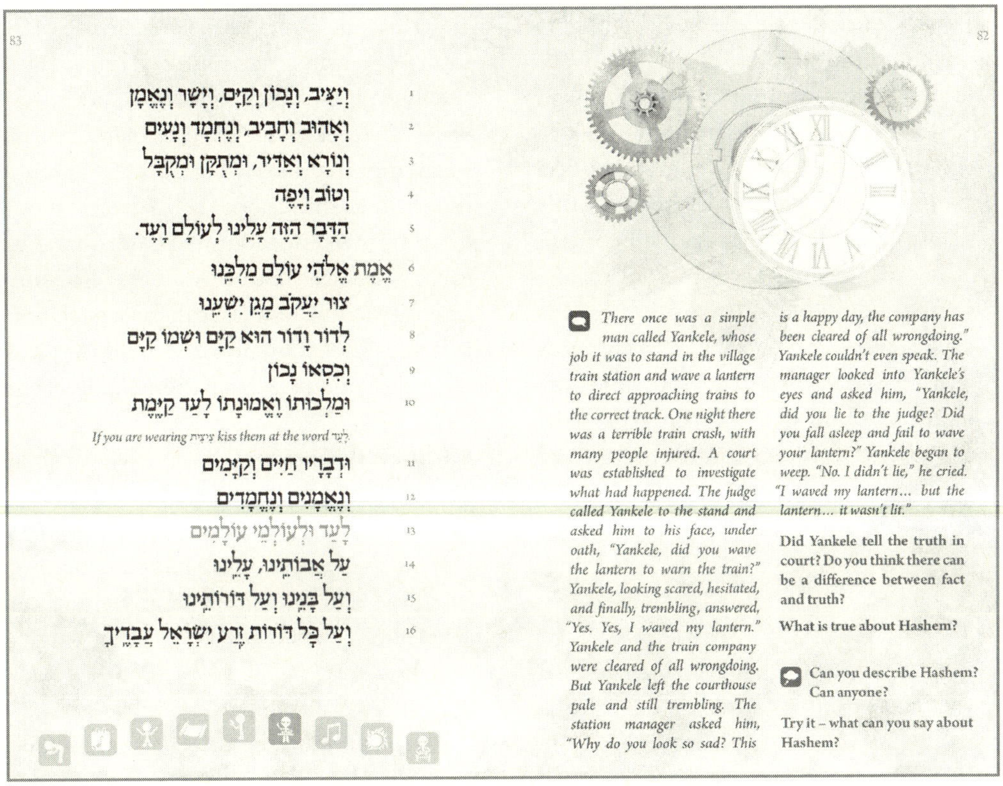

83

ויציב, ונכון וקים, וישר ונאמן
ואהוב וחביב, ונחמד ונעים
ונורא ואדיר, ומתקן ומקבל
וטוב ויפה
הדבר הזה עלינו לעולם ועד.
אמת אלהי עולם מלכנו
צור יעקב מגן ישענו
לדור ודור הוא קים ושמו קים
וכסאו נכון
ומלכותו ואמונתו לעד קימת

If you are wearing ציצית kiss them at the word לעד.

ודבריו חיים וקימים
ונאמנים ונחמדים
לעד ולעולמי עולמים
על אבותינו, עלינו
ועל בנינו ועל דורותינו
ועל כל דורות זרע ישראל עבדיך

82

There once was a simple man called Yankele, whose job it was to stand in the village train station and wave a lantern to direct approaching trains to the correct track. One night there was a terrible train crash, with many people injured. A court was established to investigate what had happened. The judge called Yankele to the stand and asked him to his face, under oath, "Yankele, did you wave the lantern to warn the train?" Yankele, looking scared, hesitated, and finally, trembling, answered, "Yes. Yes, I waved my lantern." Yankele and the train company were cleared of all wrongdoing. But Yankele left the courthouse pale and still trembling. The station manager asked him, "Why do you look so sad? This is a happy day, the company has been cleared of all wrongdoing." Yankele couldn't even speak. The manager looked into Yankele's eyes and asked him, "Yankele, did you lie to the judge? Did you fall asleep and fail to wave your lantern?" Yankele began to weep. "No. I didn't lie," he cried. "I waved my lantern… but the lantern… it wasn't lit."

Did Yankele tell the truth in court? Do you think there can be a difference between fact and truth?

What is true about Hashem?

Can you describe Hashem? Can anyone?

Try it – what can you say about Hashem?

The *Tefilla* Text

Translation:

And firm, established and enduring, right, faithful, beloved, cherished, delightful, pleasant, awesome, mighty, perfect, accepted, good and beautiful is this faith for us for ever. True is the eternal God, our King, Rock of Jacob, Shield of our salvation. He exists and His name exists through all generations. His throne is established, His kingship and faithfulness endure for ever. His words live and persist, faithful and desirable for ever and all time. So they were for our ancestors, so they are for us, and so they will be for our children and all our generations and for all future generations of the seed of Israel, Your servants.

Highlighted Text:

The word אמת is highlighted in the color of the story, and the words לעד ולעולמי עולמים are highlighted in a color from the illustration and linked to it.

Educational Themes contained in the text:

- Truth
- Faith
- Describing God

The Illustration

The illustration, with the cogs and mechanisms of a clock, represents time and, in the context of this *tefilla*, God's eternity. He was always and will always be. This is the same clock and the same idea that is expressed on the page of *Adon Olam* (page 27) which explicitly explores God's eternity, in all tenses (past, present and future).

The *Kavanot*

Story:
Truth is an abstract concept, and this story highlights that. Yankele reported the facts. He did, in fact, wave his lantern. But the lantern was not lit. So in terms of the real information the judge needed to know, Yankele did not tell the whole truth. There can sometimes be a difference between fact and truth. We often take this approach to midrash as well. Midrashim all contain truths, while they may not always represent historical fact.[29] The truth referred to in our *tefillot* here (as well as on pages 81 and 85) refer to the ultimate truth that is God. Perhaps we can argue that God is the only pure and ultimate truth, and all other truths that exist in our human world are complex, and have different sides to them, as we saw in the story.

Activity ideas:
Truth games

- Call my bluff – three volunteers are given a word each. They have to give three possible definitions for their word, one of which is true (provided by the teacher) and the other two are false. The class must vote on which is the correct definition.
- Would I lie to you – three volunteers share one interesting truth (that hopefully no one knows) and two lies about themselves and the class votes on which is the truth.

Thought Question:
According to Rambam, it is not possible to positively describe God. In Chapter 50 of the *Guide for the Perplexed*, he writes: "Those who believe that God is One and that He has many attributes declare the Unity with their lips and assume the plurality in their thoughts." Therefore, he concludes, one cannot discuss God in terms of positive attributes. This is called negative theology. We cannot say what God is, only what He isn't. However, this *tefilla* uses many descriptive words to attempt to do just that. This thought question asks the child to think about what words they can find to describe their conception of God. This is an important exercise because finding words for God turns God into an entity with whom we can form a relationship (from I–It to I–Thou). So however hard it is, it is worth trying, as a step towards relationship building.

Additional *Kavanot*:
Thought questions:

- How many describing words can you find in this *tefilla*? Can you think of any significance to this number?

The letters א-מ-ת all have wide bases or stand on two legs, while the letters ש-ק-ר all stand on one thin point.

- Why do you think this is?
  Answer: Because truth will stand for ever but lies will soon be found out and disappear.

The letters א-מ-ת are all found very far away from each other in the *Alef-Beit* but the letters ש-ק-ר are found next to one another in the *Alef-Beit*.

- Why do you think this is?
  Answer: Because lies are easily found out, but truth is harder to find.[30]

29. See Rambam's approach in the introduction to the *Guide for the Perplexed*.
30. *Shabbat* 104a

על הראשונים

pp. 84–85

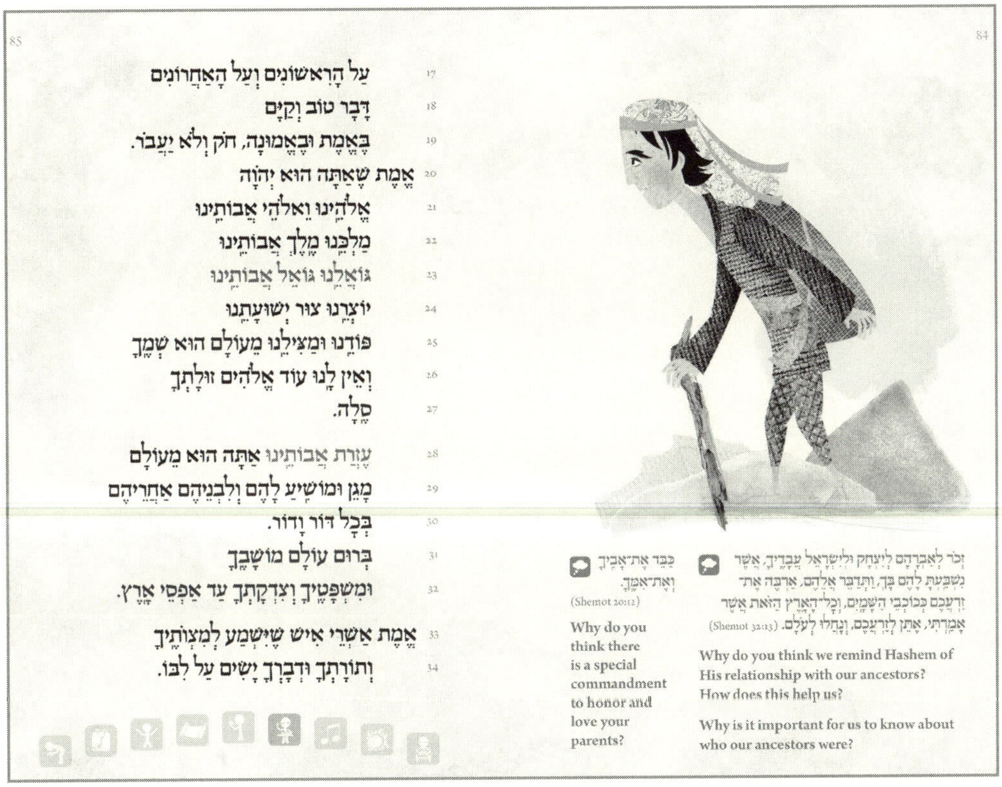

85

על הראשונים ועל האחרונים
דבר טוב וקים
באמת ובאמונה, חק ולא יעבר.
אמת שאתה הוא יהוה
אלהינו ואלהי אבותינו
מלכנו מלך אבותינו
גואלנו גואל אבותינו
יוצרנו צור ישועתנו
פודנו ומצילנו מעולם הוא שמך
ואין לנו עוד אלהים זולתך
סלה.

עזרת אבותינו אתה הוא מעולם
מגן ומושיע להם ולבניהם אחריהם
בכל דור ודור.
ברום עולם מושבך
ומשפטיך וצדקתך עד אפסי ארץ.

אמת אשרי איש שישמע למצותיך
ותורתך ודברך ישים על לבו.

84

זכר לאברהם ליצחק ולישראל עבדיך, אשר נשבעת להם בך, ותדבר אלהם, ארבה את־זרעכם ככוכבי השמים, וכל־הארץ הזאת אשר אמרתי, אתן לזרעכם, ונחלו לעלם. (Shemot 32:13)

Why do you think we remind Hashem of His relationship with our ancestors? How does this help us?

Why is it important for us to know about who our ancestors were?

כבד את־אביך ואת־אמך. (Shemot 20:12)

Why do you think there is a special commandment to honor and love your parents?

The *Tefilla* Text

Translation:

For the early and the later generations this faith has proved good and enduring truthfully and faithfully, an irrevocable law. True You are the Lord: our God and God of our ancestors, our King and King of our ancestors, our Redeemer and Redeemer of our ancestors, our Maker, Rock of our salvation, our Deliverer and Rescuer: this has ever been Your name. We have no God but You. Selah. You have always been the help of our ancestors, Shield and Savior of them and their children after them in every generation. Your dwelling is in the heights of the universe, and Your judgments and righteousness reach to the ends of the earth. True, happy is the one who obeys Your commandments and takes to heart Your teaching and Your word. True You are the Master of Your people and a mighty King who pleads the cause of parents and children.

Highlighted Text:

The words גואלנו גואל אבותינו are highlighted in a color from the illustration, and the words עזרת אבותינו are highlighted in the color of the thought questions.

Educational Themes contained in the text:

- Gratitude to previous generations
- *Zekhut Avot*
- Redemption
- God as Protector
- God as Actor in history

The Illustration

This *berakha* following the *Shema*, extending over the next three spreads in our siddur (pages 84–89), focuses on redemption, both past and future. The illustrations on these three spreads do the same. The first has a character leaving Egypt at the time of the exodus, the second has the same character entering Eretz Yisrael in the generation of Yehoshua, and the third illustration has the same character (or perhaps a direct descendant) working the land during the modern period of Zionism.

The first illustration has our friend leaving Egypt, with the pyramids in the background. His body language suggests he is physically and emotionally exhausted, and understandably so. While the miraculous redemption must have given the people strength and hope for the future, they were nevertheless a generation that had only known slavery and despair, and no doubt must have had deep fear and insecurity about the future. He leaves Egypt with trepidation and weariness from the past, but his head reaches upwards and eyes look ahead to the future, showing hope and determination.

The *Kavanot*

Thought Question 1:

כבד את-אביך, ואת-אמך
(Shemot 20:12)

The theme of both the thought questions on this page is our relationship with previous generations, based on the theme of the *tefilla*. This question asks about our responsibility to previous generations, to respect and honor them. The discussion that could be triggered here could go in many directions, and as the Torah does not give a rationale for this mitzva, all ideas are valid. Reasons could include gratitude, so that our children will do the same to us, because God told us to, etc. However, on a close reading of the question, we are asking the children why a specific commandment exists, implying that surely this is a natural emotion we would feel anyway. Sadly we know that this is not always true, and sometimes the Torah needs to help focus our emotions and give us an added motivation when our relationships are dysfunctional.

Activity ideas:
Trust games

- Pair up the students in approximate order of size (tall with tall etc. You can do this by asking them to line up in height order). Then ask partner A to stand with feet together, and partner B to stand around four feet behind them. Then partner A must fall back showing they trust partner B will catch them (they must do this without separating their feet). Then switch.
- Blindfolded obstacle course – the volunteer must trust his/her friends to guide him sensibly around the course.
- Blindfold a volunteer and tie a rope to each arm and leg. Have four classmates lead the volunteer wherever they wish.

Thought Question 2:

זכֹר לאברהם ליצחק ולישראל עבדיך, אשר נשבעת להם בך, ותדבר אלהם, ארבה את-זרעכם ככוכבי השמים; וכל-הארץ הזאת אשר אמרתי, אתן לזרעכם, ונחלו, לעלם.
(Shemot 32:13)

This discussion could just as easily take place when exploring the *berakha* of *Avot* in the *Amida*. *Zekhut Avot* means that because God had a special and close relationship with our forefathers, we stand to benefit. So that is why we remind God. We remind Him that He has contractually bound Himself to us through promises made to them. Except we know that God does not need reminding of anything. So the question is, whom are we really reminding? The answer must be ourselves. By recalling the covenant God made with our forefathers, we engender hope and faith for our own futures, and are encouraged to emulate the behavior of our forefathers, the behavior that led to the close relationship they had with Hashem.

אמת אתה הוא

pp. 86–87

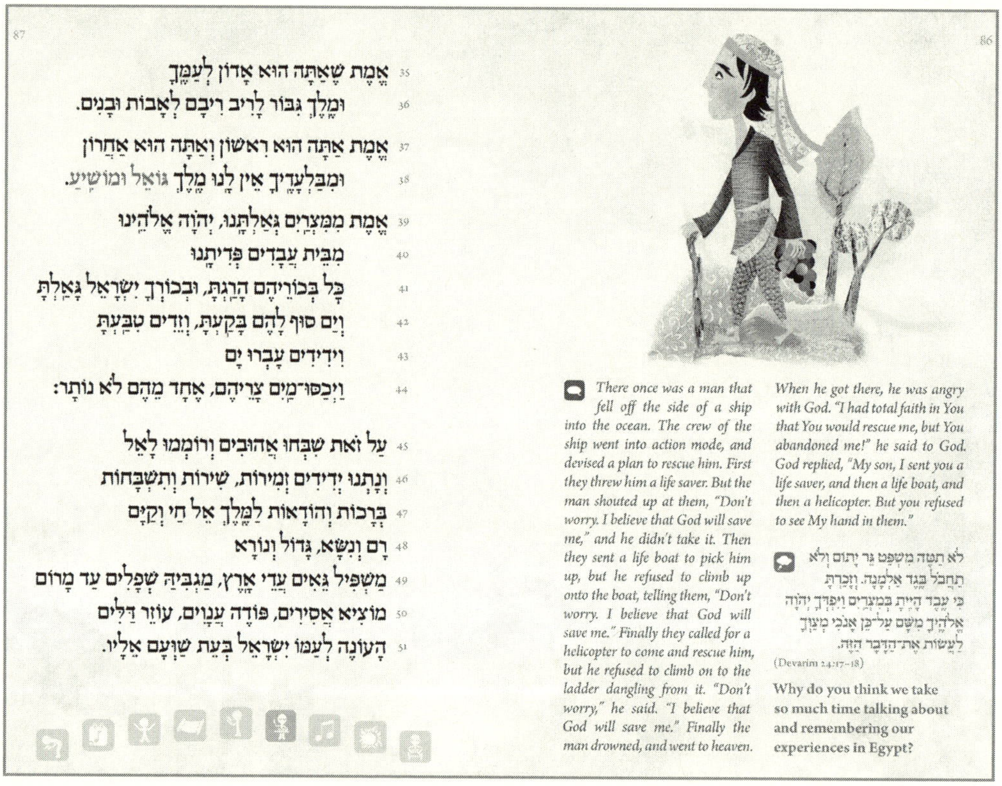

אֱמֶת שָׁאַתָּה הוּא אָדוֹן לְעַמֶּךָ
וּמֶלֶךְ גִּבּוֹר לָרִיב רִיבָם לְאָבוֹת וּבָנִים.

אֱמֶת אַתָּה הוּא רִאשׁוֹן וְאַתָּה הוּא אַחֲרוֹן
וּמִבַּלְעָדֶיךָ אֵין לָנוּ מֶלֶךְ גּוֹאֵל וּמוֹשִׁיעַ.

אֱמֶת מִמִּצְרַיִם גְּאַלְתָּנוּ, יְהוָה אֱלֹהֵינוּ
מִבֵּית עֲבָדִים פְּדִיתָנוּ
כָּל בְּכוֹרֵיהֶם הָרַגְתָּ, וּבְכוֹרְךָ יִשְׂרָאֵל גָּאָלְתָּ
וְיַם סוּף לָהֶם בָּקַעְתָּ, וְזֵדִים טִבַּעְתָּ
וִידִידִים עָבְרוּ יָם
וַיְכַסּוּ־מַיִם צָרֵיהֶם, אֶחָד מֵהֶם לֹא נוֹתָר:

עַל זֹאת שִׁבְּחוּ אֲהוּבִים וְרוֹמְמוּ לָאֵל
וְנָתְנוּ יְדִידִים זְמִירוֹת, שִׁירוֹת וְתִשְׁבָּחוֹת
בְּרָכוֹת וְהוֹדָאוֹת לַמֶּלֶךְ אֵל חַי וְקַיָּם
רָם וְנִשָּׂא, גָּדוֹל וְנוֹרָא
מַשְׁפִּיל גֵּאִים עֲדֵי אָרֶץ, מַגְבִּיהַּ שְׁפָלִים עַד מָרוֹם
מוֹצִיא אֲסִירִים, פּוֹדֶה עֲנָוִים, עוֹזֵר דַּלִּים
הָעוֹנֶה לְעַמּוֹ יִשְׂרָאֵל בְּעֵת שַׁוְּעָם אֵלָיו.

There once was a man that fell off the side of a ship into the ocean. The crew of the ship went into action mode, and devised a plan to rescue him. First they threw him a life saver. But the man shouted up at them, "Don't worry. I believe that God will save me," and he didn't take it. Then they sent a life boat to pick him up, but he refused to climb up onto the boat, telling them, "Don't worry. I believe that God will save me." Finally they called for a helicopter to come and rescue him, but he refused to climb on to the ladder dangling from it. "Don't worry," he said. "I believe that God will save me." Finally the man drowned, and went to heaven. When he got there, he was angry with God. "I had total faith in You that You would rescue me, but You abandoned me!" he said to God. God replied, "My son, I sent you a life saver, and then a life boat, and then a helicopter. But you refused to see My hand in them."

לֹא תַטֶּה מִשְׁפַּט גֵּר יָתוֹם וְלֹא תַחֲבֹל בֶּגֶד אַלְמָנָה. וְזָכַרְתָּ כִּי עֶבֶד הָיִיתָ בְּמִצְרַיִם וַיִּפְדְּךָ יְהוָה אֱלֹהֶיךָ מִשָּׁם עַל־כֵּן אָנֹכִי מְצַוְּךָ לַעֲשׂוֹת אֶת־הַדָּבָר הַזֶּה.
(Devarim 24:17–18)

Why do you think we take so much time talking about and remembering our experiences in Egypt?

The *Tefilla* Text

Translation:

True, You are the Master of Your people and a mighty King who pleads the cause of parents and children. True, You are the first and You are the last. Beside You, we have no king, redeemer or savior. True, from Egypt You redeemed us, Lord our God, and from the slave-house You delivered us. All their firstborn You killed, but Your firstborn, Israel, You redeemed. You split the Sea of Reeds for them and drowned the arrogant. You brought Your beloved ones across the sea. The water covered their foes; not one of them was left. For this, the beloved ones praised and exalted God, the cherished ones sang psalms, songs and praises, blessings and thanksgivings to the King, the living and enduring God. High and exalted, great and awesome, He lowers the haughty down to earth and raises the lowly up high, freeing captives and redeeming those in need, helping the poor and answering His people Israel when they cry out to Him.

Highlighted Text:

The words גואל ומושיע are highlighted in a color from the illustration.

Educational Themes contained in the text:

- The eternal God
- God as Redeemer
- The exodus from Egypt
- Praising God

The Illustration

The *berakha* following the *Shema*, extending over these three spreads in our siddur (pages 84–89), focuses on redemption, both past and future. The illustrations on these three spreads do the same. The first has a character leaving Egypt with the Exodus, the second has the same character entering Eretz Yisrael in the generation of Yehoshua, and the third illustration has the same character (or perhaps a direct descendent) working the land during the modern period of Zionism.

On this page our character, wearing the same clothes, has reached the Promised Land, and finally reached redemption and true freedom. His body language tells us of his pride and dignity, and hope for the future. He holds a cluster of grapes, representing one of the seven species of Eretz Yisrael, and is ready to take his place among the people asserting their independence in their own land.

The *Kavanot*

Story:
The message of this story is seeing the hand of God in our lives and in history. It is connected to this *tefilla* which speaks of God as a Redeemer, as well as the three stages of redemption in Jewish history – *Yetziat Mitzrayim*, entering Eretz Yisrael, and the modern day redemption of the contemporary State of Israel (as depicted on pages 84–89). This idea is also explored on page 70 of the siddur.

Thought Question:

לֹא תַטֶּה, מִשְׁפַּט גֵּר יָתוֹם; וְלֹא תַחֲבֹל, בֶּגֶד אַלְמָנָה. וְזָכַרְתָּ, כִּי עֶבֶד הָיִיתָ בְּמִצְרַיִם, וַיִּפְדְּךָ ה' אֱלֹהֶיךָ, מִשָּׁם; עַל-כֵּן אָנֹכִי מְצַוְּךָ, לַעֲשׂוֹת, אֶת-הַדָּבָר, הַזֶּה. (Devarim 24:17–18)

While the thought questions on pages 56 and 61 also broach the subject of remembering *Yetziat Mitzrayim*, they do so in a more experiential way. This thought question asks a more general question – why do we spend so much time on this historical event at all – whether in an experiential or cognitive way? Many answers could be given, including gratitude to Hashem, knowing our identity and history, to gain inspiration from God's role in history and the miracles that happened then. But learning lessons from history is the implied message from the verses that begin the thought question. The most central lesson to be learned from our experiences as slaves in Egypt is a sensitivity to those weaker members of our society that need to be cared for and protected. This core value, it may be argued, is the very reason our history began in slavery – so we can empathize with the weak, and create a society based on Torah values that protect all members of society, and ultimately, through modeling this ideal society (*or lagoyim*) the world can be improved (*Tikkun Olam*).

Additional *Kavanot*:
Thought questions:

- Have you ever wondered why Hashem chose to start Jewish history with slavery in Egypt? What answer did you come up with?
- What did we learn from our experiences in Egypt?

תהלות לאל עליון

pp. 88–89

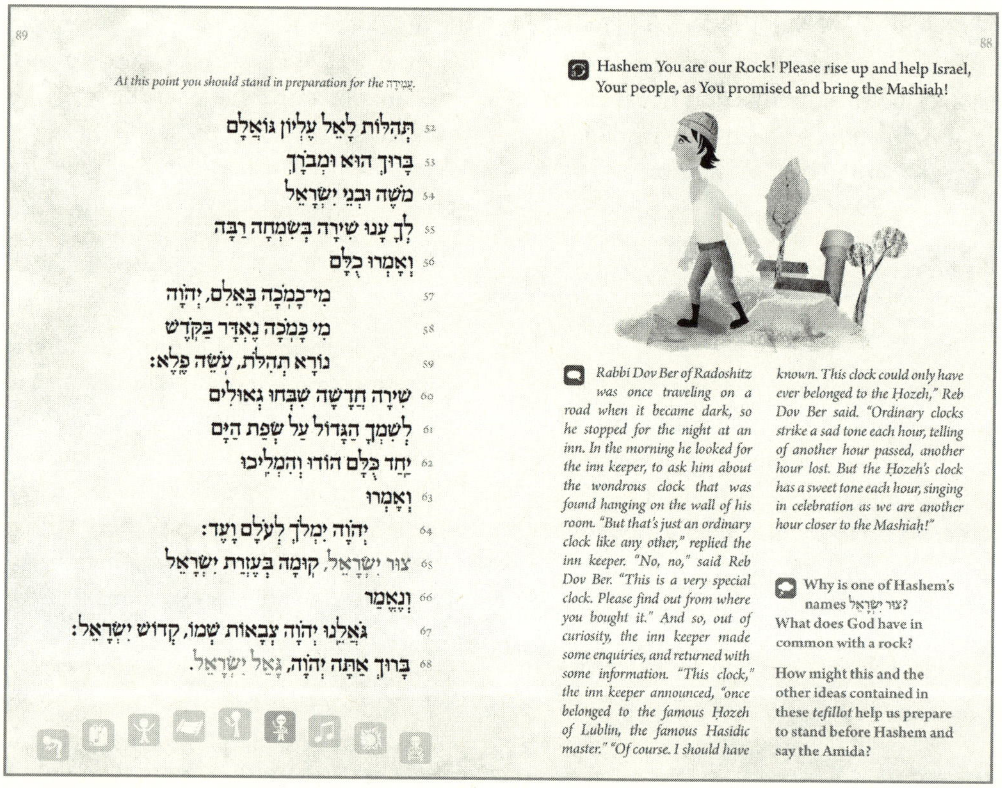

The *Tefilla* Text

Translation:
Praises to God Most High, the Blessed One who is blessed. Moses and the children of Israel recited to You a song with great joy, and they all exclaimed: "Who is like You, Lord, among the mighty? Who is like You, majestic in holiness, awesome in praises, doing wonders?" With a new song, the redeemed people praised Your name at the seashore. Together they all gave thanks, proclaimed Your kingship, and declared:

"The Lord shall reign for ever and ever."

And it is said: "Our Redeemer, the Lord of hosts is His name, the Holy One of Israel." Blessed are You, Lord, who redeemed Israel.

Highlighted Text:
The words צור ישראל are highlighted in the color of the thought question, and the words גאל ישראל are in the blue of the character's hat in the illustration.

Educational Themes contained in the text:

- Redemption
- Exodus
- The link between previous redemptions (*Shema* = exodus from Egypt) and future redemption (*Amida* = Messianic redemption)
- Redemption = a utopian vision of the world/the destiny of Jewish history

The Illustration

The *berakha* following the *Shema*, extending over these three spreads in our siddur (pages 84–89), focuses on redemption, both past and future. The illustrations on these three spreads does the same, the first has a character leaving Egypt with the Exodus, the second has the same character entering Eretz Yisrael in the generation of Yehoshua, and the third illustration has the same character (or perhaps a direct descendent) working the land during the modern period of Zionism.

On this, the third page of this *tefilla*, the text turns our attention to future redemption, the Messianic time. The illustration reflects modern Zionism as a potential beginning of that process. Our character is now wearing modern kibbutz clothes, against a backdrop of kibbutz buildings (a water tower and kibbutz houses). He wears the traditional kibbutz hat, and stands tall and proud, as he dedicates his life to working the land and building the State of Israel. The kibbutz movement was instrumental in building the foundations of the modern State of Israel, and here our character represents modern Zionism and its potential for Messianic fulfillment. The story of Zionism is not an easy one, and has not been a smooth ride. The character looks forward with faith, towards a future that he hopes will be one of peace and security for his nation.

The *Kavanot*

Conceptual Translation of:

צור ישראל, קוּמה בעזרת ישראל ופדה כנאמך יהודה וישראל.

Story:
This Hasidic story encourages us to focus on the Messianic redemption. Tied in to this *tefilla*, which asks God to hasten that time, the story does more than express a yearning for redemption. It demands of us to strive for the ideal of thinking positively towards that future time of redemption. Rather than a regular mundane and defeatist way of looking at time – minutes, hours, and days lost – the Ḥozeh of Lublin would look forward to Mashiaḥ with every passing minute, feeling closer to the Mashiaḥ's imminent arrival, and was therefore more positive about the passing time. This is the ideal we too should strive for.

Thought Question:
Few of God's names are easily understood, especially by a child. The name צור ישראל has a more concrete meaning, although why this is a name of God needs exploring. A rock gives us a sense of eternity (hence the custom to leave rocks at a Jewish grave to express our belief that the soul of the departed lives on) and a rock is strong, unbreakable, dependable. These are all character traits that can apply to God as well.

The second part of this thought question focuses us on what we are about to do, and what all of the *tefillot* of *Shaḥarit* have been preparing us to do: stand before Hashem and say the most important *tefilla* in our siddur – the *Amida*. This question asks the child to consider the themes mentioned in the *tefilla*, such as God's sublime nature, our joy in serving Him and praying to Him, the role of song in *tefilla* and service of Hashem, the historical events of the exodus and the splitting of the Yam Suf, God's eternal nature, and His role as bringer of future redemption. These are all fitting themes to focus on before we stand before Him and petition Him with our needs.

אבות

pp. 90–91

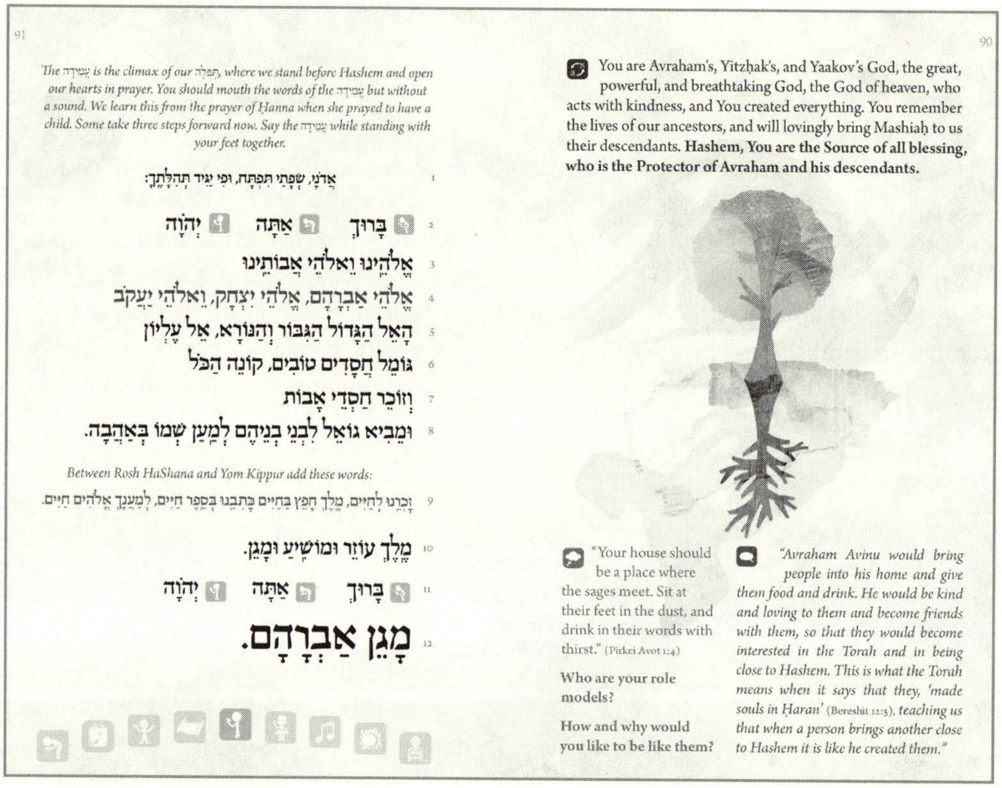

91

The עֲמִידָה is the climax of our תְּפִלָּה, where we stand before Hashem and open our hearts in prayer. You should mouth the words of the עֲמִידָה but without a sound. We learn this from the prayer of Ḥanna when she prayed to have a child. Some take three steps forward now. Say the עֲמִידָה while standing with your feet together.

1 אֲדֹנָי, שְׂפָתַי תִּפְתָּח, וּפִי יַגִּיד תְּהִלָּתֶךָ:

2 בָּרוּךְ אַתָּה יְהֹוָה

3 אֱלֹהֵינוּ וֵאלֹהֵי אֲבוֹתֵינוּ

4 אֱלֹהֵי אַבְרָהָם, אֱלֹהֵי יִצְחָק, וֵאלֹהֵי יַעֲקֹב

5 הָאֵל הַגָּדוֹל הַגִּבּוֹר וְהַנּוֹרָא, אֵל עֶלְיוֹן

6 גּוֹמֵל חֲסָדִים טוֹבִים, קוֹנֵה הַכֹּל

7 וְזוֹכֵר חַסְדֵי אָבוֹת

8 וּמֵבִיא גוֹאֵל לִבְנֵי בְנֵיהֶם לְמַעַן שְׁמוֹ בְּאַהֲבָה.

Between Rosh HaShana and Yom Kippur add these words:

9 זָכְרֵנוּ לְחַיִּים, מֶלֶךְ חָפֵץ בַּחַיִּים, וְכָתְבֵנוּ בְּסֵפֶר הַחַיִּים, לְמַעַנְךָ אֱלֹהִים חַיִּים.

10 מֶלֶךְ עוֹזֵר וּמוֹשִׁיעַ וּמָגֵן.

11 בָּרוּךְ אַתָּה יְהֹוָה

12 מָגֵן אַבְרָהָם.

90

You are Avraham's, Yitzḥak's, and Yaakov's God, the great, powerful, and breathtaking God, the God of heaven, who acts with kindness, and You created everything. You remember the lives of our ancestors, and will lovingly bring Mashiaḥ to us their descendants. **Hashem, You are the Source of all blessing, who is the Protector of Avraham and his descendants.**

"Your house should be a place where the sages meet. Sit at their feet in the dust, and drink in their words with thirst." (Pirkei Avot 1:4)

Who are your role models?

How and why would you like to be like them?

"Avraham Avinu would bring people into his home and give them food and drink. He would be kind and loving to them and become friends with them, so that they would become interested in the Torah and in being close to Hashem. This is what the Torah means when it says that they, 'made souls in Ḥaran' (Bereshit 12:5)*, teaching us that when a person brings another close to Hashem it is like he created them."*

The *Tefilla* Text

Translation:

Blessed are You, Lord our God and God of our fathers, God of Abraham, God of Isaac and God of Jacob; the great, mighty and awesome God, God Most High, who bestows acts of loving-kindness and creates all, who remembers the loving-kindness of the fathers and will bring a Redeemer to their children's children for the sake of His name, in love.

> *Between Rosh HaShana and Yom Kippur: Remember us for life, O King who desires life, write us in the book of life – for Your sake, O God of life.*

King, Helper, Savior, Shield: Blessed are You, Lord, Shield of Abraham.

Highlighted Text:

The words אלהי אברהם, אלהי יצחק, ואלהי יעקב are highlighted in the brown of the roots of the tree in the illustration.

Educational Themes contained in the text:

- Before we even start we need to ask Hashem to help us to stand before Him and ask for our needs
- Standing on the shoulders of our *Avot* when we pray
- Transcendent God (הגדול הגבור והנורה, אל עלין) vs. immanent God (גומל חסדים, זוכר חסדי אבות,מלך עוזר ומושיע ומגן)
- Hashem as Protector (of us and our *Avot*)
- *Avot* taught us how to pray/the source of our *tefillot*
- *Avot* are inside all of us
- The influence of our ancestors and parents in our lives
- History as a source of faith in God (the God of History)
- The influence of role models on our life

The Illustration

There are many metaphors available for the role of ancestors in the lives of their descendants. They are the foundation of our people, the shoulders on which we stand; they are our father and our mother, our teachers, our role models, to name but a few. The illustration uses the metaphor of the roots in the tree that is the Jewish people. For the Jewish people to thrive and be healthy, like the green carob tree in the illustration, the tree must have a sophisticated system of roots. Roots give a tree nutrition and sustain it, provide vital irrigation, and ensure stability for the tree, so it won't be blown over in the wind. So our ancestors, the *Avot* and *Imahot*, provide these things for us. They provide spiritual sustenance, in the form of inspiration and role modeling. And they provide stability and protection, through their meritorious acts and relationship with God (*Zekhut Avot*). Note that a carob tree was chosen for the illustration, hinting at the story from the Gemara (*Ta'anit* 23a; page 40 of the siddur) of Ḥoni the Circle Drawer who met an old man planting a carob tree, despite the certainty that he would not live long enough to enjoy its fruit. Said the old man to Ḥoni, *"Just as I was born into a world with fully grown fruit trees that were planted by my ancestors, so I plant a tree for my children."*

The *Kavanot*

Thought Question:

יהי ביתך בית ועד לחכמים; והוי מתאבק בעפר רגליהם, ושותה בצמא את דבריהם (*Avot* 1:4)

This mishna is presented as a trigger text to explore the concept and impact of role models. Presented in the context of the *berakha* about the *Avot*, the implication is that one should be close to religious leaders and drink in their words. At first, this mishna could be understood as encouraging exposure and access to religious leadership so one can be in a position to hear their words and learn from them. This could be a purely cognitive educational relationship. However, the question is why the mishna suggests inviting the *Ḥakhamim* into one's house, to sit in the dust of their feet? This kind of access goes above and beyond an instructional relationship. This kind of intimacy means observing their every move and hearing their every word. The mishna is encouraging a role-model relationship where we experience them as people and ultimately are inspired to emulate the *Ḥakhamim*.

The follow-up thought questions ask the child to consider who their role models are. Although the siddur provides the *Avot* and the *Ḥakhamim* as possibilities, role models can come from all areas of a child's life, and serve as a vital function in their identity formation and psychological and emotional development.

Story:
This midrash (*Bereshit Raba* 39:14) explores Avraham's character, explaining one of the reasons why he was chosen by Hashem to be the progenitor of the Jewish people – because he is synonymous with the character

trait of kindness. His behavior is worthy of emulation and he is an exemplary role model for us.

Additional *Kavanot*:
Thought questions:

- Why do you think we mention our ancestors here? Who else would you like to mention before you start praying?
- How much of who you are has been influenced by your ancestors?
- How can the *Avot* help us pray?
- Do you find stories from Jewish history inspiring and helpful for your *tefilla*? Which ones and why?
- Why do we need Hashem's help to pray (see the preface to the *Amida* – ה' שפתי תפתח)?

Story:
One day Avraham was looking after his father Teraḥ's idol shop. A woman came to visit the shop and offer a meal-offering of a bowl of fine flour to the idols. Avraham placed the bowl in front of the idols, and when the woman left he smashed up all the idols with a stick and placed the stick in the hands of the largest idol. When his father came back and saw the mess he asked Avraham to explain what happened. Avraham told him that a woman placed an offering in front of the gods, and they began to argue and fight over who would eat it. The biggest of the idols took that stick and smashed all the other idols so he could have the offering all to himself. Teraḥ screamed at Avraham, "But they are just made of clay and wood, they can't fight with each other!" Avraham replied "Aha!"[31]

31. *Bereshit Raba* 38:13

גבורות

pp. 92–93

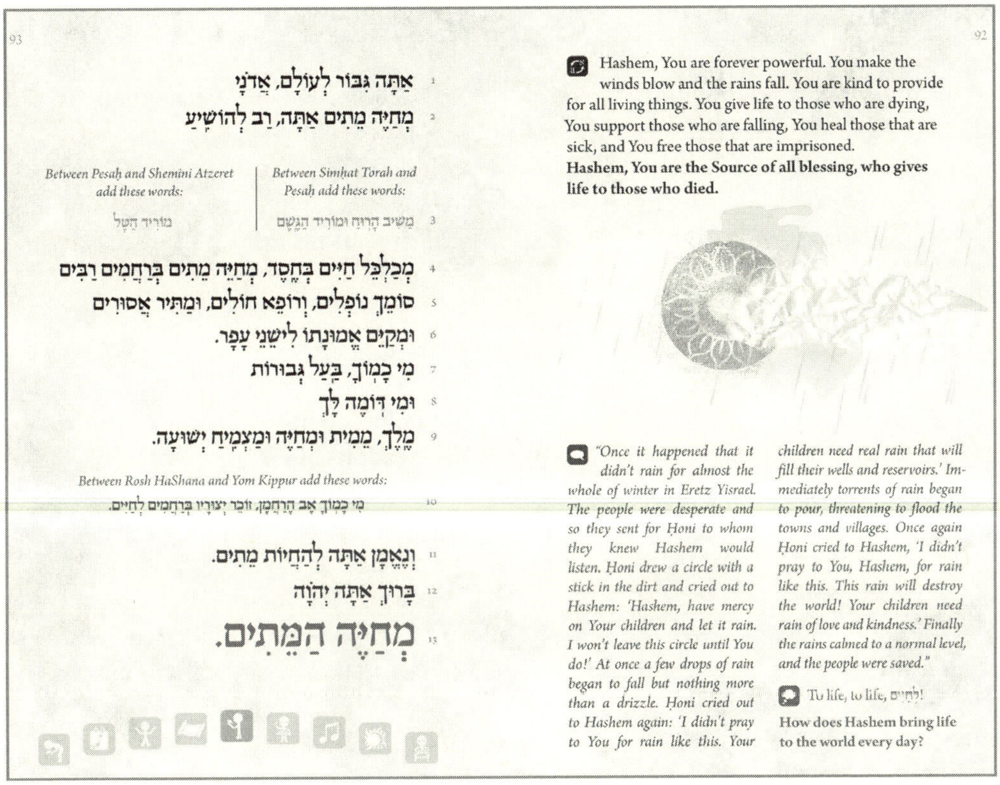
92

Hashem, You are forever powerful. You make the winds blow and the rains fall. You are kind to provide for all living things. You give life to those who are dying, You support those who are falling, You heal those that are sick, and You free those that are imprisoned.
Hashem, You are the Source of all blessing, who gives life to those who died.

"Once it happened that it didn't rain for almost the whole of winter in Eretz Yisrael. The people were desperate and so they sent for Ḥoni to whom they knew Hashem would listen. Ḥoni drew a circle with a stick in the dirt and cried out to Hashem: 'Hashem, have mercy on Your children and let it rain. I won't leave this circle until You do!' At once a few drops of rain began to fall but nothing more than a drizzle. Ḥoni cried out to Hashem again: 'I didn't pray to You for rain like this. Your children need real rain that will fill their wells and reservoirs.' Immediately torrents of rain began to pour, threatening to flood the towns and villages. Once again Ḥoni cried to Hashem, 'I didn't pray to You, Hashem, for rain like this. This rain will destroy the world! Your children need rain of love and kindness.' Finally the rains calmed to a normal level, and the people were saved."

To life, to life, לְחַיִּים!

How does Hashem bring life to the world every day?

93

1 אַתָּה גִּבּוֹר לְעוֹלָם, אֲדֹנָי
2 מְחַיֶּה מֵתִים אַתָּה, רַב לְהוֹשִׁיעַ

Between Simḥat Torah and Pesaḥ add these words:
3 מַשִּׁיב הָרוּחַ וּמוֹרִיד הַגֶּשֶׁם

Between Pesaḥ and Shemini Atzeret add these words:
מוֹרִיד הַטָּל

4 מְכַלְכֵּל חַיִּים בְּחֶסֶד, מְחַיֵּה מֵתִים בְּרַחֲמִים רַבִּים
5 סוֹמֵךְ נוֹפְלִים, וְרוֹפֵא חוֹלִים, וּמַתִּיר אֲסוּרִים
6 וּמְקַיֵּם אֱמוּנָתוֹ לִישֵׁנֵי עָפָר.
7 מִי כָמוֹךָ, בַּעַל גְּבוּרוֹת
8 וּמִי דּוֹמֶה לָּךְ
9 מֶלֶךְ, מֵמִית וּמְחַיֶּה וּמַצְמִיחַ יְשׁוּעָה.

Between Rosh HaShana and Yom Kippur add these words:
10 מִי כָמוֹךָ אָב הָרַחֲמָן, זוֹכֵר יְצוּרָיו בְּרַחֲמִים לְחַיִּים.

11 וְנֶאֱמָן אַתָּה לְהַחֲיוֹת מֵתִים.
12 בָּרוּךְ אַתָּה יְהֹוָה
13 מְחַיֵּה הַמֵּתִים.

The *Tefilla* Text

Translation:

You are eternally mighty, Lord. You give life to the dead and have great power to save.
Between Simḥat Torah and Pesaḥ: He makes the wind blow and the rain fall.
In Israel, between Pesaḥ and Shemini Atzeret: He causes the dew to fall.
He sustains the living with loving-kindness, and with great compassion revives the dead. He supports the fallen, heals the sick, sets captives free, and keeps His faith with those who sleep in the dust. Who is like You, Master of might, and to whom can You be compared, O King who brings death and gives life, and makes salvation grow?

> *Between Rosh HaShana and Yom Kippur: Who is like You, compassionate Father, who remembers His creatures in compassion, for life?*

Faithful are You to revive the dead.
Blessed are You, Lord, who revives the dead.

Highlighted Text:
The words משיב הָרוח ומוריד הגֶשם and מוריד הטל are highlighted in a color from the illustration, and the conclusion to the *berakha*, מחיה המתים, is highlighted in the color of the thought question.

Educational Themes contained in the text:

- *Gevura* (might/strength/heroism)
- Resurrection of the dead
- Water/rain as the sustainer of life (and God as its source)
- God as source of physical blessings/prosperity
- Rain = resuscitating life
- *Gevura* = force of nature

The Illustration

The weather is a powerful expression of God's *gevura* – both in terms of its power and strength, and in God's life-giving and life-sustaining role in the world. Rabbi Soloveitchik's approach to the word *gevura* is self-sacrifice.[32] In the context of God this would be contraction (*tzitzum*) – the infinite God contracts or withdraws Himself in order to create the world and to allow us to live. The illustration represents this role of God as Giver of life, through the sun and rain, essential elements necessary for life to exist on this planet.

The *Kavanot*

Conceptual Translation of:

אתה גבור לעולם, אדֹנָי... משיב הרוח ומוריד הגשם מכלכל חיים בחֶסד, מחיה מתים ברחמים רבים סומך נוֹפלים, ורוֹפא חולים, ומתיר אסורים... ברוך אתה ה׳ מחיה המתים.

Story:
One of the more concrete and everyday interactions we have with God's *gevura* is in His actions as a force of nature. When He provides rain in its season, it is life-giving and life-sustaining. So these themes, God acting through nature to bring rain, and God's *gevura*, belong together, as they are found in this *berakha*. This famous Talmudic story (*Ta'anit* 23a) about Ḥoni the Circle Drawer, who challenges God to bring rain to save His people in their land, is a colorful narrative that presents these important themes. These include the importance of rain for life (especially in Eretz Yisrael) and God as its source. It also shows how we are dependent on a very delicate balance of natural forces for life to be possible on earth – not too much rain and not too little. The story is especially powerful in how it presents the audacious Ḥoni challenging God, and holding Him to His responsibilities – to sustain His creations in life.

Thought Question:
The thought question, that starts with the familiar phrase-blessing "לחיים," builds on the themes of the story, and asks the child to think of this and other ways that Hashem provides for us and grants us life.

Activity ideas:
To gain a practical experiential understanding of the importance of rain to life on earth, plant two plants with your class. Arrange for each child to take a turn watering only one of the plants, leaving the other plant without, to compare how long it lives without water.

Additional *Kavanot*:
Thought questions:

- Why do you think we mention rain in this *berakha*?
- Look out of the window. Where do you see life?
- Why is water so important to us?

32. See Mesorat HaRav Siddur on *Birkhot HaShaḥar*.

קדושת השם

pp. 94–95

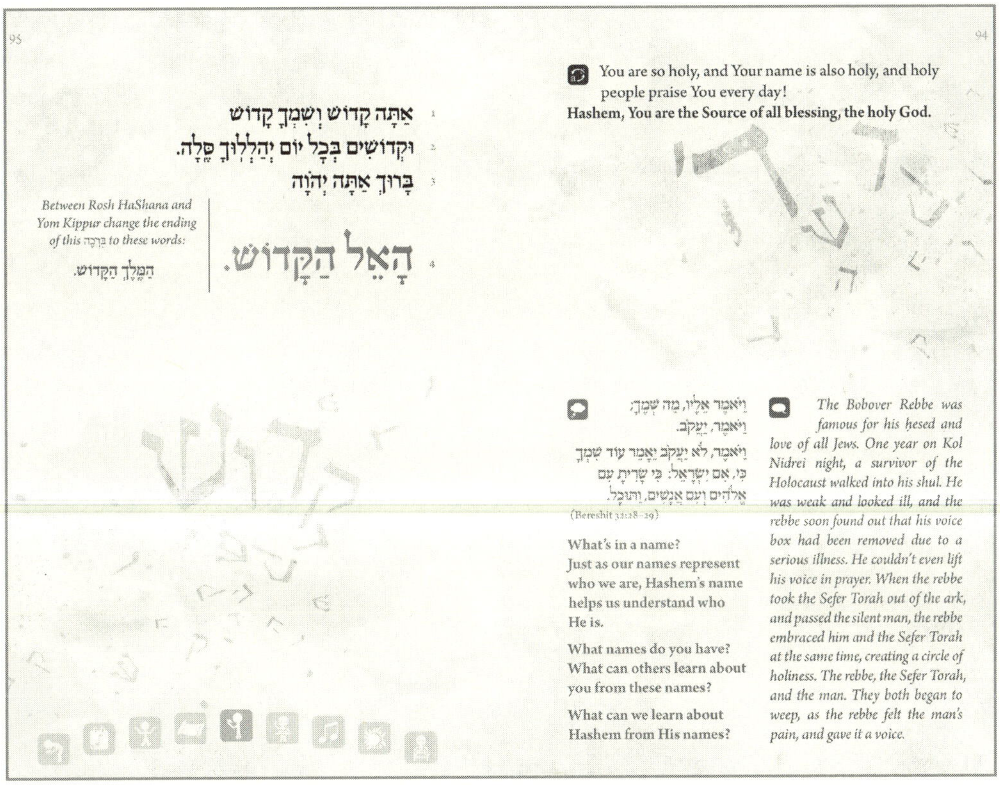

95

1 אתה קדוש ושמך קדוש
2 וקדושים בכל יום יהללוך סלה.
3 ברוך אתה יהוה
4 האל הקדוש.

Between Rosh HaShana and Yom Kippur change the ending of this ברכה *to these words:*

המלך הקדוש.

94

You are so holy, and Your name is also holy, and holy people praise You every day!
Hashem, You are the Source of all blessing, the holy God.

ויאמר אליו, מה שמך;
ויאמר, יעקב.
ויאמר, לא יעקב יאמר עוד שמך
כי, אם ישראל: כי שרית עם
אלהים ועם אנשים, ותוכל.
(Bereshit 32:28–29)

What's in a name?
Just as our names represent who we are, Hashem's name helps us understand who He is.

What names do you have? What can others learn about you from these names?

What can we learn about Hashem from His names?

The Bobover Rebbe was famous for his hesed and love of all Jews. One year on Kol Nidrei night, a survivor of the Holocaust walked into his shul. He was weak and looked ill, and the rebbe soon found out that his voice box had been removed due to a serious illness. He couldn't even lift his voice in prayer. When the rebbe took the Sefer Torah out of the ark, and passed the silent man, the rebbe embraced him and the Sefer Torah at the same time, creating a circle of holiness. The rebbe, the Sefer Torah, and the man. They both began to weep, as the rebbe felt the man's pain, and gave it a voice.

The *Tefilla* Text

Translation:
You are holy and Your name is holy, and holy ones praise You daily, Selah!

Blessed are You, Lord, the holy God. / Between Rosh HaShana and Yom Kippur: the holy King.

Highlighted Text:
The conclusion to the *berakha*, האל הקדוש, is highlighted in the gold color of the letters in the illustration.

Educational Themes contained in the text:

- Holiness
- Names – the power of a name
- The *kedoshim* that praise God are angels (or Israel)
- *Kedusha* = *kiddushin*
- *Kadosh* = Shabbat; Eretz Yisrael; Yerushalayim; the Jewish People
- *Am Segula*

The Illustration

The Hebrew language is first termed לשון הקודש in the Mishna (*Sota* 7:2), and in Talmudic and mystical sources is considered to have intrinsic holiness. For example, the Gemara (*Pesaḥim* 87b) suggests that when Moshe smashed the *Luḥot HaBerit*, "the tablets were broken and the letters are flying (live on)." *Kedusha* as an abstract concept is hard to represent visually, but the holiness of the language through its beauty is the direction we have taken here. The letters that form the word קדושה have been drawn here flying in an ethereal light. This hints at the famous story of Rabbi Teradyon's martyrdom in the Gemara (*Avoda Zara* 17b) where the letters of the *Sefer Torah* that he was wrapped in as he was burned alive flew up to heaven:

> *They found R. Ḥanina b. Teradyon sitting and occupying himself with the Torah, publicly gathering assemblies, and keeping a scroll of the Law in his bosom. Immediately they took hold of him, wrapped him in the Scroll of the Law, placed bundles of branches round him and set them on fire. They then brought tufts of wool, which they had soaked in water, and placed them over his heart, so that he should not expire quickly. His daughter exclaimed, "Father, that I should see you in this state!" He replied, "If it were I alone being burnt it would have been a thing hard to bear; but now that I am burning together with the Scroll of the Law, He who will have regard for the plight of the Torah will also have regard for my plight." His disciples called out, "Rabbi, what seest thou?" He answered them, "The parchments are being burnt but the letters are soaring on high." "Open then thy mouth" [said they] "so that the fire enter into thee." He replied, "Let Him who gave me [my soul] take it away, but no one should injure oneself." The Executioner then said to him, "Rabbi, if I raise the flame and take away the tufts of wool from over thy heart, will thou cause me to enter into the life to come?" "Yes," he replied. "Then swear unto me" [he urged]. He swore unto him. He thereupon raised the flame and removed the tufts of wool from over his heart, and his soul departed speedily. The Executioner then jumped and threw himself into the fire. And a bat-kol exclaimed: R. Ḥanina b. Teradyon and the Executioner have been assigned to the world to come. When Rabbi heard it he wept and said, "One may acquire eternal life in a single hour, another after many years."*

The *Kavanot*

Thought Question:
The abstract concept of holiness is difficult for child and adult alike to grasp and explore. This is one explanation for the focus in this *berakha* on God's name, when expressing His holiness. His name is a medium through which to relate to Him, and often expresses an aspect of His essence.

These thought questions ask the student to contemplate the function of names in our lives. Rambam writes (in *Hilkhot Teshuva* 3:14) that someone that uses a nickname for another has no portion in the World to Come. The question is why he takes such an extreme position on this. Perhaps because one's name represents one's essence; it is his identity summed up in a word. To misuse or change or abuse this is to abuse the very essence of another human being. So names have an innate sanctity, and this is the idea that these thought questions are trying to encourage the student to explore.

We can learn much about a person from their name, although often we can learn more about their society and their parents too. For example, the names of Mordekhai and Esther, both Greek Gods, show us the assimilated position of the Jewish community at the time of the Purim story (just as the Christian names in our age would do the same). This is not to say that Mordekhai and Esther themselves were assimilated, but rather they were part of a community entrenched in the culture of the wider society. Families that use Hebrew names for their children despite bringing them up outside of Israel are also making a statement. The opposite statement perhaps. That the culture that is important to that family is Jewish rather than the wider non-Jewish culture.

The verse describing how Yaakov's name was changed to Yisrael, and ultimately how we became known as the people of Israel, expresses the same idea. Hashem changed Yaakov's name (just as He did with Avraham,

Sarah, and Yehoshua) to make a statement, to them, to us, and to the world. Names make statements.

Just as we can learn a lot from a person by the name they were given at birth and the names they use (e.g., nicknames, Anglicized versions of Hebrew names), so, too, we can learn about Hashem from His names.

Activity ideas:
Name games:

- Name memory game: Everyone in the class has to think of a food that begins with the same letter as their first name (e.g., Doughnut Daniel). Then each takes a turn to say their food and their name, and remember all the food/name combinations that have gone before them.
- The same game but with a gesture: everyone says their name and a gesture that sums up their mood at that moment.
- Call my bluff: Volunteers give three explanations for their parent's choice of their name. One is true and the other two are false. The class has to guess which the true explanation is.

Story:
This heart-warming story is a physical expression of an abstract concept – holiness. The elements of the story that are "holy" are the rebbe (pious holiness), the *Sefer Torah* (ritual holiness sourced from God – the word of God), and the ill Holocaust survivor (the holiness derived from hardship – arguably also from God. To be a victim of Jewish history ascribes a holiness, and thus the reason we speak of martyrs as dying על קידוש השם). The image of the rebbe embracing both the *Sefer Torah* and the survivor, and giving the survivor a voice where he had none, is a powerful and inspiring one.

Additional *Kavanot*:
Story:

את מוצא שלשה שמות נקראו לו לאדם:
אחד מה שקוראים לו אביו ואמו,
ואחד מה שקוראין לו בני אדם,
ואחד מה שקונה הוא לעצמו.
טוב מכולן מה שקונה הוא לעצמו.
(*Midrash Tanḥuma* 35:1)

לכל איש יש שם / Everyone Has a Name[33]

Everyone has a name
given to him by God
and given to him by his parents.

Everyone has a name
given to him by his stature
and the way he smiles
and given to him by his clothing.

Everyone has a name
given to him by the mountains
and given to him by his walls.

Everyone has a name
given to him by the stars
and given to him by his neighbors.

Everyone has a name
given to him by his sins
and given to him by his longing.

Everyone has a name
given to him by his enemies
and given to him by his love.

Everyone has a name
given to him by his feasts
and given to him by his work.

Everyone has a name
given to him by the seasons
and given to him by his blindness.

Everyone has a name
given to him by the sea and
given to him
by his death.

Thought questions:

- How many things can you think of that we use the root ק-ד-ש to describe? Can you think what they all have in common?
- If Hashem is holy, how can we become holy? How will you be holy today?

33. Zelda, "Everyone has a name." Translated from the Hebrew by Marcia Falk, cited in "Generations of the Holocaust" by Bergmann and Jugovy. See http://www.zchor.org/zelda.htm

דעת

pp. 96–97

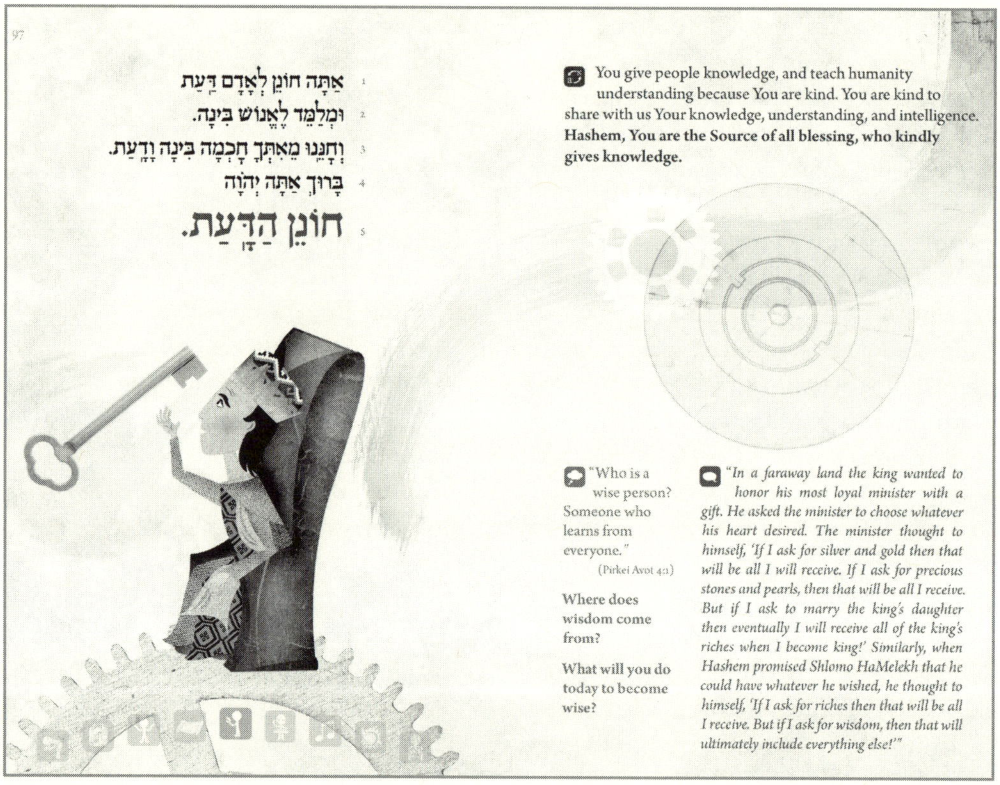

The *Tefilla* Text

Translation:
You grace humanity with knowledge and teach mortals understanding. Grace us with the wisdom, understanding, and knowledge that come from You. Blessed are You, Lord, who graciously grants knowledge.

Highlighted Text:
The words of the conclusion to the *berakha* – חונן הדעת – are highlighted in the brown of Shlomo HaMelekh's throne in the illustration.

Educational Themes contained in the text:

- חבד:
  - חכמה (השכל) = wisdom (practical judgment)
  - בינה = understanding (basic intelligence)
  - דעה = knowledge (common sense)
- Primary importance of wisdom (just as Shlomo asked for wisdom before anything else)
- Knowledge = *tzelem Elokim*
- Knowledge = abstract thought (philosophy, technology/engineering)

- *Ḥeshbon hanefesh*: who are we and what is important to us?
- *Da'at* is what separates us from animals

The Illustration

In Tanakh (*Melakhim* I 3:4–9) the story is told of how God appeared to Shlomo in a dream and offered to grant him anything his heart desires. Shlomo asks for wisdom and will forever be known for this trait. A midrashic telling of this narrative (*Shir HaShirim Raba* 1:1) is found on this page of the siddur. Just as Shlomo put knowledge and understanding before everything else, so we start our requests from Hashem in the *Amida* with the request for *Da'at*.

The illustration has a young Shlomo sitting on his royal throne, accepting the key to knowledge from Hashem. The background to the illustration portrays different expressions of other knowledge such as science (concentric circles), industry (cogs), and the arts (brushstrokes). This is an important message – there are many forms of intelligence, and each has its own importance and value.[34]

The *Kavanot*

Thought Question:
The entire mishna (*Avot* 4:1) in the original is:

בן זומא אומר, איזה הוא חכם – הלמד מכל אדם, שנאמר "מכל מלמדיי, השכלתי" (תהילים קיט,צט). איזה הוא גיבור – הכובש את יצרו, שנאמר "טוב ארך אפיים, מגיבור" (משלי טז,לב). איזה הוא עשיר – השמח בחלקו, שנאמר "יגיע כפיך, כי תאכל; אשריך, וטוב לך" (תהילים קכח,ב): "אשריך", בעולם הזה; "וטוב לך", לעולם הבא. איזה הוא מכובד – המכבד את הברייות, שנאמר "כי מכבדיי אכבד ובוזיי ייקלו" (שמואל א ב,ל).

The first three clauses of the mishna are quoted in the siddur, on pages 19, 96 and 124.

Wisdom is a good example of the partnership between us and Hashem. The source of wisdom is God. He is the absolute source of all knowledge in the world. But what we do with the available wisdom, and how wise we become, is down to us. This is the partnership between God and man personified. We ask Hashem for the opportunity to gain wisdom, but then we must make sure we take it, and this is what the thought question asks of the child – what will you do today to achieve wisdom?

The quote from the mishna in *Pirkei Avot* takes us in a slightly different direction. It tells us that real wisdom is the realization that there is something to learn from every person we encounter. So the truly wise person is someone that sees learning opportunities from every person they meet and every experience they have.

Story:
This midrashic story, from *Shir HaShirim Raba* (1:1), explains the origin of Shlomo's famed wisdom. God offered to grant him anything he wished, and he chose wisdom because he realized that it could be the source for everything else anyway. Ironically, in doing so, he proved he already had great wisdom. This should encourage the child to see the importance of wisdom and of gaining wisdom (from their school studies?) as it may lead to endless opportunities in life for success and happiness.

Additional *Kavanot*:
Thought questions:
"Everybody is a genius. But if you judge a fish by its ability to climb a tree, it will live its whole life believing that it is stupid." (Albert Einstein)[35]

34. See the quote attributed to Albert Einstein, below in the Additional *kavanot* section.
35. This quote is often attributed to Albert Einstein but it has never been verified that he actually said it. There is also concern that the word "stupid" is inappropriate language for this age. The educational message is a strong one – that there are different kinds of intelligences, and those that find school/academic study easy are not the only people who can consider themselves smart. This is an important message for school children to hear.

- What are you really good at?
- What do you want to be better at? How can you?
- What do you want to learn today? What do you think you will learn today?
- This is the first request we make of Hashem in the Amida. Why do you think the rabbis chose to ask for this first? Do you agree with them? What would you have asked for first?

Story:

A story is told of a wise old man that lived in a village far away. People would travel from all corners of the world to ask him advice for it is said that he knows the answers to all problems. Once, the children of his village decided to trick him and prove he did not have all the answers. They came to him with a butterfly in one of their hands, and they asked the man if it was dead or alive. If he replied alive they would crush it, and if he replied that it was dead they would let it free, either way proving him wrong. The wise old man thought for some moments, looked the children in their eyes and said, "The answer is in your hands!"

תשובה

pp. 98–99

99

הֲשִׁיבֵנוּ אָבִינוּ לְתוֹרָתֶךָ
וְקָרְבֵנוּ מַלְכֵּנוּ לַעֲבוֹדָתֶךָ
וְהַחֲזִירֵנוּ בִּתְשׁוּבָה שְׁלֵמָה לְפָנֶיךָ.
בָּרוּךְ אַתָּה יְהֹוָה
הָרוֹצֶה בִּתְשׁוּבָה.

98

Our Father, bring us back to Your Torah, and close to Your service, our King. Lead us back to You in sincere teshuva. **Hashem, You are the Source of all blessing, who wants teshuva.**

"There once was a king who invited all of his servants to a magnificent banquet. But he forgot to write on the invitation the exact date and time. No one was brave enough to point this out to him and so no one knew when to prepare themselves for the feast. Those who were wise prepared themselves immediately for the banquet and remained close to the palace. But the foolish among the servants did not prepare themselves. Suddenly the king called for the banquet to begin, and all the clever servants were ready to enter in their finest clothes, while the foolish were in their everyday work clothes, and embarrassed to enter the palace. When the king saw that they had come dressed so disrespectfully he was disappointed and made them stand and watch while the wise servants sat and ate and enjoyed the wonderful feast. The Rabbis tell us this is why we must do teshuva every day, because we never know when Hashem will call us before Him to judge us."

אָבִינוּ מַלְכֵּנוּ, חָטָאנוּ לְפָנֶיךָ.

Why do you think we refer to Hashem as a Parent and a King in this *berakha*?

The *Tefilla* Text

Translation:
Bring us back, our Father, to Your Torah. Draw us near, our King, to Your service. Lead us back to You in perfect repentance. Blessed are You, Lord, who desires repentance.

Highlighted Text:
The words אבינו and מלכנו are highlighted in the color of the thought question, and the conclusion of the *berakha* – הרוצה בתשובה – is highlighted in the color of the *shofar* from the illustration.

Educational Themes contained in the text:

- God as a forgiving Father bringing us back to Him
- God as a King requiring loyalty and service
- Knowledge leads to self-awareness, which then leads to action and growth
- The Days of Awe

The Illustration

The *shofar* is a powerful visual symbol of *teshuva,* and here we have the *Ba'al Tokea* blowing the *shofar* on Rosh HaShanah, stirring the community to awaken from their slumber and reach out to God in *teshuva.* Behind the *Ba'al Tokea* is a golden path, leading to him and his *shofar.* This represents the path to *teshuva* and reconnecting to God and the recognition that this is a spiritual and moral journey, and not achieved in an instant. It also connects to the illustration on page 108 where a similar path is found, this time the path itself becomes the *shofar.* This path/*shofar* is a different journey, the journey of the ingathering of the exiles. Just as that journey may be a slow and steady process, so, too, the journey of *teshuva.*

The *Kavanot*

Story:
This story from the Gemara (*Shabbat* 153a) encourages us to be prepared to come before Hashem in judgment every day. Although we have a specific time of the year that helps us to focus on this enterprise, we include this *berakha* in our daily *tefillot* so that we will be continuously aware of the need for spiritual and moral growth and preparedness to stand before Hashem and give account for our lives.

Thought Question:
We are familiar with relating to God as a Father and King from the *tefilla Avinu Malkenu,* and these two roles appear in this *berakha,* which is also in the context of *teshuva.* When contemplating *teshuva* and personal growth in this way, we relate to God in both of these paradigm roles – we are aware of God's role as Judge over us, but we ask for and expect mercy in the same way a child would from a parent. So we remind God and ourselves in this context that we are aware of His role as Judge, and pray for Him to relate to us as a parent instead.

Activity ideas:
Ask for volunteers to role-play a scenario, first as a king and then as a father, and the rest of the class guesses which role they are playing. The scenario could be given by the teacher or decided by the class, or the student.

Additional *Kavanot*:
Thought questions:

- *Teshuva* comes from the Hebrew root meaning "return." When we do *teshuva,* what are we returning to? How will you return there today?
- What do you think the connection is between the last *berakha* (knowledge) and this one (repentance)? How will you connect the two in your life today?
- Close your eyes. Imagine Hashem is standing on the other side of the room. How are you going to move closer to Him? Now imagine He is standing behind you. What must you do to become closer to Him?

סליחה

pp. 100–101

101

Some people gently tap the left side of your chest with your right fist when you say the words חָטָאנוּ and פָשָׁעְנוּ, two different words for sin. This helps us experience feeling sorry for our sins.

1 סְלַח לָנוּ אָבִינוּ כִּי חָטָאנוּ
2 מְחוֹל לָנוּ מַלְכֵּנוּ כִּי פָשָׁעְנוּ
3 כִּי אֵל טוֹב וְסַלָּח אָתָּה.
4 בָּרוּךְ אַתָּה יְהֹוָה
5 חַנּוּן הַמַּרְבֶּה לִסְלֹחַ.

100

Forgive us, Hashem our Father, we have sinned.
Pardon us, our King.
Hashem, You are the Source of all blessing, who keeps forgiving.

What do you need to say sorry for today?

Who do you need to say sorry to today?

"At first, I wanted to change the world. I tried, but the world did not change. Then I tried to change my town, but the town did not change. Then I tried to change my family, but my family did not change. Then I realized: first, I must change myself."

The *Tefilla* Text

Translation:

Forgive us, our Father, for we have sinned. Pardon us, our King, for we have transgressed; for You are the good and forgiving God. Blessed are You, Lord, the gracious One who repeatedly forgives.

Highlighted Text:

The words חטאנו and פשענו are highlighted in the green of the rubric, and the words חנון המרבה לסלח of the conclusion to the *berakha* are highlighted in the color of the thought question.

Educational Themes contained in the text:

- *Teshuva* requires forgiveness, which leads to asking for it
- God as compassionate Father
- We need a physical manifestation (beating breast) to impress this emotion on ourselves
- God as pardoning King: To receive forgiveness, *meḥila* must be achieved (pardoning – giving up on right to punish). Only the King (who has the power to punish) can do this.

The Illustration

Teshuva brings us to realize where we have gone wrong. The next stage is to make amends. *Teshuva* is also primarily about our relationship with ourselves and with Hashem. Now it is time to turn to those around us, and repair those relationships. This involves admission and confession, and the asking for forgiveness. In short, all of this meaning is found in the word "sorry."

The girl in the illustration finds herself in the middle of several concentric circles, each representing a circle of "others" in her life that she must relate to. These are her family, friends, community, nation, and beyond (the environment and humanity). The buildings on the outside of the circles represent the institutions of those circles, such as her family home, her school, her synagogue, nature, etc. But at the center of it all is the girl herself. Change must start with her. This is reflected in the well-known story attributed to Rabbi Yisrael Salanter that is found on the page too.

The *Kavanot*

Thought Questions:
These thought questions bring this *berakha* and theme to the direct personal life if the child. Everyone has something to apologize for, and someone to apologize to. These questions ask the child to realize that and contemplate to whom they need to apologize, and for what. If there is trust in the classroom then this process could be shared, and perhaps it would be ideal to start the process with the teacher sharing first.

Story:
This very famous story, attributed to Rabbi Yisrael Salanter, places *seliḥa* (and the *teshuva* of the previous *berakha*) in the context of changing oneself as a way of changing the world. We have a responsibility to make our world a better place, but sometimes, or maybe always, this should start by making ourselves better people. Before we can even start that we must try to redress the wrong we have done in our lives, and that is by repairing relationships. This is best done through asking for *seliḥa*.

Additional *Kavanot*:
Thought questions:

- Why is it important to say sorry? Who is it important for?
- They say sorry is the hardest word to say. Do you find it hard to say sorry? Why?
- Is it easier or harder to say sorry to Hashem than to a friend or member of your family? Why do you think that is?
- Why does the *tefilla* say both "forgive" and "pardon"?

גאולה

pp. 102–103

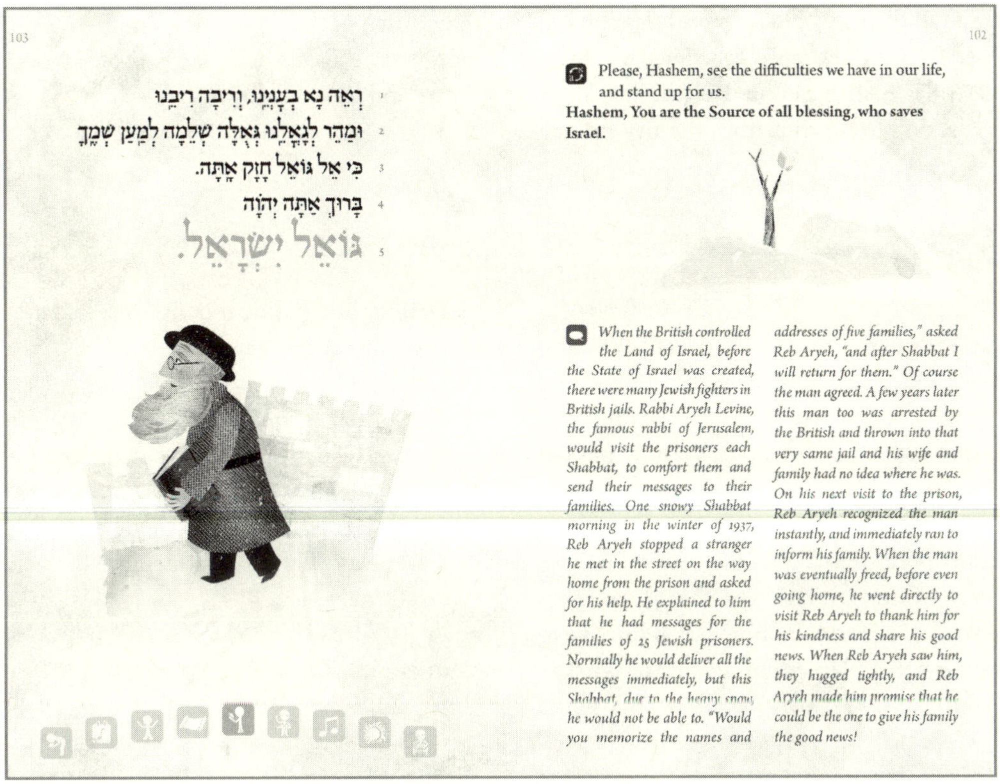

103

רְאֵה נָא בְעָנְיֵנוּ, וְרִיבָה רִיבֵנוּ
וּמַהֵר לְגָאֳלֵנוּ גְּאֻלָּה שְׁלֵמָה לְמַעַן שְׁמֶךָ
כִּי אֵל גּוֹאֵל חָזָק אָתָּה.
בָּרוּךְ אַתָּה יְהֹוָה
גּוֹאֵל יִשְׂרָאֵל.

102

Please, Hashem, see the difficulties we have in our life, and stand up for us.
Hashem, You are the Source of all blessing, who saves Israel.

When the British controlled the Land of Israel, before the State of Israel was created, there were many Jewish fighters in British jails. Rabbi Aryeh Levine, the famous rabbi of Jerusalem, would visit the prisoners each Shabbat, to comfort them and send their messages to their families. One snowy Shabbat morning in the winter of 1937, Reb Aryeh stopped a stranger he met in the street on the way home from the prison and asked for his help. He explained to him that he had messages for the families of 25 Jewish prisoners. Normally he would deliver all the messages immediately, but this Shabbat, due to the heavy snow, he would not be able to. "Would you memorize the names and addresses of five families," asked Reb Aryeh, "and after Shabbat I will return for them." Of course the man agreed. A few years later this man too was arrested by the British and thrown into that very same jail and his wife and family had no idea where he was. On his next visit to the prison, Reb Aryeh recognized the man instantly, and immediately ran to inform his family. When the man was eventually freed, before even going home, he went directly to visit Reb Aryeh to thank him for his kindness and share his good news. When Reb Aryeh saw him, they hugged tightly, and Reb Aryeh made him promise that he could be the one to give his family the good news!

The *Tefilla* Text

Translation:
Look, please, on our affliction, plead our cause, and hurry to redeem us with a complete redemption, soon, for Your name's sake, for You are a powerful God and Redeemer. Blessed are You, Lord, the Redeemer of Israel.

Highlighted Text:
The conclusion of the *berakha* – גואל ישראל – is highlighted in the brown of the Old City walls of the illustration.

Educational Themes contained in the text:

- Personal redemption from crisis (such as captivity, persecution or affliction)
- National persecution = *Ḥillul Hashem* (*lema'an shemekha*)
- Jewish history (crusades, inquisition, expulsion, pogrom, holocaust)

The Illustration

This illustration is a visual depiction of the story about Rabbi Aryeh Levine (see below). It has a representation of his image, walking in the snow through the streets of Yerushalayim, holding a holy book. His determination is apparent, to get the job done and fulfill this mitzva, despite the terrible weather (notice his beard blowing in the strong wind). The tree in the illustration is almost completely barren, except for two tiny leaves sprouting from one branch. The tree offers almost no hope for the future, and represents the sadness and depression in the hearts of the Jewish fighters incarcerated in the British prison. But there is hope. The two tiny leaves that sprout from the dry branch show there is a future for the Jewish people. Reb Aryeh gives the prisoners hope, just as the leaves give that tree hope and just as God gives us hope. Hope to those individuals in situations of distress, and hope to His people in the lowest points of their history.

The sprouting of the leaves on the barren tree also reminds us of the terminology we use in the *tefilla* for the State of Israel (page 212) – ראשית צמיחת גאֻלָּתֵנוּ – the beginning of the flowering of our redemption. This is and will be a slow and steady process, one filled with hope and determination.

The *Kavanot*

Story:
This story, taken from the book *A Tzaddik in Our Time, the Life of Rabbi Aryeh Levine*, is an inspiring tale of the love Reb Aryeh had for the Jewish fighters in pre-State Palestine, and in fact for all Jews (it is complemented by the story on the following page of the siddur that is an example of Reb Aryeh's pure *Ahavat Yisrael*). There have been many periods in Jewish history where Jews found themselves imprisoned, and this story introduces the reader to a particular time when Jews were fighting for their national freedom, against the wishes of the local authorities. Prison for many children is primarily a place where criminals are incarcerated, yet this *berakha* asks Hashem for help redeeming Jewish captives who may also find themselves there for non-criminal reasons. It is a perfect opportunity to share with your students some of the periods in Jewish history when Jews were incarcerated simply because they were Jewish (such as Czarist Russia) or for practicing Judaism (such as Soviet Russia) or for asserting their political rights as Jews (such as British Mandatory Palestine).

The role Reb Aryeh plays in the story represents the agent of Hashem working towards the fulfillment of this *berakha*, and the mitzva of *Pidyon Shevuyim*. As well as bringing comfort to the fighters and their families, Reb Aryeh also petitioned the British authorities for their release.

Additional *Kavanot*:
Thought questions:

"Everyone you meet is fighting a battle you know nothing about. Be kind always."[36]

- What difficulties do you have in your life? Turn to Hashem and share them.
- Who are you going to help that is having difficulties today?

36. This profound quote is anonymous but is often seen shared in social media.

רפואה

pp. 104–105

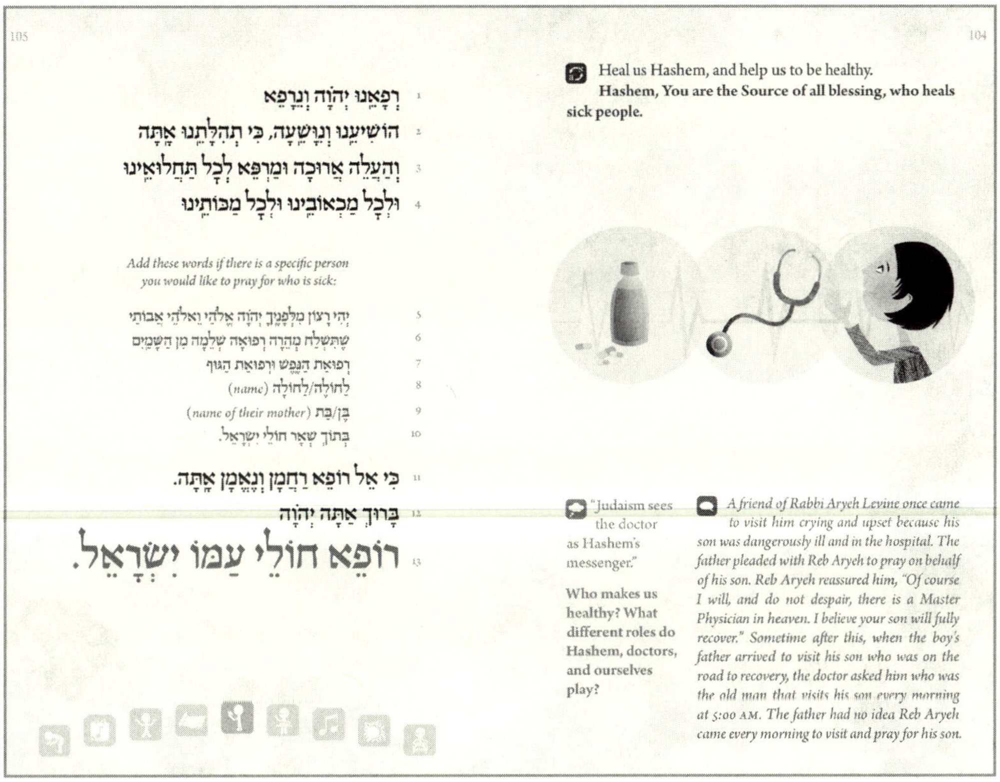

105

104

Heal us Hashem, and help us to be healthy.

Hashem, You are the Source of all blessing, who heals sick people.

רפאנו יהוה ונרפא
הושיענו ונושעה, כי תהלתנו אתה
והעלה ארוכה ומרפא לכל תחלואינו
ולכל מכאובינו ולכל מכותינו

Add these words if there is a specific person you would like to pray for who is sick:

יהי רצון מלפניך יהוה אלהי ואלהי אבותי
שתשלח מהרה רפואה שלמה מן השמים
רפואת הנפש ורפואת הגוף
לחולה/לחולה (*name*)
בן/בת (*name of their mother*)
בתוך שאר חולי ישראל.

כי אל רופא רחמן ונאמן אתה.
ברוך אתה יהוה
רופא חולי עמו ישראל.

"Judaism sees the doctor as Hashem's messenger."

Who makes us healthy? What different roles do Hashem, doctors, and ourselves play?

A friend of Rabbi Aryeh Levine once came to visit him crying and upset because his son was dangerously ill and in the hospital. The father pleaded with Reb Aryeh to pray on behalf of his son. Reb Aryeh reassured him, "Of course I will, and do not despair, there is a Master Physician in heaven. I believe your son will fully recover." Sometime after this, when the boy's father arrived to visit his son who was on the road to recovery, the doctor asked him who was the old man that visits his son every morning at 5:00 AM. The father had no idea Reb Aryeh came every morning to visit and pray for his son.

The *Tefilla* Text

Translation:

Heal us, Lord, and we shall be healed. Save us and we shall be saved, for You are our praise. Bring remedy and healing to all our illnesses and all our pains, and for all our ailments.

The following prayer for a sick person may be said here:

May it be Your will, O Lord my God and God of my ancestors, that You speedily send a complete recovery from heaven, a healing of both soul and body, to the patient (name), son/daughter of (mother's name) among the other afflicted of Israel.

For You, God, are a compassionate and faithful Healer.

Blessed are You, Lord, Healer of the sick of His people Israel.

Highlighted Text:

The conclusion to the *berakha* – רופא חולי עמו ישראל – is highlighted in the color of the medicine in the illustration and the added יהי רצון we say for sick people.

Educational Themes contained in the text:

- Humans (doctors) vs. God as primary healer (partnership!)
- Is health *the* most important *berakha* we ask for?
- Health = body and soul
- Praying for the collective and individuals

The Illustration

The three circles in this illustration depict three elements of healing in a Torah world-view. The first, medicine, represents medical technology and innovation – the intelligence of man. The second, the stethoscope of the medical practitioner, is the emotional intelligence that it takes to care for a patient and the brilliance of man to apply the knowledge he has to the welfare of a human being. And finally we have our character looking up at the heavens and praying to Hashem for the healing of the loved one. This is the direct role of Hashem in this process, and the part that we can play in this. The ECG heart-rate monitor line that runs through each circle is the metaphor for Hashem, the source of all three, and links all three together.

The *Kavanot*

Thought Question:
This is a paraphrased quote from J. David Bleich in his book *Judaism and Healing* (although it can be considered a generally accepted normative idea in Jewish thought). This asks the child to consider how Hashem provides and protects for us, and to explore the partnership we have with Him in our lives to look after ourselves and the world. Additional concepts that can be discussed as an outgrowth of this could be the injunction to not rely on miracles, Hashem as the source of mankind's inspiration and knowledge, Divine Providence and God's role in the world and our lives, supernatural and natural miracles.

The thought questions that follow the quote ask the child to consider the people involved in maintaining our health – Hashem, ourselves and our doctors. We have a religious responsibility to Hashem to look after the bodies He gave us, and doctors and medical science is a way that Hashem acts in our lives to help us stay healthy. When we pray for health and recovery in this *berakha*, we are not necessarily asking for a divine intervention, but rather for nature and science to take its natural course, with the help of Hashem.

Story:
This story, taken from the book *A Tzaddik in Our Time, the Life of Rabbi Aryeh Levine*, exposes the student to a saintly and pure faith in Hashem's role as Master Physician, healing those who are ill. With this faith and our prayers we hope that our loved ones who are ill will fully recover. This is the implied *tefilla* in the wish "*Refua Shelema*," as it is customary to say when someone is ill. Reb Aryeh not only models faith in Hashem as Healer, but also the mitzva of *Bikur Ḥolim*" – visiting the sick. While Hashem has his role to play, we have ours too!

Additional *Kavanot*:
Thought Questions:

- Do you know someone who is unwell? Pray for them in your own words now.
- Is there anything more important in your life than health?
- How can you make sure you stay healthy?
- "Our prayers are in the plural, because our prayers are not just for us here and now but for all the Jewish people… But we can say personal prayers, for example, for a sick relative, in this *berakha*."[37]

37. Paraphrased quote from Rabbi Adin Steinsaltz (in *A Guide to Jewish Prayer*, pp. 19–20).

ברכת השנים

pp. 106–107

107

During the summer say this בְּרָכָה:

בָּרְכֵנוּ יְהֹוָה אֱלֹהֵינוּ בְּכָל מַעֲשֵׂי יָדֵינוּ
וּבָרֵךְ שְׁנָתֵנוּ בְּטַלְלֵי רָצוֹן בְּרָכָה וּנְדָבָה
וּתְהִי אַחֲרִיתָהּ חַיִּים וְשָׂבָע וְשָׁלוֹם כַּשָּׁנִים הַטּוֹבוֹת לִבְרָכָה
כִּי אֵל טוֹב וּמֵטִיב אַתָּה וּמְבָרֵךְ הַשָּׁנִים.
בָּרוּךְ אַתָּה יְהֹוָה
מְבָרֵךְ הַשָּׁנִים.

During the winter say this בְּרָכָה:

בָּרֵךְ עָלֵינוּ יְהֹוָה אֱלֹהֵינוּ אֶת הַשָּׁנָה הַזֹּאת
וְאֶת כָּל מִינֵי תְבוּאָתָהּ לְטוֹבָה
וְתֵן טַל וּמָטָר לִבְרָכָה עַל כָּל פְּנֵי הָאֲדָמָה
וְרַוֵּה פְּנֵי תֵבֵל, וְשַׂבַּע אֶת הָעוֹלָם כֻּלּוֹ מִטּוּבָךְ
וּמַלֵּא יָדֵינוּ מִבִּרְכוֹתֶיךָ, וּמֵעֹשֶׁר מַתְּנוֹת יָדֶיךָ
שָׁמְרָה וְהַצִּילָה שָׁנָה זוֹ מִכָּל דָּבָר רָע
וּמִכָּל מִינֵי מַשְׁחִית, וּמִכָּל מִינֵי פֻרְעָנוּת
וַעֲשֵׂה לָהּ תִּקְוָה טוֹבָה וְאַחֲרִית שָׁלוֹם
חוּס וְרַחֵם עָלֶיהָ וְעַל כָּל תְּבוּאָתָהּ וּפֵרוֹתֶיהָ
וּבָרְכָהּ בְּגִשְׁמֵי רָצוֹן בְּרָכָה וּנְדָבָה
וּתְהִי אַחֲרִיתָהּ חַיִּים וְשָׂבָע וְשָׁלוֹם כַּשָּׁנִים הַטּוֹבוֹת לִבְרָכָה
כִּי אֵל טוֹב וּמֵטִיב אַתָּה וּמְבָרֵךְ הַשָּׁנִים.
בָּרוּךְ אַתָּה יְהֹוָה
מְבָרֵךְ הַשָּׁנִים.

106

Hashem, bless this year for us. Make it a very successful year and help the land provide the food we need.
Hashem, You are the Source of all blessing, who provides blessings.

There once was a drought, and the people of the town had no water to drink. The Rabbi called everyone together to pray for rain. The people came together and cried out with emotion and sincerity to ask Hashem to send the rains they so desperately needed. A small girl tugged on her father's hand and asked him, "Abba, if we have all come to pray to Hashem for rain, then how come nobody has brought an umbrella?"

The umbrella represents *Emuna*. When you pray to Hashem today, do you have your "umbrella"?

בָּרוּךְ אַתָּה ה'...
הַמּוֹצִיא לֶחֶם מִן הָאָרֶץ.

Look at the food you are going to eat for lunch today.

How did it get into your hand?

Trace its journey from your hand all the way back to where it came from.

What role did Hashem play in that journey?

The *Tefilla* Text

Translation:

During the summer:

Bless us, LORD our God, in all of our handiwork, and bless our years with dew of favor, blessing and generosity, and let it culminate in life, satisfaction and peace like all good years, for a blessing. For You are the good and beneficent God, who gives the years their blessing. Blessed are You, Lord, who blesses the years.

During the winter:

Bless this year for us, LORD our God, and all its types of produce for good. Grant dew and rain as a blessing on the face of the land, saturate the earth and satiate the entire world with Your goodness, and fill our hands with Your blessings and with the wealth of Your gifts. Protect and save this year from all evil matters, from all types of destruction, and all types of misfortune, and grant it good hope and a peaceful conclusion. Spare it and have compassion on it, and on all of its produce and fruit, and bless it with rains of favor, blessing and generosity, and let it culminate in life, satisfaction and peace like all good years, for a blessing. For You are the good and beneficent God, who gives the years their blessing. Blessed are You, Lord, who blesses the years.

Educational Themes contained in the text:

- God as source of physical blessings/prosperity
- Partnership between the farmer and God
- Water/rain as the sustainer of life (and God as its source)
- Need for rains of blessing (rain can be destructive)
- Creating prosperity is not enough; we need access to it and to benefit from it (*aleinu*)
- The Land of Israel (focus on)

The Illustration

The illustration on this page interprets the ברכה promised in the *tefilla* as physical sustenance, in the form of produce. While blessing and agricultural prosperity is an ancient association, it is an important message for today's students – that ultimately the *berakhot* we need and ask for from Hashem are our basic needs, such as food. And the food we eat does not come from the supermarket, but from the ground. It is easier for them to conceptualize the role of God in that process when we start at the harvesting stage of production (or even before). The illustration shows the rain allowing the crops to grow, and the rain obviously represents God's intervention on our behalf in the process. Another message behind the ears of wheat in the illustration is the focus of this *berakha* on Eretz Yisrael. We alter the content of the *berakha* based on the agricultural seasons in Israel, and ultimately are praying for plentiful rain in Eretz Yisrael. For this reason, one of the *Shivat HaMinim* was chosen to represent this blessing.

The *Kavanot*

Thought Questions:
The thought questions start with the *berakha* for bread – הַמּוֹצִיא לֶחֶם מִן הָאָרֶץ – in which we thank Hashem for bringing forth bread from the ground. But did Hashem really do that or was it man? What role does God play in the process and what role does man?

The first challenge is for our urbanized children to understand what went into bringing the slice of bread into their hands. Some of them will perhaps need help tracing that bread's journey before it reached the supermarket or bakery. Then the question of God's role vs. man's role in that process needs to be debated and explored. The ideal conclusion will be an understanding of the partnership between man and God in the creation of all things, especially food. In this *berakha* we ask for Hashem to do His part so we can do ours.

Activity idea:
Bake bread (*ḥalla* for Shabbat would be extra special) with your children, to give them an idea of what goes into the creation of bread. Start the activity with as much practical and visual explanation of the process of creating flour to make the bread, followed by the processes of kneading, yeast fermentation, proofing etc.

Story:
This wonderful story that revolves around the *tefilla* for rain pushes us to think about how much we really have faith in what we are asking for. When we say these words do we have our umbrellas with us? If we do not, then what value are our words, to both us and Hashem? This idea can be applied to every *tefilla* in the siddur not just this one.

Activity ideas:
Trust games

- Pair up the students in rough size order (tall with tall etc. you can do this by asking them to line up in height order). Then ask partner A to stand with feet together, and partner B to stand around 4 feet behind them. Then partner A must fall back showing they trust partner B will catch them (they must do this without separating their feet). Then switch roles.

- Blind folded obstacle course – the volunteer must trust his/her friends to guide him sensibly around it.
- Blindfold a volunteer and tie a rope to each arm and leg. Have four classmates lead the volunteer wherever they wish.

Additional *Kavanot*:
Thought questions:

- Do you live in a rainy place? Imagine living in a place with little rain. How happy would you be when it did rain? Now thank Hashem for the rain as if you lived in that place.
- Close your eyes and imagine rain drops gently falling on your face. Think about why rain is important for us. Now thank Hashem for it.

Story:
Ḥanan "the Hidden One" was a grandson of Ḥoni the Circle Maker. Whenever the world needed rain the rabbis would send schoolchildren to pull gently on his [Hanan's] clothing and cry, "Abba, Abba, give us rain!" He would then cry out to Hashem and say, "Hashem, Master of the Universe, give them rain, because they don't even know the difference between a Father who has the power to give rain [Hashem] and a father that does not"[38]

38. *Ta'anit* 23b

קבוץ גלוית

pp. 108–109

109

1 תקע בשופר גדול לחרותנו
2 ושא נס לקבץ גליותינו
3 וקבצנו יחד מארבע כנפות הארץ לארצנו.
4 ברוך אתה יהוה
5 מקבץ נדחי עמו ישראל.

108

Blow the great shofar to announce the arrival of the Mashiaḥ, and show a sign to gather us together in Israel from the four corners of the earth.
Hashem, You are the Source of all blessing, who brings all Jews together in Israel.

In 1991 Ethiopia had a terrible civil war – people in the same country fought against each other. The State of Israel wanted to save the Jewish community in the country. During Operation Shlomo, 35 Israeli aircraft brought 14,000 Ethiopian Jews to safety over a period of 36 hours. This ancient Jewish community always dreamt of joining our people in our ancient homeland, despite the obvious dangers involved. The seats were ripped out of the planes to make as much room as possible and 1,200 people managed to cram aboard each plane. Many of the passengers only brought with them clothes and cooking utensils, and during the flights seven babies were born on the planes. Everyone felt that this was the fulfillment of the promise to gather all the Jewish people from the four corners of the earth.

ויאמר יהוה אל־אברם,
לך־לך מארצך וממולדתך
ומבית אביך אל־הארץ אשר אראך.
(Bereshit 12:1)

What signs has Hashem already shown us that the process mentioned in this *berakha* has already begun?

The *Tefilla* Text

Translation:
Sound the great shofar for our freedom, raise high the banner to gather our exiles, and gather us together from the four quarters of the earth. Blessed are You, Lord, who gathers the dispersed of His people Israel.

Highlighted Text:
The words תקע בשופר גדול לחרותנו are highlighted in the golden brown of the *shofar*/path in the illustration, and the words מקבץ נדחי עמו ישראל are highlighted in the color of the story.

Educational Themes contained in the text:

- The *shofar* of national redemption
- *Nes* = *Degel Yisrael*
- *Kibbutz galuyot* = historical and contemporary *aliya*
- Natural redemption (Zionism) vs. divine redemption (Mashiaḥ)

The Illustration

This *berakha* petitions God to bring the dispersed of the people of Israel back to their land – the Ingathering of the Exiles – as part of the process of the Messianic redemption. The *shofar* referenced in the text is the *tekiat shofar* that will accompany Mashiaḥ when he comes. The path for the dispersed exiles may be a long and winding one, like the path in the illustration, but ultimately we pray that it will lead to redemption and to the blowing of that *shofar*, just like the path in the illustration. As on page 102, the tree and vegetation here hint to the terminology we use in the *tefilla* for the State of Israel (page 212) – ראשית צמיחת גאלתנו – the beginning of the flowering of our redemption. This process, redemption in general, and the ingathering of the exiles in particular, will be a slow and steady process. We are living in a generation where we believe this has clearly started, and we pray it will continue, ultimately leading to the national redemption God has promised us.

The *Kavanot*

Story:
This inspiring story is one of many examples of communities in the Diaspora that have made their way en masse to Eretz Yisrael since the beginning of the era of modern Zionism. There were five pre-State waves of *aliya*, and several post-State waves of *aliya*, this being one of the more recent and famous of the latter. Religious Zionists believe that these historical events are the partial fulfillment of this *tefilla* and of the prophecies and promises made throughout Jewish history for the ingathering of the exiles of the Jewish people to their homeland. While this process is far from over, our students live in an era when almost half the population of the Jewish people lives in Israel.

Activity idea:
Arrange for your class to embark on a pen-pal project with Israeli children who have made *aliya* themselves (or are the children of *olim*) from as many communities in the Diaspora as possible. Your students can ask them about their experiences making *aliya*/living in Israel, and also questions about the communities they originated from.

Thought Question:
This quote is the first reference to an *aliya* to Eretz Yisrael. Hashem commands Avraham to leave the land of his birth and everything he knows, and make the long and difficult journey to Eretz Yisrael. *Aliya* as a modern phenomenon is one that your students are probably familiar with even if they have no first-hand experience of anyone that has made *aliya* (if they do then it would be a great opportunity for them to share this with the class in this discussion). The thought question here asks the child to consider the phenomenon of *aliya* in modern times (from the beginning of modern Zionism in the 1880s until the present day) as the process that we are praying for in this *berakha*. The נס (sign) that we ask Hashem to show us to signify that the ingathering of the exiles is taking place could well be the events of modern Zionist history, and this thought question asks the students to consider that.

Activity idea:
The Nefesh B'Nefesh YouTube channel has many inspiring and emotional videos about *aliya* that could be shared with your class.

Additional *Kavanot*:
Thought questions:

ויש-תקווה לאחריתך, נאום-ה׳; ושבו בנים, לגבולם
(Yirmiyahu 31:16)

- Do you know anyone who has made *aliya*? Why do you think they did it?
- What is different about the request in this *berakha* from the previous requests? Clue: compare who benefits in this *berakha* to the previous ones.
- Has Hashem answered this *berakha* already?
- Have you ever been to Israel to visit? Do you think you would like to live there one day?

משפט

pp. 110–111

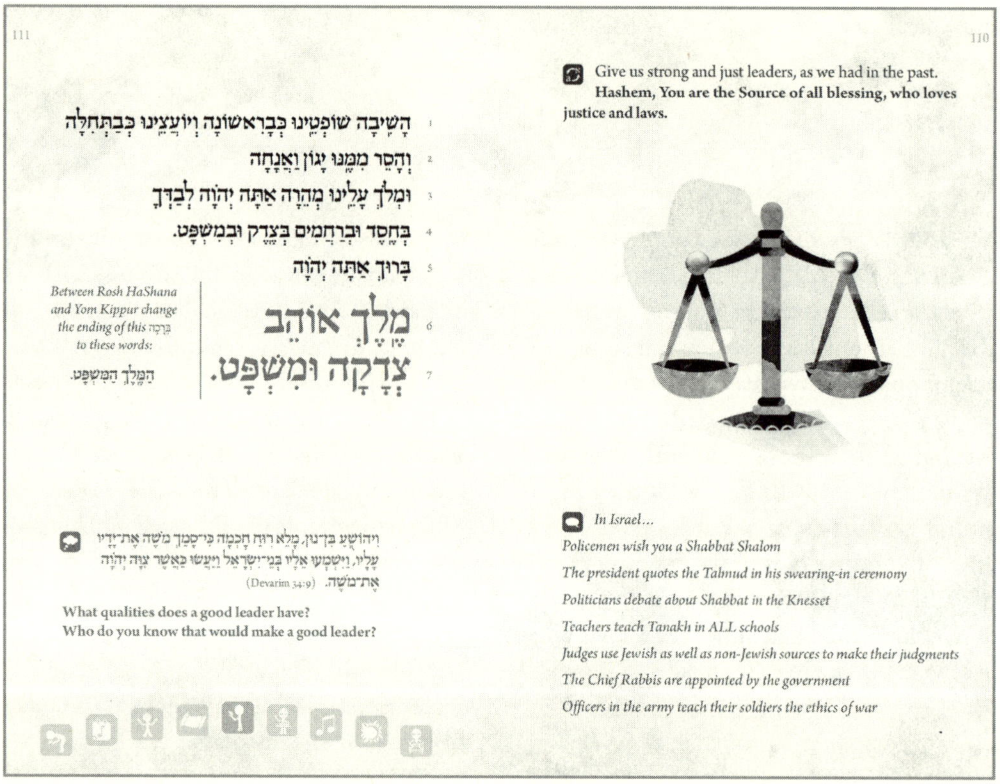
111

הָשִׁיבָה שׁוֹפְטֵינוּ כְּבָרִאשׁוֹנָה וְיוֹעֲצֵינוּ כְּבַתְּחִלָּה
וְהָסֵר מִמֶּנּוּ יָגוֹן וַאֲנָחָה
וּמְלֹךְ עָלֵינוּ מְהֵרָה אַתָּה יְהֹוָה לְבַדְּךָ
בְּחֶסֶד וּבְרַחֲמִים בְּצֶדֶק וּבְמִשְׁפָּט.
בָּרוּךְ אַתָּה יְהֹוָה
מֶלֶךְ אוֹהֵב
צְדָקָה וּמִשְׁפָּט.

Between Rosh HaShana and Yom Kippur change the ending of this בְּרָכָה *to these words:*

הַמֶּלֶךְ הַמִּשְׁפָּט.

וִיהוֹשֻׁעַ בִּן־נוּן, מָלֵא רוּחַ חָכְמָה כִּי־סָמַךְ מֹשֶׁה אֶת־יָדָיו
עָלָיו, וַיִּשְׁמְעוּ אֵלָיו בְּנֵי־יִשְׂרָאֵל וַיַּעֲשׂוּ כַּאֲשֶׁר צִוָּה יְהֹוָה
אֶת־מֹשֶׁה. (Devarim 34:9)

What qualities does a good leader have?
Who do you know that would make a good leader?

110

Give us strong and just leaders, as we had in the past.
Hashem, You are the Source of all blessing, who loves justice and laws.

In Israel…
Policemen wish you a Shabbat Shalom
The president quotes the Talmud in his swearing-in ceremony
Politicians debate about Shabbat in the Knesset
Teachers teach Tanakh in ALL schools
Judges use Jewish as well as non-Jewish sources to make their judgments
The Chief Rabbis are appointed by the government
Officers in the army teach their soldiers the ethics of war

The *Tefilla* Text

Translation:
Restore our judges as at first, and our counselors as at the beginning, and remove from us sorrow and sighing. May You alone, Lord, reign over us soon with loving-kindness and compassion, with righteousness and justice.
Blessed are You, Lord, the King who loves righteousness and justice/the King of justice.

Highlighted Text:
The conclusion to the *berakha* – מלך אוהב צדקה ומשפט – is highlighted in the brown of the weighing scales in the illustration.

Educational Themes contained in the text:

- Political redemption (*shofetim* = political and military leaders)

- Sorrow and sighing is caused by lack of self-determination (*galut*)
- A prayer for leadership
- The reestablishment of the Sanhedrin will precede redemption
- Activism – championing justice in the world
- Justice

The Illustration

Scales of Justice is the universal symbol for justice and an appropriate image for the illustration on the page of the siddur where we petition God to return judges and a justice system to our national autonomy in our land. But the scales are also a common theme of civil halakha. In Vayikra, the Torah commands justice in weights and measures: לֹא-תַעֲשׂוּ עָוֶל, בַּמִּשְׁפָּט, בַּמִּדָּה, בַּמִּשְׁקָל וּבַמְּשׂוּרָה, and develops this law in *Devarim* 25:13–16. The Mishna even goes as far as to legislate careful and regular cleaning of weights, measures and scales to ensure their accuracy (Mishna, *Bava Batra* 5:10). The scales are clearly representative of the values of fairness and justice, and we pray that God help us to return to a national autonomous existence in our own land based on these values.

The *Kavanot*

Conceptual Translation of:

הָשִׁיבָה שׁוֹפְטֵינוּ כְּבָרִאשׁוֹנָה, וְיוֹעֲצֵינוּ כְּבַתְּחִלָּה... בָּרוּךְ אַתָּה ה׳ מֶלֶךְ אוֹהֵב צְדָקָה וּמִשְׁפָּט

Story:
This *berakha* asks God to restore Jewish leadership and autonomy to us in our land as in previous eras. The *Shofetim* referred to in the text are the leaders of the people as described in *Sefer Shofetim* – military and political leaders as much as judicial authorities. This short text here describes several types of leadership present in the modern State of Israel. It cites examples when these leaders use Jewish culture and values to demonstrate their leadership. The claim here is certainly not that the State of Israel is the full realization of the petition in this *berakha*, or that Israel's modern-day leaders are comparable religiously or spiritually to the leadership found in *Tanakh* times. However, for the child living in the Diaspora to consider just how Jewish the leadership in modern Israel is should be an inspiring thought, and one that we are comfortable saying leads us to conclude that we are closer to the dream that we describe and pray for in these *berakhot*.

Thought Question:
This verse is the transmission of the mantle of leadership from Moshe to Yehoshua before the former's death and the latter leads the Benei Yisrael into Eretz Yisrael and into a new period of Jewish history. The verse suggests that Yehoshua was chosen to be Moshe's successor for two reasons – that he was "full of the spirit of wisdom" and because Moshe transmitted the mantle of leadership (literally by placing his hands on Yehoshua (*semikha*). Did the skills and leadership ability of Yehoshua come from his own innate abilities or from the training and apprenticeship that Moshe gave him? More than likely we can say it was both, and a leader needs both natural ability and experience and training.

The thought questions that follow ask the student to consider what makes a good leader, and if they know anyone (adult or child) who has these skills and would make a good leader. Our students see leadership at every turn in their lives, from their teachers and the school's administrative leadership, to their parents, siblings, and peers. These thought questions ask them to consider what kind of leaders we are asking Hashem to return to us so we can have autonomy in our land.

Activity ideas:
Leadership games

- Guess the leader – Class sits in a circle formation. A volunteer leaves the room. A leader is chosen to lead the class in an action and to keep a rhythm. Start with clapping, and change at any time (for example, patting his/her head, clicking fingers, rubbing stomach, etc.). When the leader changes the action the rest of the class must follow. The volunteer is called in and must try and guess who the leader is.

- Shimon says – A variation on "Simon Says": one person is chosen to lead the class in various actions preceded with the phrase, "Shimon says…" (e.g., "Shimon says stamp your feet"). At some point the leader announces an action without the prefix "Shimon says." Those classmates that follow the action are out.
- Follow the leader – take the class outside. Choose a volunteer to be the leader. They can lead the class anywhere they wish and the class has to follow and mimic their actions/walking style.
- Guess the Jewish leader – write the name of a Jewish leader (national or local) on a sticky note and place it on the forehead of each student. They must find out who they are by asking their friends questions about their character. No one is allowed to say explicitly who they are but must admit when they have guessed correctly.

Additional *Kavanot*:
Thought questions:

- Have you ever experienced injustice? How did that feel?
- Why is justice important? What would you like to do in your life to ensure there is justice?
- When do you think כבתחילה refers to? Why do you think the leadership was so good then?
- Why is it important for a leader to value justice?

ברכת המינים

pp. 112–113

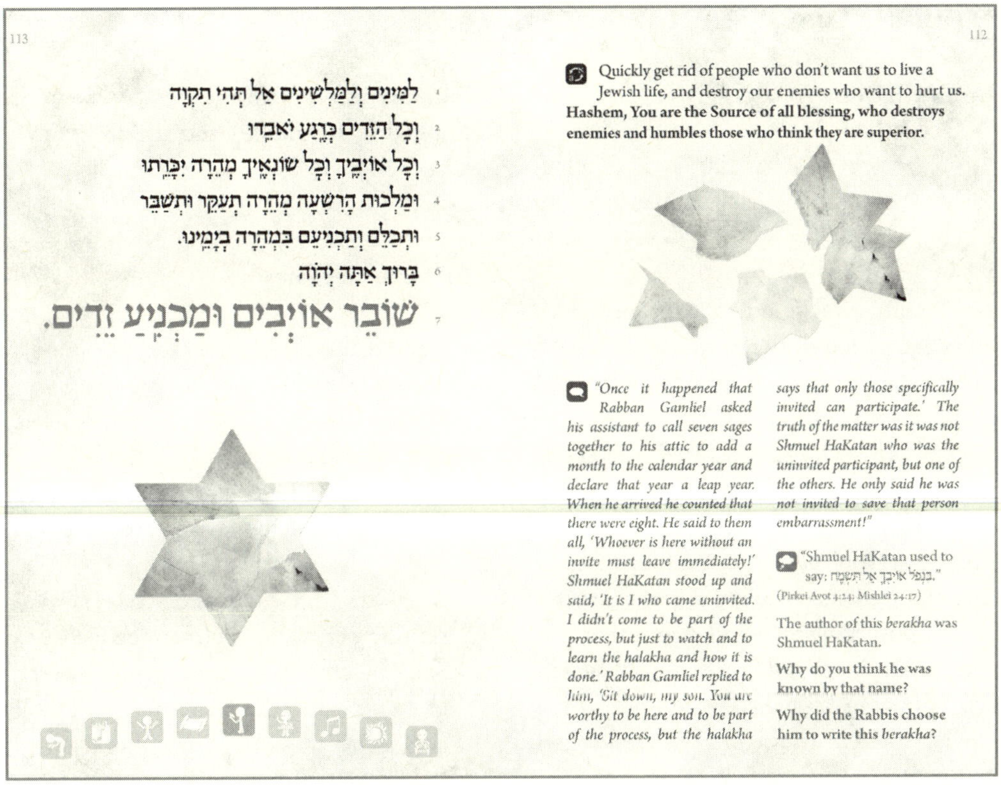

113

1 לַמִּינִים וְלַמַּלְשִׁינִים אַל תְּהִי תִקְוָה

2 וְכָל הַזֵּדִים כְּרֶגַע יֹאבֵדוּ

3 וְכָל אוֹיְבֶיךָ וְכָל שׂוֹנְאֶיךָ מְהֵרָה יִכָּרֵתוּ

4 וּמַלְכוּת הָרִשְׁעָה מְהֵרָה תְעַקֵּר וּתְשַׁבֵּר

5 וּתְכַלֵּם וְתַכְנִיעֵם בִּמְהֵרָה בְיָמֵינוּ.

6 בָּרוּךְ אַתָּה יְהֹוָה

7 שׁוֹבֵר אוֹיְבִים וּמַכְנִיעַ זֵדִים.

112

Quickly get rid of people who don't want us to live a Jewish life, and destroy our enemies who want to hurt us. **Hashem, You are the Source of all blessing, who destroys enemies and humbles those who think they are superior.**

"Once it happened that Rabban Gamliel asked his assistant to call seven sages together to his attic to add a month to the calendar year and declare that year a leap year. When he arrived he counted that there were eight. He said to them all, 'Whoever is here without an invite must leave immediately!' Shmuel HaKatan stood up and said, 'It is I who came uninvited. I didn't come to be part of the process, but just to watch and to learn the halakha and how it is done.' Rabban Gamliel replied to him, 'Sit down, my son. You are worthy to be here and to be part of the process, but the halakha says that only those specifically invited can participate.' The truth of the matter was it was not Shmuel HaKatan who was the uninvited participant, but one of the others. He only said he was not invited to save that person embarrassment!"

"Shmuel HaKatan used to say: בִּנְפֹל אוֹיִבְךָ אַל תִּשְׂמָח."
(Pirkei Avot 4:24; Mishlei 24:17)

The author of this *berakha* was Shmuel HaKatan.

Why do you think he was known by that name?

Why did the Rabbis choose him to write this *berakha*?

The *Tefilla* Text

Translation:

For the heretics and slanderers let there be no hope, let all the arrogant ones perish in an instant, and may all of the arrogant ones perish in an instant. May all of Your enemies and all those who hate You be swiftly cut down. May You speedily uproot, smash, humble and subdue the regime of evil swiftly in our days. Blessed are You, Lord, who destroys enemies and humbles the arrogant.

Highlighted Text:

The words concluding the *berakha* – שובר אויבים ומכניע זדים – are highlighted in the turquoise of the *Magen David* in the illustration.

Educational Themes contained in the text:

- Statement against sectarianism (pro-unity)
- Shmuel HaKatan was asked to author this because he was totally free of animosity towards his opponents
- Separating sin from sinners (hate the sin not the sinner)

The Illustration

This *berakha*, added to the *Amida* during the Second Temple period as a response to Jewish sectarianism, petitions God to eradicate the evil wishes of apostates who conspired with external enemies against the people, both spiritually and physically. Essentially it is a plea against civil war and fraternal fighting. The pain and sadness of Jew fighting Jew is expressed here through a torn and broken *Magen David*. However, the illustration is its own prayer for unity and peace, with a pristine and whole *Magen David* on the facing page, echoing the general themes of the national *berakhot* of the *Amida* – a prayer for a peaceful and united autonomous Jewish people in their own land.

The *Kavanot*

Conceptual Translation of:

וכל הרשעה כְּרֶגַע תֹּאבד וכל אויבי עמך מהרה יִכָּרֵתוּ. ברוך אתה ה׳ שובר אויבים ומַכְנִיעַ זדים.

Story:
This is the "nineteenth" *berakha* added to the *Shemoneh Esreh* after the destruction of the Second Temple, to address the sectarianism of many apostates who had become estranged from Judaism and had made peace with the foreign oppressors, and conspired against our people both spiritually and physically. Rabban Gamliel asked Shmuel HaKatan to compose the extra *berakha*, as the appropriate person who was entirely enveloped in the attribute of mercy and humility. These character traits are seen in both the story and quote that precedes the thought questions, and in the name by which he was known. While the *berakha* is uncompromising in its approach to the enemies of Israel, even when they are the enemy within, the message of its chosen author is a powerful and important one. This story, found in the Gemara (*Sanhedrin* 11a), demonstrates the humility and *Ahavat Yisrael* of Shmuel HaKatan.

Thought Question:
Shmuel HaKatan was famous for quoting and living by this verse in Mishlei – "If your enemy falls, do not rejoice."[39] To live by this statement means that you can consider the humanity of your enemy, and separate the sin from the sinner, hating only the sin. While profoundly challenging, this is clearly the ideal, and the reason why Shmuel HaKatan was asked to be the author of this *berakha*. There is a clear link to the humility he was famous for (as seen in the story and implied by his name) and the ability to achieve this higher state.

Activity ideas:
Unity/team games

- Bonding belt: Teams of four people are tied together with a large belt (made from rope or something similar). They then race each other along a predetermined course.
- *Maḥanayim*: There are various forms of this game, which is in essence a two-team ball game. One example: two teams start in opposite halves of a basketball court (or similar space). Each team has a goalkeeper standing on a chair at the opposite side of the court. The objective is to score a goal by getting the ball to your goalkeeper (and to defend the other team's goalkeeper preventing the other team from scoring). Any player who has the ball is not allowed to move (no traveling).
- Human knot: The class stands in a large circle, and everyone puts their left hand in the middle, and holds hands with someone in the circle, not directly next to them. Repeat with the right hand, being sure to hold hands with a different person who is not directly next to them. Then the group must use teamwork to unravel themselves into a circle again without becoming disconnected.
- Human machine: Divide the class into groups of 6–8. Ask each team to make themselves into a machine, with as many parts (gears, levers, etc.) as they can devise. The machine should have motion and sound,

39. The Mishna quotes Mishlei 24:17–18. The full text of the verses is:
בנפל אויבך, אל-תשמח; ובכשלו, אל-יגל לבך. פן-יראה ה׳, ורע בעיניו; והשיב מעליו אפו.

and include all team members (each with their own unique function). The machines can be based on real machines that exist, or imaginary machines. Give the teams five minutes to prepare their machine, and then the teams take turns presenting and guessing the function of each other's machine.

- 1–100: The whole class must count to 100 together as a team. But only one person may say a number aloud at a time, and the counting must be random. If more than one person begins saying the next number, the task must begin again from 1.
- Earthball: The class must keep a beach ball or balloon in the air for a specified number of hits without letting it hit the ground. No one person can touch the object twice in a row. Set a goal of how many hits the class can make. After the class meets its goal, it can increase the target number or go for the class all-time record.

Additional *Kavanot*:
Thought questions:

- Jews like to argue a lot! What will you do today to bring Jewish people closer together?
- Are there people in the world today who wish to hurt the Jewish people? Think about them when you say this *berakha*.

על הצדיקים

pp. 114–115

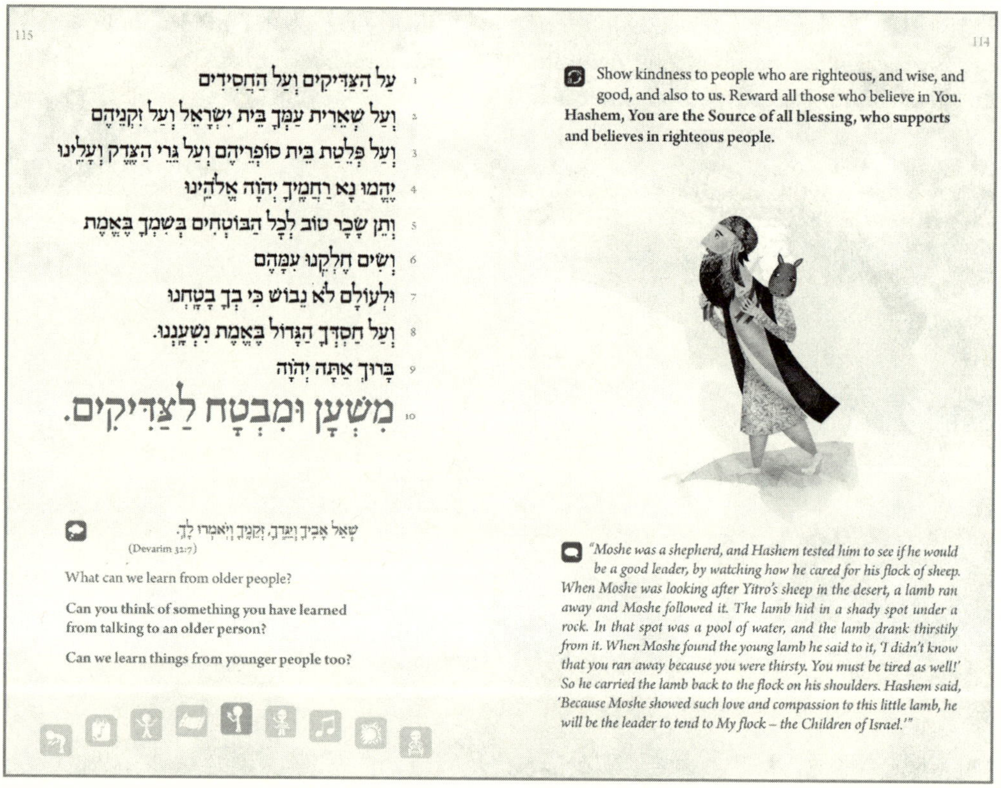

114

Show kindness to people who are righteous, and wise, and good, and also to us. Reward all those who believe in You. **Hashem, You are the Source of all blessing, who supports and believes in righteous people.**

"Moshe was a shepherd, and Hashem tested him to see if he would be a good leader, by watching how he cared for his flock of sheep. When Moshe was looking after Yitro's sheep in the desert, a lamb ran away and Moshe followed it. The lamb hid in a shady spot under a rock. In that spot was a pool of water, and the lamb drank thirstily from it. When Moshe found the young lamb he said to it, 'I didn't know that you ran away because you were thirsty. You must be tired as well!' So he carried the lamb back to the flock on his shoulders. Hashem said, 'Because Moshe showed such love and compassion to this little lamb, he will be the leader to tend to My flock – the Children of Israel.'"

115

על הצדיקים ועל החסידים
ועל שארית עמך בית ישראל ועל זקניהם
ועל פליטת בית סופריהם ועל גרי הצדק ועלינו
יהמו נא רחמיך יהוה אלהינו
ותן שכר טוב לכל הבוטחים בשמך באמת
ושים חלקנו עמהם
ולעולם לא נבוש כי בך בטחנו
ועל חסדך הגדול באמת נשענו.
ברוך אתה יהוה
משען ומבטח לצדיקים.

שאל אביך ויגדך, זקניך ויאמרו לך.
(Devarim 32:7)

What can we learn from older people?

Can you think of something you have learned from talking to an older person?

Can we learn things from younger people too?

The *Tefilla* Text

Translation:

To the righteous, the pious, the remnant of Your nation, the house of Israel and their elders, the remnant of their scholars, the righteous converts, and to us, may Your compassion be aroused, Lord our God. Grant a good reward to all who sincerely trust in Your name. Set our lot with them, so that we may never be ashamed, for in You we trust, and it is upon Your great mercy that we truly rely. Blessed are You, Lord, who is the support and trust of the righteous.

Highlighted Text:

The words that conclude this *berakha* – משען ומבטח לצדיקים – are highlighted in the color of the clothing of Moshe in the illustration.

Educational Themes contained in the text:

- Leadership and leaders
- Chain of tradition
- Today's leadership standing on the shoulders of previous generations
- Conversion is not prohibitive to this exclusive group

The Illustration

With another prayer for strong and just leadership for our people, this illustration gives a visual representation of the midrash found below it (from *Shemot Raba* 2:2) that explores Moshe's leadership potential, as seen in his skills as a shepherd.

The *Kavanot*

Story:
This *berakha* turns to the spiritual leadership needed for an autonomous Jewish State, and this midrashic story from *Shemot Raba* (2:2) gives us the narrative that explains why God chose Moshe to be the quintessential leader in Jewish history, and what leadership skills are necessary for the role. In the story Moshe shows love and concern for his flock, especially for the weaker members, and it is these characteristics as a shepherd that show Moshe has the ability to lead God's flock.

Thought Questions:
These thought questions focus on the concept of the elder as a leader, and what we can learn from people with life experience. While life experience isn't always enough to make a good leader, we all have much to learn from older people, and the verse encourages us to be open to that. The thought questions ask the child to consider what they have learnt from an older person, in a real and tangible way in their life, encouraging them to be open to future learning experiences like this. However, the second thought question also empowers them as a younger person to be someone whom others can learn from, and to be open to learning things from younger people, such as their younger siblings. This openness to learning from all people is found in *Mishna Avot* 4:1 (see page 96 of the siddur).

Activity ideas:
Leadership games

- Guess the leader – Class sits in a circle formation. A volunteer leaves the room. A leader is chosen to lead the class in an action and to keep a rhythm. Start with clapping, and change at any time (for example, patting his/her head, clicking fingers, rubbing stomach, etc.). When the leader changes the action the rest of the class must follow. The volunteer is called in and must try and guess who the leader is.
- Shimon says – A variation on "Simon Says": one person is chosen to lead the class in various actions preceded with the phrase, "Shimon says…" (e.g., "Shimon says stamp your feet"). At some point the leader announces an action without the prefix "Shimon says." Those classmates that follow the action are out.
- Follow the leader – take the class outside. Choose a volunteer to be the leader. They can lead the class anywhere they wish and the class has to follow and mimic their actions/walking style.
- Guess the Jewish leader – write the name of a Jewish leader (national or local) on a sticky note and place it on the forehead of each student. They must find out who they are by asking their friends questions about their character. No one is allowed to say explicitly who they are but must admit when they have guessed correctly.

Additional *Kavanot*:
Thought questions:

- What does it mean for someone to be a *tzaddik*?
- Why is it important to ask Hashem to reward and look after righteous people?

מפני שיבה תקום, והדרת פני זקן
(Vayikra 19:32)

- Why is it important to respect our elders?

Story:
This is a little story about four people named Everybody, Somebody, Anybody, and Nobody. There was an important job to be done and Everybody was sure that Somebody would do it. Anybody could have done it, but Nobody did it. Somebody got angry about that because it was Everybody's job. Everybody thought that Anybody could do it. It ended up that Everybody blamed Somebody when Nobody did what Everybody could have done!

בנין ירושלים

pp. 116–117

116

Please return to Yerushalayim and live there as You promised. Rebuild Your Temple there now and have it last forever. Put a king there who is a descendant of King David. **Hashem, You are the Source of all blessing, who rebuilds Yerushalayim.**

"Once, after the destruction of the Beit HaMikdash, Rabban Gamliel, Rabbi Elazar ben Azaria, Rabbi Yehoshua, and Rabbi Akiva were walking on Mount Scopus in Yerushalayim. When they reached the top and saw Har HaBayit where the Beit HaMikdash once stood, they noticed a fox leaving from where the Kodesh HaKodashim used to be. Rabbi Akiva began to laugh while his friends were crying at what they had seen. They asked Rabbi Akiva, 'How can you laugh at such a time, when a lowly fox is walking around the holiest place on earth, a place where only the Kohen Gadol could enter on the holiest day of the year?!' Rabbi Akiva replied, 'Now that I have seen the prophecies of the destruction of the Beit HaMikdash fulfilled, I know the prophecies of redemption and return will be fulfilled. As it says in Zekharia: "One day old men and women will once again sit in peace in the streets of Jerusalem."'"

לְשָׁנָה הַבָּאָה
בִּירוּשָׁלַיִם הַבְּנוּיָה

Isn't Yerushalayim rebuilt already? So what are we still praying for?

117

תִּשְׁכּוֹן בְּתוֹךְ יְרוּשָׁלַיִם עִירְךָ כַּאֲשֶׁר דִּבַּרְתָּ
וְכִסֵּא דָוִד עַבְדְּךָ מְהֵרָה בְּתוֹכָהּ תָּכִין
וּבְנֵה אוֹתָהּ בִּנְיַן עוֹלָם בִּמְהֵרָה בְיָמֵינוּ.
בָּרוּךְ אַתָּה יְהֹוָה
בּוֹנֵה יְרוּשָׁלָיִם.

The *Tefilla* Text

Translation:
Dwell within Jerusalem, Your city, as You promised, and install within it soon the throne of David, Your servant. May You rebuild it as an everlasting structure, rapidly in our days. Blessed are You, Lord, who builds Jerusalem.

Highlighted Text:
The concluding words of the *berakha* – בונה ירושלים – are highlighted in the brown of the stones of Yerushalayim in the illustration.

Educational Themes contained in the text:

- Yerushalayim (*habenuya*)
- *Beit HaMikdash*
- Davidic throne of kingship
- Yerushalayim = the direction to which all Jews around the world turn in prayer
- Kotel

The Illustration

In this *berakha* the Jewish people have prayed for 2000 years, three times a day, for the rebuilding of their holy city Yerushalayim, and the return there of the Divine Presence. This *berakha* alone has kept the Jewish heart firmly focused on a future that contains a rebuilt Jerusalem, and full of hope. The illustration presents a visual representation of the well-known story (in *Makkot* 24a) of when Rabbi Akiva saw a fox walking out of the location of where the *Kodesh HaKodashim* was on *Har HaBayit*. The message of the story is also one of hope and faith.

The *Kavanot*

Story:
This famous aggadic story from the Gemara (*Makkot* 24a) shows us an inspiring model for coping with the destruction of the Temple and exile from our land. Rabbi Akiva witnesses a sight that causes sadness and despair in his colleagues, but because of his optimism and faith it brings him joy. Just as he now sees the prophecies of destruction fulfilled, so he knows for sure that the prophecies of return and of the rebuilding of Yerushalayim will be fulfilled.

Activity idea:

- Using Google Earth or even Google Images (try entering "the view from mount Scopus"), give your students a visual image of what Rabbi Akiva and his colleagues saw.
- Arts and crafts project – building a model of Yerushalayim.

Thought Question:
Our students live in a period of Jewish history where the fulfillment of these *berakhot* and age-old dreams are happening in front of their eyes. No doubt many of them have visited modern-day Yerushalayim, which to all intents and purposes could be considered rebuilt. However, we still say this renowned *tefilla* every year at the conclusion of the two most central family-and community-focused days of the year – Yom Kippur and Seder night – לשנה הבאה בירושלים הבנויה. Why? Because the rebuilt Yerushalayim of our generation is not complete, and still lacks full redemption. This is important for us to realize and continuously focus on.

Additional *Kavanot*:
Thought questions:

והתפללו אל-ה׳, דרך העיר אשר בחרת בה, והבית, אשר-בנתי לשמך
(*Melakhim* I 8:44)

- Why is it important that everyone faces Yerushalayim when we pray? What if you don't know which direction to face?
- Have you ever been to Yerushalayim? Imagine you are there now. What can you see? How do you feel?
- Which direction are you facing in right now? Why?
- What do you think is so holy about the Kotel?

מלכות בן דוד

pp. 118–119

119

אֶת צֶמַח דָּוִד עַבְדְּךָ מְהֵרָה תַצְמִיחַ
וְקַרְנוֹ תָּרוּם בִּישׁוּעָתֶךָ
כִּי לִישׁוּעָתְךָ קִוִּינוּ כָּל הַיּוֹם.
בָּרוּךְ אַתָּה יְהוָה
מַצְמִיחַ קֶרֶן יְשׁוּעָה.

118

Bring back the Kingdom of David's family, because we hope for You to bring the Mashiaḥ every day. **Hashem, You are the Source of all blessing, who already started saving us.**

Once upon a time, Hashem called for the Melekh HaMashiaḥ to tell him that the time had come for the final redemption. So the Mashiaḥ got dressed in his very best clothes, and entered the first Beit Kenesset he came to, to announce the good news. Everyone there immediately stopped their learning and stared at him in disbelief. One person called out, "That cannot be the Mashiaḥ. Just look at his hat… it has pinches and the brim is down!" So the Mashiaḥ changed his hat, and put the brim up, and traveled to the next shul on the way. But there he was also received with surprise. "What a strange thought, Mashiaḥ wearing a hat!" they said. "If you were really the Mashiaḥ you would have a knitted kippa!" So the Mashiaḥ took off his hat and placed a knitted kippa on his head, for he didn't mind what he wore on his head. At the next shul they said to him, "Who ever heard of a Mashiaḥ without a black hat?" "But I have a black hat," he replied. And as he placed it on his head they all laughed and said, "The Mashiaḥ wearing a hat with pinches and the brim down!" With sadness in his eyes the Mashiaḥ realized that his time had not yet come, and he began his journey back to heaven. As he was leaving, Jews of every type ran after him crying, "Wait! Don't leave. It was their fault!" But the Mashiaḥ just continued slowly and sadly walking, saying, "Don't you see? Hashem loves each and every one of you. But my time will only come when you do too!"

The *Tefilla* Text

Translation:
May the offshoot of Your servant David soon flower, and may his pride be raised high by Your salvation, for we wait for Your salvation all day. Blessed are You, Lord, who makes the glory of salvation flourish.

Highlighted Text:
The conclusion to the *berakha* – מצמיח קרן ישועה – is highlighted in green to link to the sprouting buds in the illustration.

Educational Themes contained in the text:

- Mashiaḥ
- Davidic dynasty
- *Tzemiḥa* = gradual redemption (Zionism) – *reshit tzemiḥat geulateinu*

The Illustration

The culmination of the previous five *berakhot*, which all asked for different aspects of a return to national independence and autonomy, this *berakha* asks for the final piece of the national redemption puzzle – Mashiaḥ. The restoration of the Davidic monarchy is one of the accepted elements of the Messianic redemption, and the language chosen in the *berakha* is of flowering and gradual sprouting. The illustration expresses this through the easily recognizable Harp of David, with musical notes in the background emanating from the harp, and with shoots of vegetation flowering from it.

The harp (כנור in Hebrew) is synonymous with David HaMelekh, who was a talented poet and musician. In Shmuel I 16:23 we have a young David playing his harp to sooth Shaul HaMelekh (והיה, בהיות רוח-אלהים אל-שאול, ולקח דוד את-הכנור, ונגן בידו; ורוח לשאול וטוב לו, וסרה מעליו רוח הרעה), and the influence of David's harp throughout his life is also referenced in the gemara (*TB Berakhot* 3b) – *"Rabbi Shim'on Ḥasida said: 'David hung his harp above his bed and when midnight would arrive the north wind would blow upon the harp (vibrating the strings) and causing music to emanate. David would immediately rise and begin studying Torah. He would continue his studies even as the first light of dawn appeared in the sky.'"*

The language of צמיחה in this *berakha* was the inspiration of the choice of terminology used in the *Tefilla* for the State of Israel (page 212) – ראשית צמיחת גאלתנו – the beginning of the flowering of our redemption. This language suggests that we believe that the modern State of Israel is the initial stage of the redemption process, but by no means the completion of it (nor are we saying it is a process that cannot be reversed if we do not merit it). While the process has begun, it will be slow and steady, and require investment, patience, hope and faith. We are living in a generation where we believe this has clearly started, and we pray it will continue, ultimately leading to the national redemption God has promised us.

David's harp is also featured on page 38 of the siddur in the context of the beginning of *Pesukei DeZimra* that largely consists of chapters of his poetry (*Sefer Tehillim*).

The *Kavanot*

Story:
This story is an adaptation of the often quoted poem "Mashiaḥ's Hat,"[40] which introduces to the reader important concepts such as yearning for the coming of Mashiaḥ, transcending the petty divisions within the religious Jewish world, looking beyond the superficial trappings of one's clothing (and not judging a book by its cover), taking responsibility, among others.

Additional *Kavanot*:
Thought questions:

אני מאמין באמונה שלמה בביאת המשיח
ואף על פי שיתמהמה
עם כל זה אחכה לו בכל יום
שיבוא

- What changes in the world would you like to see Mashiaḥ bring?
- How can we help to make that happen?
- When do you think Mashiaḥ will come? What do we have to do to make that happen?
- How will we know when Mashiaḥ has come?
- This *berakha* uses the word צמח (like the flowering of a plant) to describe the coming of Mashiaḥ. Why do you think that is? What similarities are there between a flowering plant and the coming of Mashiaḥ?
- What is the connection between King David and Mashiaḥ?

40. The original and some background to it can be found here: http://beingmoshiach.blogspot.co.il/2013/09/a-lubavitch-teenager-told-me-recently.html

שומע תפילה

pp. 120–121

121

שְׁמַע קוֹלֵנוּ יְהוָה אֱלֹהֵינוּ
אָב הָרַחֲמָן חוּס וְרַחֵם עָלֵינוּ
וְקַבֵּל בְּרַחֲמִים וּבְרָצוֹן אֶת תְּפִלָּתֵנוּ
כִּי אֵל שׁוֹמֵעַ תְּפִלּוֹת וְתַחֲנוּנִים אָתָּה
וּמִלְּפָנֶיךָ מַלְכֵּנוּ רֵיקָם אַל תְּשִׁיבֵנוּ
חָנֵּנוּ וַעֲנֵנוּ וּשְׁמַע תְּפִלָּתֵנוּ
כִּי אַתָּה שׁוֹמֵעַ תְּפִלַּת כָּל פֶּה.
בָּרוּךְ אַתָּה יְהוָה
שׁוֹמֵעַ תְּפִלָּה.

120

Hashem, please listen to our prayers, and accept them with kindness and understanding.
Hashem, You are the Source of all blessing, who listens to prayer.

"Here one should turn to Hashem with all of his needs, whether big or small… in his own words."

What do you want to ask Hashem for today?

In 1932 Rabbi Soloveitchik prayed to Hashem to allow him to stay in Europe with his family and friends. His life instead brought him to America. When he heard news of the Shoah in Europe that began in 1939 he realized that while Hashem always listens to our tefillot, He knows what is best for us better than we do ourselves, and sometimes decides not to answer them how we would wish. But He always listens.

The *Tefilla* Text

Translation:
Listen to our voice, Lord our God, compassionate Father. Spare us and have compassion on us, and in compassion and favor accept our prayer, for You, God, listen to prayers and pleas. Do not turn us away, O our King, empty-handed from Your presence, show us grace, answer us, and listen to our prayers, for You listen with compassion to the prayer of all people. Blessed are You, Lord, who listens to prayer.

Highlighted Text:
The words ומלפניך מלכנו ריקם אל תשיבנו are highlighted in the color of the thought question, and the conclusion to the *berakha* – שׁוֹמֵעַ תפלה – is highlighted in the color of the letters in the illustration.

Educational Themes contained in the text:

- Personal prayers vs. collective prayers
- Hashem answers our prayers because that is what He does (He is אל שומע תפילות)

- Asking God to accept our prayers with "compassion and favor" suggests that He should accept only the prayers that He thinks appropriate

The Illustration

Our character here is in the midst of her *tefilla*, singing from her heart words that fly directly up to heaven. She is being drawn closer to God as she says them. It is almost as if the words themselves are drawing her closer and closer to Hashem. Note that the words she is saying are *שמע תפילתי*, a more personalized version of the text of the *berakha* which asks for Hashem to listen to our prayers. This is her very personal *tefilla* that she pours towards heaven during this *berakha*, which is the time for the most personal of prayers as we make our own personal additions to our *tefillot*, in whichever language we are most comfortable.

The *Kavanot*

Conceptual Translation of:

שמע קולנו ה׳ אלהינו, חוס ורחם עלינו, וקבל ברחמים וברצון את תפלתנו... ברוך אתה ה׳ שומע תפלה.

Thought Question:

"Here one should turn to Hashem with all of his needs, whether big or small... in his own words."

This quote from *Ya'arot Devash*, reflecting the halakha that one can insert one's own *tefilla* in this *berakha* in any language, encourages the child to feel empowered to ask Hashem for whatever their heart desires. This should help to foster a connection with Hashem, and an understanding that Hashem is the source of all blessings in our lives, and the address for prayers. The thought question that follows asks the child to consider what they want and need from Hashem today.

Activity idea:

Have your students compose their own *tefillot* for whatever they wish. These could be for notes to place in the Kotel (perhaps someone traveling to Israel could deliver them).

Story:

This story, taken from the Mesorat HaRav Siddur, explores the language of *שומע תפלה* – why don't we say that Hashem answers our prayers? Why is it good to know He listens even if we don't get a response? The answer is we are declaring that although Hashem may choose not to answer in the affirmative to our requests and *tefillot*, it is comforting to know He is always listening and considering our lives for our benefit. Rabbi J.B. Soloveitchik fervently prayed for circumstances that would have allowed him to remain in Europe in 1932 rather than immigrate to America. God, in His compassion, did not accept his prayer. But He was certainly listening!

Activity ideas:

Listening game: Concentric circles. Have half the class sit in a circle sitting facing outwards, and the other half in a circle outside them facing inwards (each child face-to-face with another). Without the outer circle seeing, send a message to the inner circle to listen in one or more of the following styles while the outer circle discusses something (a topic of your choice):

1. Do not pay attention and do not maintain eye contact
2. Over listen
3. Talk at the same time as your partner
4. Fall asleep
5. Ask too many questions
6. Listen normally/empathetically

Ask the outside circle to switch places to the left after a couple of minutes, and change the topic and listening style each time.

Additional *Kavanot*:
Thought questions:

- Why do we ask Hashem to listen to our *tefillot*? Why not to answer them or fulfill them?
- Do we always know what is best for us? Can you think of an example where you wanted something that you now realize wasn't in your best interest?
- Stop what you are doing for a moment and listen? What can you hear?
- Are you a good listener? Who will you pay close attention to today?
- How does it feel when someone listens to you? How does it feel when you listen to someone else? How does it feel when someone doesn't listen to you? How will you be a good listener today?

עבודה

pp. 122–123

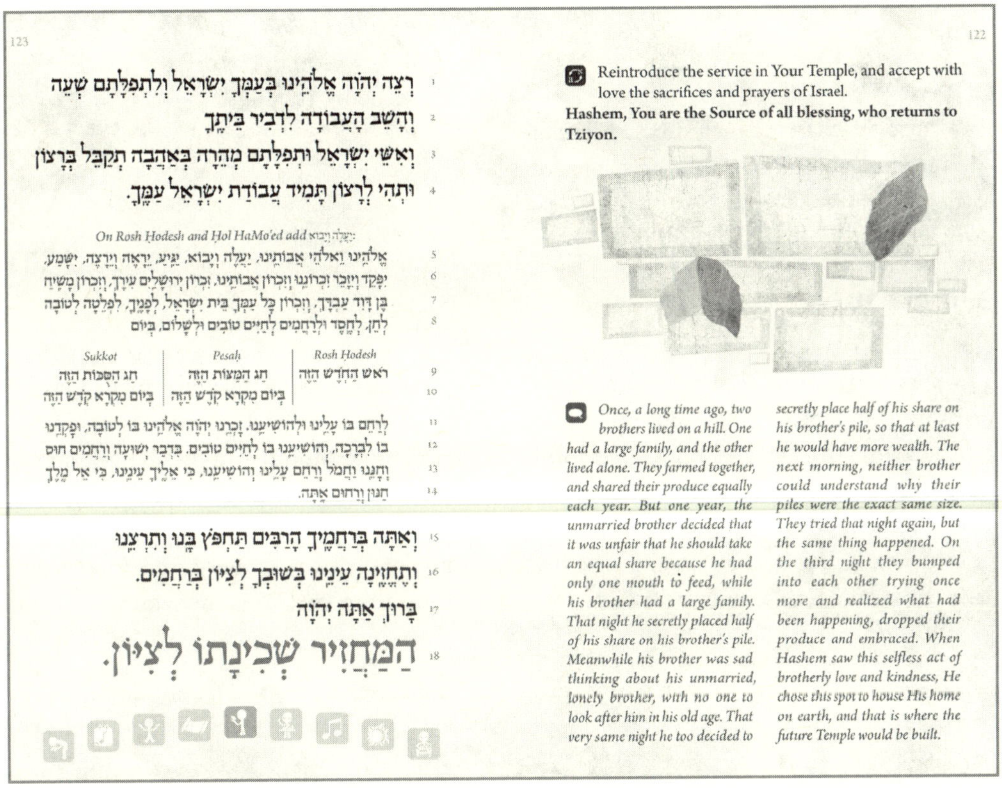
123

122

Reintroduce the service in Your Temple, and accept with love the sacrifices and prayers of Israel.
Hashem, You are the Source of all blessing, who returns to Tziyon.

Once, a long time ago, two brothers lived on a hill. One had a large family, and the other lived alone. They farmed together, and shared their produce equally each year. But one year, the unmarried brother decided that it was unfair that he should take an equal share because he had only one mouth to feed, while his brother had a large family. That night he secretly placed half of his share on his brother's pile. Meanwhile his brother was sad thinking about his unmarried, lonely brother, with no one to look after him in his old age. That very same night he too decided to secretly place half of his share on his brother's pile, so that at least he would have more wealth. The next morning, neither brother could understand why their piles were the exact same size. They tried that night again, but the same thing happened. On the third night they bumped into each other trying once more and realized what had been happening, dropped their produce and embraced. When Hashem saw this selfless act of brotherly love and kindness, He chose this spot to house His home on earth, and that is where the future Temple would be built.

רְצֵה יְהֹוָה אֱלֹהֵינוּ בְּעַמְּךָ יִשְׂרָאֵל וְלִתְפִלָּתָם שְׁעֵה
וְהָשֵׁב הָעֲבוֹדָה לִדְבִיר בֵּיתֶךָ
וְאִשֵּׁי יִשְׂרָאֵל וּתְפִלָּתָם מְהֵרָה בְּאַהֲבָה תְקַבֵּל בְּרָצוֹן
וּתְהִי לְרָצוֹן תָּמִיד עֲבוֹדַת יִשְׂרָאֵל עַמֶּךָ.

On Rosh Hodesh and Hol HaMo'ed add יַעֲלֶה וְיָבוֹא:

אֱלֹהֵינוּ וֵאלֹהֵי אֲבוֹתֵינוּ, יַעֲלֶה וְיָבוֹא, יַגִּיעַ, יֵרָאֶה וְיֵרָצֶה, יִשָּׁמַע,
יִפָּקֵד וְיִזָּכֵר זִכְרוֹנֵנוּ וְזִכְרוֹן אֲבוֹתֵינוּ, זִכְרוֹן יְרוּשָׁלַיִם עִירָךְ, וְזִכְרוֹן מָשִׁיחַ
בֶּן דָּוִד עַבְדָּךְ, וְזִכְרוֹן כָּל עַמְּךָ בֵּית יִשְׂרָאֵל, לְפָנֶיךָ, לִפְלֵטָה לְטוֹבָה
לְחֵן, לְחֶסֶד וּלְרַחֲמִים לְחַיִּים טוֹבִים וּלְשָׁלוֹם, בְּיוֹם

Rosh Hodesh	Pesah	Sukkot
רֹאשׁ הַחֹדֶשׁ הַזֶּה	חַג הַמַּצּוֹת הַזֶּה	חַג הַסֻּכּוֹת הַזֶּה
	בְּיוֹם מִקְרָא קֹדֶשׁ הַזֶּה	בְּיוֹם מִקְרָא קֹדֶשׁ הַזֶּה

לְרַחֵם בּוֹ עָלֵינוּ וּלְהוֹשִׁיעֵנוּ. זָכְרֵנוּ יְהֹוָה אֱלֹהֵינוּ בּוֹ לְטוֹבָה, וּפָקְדֵנוּ
בוֹ לִבְרָכָה, וְהוֹשִׁיעֵנוּ בוֹ לְחַיִּים טוֹבִים. בִּדְבַר יְשׁוּעָה וְרַחֲמִים חוּס
וְחָנֵּנוּ וַחֲמֹל וְרַחֵם עָלֵינוּ וְהוֹשִׁיעֵנוּ, כִּי אֵלֶיךָ עֵינֵינוּ, כִּי אֵל מֶלֶךְ
חַנּוּן וְרַחוּם אָתָּה.

וְאַתָּה בְּרַחֲמֶיךָ הָרַבִּים תַּחְפֹּץ בָּנוּ וְתִרְצֵנוּ
וְתֶחֱזֶינָה עֵינֵינוּ בְּשׁוּבְךָ לְצִיּוֹן בְּרַחֲמִים.
בָּרוּךְ אַתָּה יְהֹוָה
הַמַּחֲזִיר שְׁכִינָתוֹ לְצִיּוֹן.

The *Tefilla* Text

Translation:
Find favor, Lord our God, in Your people Israel and heed their prayer. Restore the service to Your most holy House, and accept in love and favor the fire-offerings of Israel and their prayer. May the service of Your people Israel always find favor with You.

On Rosh Hodesh and Hol HaMo'ed, say:
Our God and God of our ancestors, may there rise, come, reach, appear, be favored, heard, regarded and remembered before You, our recollection and remembrance, as well as the remembrance of our ancestors, and of the Messiah son of David Your servant, and of Jerusalem Your holy city, and of all Your people the house of Israel – for deliverance and well-being, grace, loving-kindness and compassion, life and peace, on this day of:

On Rosh Hodesh: Rosh Hodesh.
On Pesah: the Festival of Matzot.
On Sukkot: the Festival of Sukkot.

To show compassion to us and to save us. On it remember us, Lord our God, for good; recollect us for blessing, and deliver us for life. In accord with Your promise of salvation and compassion, spare us and be gracious to us; have compassion on us and deliver us, for our eyes are turned to You because You, God, are a gracious and compassionate King.

And may You, with Your abundant compassion, desire us and be pleased with us. And may our eyes witness Your return to Zion in compassion. Blessed are You, Lord, who restores His Presence to Zion.

Highlighted Text:
The words המחזיר שכינתו לציון that conclude the *berakha* are highlighted in the golden brown of the stones of the Kotel in the illustration.

Educational Themes contained in the text:

- Thanksgiving as central to Temple service
- First take pleasure in us and then our *tefillot*, because we must embody the values of our *tefillot*
- *Tefilla* is in place of sacrificial worship
- The modern State of Israel as a fulfillment of this desire (return of the Divine Presence to Israel)
- This blessing could be seen as a request, and out of place here. However it should be seen as a statement of faith, and therefore a thanksgiving.
- *Hashgaḥa* (*kelalit/peratit*)
- *Ḥagim* = God in history
- Jerusalem/Temple

The Illustration

This *berakha* refers to the Temple service and asks for God to restore it in a rebuilt *Beit HaMikdash* in a rebuilt Yerushalayim. The closest tangible site and relatable concept we have for our students to relate to is the Kotel – a segment of the western outside wall to the Temple Mount complex. For Jews, this is the holiest site that we have access to, and we focus on this location as a visual relatable image to which we direct our *tefillot*. The illustration does the same – hinting at the Temple Mount and the Temple service by depicting the closest we can get to those concepts. Make sure to notice the small pieces of paper (*kvitelach*) between some of the stones. These are written *tefillot* left by visitors to the Kotel, as is the widespread custom.

The *Kavanot*

Conceptual Translation of:

והשב את העבודה לדביר ביתך ואשי ישראל ותפלתם באהבה תקבל ב רצון ברוך אתה ה׳ המחזיר שכינתו לציון.

Story:
This beautiful, anonymously written story expresses a traditional connection between the Temple Mount and peace and love. The Temple and the Temple service are difficult concepts for children in modern times to grasp, and this gives them a connection to this site through a utopian vision that they can relate to.

The story on page 238 from *Pesaḥim* 8b is also an appropriate one to share with your students here, especially on a day when *Ya'aleh Veyavo* is said.

Activity ideas:

- Arts and crafts project: Design a house for God – the message ultimately being God doesn't need a physical abode; it is for us to be able to focus on Him.
- Watch a live stream of the Kotel on the "Kotel Cam" (http://english.thekotel.org/cameras.asp)
- Have your students write their own *tefillot* on small pieces of paper for someone from the community to take and place in the Kotel.

Additional *Kavanot*:
Thought questions:

- Have you ever been to the Kotel? Did you feel anything special there? Why do you think people feel emotional and spiritual there?

- Today there is no *Beit HaMikdash*. How do we connect to Hashem?
- Where is Zion? Have you been there? Close your eyes and go there now.
- What are we celebrating on Rosh Ḥodesh?
- Look back over the last month. What was your highlight? What are your hopes for the next month?
- We are asking in this *tefilla* for Hashem to look after us at this time. Can you feel Hashem looking after you at this time?

הודאה 1

pp. 124–125

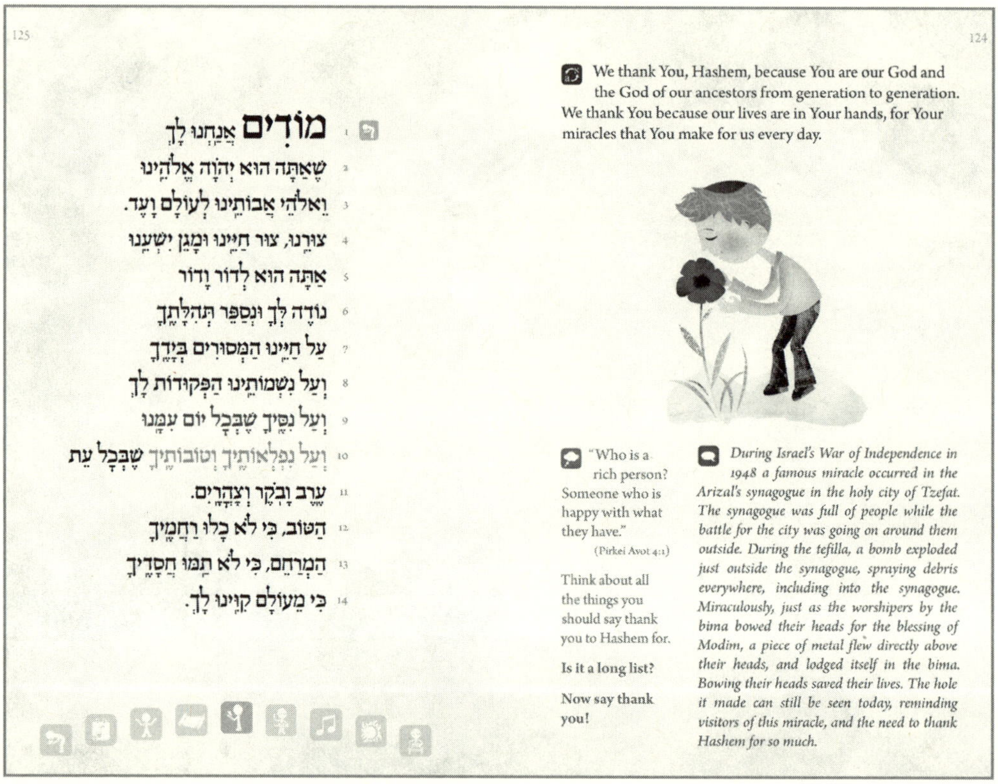
125

מוֹדִים אֲנַחְנוּ לָךְ
שָׁאַתָּה הוּא יְהוָה אֱלֹהֵינוּ
וֵאלֹהֵי אֲבוֹתֵינוּ לְעוֹלָם וָעֶד.
צוּרֵנוּ, צוּר חַיֵּינוּ וּמָגֵן יִשְׁעֵנוּ
אַתָּה הוּא לְדוֹר וָדוֹר
נוֹדֶה לְּךָ וּנְסַפֵּר תְּהִלָּתֶךָ
עַל חַיֵּינוּ הַמְּסוּרִים בְּיָדֶךָ
וְעַל נִשְׁמוֹתֵינוּ הַפְּקוּדוֹת לָךְ
וְעַל נִסֶּיךָ שֶׁבְּכָל יוֹם עִמָּנוּ
וְעַל נִפְלְאוֹתֶיךָ וְטוֹבוֹתֶיךָ שֶׁבְּכָל עֵת
עֶרֶב וָבֹקֶר וְצָהֳרָיִם.
הַטּוֹב, כִּי לֹא כָלוּ רַחֲמֶיךָ
הַמְרַחֵם, כִּי לֹא תַמּוּ חֲסָדֶיךָ
כִּי מֵעוֹלָם קִוִּינוּ לָךְ.

124

We thank You, Hashem, because You are our God and the God of our ancestors from generation to generation. We thank You because our lives are in Your hands, for Your miracles that You make for us every day.

"Who is a rich person? Someone who is happy with what they have."
(Pirkei Avot 4:1)

Think about all the things you should say thank you to Hashem for.

Is it a long list?

Now say thank you!

During Israel's War of Independence in 1948 a famous miracle occurred in the Arizal's synagogue in the holy city of Tzefat. The synagogue was full of people while the battle for the city was going on around them outside. During the tefilla, a bomb exploded just outside the synagogue, spraying debris everywhere, including into the synagogue. Miraculously, just as the worshipers by the bima bowed their heads for the blessing of Modim, a piece of metal flew directly above their heads, and lodged itself in the bima. Bowing their heads saved their lives. The hole it made can still be seen today, reminding visitors of this miracle, and the need to thank Hashem for so much.

The *Tefilla* Text

Translation:
We give thanks to You, for You are the Lord our God and God of our ancestors for ever and all time. You are our Rock, the Rock of our lives, and the Shield of our salvation from generation to generation. We will thank You and declare Your praise for our lives, which are entrusted into Your hand; for our souls, which are placed in Your charge; for Your miracles which are with us every day; and for Your wonders and favors at all times, evening, morning and midday. You are good – for Your compassion never fails. You are compassionate – for Your loving-kindnesses never cease. For we have always placed our hope in You.

Highlighted Text:
The words ועל נסיך שבכל יום עמנו are highlighted in the color of the flower in the illustration, and the words ועל נפלאותיך וטובותיך are highlighted in the green of the boy's sweater in the illustration.

Educational Themes contained in the text:

- Importance of giving thanks and *hakarat hatov*
- Thanksgiving as central to Temple service
- Bowing = physical act of subservience and admission of dependence
- Miracles = extraordinary events that are universally recognized as an act of God
- Wonders = happen every day and run the risk of being taken for granted

The Illustration

This *tefilla* uses two terms to describe miracles – נסים and נפלאות. The term נס can mean extraordinary miracles and נפלאות can refer to the wonders of nature. The illustration has our character smelling the fragrance of a beautiful flower – a natural and everyday feature of our world. Nothing out of the ordinary, but still a wonder of God. We must make sure we appreciate both kinds of God-given miracles, and give thanks for both as well. The body language of the boy, almost bowing as he bends to smell the flower, reminds us of the choreography of this *tefilla*. Bowing before someone is a humbling experience, reminding us of our subservience to them. When we bow to Hashem at this *berakha* we are saying we appreciate the world He created and everything He does for us, and are humbled in His presence. And that is what we feel when we appreciate nature, like the boy in the illustration.

The *Kavanot*

Conceptual Translation:

מודים אנחנו לך שאתה הוא ה׳ אלהינו ואלהי אבותינו לעולם ועד, צור חיינו, מגן ישענו אתה הוא לדור ודור. נודה לך ונספר תהלתך על חיינו המסורים בידך ועל נשמותינו הפקודות לך, ועל נסיך שבכל יום עמנו, ועל נפלאותיך וטובותיך שבכל עת, ערב ובקר וצהרים.

Thought Question:
The entire Mishna (*Avot* 4:1) in the original is:

בן זומא אומר, איזה הוא חכם – הלמד מכל אדם, שנאמר ״מכל מלמדיי, השכלתי״ (תהילים קיט,צט). איזה הוא גיבור – הכובש את יצרו, שנאמר ״טוב ארך אפיים, מגיבור״ (משלי טז,לב). איזה הוא עשיר – השמח בחלקו, שנאמר ״יגיע כפיך, כי תאכל; אשריך, וטוב לך״ (תהילים קכח,ב): ״אשריך״, בעולם הזה; ״וטוב לך״, לעולם הבא. איזה הוא מכובד – המכבד את הברייות, שנאמר ״כי מכבדיי אכבד ובוזיי ייקלו״ (שמואל א׳ ב,ל).

The first three clauses of the Mishna are quoted in the siddur, on pages 31, 96 and 124.

The excerpt quoted on this page encourages us to be truly grateful for what we have, and not constantly searching for more as a route to happiness. If we can achieve this, contentment and fulfillment from what we already have in our lives, then gratitude to Hashem will come much more easily. The thought question that follows the quote asks the child to consider this in a tangible real way in their lives – list what they have to be grateful for, and then thank Hashem for it.

Activity idea:
Everyone in the room takes a turn to thank someone else in the room for something specific. Or, if preferred, this could be done in written form – everyone writes a thank-you note and places it in a central place for that person to pick up.

Story:
This amazing story that took place in Tzefat ties into to this *tefilla* on many levels. The story relates an extraordinary miracle that happened to take place at the very moment when a community was saying this prayer (and therefore bowing), and one that we must be thankful for. The text of the *tefilla* uses two terms to describe miracles – נסים and נפלאות. The term נס can mean extraordinary miracles, and נפלאות (such as nature – the flower in the illustration) can refer to

the wonders of nature. Although this story does not involve a supernatural miracle, it is an extraordinary one that falls into the category of נסים.

Additional *Kavanot*:
Thought questions:

- Why do you think we bow when we say thank you in this *berakha*? How do you feel when you bow?
- Apart from Hashem, who else do you need to say thank you to today?

See also the thought questions on the following page of the siddur (page 126 – על הנסים).

על הנסים

pp. 126–127

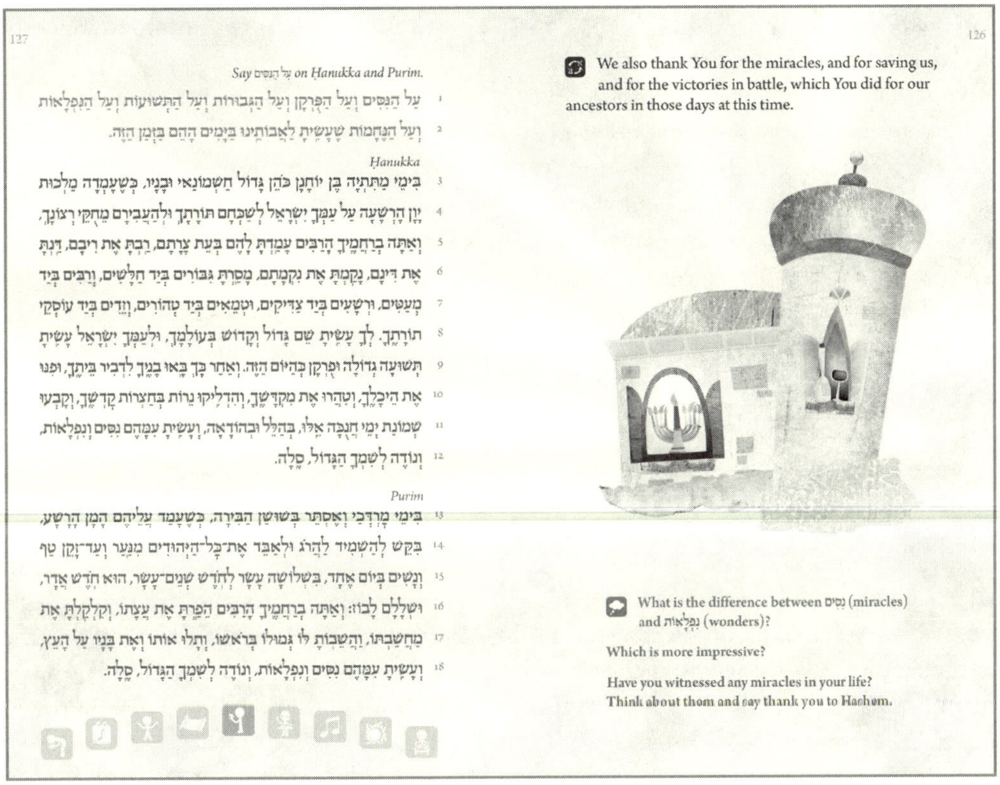
127

Say עַל הַנִּסִּים *on Ḥanukka and Purim.*

עַל הַנִּסִּים וְעַל הַפֻּרְקָן וְעַל הַגְּבוּרוֹת וְעַל הַתְּשׁוּעוֹת וְעַל הַנִּפְלָאוֹת וְעַל הַנֶּחָמוֹת שֶׁעָשִׂיתָ לַאֲבוֹתֵינוּ בַּיָּמִים הָהֵם בִּזְּמַן הַזֶּה.

Ḥanukka

בִּימֵי מַתִּתְיָה בֶּן יוֹחָנָן כֹּהֵן גָּדוֹל חַשְׁמוֹנַאי וּבָנָיו, כְּשֶׁעָמְדָה מַלְכוּת יָוָן הָרְשָׁעָה עַל עַמְּךָ יִשְׂרָאֵל לְשַׁכְּחָם תּוֹרָתָךְ וּלְהַעֲבִירָם מֵחֻקֵּי רְצוֹנָךְ, וְאַתָּה בְּרַחֲמֶיךָ הָרַבִּים עָמַדְתָּ לָהֶם בְּעֵת צָרָתָם, רַבְתָּ אֶת רִיבָם, דַּנְתָּ אֶת דִּינָם, נָקַמְתָּ אֶת נִקְמָתָם, מָסַרְתָּ גִבּוֹרִים בְּיַד חַלָּשִׁים, וְרַבִּים בְּיַד מְעַטִּים, וּרְשָׁעִים בְּיַד צַדִּיקִים, וּטְמֵאִים בְּיַד טְהוֹרִים, וְזֵדִים בְּיַד עוֹסְקֵי תוֹרָתָךְ. לְךָ עָשִׂיתָ שֵׁם גָּדוֹל וְקָדוֹשׁ בְּעוֹלָמָךְ, וּלְעַמְּךָ יִשְׂרָאֵל עָשִׂיתָ תְּשׁוּעָה גְדוֹלָה וּפֻרְקָן כְּהַיּוֹם הַזֶּה. וְאַחַר כָּךְ בָּאוּ בָנֶיךָ לִדְבִיר בֵּיתֶךָ, וּפִנּוּ אֶת הֵיכָלֶךָ, וְטִהֲרוּ אֶת מִקְדָּשֶׁךָ, וְהִדְלִיקוּ נֵרוֹת בְּחַצְרוֹת קָדְשֶׁךָ, וְקָבְעוּ שְׁמוֹנַת יְמֵי חֲנֻכָּה אֵלּוּ, בְּהַלֵּל וּבְהוֹדָאָה, וְעָשִׂיתָ עִמָּהֶם נִסִּים וְנִפְלָאוֹת, וְנוֹדֶה לְשִׁמְךָ הַגָּדוֹל, סֶלָה.

Purim

בִּימֵי מָרְדְּכַי וְאֶסְתֵּר בְּשׁוּשַׁן הַבִּירָה, כְּשֶׁעָמַד עֲלֵיהֶם הָמָן הָרָשָׁע, בִּקֵּשׁ לְהַשְׁמִיד לַהֲרֹג וּלְאַבֵּד אֶת־כָּל־הַיְּהוּדִים מִנַּעַר וְעַד־זָקֵן טַף וְנָשִׁים בְּיוֹם אֶחָד, בִּשְׁלוֹשָׁה עָשָׂר לְחֹדֶשׁ שְׁנֵים־עָשָׂר, הוּא חֹדֶשׁ אֲדָר, וּשְׁלָלָם לָבוֹז: וְאַתָּה בְּרַחֲמֶיךָ הָרַבִּים הֵפַרְתָּ אֶת עֲצָתוֹ, וְקִלְקַלְתָּ אֶת מַחֲשַׁבְתּוֹ, וַהֲשֵׁבוֹתָ לּוֹ גְּמוּלוֹ בְּרֹאשׁוֹ, וְתָלוּ אוֹתוֹ וְאֶת בָּנָיו עַל הָעֵץ, וְעָשִׂיתָ עִמָּהֶם נִסִּים וְנִפְלָאוֹת, וְנוֹדֶה לְשִׁמְךָ הַגָּדוֹל, סֶלָה.

126

We also thank You for the miracles, and for saving us, and for the victories in battle, which You did for our ancestors in those days at this time.

What is the difference between נִסִּים (miracles) and נִפְלָאוֹת (wonders)?

Which is more impressive?

Have you witnessed any miracles in your life? Think about them and say thank you to Hashem.

The *Tefilla* Text

Translation:

[We thank You also] for the miracles, the redemption, the mighty deeds, the salvations, and the wonders and consolations which You performed for our ancestors in those days, at this time.

On Ḥanukka:

In the days of Mattityahu, son of Yoḥanan, the High Priest, the Hasmonean, and his sons, the wicked Greek kingdom rose up against Your people Israel to make them forget Your Torah and to force them to transgress the statutes of Your will. It was then that You in Your great compassion stood by them in the time of their distress. You championed their cause, judged their claim, and avenged their wrong. You delivered the strong into the hands of the weak, the many into the hands of the few, the impure into the hands of the pure, the wicked into the hands of the righteous, and the arrogant into the hands of those who were engaged in the study of Your Torah. You made for Yourself great and holy renown in Your world, and for Your people Israel You performed a great salvation and redemption as of this very day. Your children then entered the holiest part of Your House, cleansed Your Temple, purified Your Sanctuary, kindled lights in Your holy courts, and designated these eight days of Ḥanukka with praise and gratitude. For you performed miracles and wonders for them, and we give thanks to Your great name, Selah.

On Purim:

In the days of Mordekhai and Esther, in Shushan the capital, the wicked Haman rose up against them and sought to destroy, slay and exterminate all the Jews, young and old, children and women, on one day, the thirteenth day of the twelfth month, which is the month of Adar, and to plunder their possessions. Then You in Your great compassion thwarted his counsel, frustrated his plans, and caused his scheme to recoil on his own head, so that they hanged him and his sons on the gallows. For you performed miracles and wonders for them, and we give thanks to Your great name, Selah.

Highlighted Text:
The first line that precedes both versions of this *tefilla* is highlighted in the color of the flames in the illustration:

עַל הנסים ועל הפרקן ועל הגבורות ועל התשועות ועל המלחמות שֶׁעָשִׂית לאבוֹתֵינו בימים ההם בזמן הזה.

Educational Themes contained in the text:

- Miracles – the interplay between our role and the role of God
- Miracles through nature and supernatural miracles
- The God of history – Divine Providence/*Hashgaḥa*
- "In those days, at this time" – Historical national miracles as a template for modern national miracles
- The theme of light in Ḥanukka and Purim

The Illustration

Al HaNissim celebrates and expresses our gratitude for the miracles of the Ḥanukka and Purim stories. In the illustration there are houses (that look like they could be contemporary to the Ḥanukka and Purim stories) where the occupants are clearly celebrating these two festivals. The house on the left has a *ḥanukkia* in the window, publicizing the miracles of Ḥanukka, as the halakha demands. The house on the right is in the middle of a Purim *seuda*, with wine, as the halakha demands. However, there is light emanating from behind the houses (as well as within), hinting at the common theme that runs through these two festivals. The miracle of Ḥanukka was obviously the discovery of the cruse of oil that then lasted for eight days, and light is also an important theme in the Purim story that we remember each Motza'ei Shabbat in *Havdala* when we say the words: ליהודים, היתה אורה ושמחה, וששן, ויקר (Ester 8:16).

The *Kavanot*

Conceptual Translation of:

עַל הנסים ועל הפרקן ועל הגבורות ועל התשועות ועל המלחמות שֶׁעָשִׂית לאבוֹתֵינו בימים ההם בזמן הזה.

Thought Questions:
The previous *tefilla* (מודים) uses two terms to describe miracles – נסים and נפלאות. As we have mentioned, the term נס can refer to extraordinary miracles, either supernatural or just historically exceptional, and נפלאות can refer to the wonders of nature and natural miracles. This *tefilla*, על הנסים, only uses the first term – נסים. The miracles in both the stories of Ḥanukka and Purim are extraordinary. While there was a supernatural miracle in the Ḥanukka story (the burning of the cruse of oil for eight days), the military battle and the entire political narrative of the Purim story are miracles through natural means, yet they are extraordinary and historically exceptional. The thought questions ask the student to compare and explore these two different

categories of miracles, and arrive at an understanding that we should be thankful for both types: the everyday wonders of nature, and the extraordinary miracles of history that are exceptional.

Activity ideas:
In a classroom discussion, breakdown the stories of Ḥanukka and/or Purim into נסים and נפלאות. Then ask your students to draw/paint two pictures telling the events of these stories – one entitled נסים and the other נפלאות.

Additional *Kavanot*:
Stories:
Private Winneger was a soldier in the US army during the Second World War. He was on patrol one night when he saw a dark figure running through a field. He shouted, "Halt, or I'll shoot!" but the figure ran away and hid behind a tree. He chased the figure until he had caught up with him and tackled him to the ground. To his surprise it was a young boy. As the boy fell to the ground a silver *ḥanukkia* fell out of his hand. Private Winneger picked it up and the boy tried to grab it back shouting, "It's mine. Give it back!" The soldier reassured the boy he was among friends, and that he too was Jewish, as he found out that the boy had survived a concentration camp. He had witnessed his father's death but had no idea of his mother's whereabouts, and was all alone in the world. Over time, they became close, and the boy, who was called David, explained that the *ḥanukkia* was a family heirloom, passed down through the generations for over 200 years. Winneger offered to bring the boy home with him to New York and officially adopt him, and David accepted the offer. Some years later, on Ḥanukka, as they lit that special *ḥanukkia*, there was a knock on the door. A German lady said she had seen the beautiful *ḥanukkia*, and it seemed to be an exact replica of one that was in her family in Germany. Winneger asked David to explain the history of the *ḥanukkia* to the woman, but he had no need; for David was looking at his mother for the first time in many years, and ran to hug her.

הודאה 2

pp. 128–129

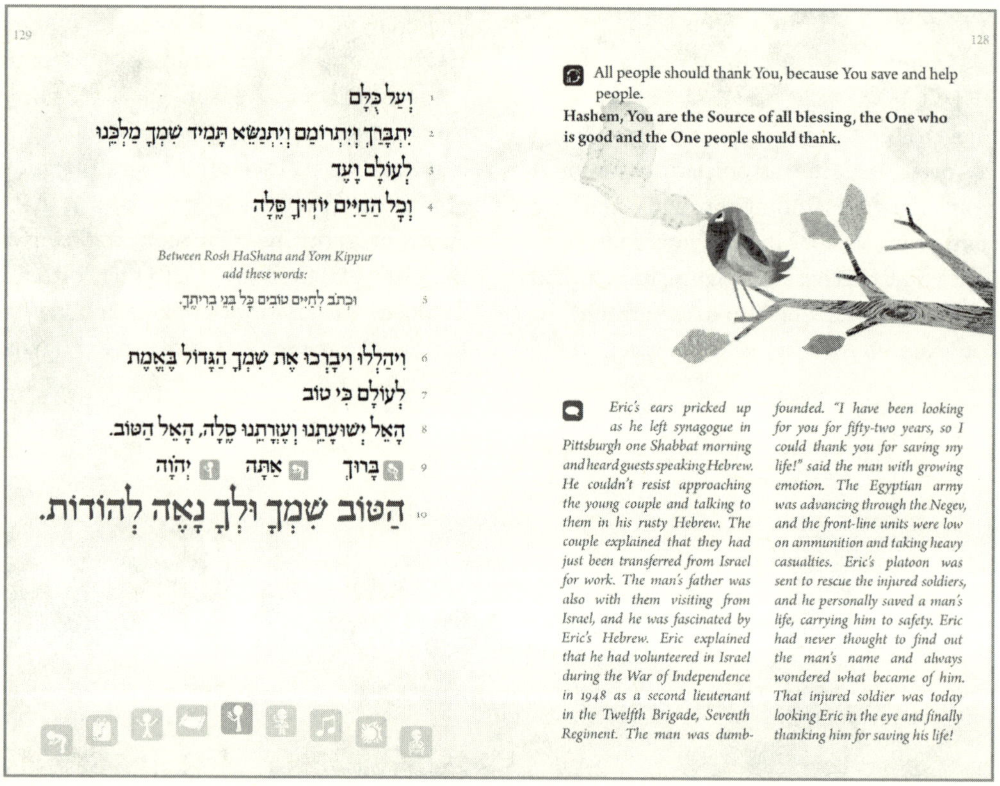

129

וְעַל כֻּלָּם
יִתְבָּרַךְ וְיִתְרוֹמַם וְיִתְנַשֵּׂא תָּמִיד שִׁמְךָ מַלְכֵּנוּ
לְעוֹלָם וָעֶד
וְכָל הַחַיִּים יוֹדְוּךָ סֶּלָה

Between Rosh HaShana and Yom Kippur add these words:

וּכְתֹב לְחַיִּים טוֹבִים כָּל בְּנֵי בְרִיתֶךָ.

וִיהַלְלוּ וִיבָרְכוּ אֶת שִׁמְךָ הַגָּדוֹל בֶּאֱמֶת
לְעוֹלָם כִּי טוֹב
הָאֵל יְשׁוּעָתֵנוּ וְעֶזְרָתֵנוּ סֶלָה, הָאֵל הַטּוֹב.
בָּרוּךְ אַתָּה יְהֹוָה
הַטּוֹב שִׁמְךָ וּלְךָ נָאֶה לְהוֹדוֹת.

128

All people should thank You, because You save and help people.

Hashem, You are the Source of all blessing, the One who is good and the One people should thank.

Eric's ears pricked up as he left synagogue in Pittsburgh one Shabbat morning and heard guests speaking Hebrew. He couldn't resist approaching the young couple and talking to them in his rusty Hebrew. The couple explained that they had just been transferred from Israel for work. The man's father was also with them visiting from Israel, and he was fascinated by Eric's Hebrew. Eric explained that he had volunteered in Israel during the War of Independence in 1948 as a second lieutenant in the Twelfth Brigade, Seventh Regiment. The man was dumbfounded. "I have been looking for you for fifty-two years, so I could thank you for saving my life!" said the man with growing emotion. The Egyptian army was advancing through the Negev, and the front-line units were low on ammunition and taking heavy casualties. Eric's platoon was sent to rescue the injured soldiers, and he personally saved a man's life, carrying him to safety. Eric had never thought to find out the man's name and always wondered what became of him. That injured soldier was today looking Eric in the eye and finally thanking him for saving his life!

The *Tefilla* Text

Translation:
For all these things may Your name be blessed, glorified and exalted, our King, continually, for ever and all time. Let all that lives thank You, Selah!

> *Between Rosh HaShana and Yom Kippur: And write, for a good life, all the children of Your covenant.*

And praise and bless Your great name in truth for ever, for it is good. God, our Savior and Help, Selah, God who is good! Blessed are You, Lord, whose name is "the Good" and to whom thanks are due.

Highlighted Text:
The words that conclude this *berakha* – הטוב שמך ולך נאה להודות – are highlighted in the color of the story.

Educational Themes contained in the text:

- Importance of giving thanks and *hakarat hatov*

- Bowing = physical act of subservience and admission of dependence
- God's goodness

The Illustration

This illustration has a bird singing the praises of Hashem with his song, musical notes emanating from his beak. This takes us back to the illustration on page 42 that explores the verse from *Ashrei* – יוֹדוּךָ ה׳ כׇּל־מַעֲשֶׂיךָ, וַחֲסִידֶיךָ יְבָרְכוּכָה: – that all of God's creations will praise and thank Him (the word יודוך is found in that verse and in this *berakha*), and chapter 148 of *Sefer Tehillim* (page 49) is an explanation of that verse, according to the *Tehillot Hashem*.

The *Kavanot*

Conceptual Translation of:

וכל החיים יוֹדוּךָ סֶּלָה ויהללו את שמך באמת האל ישועתֵנו ועזרתֵנו סֶלָה. ברוך אתה ה׳ הטוב שמך ולך נאה להודות.

Story:
An inspiring story of gratitude and the desire to show it that stayed with a person for years, until eventually he had the opportunity to show the gratitude.

שלום

pp. 130–131

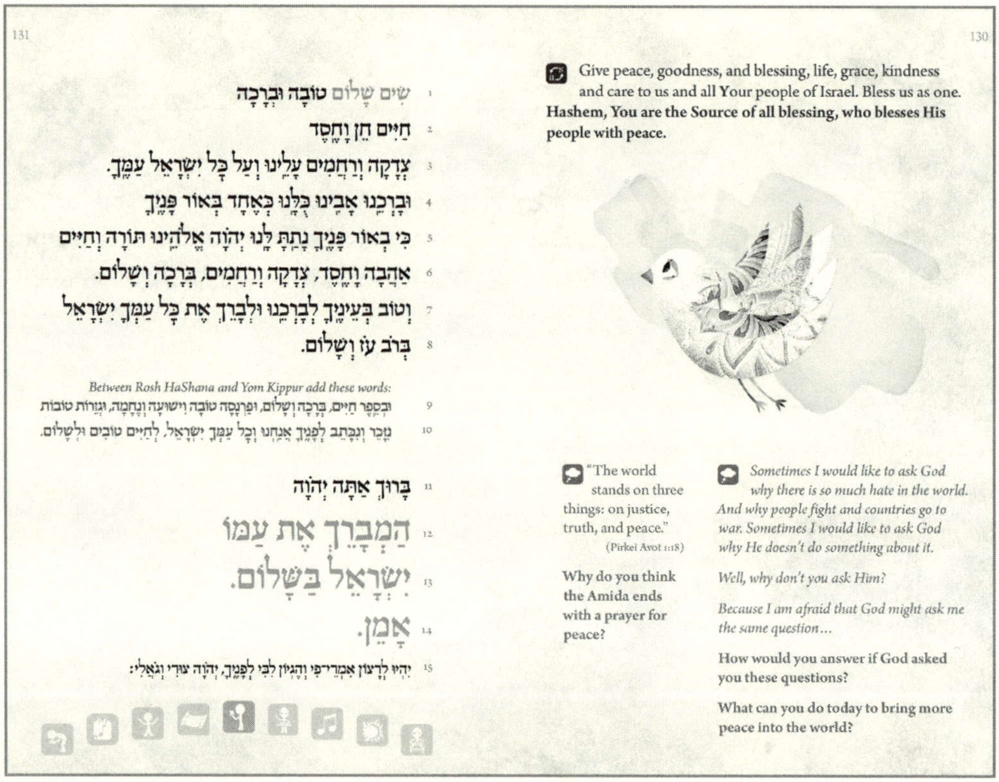

131

שִׂים שָׁלוֹם טוֹבָה וּבְרָכָה
חַיִּים חֵן וָחֶסֶד
צְדָקָה וְרַחֲמִים עָלֵינוּ וְעַל כָּל יִשְׂרָאֵל עַמֶּךָ.
וּבָרְכֵנוּ אָבִינוּ כֻּלָּנוּ כְּאֶחָד בְּאוֹר פָּנֶיךָ
כִּי בְאוֹר פָּנֶיךָ נָתַתָּ לָּנוּ יְהוָה אֱלֹהֵינוּ תּוֹרָה וְחַיִּים
אַהֲבָה וָחֶסֶד, צְדָקָה וְרַחֲמִים, בְּרָכָה וְשָׁלוֹם.
וְטוֹב בְּעֵינֶיךָ לְבָרְכֵנוּ וּלְבָרֵךְ אֶת כָּל עַמְּךָ יִשְׂרָאֵל
בְּרֹב עֹז וְשָׁלוֹם.

Between Rosh HaShana and Yom Kippur add these words:

וּבְסֵפֶר חַיִּים, בְּרָכָה וְשָׁלוֹם, וּפַרְנָסָה טוֹבָה וִישׁוּעָה וְנֶחָמָה, וּגְזֵרוֹת טוֹבוֹת
נִזָּכֵר וְנִכָּתֵב לְפָנֶיךָ אֲנַחְנוּ וְכָל עַמְּךָ יִשְׂרָאֵל, לְחַיִּים טוֹבִים וּלְשָׁלוֹם.

בָּרוּךְ אַתָּה יְהוָה
הַמְבָרֵךְ אֶת עַמּוֹ
יִשְׂרָאֵל בַּשָּׁלוֹם.
אָמֵן.

יִהְיוּ לְרָצוֹן אִמְרֵי־פִי וְהֶגְיוֹן לִבִּי לְפָנֶיךָ, יְהוָה צוּרִי וְגֹאֲלִי:

130

Give peace, goodness, and blessing, life, grace, kindness and care to us and all Your people of Israel. Bless us as one. **Hashem, You are the Source of all blessing, who blesses His people with peace.**

"The world stands on three things: on justice, truth, and peace." (Pirkei Avot 1:18)

Why do you think the Amida ends with a prayer for peace?

Sometimes I would like to ask God why there is so much hate in the world. And why people fight and countries go to war. Sometimes I would like to ask God why He doesn't do something about it.

Well, why don't you ask Him?

Because I am afraid that God might ask me the same question…

How would you answer if God asked you these questions?

What can you do today to bring more peace into the world?

The *Tefilla* Text

Translation:
Grant peace, goodness and blessing, life, grace, loving-kindness, righteousness and compassion to us and all Israel Your people. Bless us, our Father, all as one, with the light of Your face, for by the light of Your face You have given us, Lord our God, Torah and life, love and kindness, righteousness, compassion, blessing, and peace. May it be good in Your eyes to bless us and to bless all of Your people Israel with much strength and peace.

Between Rosh HaShana and Yom Kippur: *And in the book of life, blessing, peace and prosperity, salvation and comfort, and favorable decrees, may we and all Your people the house of Israel be remembered and written before You for a good life, and for peace.*

Blessed are You, Lord, who blesses His people Israel with peace.

May the words of my mouth and the meditation of my heart find favor before You, Lord, my Rock and Redeemer.

Highlighted Text:
The words שים שלום and the concluding words to the *berakha* – המברך את עמו ישראל בשלום – are highlighted in the color of the dove from the illustration.

Educational Themes contained in the text:

- "Bless us as one" = peace can only be established on true equality of people. These are the values upon which peace will be established: grace; loving-kindness; compassion; [values of] life
- Peace is the ultimate hope of Judaism and therefore the way the ultimate prayer concludes
- A tranquil conclusion to a *tefilla* of emotional highs and lows (love, mercy, dread, helplessness, yearning, confusion, terror)
- The relationship between the Torah, and *ḥesed,* and peace

The Illustration

Here we meet a new friend who will return to us on almost every page of the siddur that discusses peace – the *yona* (dove). The white dove is traditionally seen as a symbol of peace. This comes from the story of Noaḥ and the flood. At the conclusion of the flood Noaḥ let a dove fly free to determine if the waters were abating. The dove returned to him with an olive branch (also a symbol of peace for the same reason) to demonstrate that the waters were in fact receding, and the world was entering a new peaceful age after the destruction of the flood. Our friend the *yona* can also be found on pages 132, 169, 209, and 256.

The *Kavanot*

Conceptual Translation of:

שים שלום טובה וברכה, חן וחסד ורחמים עלינו ועל כל ישראל עמך.
ברכנו אבינו כלנו כאחד... ברוך אתה ה׳ המברך את עמו ישראל בשלום.

Thought Question 1:

רבן שמעון בן גמליאל אומר, על שלושה דברים העולם קיים – על הדין, ועל האמת, ועל השלום.
(*Avot* 1:18)

This mishna gives us three core concepts of the world and the way it functions. Each one best personifies a category of relationship we have in our lives. Truth is the concept that governs our relationship with God. God represents truth and we strive to understand it in order to develop a relationship with Him. Justice is the concept that we need to govern our world in order to be at peace within ourselves – we need justice to exist for our own well-being within the relationship we have with ourselves. And finally, peace is the concept that governs and develops relationships between man and his fellow man. This is parallel to the second mishna in *Avot* that states that the world stands on the following three concepts – *Torah, avoda,* and *gemilut ḥasadim.* Torah is about man improving himself, *avoda* is about man worshiping God, and acts of loving-kindness is about man and his fellow man.

The *Amida* ends with the *berakha* for peace; having stood before Hashem and asked for numerous personal and national requests, we end and climax with the request for peace. Peace is a core value in Judaism, and every single *Amida* in every single *tefilla* ends with a request for it.

Activity ideas:
Science experiment with the mishna: Ask your students to build a support for a small ball (the world) with three legs. Label each leg one of the three concepts from the mishna. Then take away one of the legs and see what happens to the ball.

Thought Question 2:
The second thought question builds on this, and challenges the child to realize that we cannot sit back and petition God for peace only, but we must partner Him, and do our utmost, to achieve peace in the world ourselves.

There are other *kavanot* that explore the concept of peace on the following pages of the siddur: pages 132, 167, and 225.

Additional *Kavanot*:

Story:

When Hashem was about to create man, the angels in heaven arranged themselves into two groups, one shouting, "Don't do it!" and the other shouting, "Do it!" Some used love as their argument, and said, "Let man be created because he will do acts of love." Others used truth and said, "Don't create man because he will bring lies into the world." Others used righteousness and argued, "Let him be created because he will do righteous acts." And others used peace and said, "Don't create him because he will only fight!" When Hashem heard the angels arguing these points he took truth and threw it to the ground, showing them that love, righteousness and peace were more important.[41]

Thought questions:

דרכיה דרכי-נֹעַם; וכל-נתיבותיה שלום
(Mishlei 3:17)

- Which mitzvot can lead to peace?

41. *Bereshit Raba* 8:5

אלהי נצור

pp. 132–133

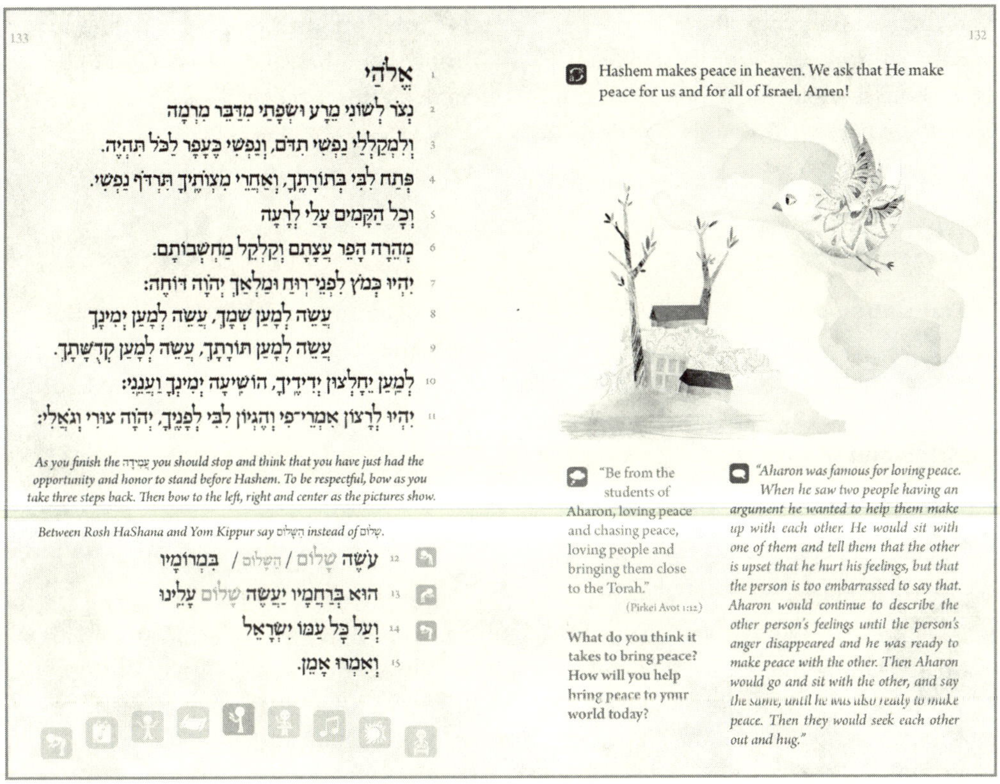
132

Hashem makes peace in heaven. We ask that He make peace for us and for all of Israel. Amen!

"Be from the students of Aharon, loving peace and chasing peace, loving people and bringing them close to the Torah."
(Pirkei Avot 1:12)

What do you think it takes to bring peace? How will you help bring peace to your world today?

"Aharon was famous for loving peace. When he saw two people having an argument he wanted to help them make up with each other. He would sit with one of them and tell them that the other is upset that he hurt his feelings, but that the person is too embarrassed to say that. Aharon would continue to describe the other person's feelings until the person's anger disappeared and he was ready to make peace with the other. Then Aharon would go and sit with the other, and say the same, until he was also ready to make peace. Then they would seek each other out and hug."

133

1 אֱלֹהַי

2 נְצֹר לְשׁוֹנִי מֵרָע וּשְׂפָתַי מִדַּבֵּר מִרְמָה

3 וְלִמְקַלְלַי נַפְשִׁי תִדֹּם, וְנַפְשִׁי כֶּעָפָר לַכֹּל תִּהְיֶה.

4 פְּתַח לִבִּי בְּתוֹרָתֶךָ, וְאַחֲרֵי מִצְוֹתֶיךָ תִּרְדֹּף נַפְשִׁי.

5 וְכָל הַקָּמִים עָלַי לְרָעָה

6 מְהֵרָה הָפֵר עֲצָתָם וְקַלְקֵל מַחְשְׁבוֹתָם.

7 יִהְיוּ כְּמֹץ לִפְנֵי־רוּחַ וּמַלְאַךְ יְהֹוָה דּוֹחֶה:

8 עֲשֵׂה לְמַעַן שְׁמֶךָ, עֲשֵׂה לְמַעַן יְמִינֶךָ

9 עֲשֵׂה לְמַעַן תּוֹרָתֶךָ, עֲשֵׂה לְמַעַן קְדֻשָּׁתֶךָ.

10 לְמַעַן יֵחָלְצוּן יְדִידֶיךָ, הוֹשִׁיעָה יְמִינְךָ וַעֲנֵנִי:

11 יִהְיוּ לְרָצוֹן אִמְרֵי־פִי וְהֶגְיוֹן לִבִּי לְפָנֶיךָ, יְהֹוָה צוּרִי וְגֹאֲלִי:

As you finish the עֲמִידָה you should stop and think that you have just had the opportunity and honor to stand before Hashem. To be respectful, bow as you take three steps back. Then bow to the left, right and center as the pictures show.

Between Rosh HaShana and Yom Kippur say הַשָּׁלוֹם *instead of* שָׁלוֹם.

12 עֹשֶׂה שָׁלוֹם / הַשָּׁלוֹם / בִּמְרוֹמָיו

13 הוּא בְּרַחֲמָיו יַעֲשֶׂה שָׁלוֹם עָלֵינוּ

14 וְעַל כָּל עַמּוֹ יִשְׂרָאֵל

15 וְאִמְרוּ אָמֵן.

The *Tefilla* Text

Translation:

My God, guard my tongue from evil and my lips from deceitful speech. To those who curse me, let my soul be silent; may my soul be to all like the dust. Open my heart to Your Torah and let my soul pursue Your commandments. As for all who rise up against me with evil intent, swiftly thwart their counsel and frustrate their plans. May they be like chaff before the wind, with the angel of the Lord driving them on. Act for the sake of Your name; act for the sake of Your right hand; act for the sake of Your holiness; act for the sake of Your Torah. That Your beloved ones may be delivered, save with Your right hand and answer me. May the words of my mouth and the meditation of my heart find favor before You, Lord, my Rock and Redeemer. May He who makes peace in His high places, may He, in His compassion, make peace for us and for all His people Israel – and say: Amen.

Highlighted Text:

The word שלום is highlighted in the color of the dove from the illustration.

Educational Themes contained in the text:

- Peace on High (Heaven) and peace below on earth
- Peace is the ultimate hope of Judaism and therefore the way the ultimate prayer concludes
- A tranquil conclusion to a *tefilla* of emotional highs and lows (love, mercy, dread, helplessness, yearning, confusion, terror)
- *Lashon HaRa* and the power of speech
- The power of speech for good (peace) and for bad (strife)

The Illustration

In the second half of the *berakha* of *Shalom*, on this second spread focused on peace, the *yona* (see the previous page for an explanation of its significance) flies towards the houses where the people are waiting for him to bring them peace. The houses look desolate and the trees barren and the scene is cold and in need of hope and warmth. The *yona* flies towards them to bring them that, and we ask God to bring us the very same in this *berakha*.

The *Kavanot*

Conceptual Translation of:

עֹשֶׂה שלום במרומיו, הוא יעשה שלום עלינו ועל כל ישראל, ואמרו אמן

Thought Question and story:
The full text of the mishna:

הלל ושמאי קיבלו מהם. הלל אומר, הוי כתלמידיו של אהרן – אוהב שלום ורודף שלום, אוהב את הברייות ומקרבן לתורה.

Aharon was a practical role model when it came to bringing peace into the world. The Talmud uses him as a model for both inspiration, and for practical advice how to bring peace into the world – by bringing peace between people. He didn't just love the concept of peace, he pursued it, and the story, from *Avot deRabbi Natan* 12, describes how he achieved this. Up until now peace has been presented as an abstract concept and as a value and an ideal to strive for. But these *kavanot*, with the help of Aharon, take the concept and make it real for the students, and ask them to bring a concrete peace into their world.

Activity ideas:
Create a Peace Corps among your students, to roam the school (under supervision of course) bringing peace to your school community. Plan the way your students think they can do this, with well-planned activities, coordinated with the school administration. Perhaps the initiative can be brought to the wider community outside of the school campus.

There are other *kavanot* that explore the concept of peace on the following pages of the siddur: pages 130, 167, and 225.

אבינו מלכנו

pp. 134–135

134

Our Father, our King, we have sinned, be forgiving to us.
Our Father, our King, You are our only King!

A long time ago, when there were no fire engines and fire alarms, and buildings were made of wood, a small fire could spread to the whole town. One town built a tower so a watchman could blow his bugle loudly to warn the residents that there was a fire in the town. This way, everyone would drop what they were doing as soon as they heard the bugle and run to help put out the fire. Once a boy from a village came to stay in the town. When he heard the noise of the bugle he asked the innkeeper about it. When the innkeeper explained, the boy said to himself, "What an amazing idea." So on his way home he bought a bugle and returned to his village. When he got there he showed the villagers what he had bought. He set fire to the straw roof of the nearest hut, and told the villagers not to worry, the fire will be out in no time, just watch. He began to blow his bugle with gusto, but with no success. The fire refused to obey the sound of his bugle, and instead quickly spread. The villagers screamed at the boy, "Did you think just the sound of the bugle would put out the fire? It is only a wakeup call for those asleep or at work to come and help put out the fire!"

135

Between Rosh HaShana and Yom Kippur we say אבינו מלכנו.
We open the ארון קדש and stand for this תפלה.

1 אבינו מלכנו, חטאנו לפניך רחם עלינו.
2 אבינו מלכנו, אין לנו מלך אלא אתה.
3 אבינו מלכנו, עשה עמנו למען שמך.
4 אבינו מלכנו, קרע רוע גזר דיננו.
5 אבינו מלכנו, שלח רפואה שלמה לכל חולי עמך.
6 אבינו מלכנו, כתבנו בספר חיים טובים.
7 אבינו מלכנו, כתבנו בספר צדיקים וחסידים.
8 אבינו מלכנו, כתבנו בספר ישרים ותמימים.
9 אבינו מלכנו, כתבנו בספר פרנסה וכלכלה טובה.
10 אבינו מלכנו, כתבנו בספר מחילה וסליחה וכפרה.
11 אבינו מלכנו, כתבנו בספר גאלה וישועה.
12 אבינו מלכנו, חננו ועננו.
13 אבינו מלכנו, החזירנו בתשובה שלמה לפניך.
14 אבינו מלכנו, שמע קולנו חוס ורחם עלינו.
15 אבינו מלכנו, עשה למענך אם לא למעננו.
16 אבינו מלכנו, קבל ברחמים וברצון את תפלתנו.
17 אבינו מלכנו, אל תשיבנו ריקם מלפניך.

The *Tefilla* Text

Translation:

Our Father, our King, we have sinned before You, be compassionate to us.
Our Father, our King, we have no king but You.
Our Father, our King, deal kindly with us for the sake of Your name.
Our Father, our King, tear up the evil decree against us.
Our Father, our King, send a complete healing to the sick of Your people.
Our Father, our King, write us in the book of good life.
Our Father, our King, write us in the book of the righteous and faithful.
Our Father, our King, write us in the book of the upright and innocent.
Our Father, our King, write us in the book of livelihood and abundant sustenance.
Our Father, our King, write us in the book of pardon, forgiveness and atonement.
Our Father, our King, write us in the book of redemption and salvation.
Our Father, our King, be gracious to us and answer us.
Our Father, our King, bring us back to You in perfect repentance.

Our Father, our King, hear our voice, pity and be compassionate to us.
Our Father, our King, act for Your sake, if not for ours.
Our Father, our King, accept, with compassion and favor, our prayer.
Our Father, our King, do not turn us away from You empty-handed.

Educational Themes contained in the text:

- God as King (Justice, power, demands obedience)
- God as parent/father (love, compassion, forgiveness, intimacy)
- Source of this prayer = a story from Rabbi Akiva's life (*Ta'anit* 25b – see below)

The Illustration

This illustration is a visual depiction of the story found on this page. The boy is blowing his bugle as loud as his lungs will allow him, trying with all his might to put out the fire, which refuses to obey the command.

The *Kavanot*

Conceptual Translation of:

אבינו מלכנו, חטאנו לפניך רחם עלינו.
אבינו מלכנו, אין לנו מלך אלא אתה.

Activity ideas:
Ask for volunteers to role play a scenario, first as a King and then as a father, and the rest of the class guesses which role they are playing. The scenario could be given by the teacher or decided by the class, or the student.

Story:
This story is really about the blowing of the *shofar* during the month of Elul, and of course on Rosh HaShana. It is placed here because *Avinu Malkenu* is said during the Ten Days of Repentance between Rosh HaShana and Yom Kippur. It reminds us that *teshuva* is an internal process that we must embark on, not an external one that can be accomplished simply by carrying out the external rituals of this period of the year, such as blowing the *shofar*. The *shofar* only serves as a wakeup call. We must wake ourselves up to actually do *teshuva* in our hearts, and change our behavior as a result of that.

Additional *Kavanot*:
Story:
It is related of Rabbi Eliezer that he once stepped before the Ark [to lead the congregation in prayer] and recited the twenty-four benedictions [of the *Amida* for fast days declared on account of drought], and his prayer was not answered. Rabbi Akiva stepped before the Ark after him and exclaimed: "Our Father, our King! We have no king but You! Our Father, our King! For Your sake, have compassion for us!" And rain fell.[42]

Niels Bohr was a Danish scientist who won the Nobel Prize for physics for a theory that came to him when his young son once told him that he had stolen something from a shop, and he realized that he could think of his son with love as a father, or in terms of justice and right and wrong, like a judge. But he could not manage to do both at the same time. But Hashem manages to be both to us at the very same time![43]

Thought questions:

- What is the difference between a parent and a king? What is similar?
- How do you see Hashem today, more like a king or a parent?
- Could a person who has never done something wrong say this *tefilla*?
- What is the difference between writing something and remembering something? Which is a stronger phrase?

42. *Ta'anit* 25b
43. Koren Sacks Rosh HaShana Maḥzor

קריאת התורה

pp. 136–137

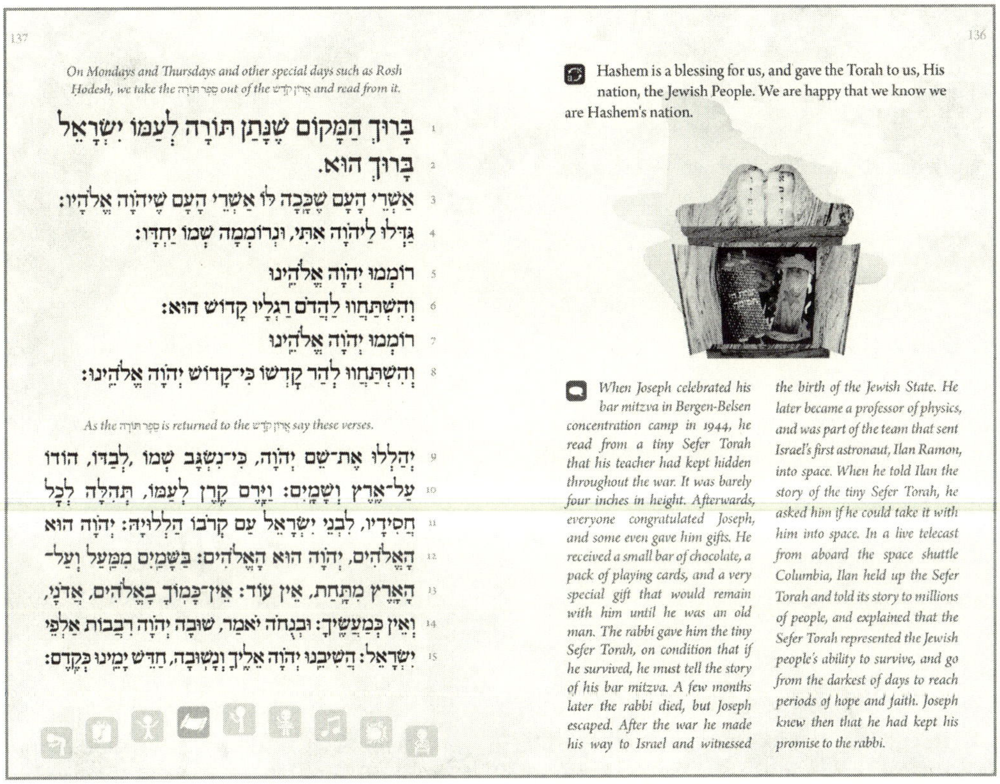

137

On Mondays and Thursdays and other special days such as Rosh Ḥodesh, we take the ספר תורה *out of the* ארון קודש *and read from it.*

בָּרוּךְ הַמָּקוֹם שֶׁנָּתַן תּוֹרָה לְעַמּוֹ יִשְׂרָאֵל
בָּרוּךְ הוּא.
אַשְׁרֵי הָעָם שֶׁכָּכָה לּוֹ אַשְׁרֵי הָעָם שֶׁיהוָה אֱלֹהָיו:
גַּדְּלוּ לַיהוָה אִתִּי, וּנְרוֹמְמָה שְׁמוֹ יַחְדָּו:
רוֹמְמוּ יְהוָה אֱלֹהֵינוּ
וְהִשְׁתַּחֲווּ לַהֲדֹם רַגְלָיו קָדוֹשׁ הוּא:
רוֹמְמוּ יְהוָה אֱלֹהֵינוּ
וְהִשְׁתַּחֲווּ לְהַר קָדְשׁוֹ כִּי־קָדוֹשׁ יְהוָה אֱלֹהֵינוּ:

As the ספר תורה *is returned to the* ארון קודש *say these verses.*

יְהַלְלוּ אֶת־שֵׁם יְהוָה, כִּי־נִשְׂגָּב שְׁמוֹ ,לְבַדּוֹ, הוֹדוֹ
עַל־אֶרֶץ וְשָׁמָיִם: וַיָּרֶם קֶרֶן לְעַמּוֹ, תְּהִלָּה לְכָל
חֲסִידָיו, לִבְנֵי יִשְׂרָאֵל עַם קְרֹבוֹ הַלְלוּיָהּ: יְהוָה הוּא
הָאֱלֹהִים, יְהוָה הוּא הָאֱלֹהִים: בַּשָּׁמַיִם מִמַּעַל וְעַל־
הָאָרֶץ מִתָּחַת, אֵין עוֹד: אֵין־כָּמוֹךָ בָאֱלֹהִים, אֲדֹנָי,
וְאֵין כְּמַעֲשֶׂיךָ: וּבְנֻחֹה יֹאמַר, שׁוּבָה יְהוָה רִבְבוֹת אַלְפֵי
יִשְׂרָאֵל: הֲשִׁיבֵנוּ יְהוָה אֵלֶיךָ וְנָשׁוּבָה, חַדֵּשׁ יָמֵינוּ כְּקֶדֶם:

136

Hashem is a blessing for us, and gave the Torah to us, His nation, the Jewish People. We are happy that we know we are Hashem's nation.

When Joseph celebrated his bar mitzva in Bergen-Belsen concentration camp in 1944, he read from a tiny Sefer Torah that his teacher had kept hidden throughout the war. It was barely four inches in height. Afterwards, everyone congratulated Joseph, and some even gave him gifts. He received a small bar of chocolate, a pack of playing cards, and a very special gift that would remain with him until he was an old man. The rabbi gave him the tiny Sefer Torah, on condition that if he survived, he must tell the story of his bar mitzva. A few months later the rabbi died, but Joseph escaped. After the war he made his way to Israel and witnessed the birth of the Jewish State. He later became a professor of physics, and was part of the team that sent Israel's first astronaut, Ilan Ramon, into space. When he told Ilan the story of the tiny Sefer Torah, he asked him if he could take it with him into space. In a live telecast from aboard the space shuttle Columbia, Ilan held up the Sefer Torah and told its story to millions of people, and explained that the Sefer Torah represented the Jewish people's ability to survive, and go from the darkest of days to reach periods of hope and faith. Joseph knew then that he had kept his promise to the rabbi.

The *Tefilla* Text

Translation:

Blessed is the All-present, who gave the Torah to his people Israel, Blessed is He.
Happy are the people for whom this is so; happy are the people whose God is the Lord.
Magnify the Lord with me, and let us exalt His name together.
Exalt the Lord our God and bow to His footstool; He is holy. Exalt the Lord our God, and bow at His holy mountain, for holy is the Lord our God.
Let them praise the name of the Lord, for His name alone is sublime. His majesty is above earth and heaven. He has raised the horn of His people, for the glory of all His devoted ones, the children of Israel, the people close to Him. Halleluya! The Lord is God, the Lord is God. In heaven above and on earth below, there is no other. There is none like You among the heavenly powers, Lord, and there are no works like Yours. When the Ark came to rest, Moses would say: "Return, O Lord, to the myriad thousands of Israel." Turn us back, O Lord, to You, and we will return. Renew our days as of old.

Educational Themes contained in the text:

- Public Torah reading = A reenactment of the revelation at Sinai
- Prayer = speaking; *Keriat HaTorah* = listening
- *Aron Kodesh* (today's or from the *Beit HaMikdash/Mishkan*)
- Yerushalayim (Torah emanating from Israel today)
- Public Torah reading = democratization of Torah knowledge
- The experience of *Keriat HaTorah* is reaffirming commitment and connection to people, tradition and God

The Illustration

The *Aron Kodesh* in this illustration asserts the connection between the *Sefer Torah* that we have today in our synagogues and schools, and the original *Luḥot HaBerit* given to Moshe on Sinai. Here, on the top of the *Aron*, are the same *luḥot* we find on page 28 (*Yigdal*) which represent the original Torah from Sinai. Notice the two *Sifrei Torah* inside the *Aron*. The one on the left is an Ashkenazi Torah, and the one on the right the traditional Sephardi *Sefer Torah* in a hard case.

The *Kavanot*

Conceptual Translation of:

בָּרוּךְ הַמָּקוֹם שֶׁנָּתַן תּוֹרָה לְעַמּוֹ יִשְׂרָאֵל, בָּרוּךְ הוּא. אַשְׁרֵי הָעָם שֶׁכָּכָה לּוֹ, אַשְׁרֵי הָעָם שֶׁה׳ אֱלֹהָיו:

Activity idea:
This is a good opportunity for your students to become more intimately acquainted with a *Sefer Torah* (have they all seen inside a *Sefer Torah* close up?). Take your class to the synagogue in your school and take out the *Sefer Torah* on the *bima*, ensuring each one has sufficient access to it, and take this opportunity to explain all the details of how a *Sefer Torah* is made and written and the laws surrounding handling it.

Story:
This very inspiring story about a tiny *Sefer Torah* that survived the Shoah, presents the *Sefer Torah* as a symbol of Jewish survival and continuity. The *Sefer Torah* the children are about to see taken from the *Aron* is the same *Sefer Torah* from this story, and the same *Sefer Torah* that our people have been reading from for generations and generations.

The notion also that Ilan Ramon broadcast the message behind this *Sefer Torah* to the world, almost via Jerusalem (as the first astronaut of the Jewish State), is a modern fulfillment and interpretation of the verse כי מציון תצא תורה ודבר ה׳ מירושלם. Further details to the story make it an even richer narrative, which you may wish to share with your students. Ilan's mother and grandmother were both survivors of Auschwitz. Yad Vashem asked him to also carry with him into space a drawing by 16-year-old Petr Ginz, who died in Auschwitz. The drawing was called "Moon Landscape." He also took a dollar given to him by the Lubavitcher Rebbe.

Sadly there is a postscript to the story that you may also wish to share with your students. On the space shuttle Columbia's return journey, as it reentered Earth's atmosphere, the space shuttle disintegrated, killing all seven crew members who were aboard. While this is a sad and tragic ending to the story, it does not take away from the powerful message of the story. Although the *Sefer Torah* from the story was destroyed in the tragic accident, it had fulfilled the mission that Joseph's teacher, the Chief Rabbi of Holland, had made him promise.

Additional *Kavanot*:

Thought Questions:

Keriat HaTorah is a reenactment of the original experience of *Matan Torah.*[44]

- Why do you think we read the Torah in public? Why not just at home on our own?
- Which direction are you facing in right now? Why?

44. Rav Soloveitchik – http://www.vbm-torah.org/shavuot/shav69-mt.htm – This *kavana* is found on p.214 of the siddur

שיר של יום

pp. 140–141

141

Each day the Levi'im would sing a different song from סֵפֶר תְּהִלִּים *in the* בֵּית הַמִּקְדָּשׁ. *Say the beginning of the song for today.*

Sunday:

1 הַיּוֹם יוֹם אֶחָד בְּשַׁבַּת קֹדֶשׁ, הַשִּׁיר שֶׁהָיוּ הַלְוִיִּם אוֹמְרִים עַל הַדּוּכָן:

2 לְדָוִד מִזְמוֹר, לַיהוָה הָאָרֶץ וּמְלוֹאָהּ, תֵּבֵל וְיֹשְׁבֵי בָהּ:

Monday

3 הַיּוֹם יוֹם שֵׁנִי בְּשַׁבַּת קֹדֶשׁ, הַשִּׁיר שֶׁהָיוּ הַלְוִיִּם אוֹמְרִים עַל הַדּוּכָן:

4 שִׁיר מִזְמוֹר לִבְנֵי־קֹרַח:

5 גָּדוֹל יְהוָה וּמְהֻלָּל מְאֹד, בְּעִיר אֱלֹהֵינוּ, הַר־קָדְשׁוֹ:

Tuesday

6 הַיּוֹם יוֹם שְׁלִישִׁי בְּשַׁבַּת קֹדֶשׁ, הַשִּׁיר שֶׁהָיוּ הַלְוִיִּם אוֹמְרִים עַל הַדּוּכָן:

7 מִזְמוֹר לְאָסָף, אֱלֹהִים נִצָּב בַּעֲדַת־אֵל, בְּקֶרֶב אֱלֹהִים יִשְׁפֹּט:

Wednesday:

8 הַיּוֹם יוֹם רְבִיעִי בְּשַׁבַּת קֹדֶשׁ, הַשִּׁיר שֶׁהָיוּ הַלְוִיִּם אוֹמְרִים עַל הַדּוּכָן:

9 אֵל־נְקָמוֹת יְהוָה, אֵל נְקָמוֹת הוֹפִיעַ:

Thursday:

10 הַיּוֹם יוֹם חֲמִישִׁי בְּשַׁבַּת קֹדֶשׁ, הַשִּׁיר שֶׁהָיוּ הַלְוִיִּם אוֹמְרִים עַל הַדּוּכָן:

11 לַמְנַצֵּחַ עַל־הַגִּתִּית לְאָסָף:

12 הַרְנִינוּ לֵאלֹהִים עוּזֵּנוּ, הָרִיעוּ לֵאלֹהֵי יַעֲקֹב:

Friday:

13 הַיּוֹם יוֹם הַשִּׁשִּׁי בְּשַׁבַּת קֹדֶשׁ, הַשִּׁיר שֶׁהָיוּ הַלְוִיִּם אוֹמְרִים עַל הַדּוּכָן:

14 יְהוָה מָלָךְ, גֵּאוּת לָבֵשׁ, לָבֵשׁ יְהוָה עֹז הִתְאַזָּר, אַף־תִּכּוֹן

15 תֵּבֵל בַּל־תִּמּוֹט:

Between Rosh Ḥodesh Elul and Yom Kippur, and on Hoshana Rabba, say these verses from סֵפֶר תְּהִלִּים.

16 אַחַת שָׁאַלְתִּי מֵאֵת־יְהוָה, אוֹתָהּ אֲבַקֵּשׁ שִׁבְתִּי בְּבֵית־

17 יְהוָה כָּל־יְמֵי חַיַּי, לַחֲזוֹת בְּנֹעַם־יְהוָה וּלְבַקֵּר בְּהֵיכָלוֹ:

140

"Shammai would eat for Shabbat every day of the week. What does that mean? If he found a tasty piece of meat in the market he would buy it and say, 'This will be for Shabbat!' But, on the next day if he found an even better piece of meat he would buy it for Shabbat, and eat the first one that day. So for Shammai, he was focused on Shabbat starting already on Sunday!"

Why do you think we mention Shabbat before each of these songs?

The *Tefilla* Text

Translation:

Today is the first day of the week, on which the Levites used to say this psalm in the Temple:
A psalm of David. The earth is the Lord's and all it contains, the world and all who live in it.

Today is the second day of the week, on which the Levites used to say this psalm in the Temple:
A song. A psalm of the sons of Koraḥ. Great is the Lord and greatly to be praised in the city of God, on His holy mountain.

Today is the third day of the week, on which the Levites used to say this psalm in the Temple:
A psalm of Asaph. God stands in the Divine assembly. Among the judges He delivers judgment.

Today is the fourth day of the week, on which the Levites used to say this psalm in the Temple:
God of retribution, Lord, God of retribution, appear!

Today is the fifth day of the week, on which the Levites used to say this psalm in the Temple:

For the conductor of music. On the Gittit. By Asaph. Sing for joy to God, our strength. Shout aloud to the God of Jacob.

Today is the sixth day of the week, on which the Levites used to say this psalm in the Temple:
The Lord reigns. He is robed in majesty. The Lord is robed, girded with strength. The world is firmly established; it cannot be moved.

Between Rosh Ḥodesh Elul and Shemini Atzeret: One thing I ask of the Lord, only this do I seek: to live in the House of the Lord all the days of my life, to gaze on the beauty of the Lord and worship in His Temple.

Highlighted Text:
The word בשבת, each time it appears in the introduction to each day's chapter of Tehillim, is highlighted in the color of the flames from the *Menora* in the illustration.

Educational Themes contained in the text:

- Messianic times (third *Beit HaMikdash*)
- *Levi'im*
- Song as *Avodat Hashem*
- Focus on Shabbat every day of the week
- Temple/Yerushalayim
- Living in God's presence
- Rosh HaShana, Yom Kippur, Sukkot
- *Shofar/Teshuva*

The Illustration

Rabbi Soloveitchik says that the mitzva of remembering Shabbat begins on Sunday, and lasts all week long. "In anticipating Shabbat the Jew is waiting for Infinity to embrace him."[45] There is a tradition that says that this idea was represented in the *Menora* in the *Beit HaMikdash*, where all the flames and wicks would face inwards towards the center branch. The center branch of the *Menora* represents Shabbat, and each of the others a day of the week, telling us that we should maintain a focus on Shabbat on every other day of the week. One of the ways we do this is by mentioning each day of the week in relation to Shabbat when we introduce the daily psalm that the *Levi'im* would sing in the *Beit HaMikdash*.

The illustration has the *Menora* from the *Beit HaMikdash* (in the same gold pattern of the *mizbe'aḥ* on page 34 and the *Aron HaBerit* on page 68) with the *Kohen* lighting it. Each of the flames is reaching towards the center branch, reminding us of our daily focus on the coming Shabbat.

The *Kavanot*

Story:
This story, from the Gemara (*Beitza* 16a), shows how Shammai was always focused on Shabbat, every day of the week. His entire week revolved around and culminated in the climax that is Shabbat. In much the same way as we mention each day of the week in the *Shir shel Yom* in relation to Shabbat, continuously focusing on the coming Shabbat, so Shammai was continuously focused on the coming Shabbat.

Thought Question:
The thought question asks why we refer to Shabbat when mentioning the day of the week in relation to the *Shir shel Yom*. The answer is demonstrated by Shammai in the story – to continuously focus us on the coming Shabbat, and elevating it to the climax of our week (not a break from our week).

Activity idea:
Ask every child to commit to making a preparation that day for the coming Shabbat, and ask them to share with the class what it is.

45. Siddur Mesorat HaRav

עלינו 1

pp. 142–143

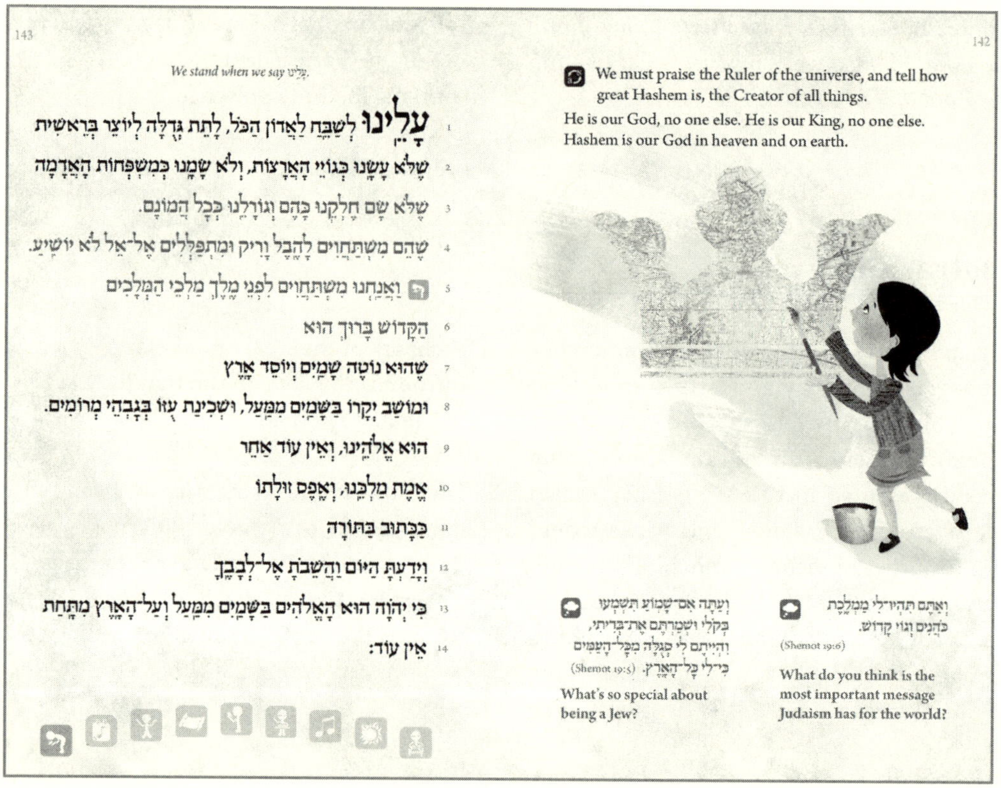

The *Tefilla* Text

Translation:
It is our duty to praise the Master of all, and ascribe greatness to the Author of creation, who has not made us like the nations of the lands nor placed us like the families of the earth; who has not made our portion like theirs, nor our destiny like all their multitudes. For they worship vanity and emptiness, and pray to a god who cannot save. But we bow in worship and thank the Supreme King of kings, the Holy One, blessed be He, who extends the heavens and establishes the earth, whose throne of glory is in the heavens above, and whose power's Presence is in the highest of heights. He is our God; there is no other. Truly He is our King, there is none else, as it is written in His Torah: "You shall know and take to heart this day that the Lord is God, in heaven above and on earth below. There is no other."

Highlighted Text:
The words שלֹא שם חלקנו כהם וגורלנו ככל המונם. שהם משתחוים להבל וריק ומתפללים אל אל לֹא יושיע. are highlighted in the color of the thought question, and the words ואנחנו כורעים ומשתחוים ומודים לפני מלך מלכי המלכים,

הקדוש ברוך הוא are highlighted in gold to suggest the crown in the illustration.

Educational Themes contained in the text:

- *Malkhut* – God as King of the Universe
- One day, in Messianic times, all will acknowledge God
- National mission to bring about universal message/vision

The Illustration

According to Rabbi Sacks, in his commentary to the Koren Siddur, the first paragraph of *Aleinu*, coming from the *Malkhiyot* section of the Rosh HaShana *Musaf* liturgy, explores Jewish particularistic national destiny. The second paragraph describes a future time when the whole of humanity will acknowledge one God. Together, he says, they express the dual nature of the destiny of the Jewish people: "Its singular history as the nation chosen to be God's witness on earth, and its universal aspiration for the time when all inhabitants of earth will recognize the God in whose image we are formed."

In this illustration for the first paragraph of *Aleinu*, we have our character revealing God's *malkhut* in the world, slowly, brushstroke by brushstroke. This is represented by the crown that is really a map of the world. The girl's brushstrokes are a metaphor for the acts of the Jewish people as they observe the Torah, and by being a light unto the nations, slowly bring the world to the knowledge of God's existence. In the second illustration (on the next page) the Jewish people have fulfilled their job, and the world is complete. This is the fulfillment of *Tikkun Olam*, and the future Messianic era of peace on earth.

The *Kavanot*

Conceptual Translation of:

עלינו לשבח לאדון הכל, לתת גדלה ליוצר בראשית... הוא אלֹהינו,
אין עוד. אמת מלכנו, אפס זולתו.

Thought Questions:
The first thought question presented here explores the concept of a "Chosen People," an expression of our particularistic national identity. The verse from Shemot describes the Jewish people as a "*segula*" – a treasure. We interpret this to be "chosen." But the question is, chosen for what? The second thought question quotes the very next verse which can be seen as an answer – to be a holy nation of priests. The priestly tribe of Levi was traditionally the origin of the educators in biblical times, and this verse suggests that we have a national role to play as educators – "a light unto the nations" (see the verse from Yeshayahu 42:6 on page 24). This national role is how the Jewish people can make a universal impact, in line with the second paragraph of *Aleinu*, which also mentions the concept of *Tikkun Olam*, an idea central to these concepts. The second thought question asks the student to consider what the core message of Judaism is that as a nation we must spread in order to be a light unto the nations, and to work towards *Tikkun Olam*. The answer, in a phrase, is ethical monotheism, but this can be expressed in many ways.

Additional *Kavanot*:
Story:
There once was a king who ordered his servants to plant a beautiful orchard with rows and rows of trees. There was a row of fig trees, and a row of grapevines, and a row of pomegranate trees, and a row of apple trees. Then the king arranged for a keeper to tend to the orchard. Months later when the king returned to enjoy his orchard he found it overgrown with thorns and weeds. Because he was so angry, he called for the woodcutters to come and cut the trees down and destroy the orchard. But before they could arrive he noticed a rose-colored flower growing in the orchard. He picked the beautiful flower and smelled it. He breathed in its beautiful smell, and he was calmed. The

king said, "Because of this flower, the orchard will be spared." The same is true for our world. Our world continues because of the Jews, God's rose-colored flower.[46]

Thought questions:

- Have you ever thought about what the world would be like when Mashiaḥ comes? Think about it now.
- What can you do today to make the world more perfect?
- What can you do today to help the world see Hashem is God?

46. *Vayikra Raba* 23:3; *Shir HaShirim Raba* 2:2

עלינו 2

pp. 144–145

145

עַל כֵּן נְקַוֶּה לְךָ, יְהֹוָה אֱלֹהֵינוּ, לִרְאוֹת מְהֵרָה בְּתִפְאֶרֶת עֻזָּךְ
לְהַעֲבִיר גִּלּוּלִים מִן הָאָרֶץ וְהָאֱלִילִים כָּרוֹת יִכָּרֵתוּן
לְתַקֵּן עוֹלָם בְּמַלְכוּת שַׁדַּי
וְכָל בְּנֵי בָשָׂר יִקְרְאוּ בִשְׁמֶךָ לְהַפְנוֹת אֵלֶיךָ כָּל רִשְׁעֵי אָרֶץ
יַכִּירוּ וְיֵדְעוּ כָּל יוֹשְׁבֵי תֵבֵל
כִּי לְךָ תִכְרַע כָּל בֶּרֶךְ, תִּשָּׁבַע כָּל לָשׁוֹן.
לְפָנֶיךָ יְהֹוָה אֱלֹהֵינוּ יִכְרְעוּ וְיִפֹּלוּ, וְלִכְבוֹד שִׁמְךָ יְקָר יִתֵּנוּ
וִיקַבְּלוּ כֻלָּם אֶת עוֹל מַלְכוּתֶךָ
וְתִמְלֹךְ עֲלֵיהֶם מְהֵרָה לְעוֹלָם וָעֶד
כִּי הַמַּלְכוּת שֶׁלְּךָ הִיא וּלְעוֹלְמֵי עַד תִּמְלֹךְ בְּכָבוֹד
כַּכָּתוּב בְּתוֹרָתֶךָ, יְהֹוָה יִמְלֹךְ לְעֹלָם וָעֶד:
וְנֶאֱמַר, וְהָיָה יְהֹוָה לְמֶלֶךְ עַל־כָּל־הָאָרֶץ
בַּיּוֹם הַהוּא יִהְיֶה יְהֹוָה אֶחָד וּשְׁמוֹ אֶחָד:

144

Therefore we hope that You will let us see Your amazing power, when all evil and misunderstanding will be removed from the world, and the world will be perfect with every person recognizing You as King.

Aaron Feuerstein owned a textile mill in a small town in Massachusetts, at a time when most of the textile mills had closed down because it was cheaper to have them in other countries such as India and Mexico. His mill was destroyed in a fire, and most people assumed he would take this opportunity to take the insurance money and close it down. But the mill had employed 1,800 people from the local town, who would all be out of a job if the mill closed. Aaron felt a responsibility to them, and refused to close the mill. Not only did he rebuild the mill, making their jobs safe, but he paid them full salaries while the mill was being rebuilt and they couldn't work. Aaron had made a tremendous Kiddush Hashem and made the world a better place.

The *Tefilla* Text

Translation:
Therefore, we place our hope in You, Lord our God, that we may soon see the glory of Your power, when You will remove abominations from the earth, and idols will be utterly destroyed, when the world will be perfected under the sovereignty of the Almighty, when all humanity will call on Your name, to turn all the earth's wicked toward You. All the world's inhabitants will realize and know that to You every knee must bow and every tongue swear loyalty. Before You, Lord our God, they will kneel and bow down and give honor to Your glorious name. They will all accept the yoke of Your kingdom, and You will reign over them soon and for ever. For the kingdom is Yours, and to all eternity You will reign in glory, as it is written in Your Torah: "The Lord will reign for ever and ever." And it is said: "Then the Lord shall be King over all the earth; on that day the Lord shall be One and His name One."

Highlighted Text:
The words לתקן עולם במלכות שדי are highlighted in the turquoise of the brushstrokes in the illustration.

Educational Themes contained in the text:

- *Malkhut* – God as King of the Universe
- One day, in Messianic times, all will acknowledge God
- National mission to bring about universal message/vision
- *Am Segula*
- *Tikkun Olam*
- Messianic times

The Illustration

As we mentioned on the previous page, Rabbi Sacks believes the first paragraph of *Aleinu* explores Jewish particularistic national destiny. The second paragraph describes a future time when the whole of humanity will acknowledge one God. Together they express the dual nature of the destiny of the Jewish people: "Its singular history as the nation chosen to be God's witness on earth, and its universal aspiration for the time when all inhabitants of earth will recognize the God in whose image we are formed."

In the illustration for the first paragraph of *Aleinu*, we have our character revealing God's *malkhut* in the world, slowly, brushstroke by brushstroke. This is represented by the crown that is really a map of the world. The girl's brushstrokes are a metaphor for the acts of the Jewish people as they observe the Torah and bring the world to the knowledge of God's existence, slowly and steadily, through being a light unto the nations.

In this, the second illustration, through becoming an exemplary people, and creating a model society based on the values of the Torah, the Jewish people have fulfilled their job as a chosen nation and a light unto the nations, and now the world is "complete" and redeemed (she has placed the paint and brush on the side now her job is complete). This is the fulfillment of *Tikkun Olam*, and the arrival of the future Messianic era.

The *Kavanot*

Conceptual Translation of:

על כן נקוה לך ה׳ אלהינו לראות מהרה בתפארת עזך, להעביר גלולים
מן הארץ והאלילים כרות יכרתון לתקן עולם במלכות שדי. וכל בני בשר
יקראו בשמך להפנות אליך כל רשעי ארץ. יכירו וידעו כל יושבי תבל

Story:
This story is adapted from one told by Rabbi Sacks in his book *To Heal a Fractured World* (p. 58) and offers a great example of *Kiddush Hashem*. It is placed here in the context of the Jewish people's universalistic role as an *Am Segula*, being an *Or LaGoyim*. Aaron Feuerstein models core Jewish values in his behavior here, such as protecting the weak in society, maintaining human dignity, and fairness and justice, even at his own expense. He was within his rights to make business decisions that put his own economic welfare before that of his workers, but he chose not to. In his small way, he is making the world a better place (*Tikkun Olam*) by modeling Torah values and fulfilling his part in our national calling.

Additional *Kavanot*:
Thought questions:

- Have you ever thought about what the world would be like when Mashiaḥ comes? Think about it now.
- What can you do today to make the world more perfect?
- What can you do today to help the world see Hashem is God?

הדלקת נרות שבת/ידיד נפש

pp. 148–149

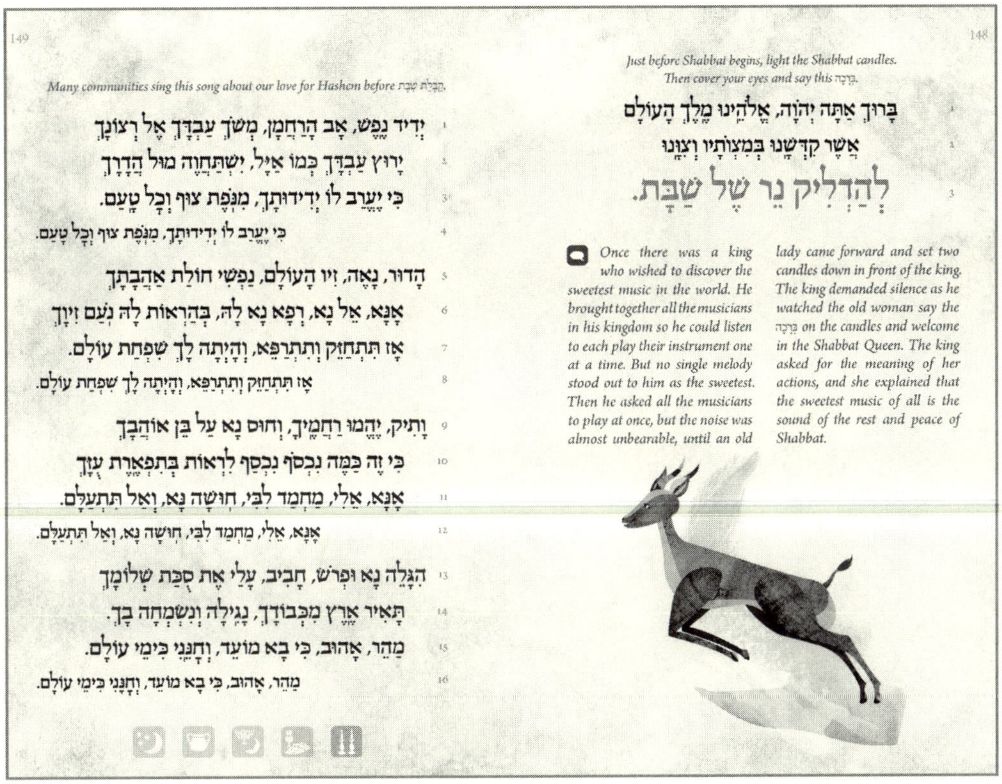
148

Just before Shabbat begins, light the Shabbat candles. Then cover your eyes and say this בְּרָכָה.

בָּרוּךְ אַתָּה יְהֹוָה, אֱלֹהֵינוּ מֶלֶךְ הָעוֹלָם
אֲשֶׁר קִדְּשָׁנוּ בְּמִצְוֹתָיו וְצִוָּנוּ
לְהַדְלִיק נֵר שֶׁל שַׁבָּת.

Once there was a king who wished to discover the sweetest music in the world. He brought together all the musicians in his kingdom so he could listen to each play their instrument one at a time. But no single melody stood out to him as the sweetest. Then he asked all the musicians to play at once, but the noise was almost unbearable, until an old lady came forward and set two candles down in front of the king. The king demanded silence as he watched the old woman say the בְּרָכָה *on the candles and welcome in the Shabbat Queen. The king asked for the meaning of her actions, and she explained that the sweetest music of all is the sound of the rest and peace of Shabbat.*

149

Many communities sing this song about our love for Hashem before קַבָּלַת שַׁבָּת.

יְדִיד נֶפֶשׁ, אָב הָרַחֲמָן, מְשֹׁךְ עַבְדָּךְ אֶל רְצוֹנָךְ
יָרוּץ עַבְדָּךְ כְּמוֹ אַיָּל, יִשְׁתַּחֲוֶה מוּל הֲדָרָךְ
כִּי יֶעֱרַב לוֹ יְדִידוּתָךְ, מִנֹּפֶת צוּף וְכָל טָעַם.
כִּי יֶעֱרַב לוֹ יְדִידוּתָךְ, מִנֹּפֶת צוּף וְכָל טָעַם.

הָדוּר, נָאֶה, זִיו הָעוֹלָם, נַפְשִׁי חוֹלַת אַהֲבָתָךְ
אָנָּא, אֵל נָא, רְפָא נָא לָהּ, בְּהַרְאוֹת לָהּ נֹעַם זִיוָךְ
אָז תִּתְחַזֵּק וְתִתְרַפֵּא, וְהָיְתָה לָךְ שִׁפְחַת עוֹלָם.
אָז תִּתְחַזֵּק וְתִתְרַפֵּא, וְהָיְתָה לָךְ שִׁפְחַת עוֹלָם.

וָתִיק, יֶהֱמוּ רַחֲמֶיךָ, וְחוּס נָא עַל בֵּן אוֹהֲבָךְ
כִּי זֶה כַּמֶּה נִכְסֹף נִכְסַף לִרְאוֹת בְּתִפְאֶרֶת עֻזָּךְ
אָנָּא, אֵלִי, מַחְמַד לִבִּי, חוּשָׁה נָּא, וְאַל תִּתְעַלָּם.
אָנָּא, אֵלִי, מַחְמַד לִבִּי, חוּשָׁה נָּא, וְאַל תִּתְעַלָּם.

הִגָּלֶה נָא וּפְרֹשׂ, חָבִיב, עָלַי אֶת סֻכַּת שְׁלוֹמָךְ
תָּאִיר אֶרֶץ מִכְּבוֹדָךְ, נָגִילָה וְנִשְׂמְחָה בָךְ.
מַהֵר, אָהוּב, כִּי בָא מוֹעֵד, וְחָנֵּנִי כִּימֵי עוֹלָם.
מַהֵר, אָהוּב, כִּי בָא מוֹעֵד, וְחָנֵּנִי כִּימֵי עוֹלָם.

The *Tefilla* Text

The conclusion to the *berakha* for *Hadlakat Nerot* – להדליק נר של שבת – is highlighted in the color of flames.

The words ירוץ עבדך כמו איל, from *Yedid Nefesh,* are highlighted in the brown of the deer in the illustration.

The Illustration

Yedid Nefesh was written by Rabbi Elazar Azikri in the sixteenth century in language that is reminiscent of *Shir HaShirim.* It describes the intimate relationship between man and God. The illustration of the deer, gracefully bounding across the fields in majestic flight is a metaphor for man who runs to serve and draw close to God.

The *Kavanot*

Story:
In meter (music and poetry) an audible pause is called a caesura. This is not an absence of sound (a negative), but rather a pause that adds to the meter and functions in the same way as a musical note (a positive). Rest on Shabbat is the same. It is not an absence of work, but should be seen as a positive creative experience in itself. Hence the positive framing of Shabbat observance in the verses we say for the *Kiddush* of Shabbat day – לַעֲשׂוֹת אֶת-הַשַּׁבָּת (*Shemot* 31:16, found in the siddur on page 158). Observing Shabbat is a positive active enterprise, not a refraining from positive acts. This story brings these ideas together. The king wishes to hear the sweetest music in the world, and the old lady showed him that the tranquility of Shabbat was in fact the sweetest audible silence of all. There are other music related questions and stories in the siddur found on pages 39, 50, 52, 184, and 229.

לכה דודי 1

pp. 150–151

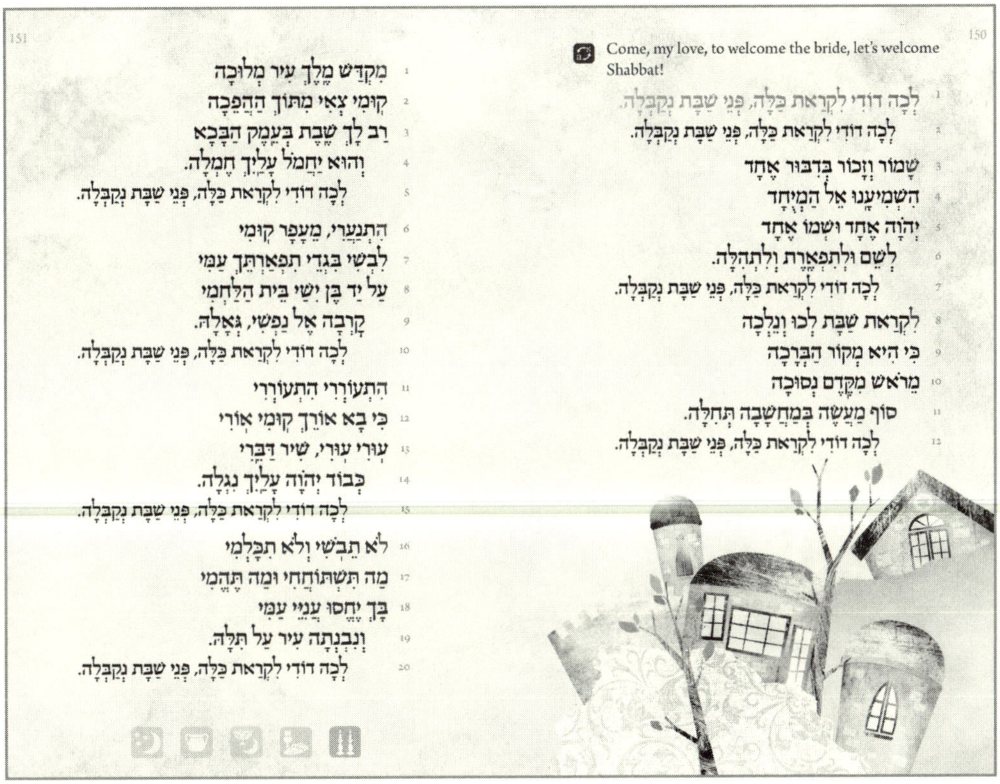

150

Come, my love, to welcome the bride, let's welcome Shabbat!

לְכָה דוֹדִי לִקְרַאת כַּלָּה, פְּנֵי שַׁבָּת נְקַבְּלָה.
לְכָה דוֹדִי לִקְרַאת כַּלָּה, פְּנֵי שַׁבָּת נְקַבְּלָה.

שָׁמוֹר וְזָכוֹר בְּדִבּוּר אֶחָד
הִשְׁמִיעָנוּ אֵל הַמְיֻחָד
יְהֹוָה אֶחָד וּשְׁמוֹ אֶחָד
לְשֵׁם וּלְתִפְאֶרֶת וְלִתְהִלָּה.
לְכָה דוֹדִי לִקְרַאת כַּלָּה, פְּנֵי שַׁבָּת נְקַבְּלָה.

לִקְרַאת שַׁבָּת לְכוּ וְנֵלְכָה
כִּי הִיא מְקוֹר הַבְּרָכָה
מֵרֹאשׁ מִקֶּדֶם נְסוּכָה
סוֹף מַעֲשֶׂה בְּמַחֲשָׁבָה תְּחִלָּה.
לְכָה דוֹדִי לִקְרַאת כַּלָּה, פְּנֵי שַׁבָּת נְקַבְּלָה.

151

מִקְדַּשׁ מֶלֶךְ עִיר מְלוּכָה
קוּמִי צְאִי מִתּוֹךְ הַהֲפֵכָה
רַב לָךְ שֶׁבֶת בְּעֵמֶק הַבָּכָא
וְהוּא יַחֲמֹל עָלַיִךְ חֶמְלָה.
לְכָה דוֹדִי לִקְרַאת כַּלָּה, פְּנֵי שַׁבָּת נְקַבְּלָה.

הִתְנַעֲרִי, מֵעָפָר קוּמִי
לִבְשִׁי בִּגְדֵי תִפְאַרְתֵּךְ עַמִּי
עַל יַד בֶּן יִשַׁי בֵּית הַלַּחְמִי
קָרְבָה אֶל נַפְשִׁי, גְּאָלָהּ.
לְכָה דוֹדִי לִקְרַאת כַּלָּה, פְּנֵי שַׁבָּת נְקַבְּלָה.

הִתְעוֹרְרִי הִתְעוֹרְרִי
כִּי בָא אוֹרֵךְ קוּמִי אוֹרִי
עוּרִי עוּרִי, שִׁיר דַּבֵּרִי
כְּבוֹד יְהֹוָה עָלַיִךְ נִגְלָה.
לְכָה דוֹדִי לִקְרַאת כַּלָּה, פְּנֵי שַׁבָּת נְקַבְּלָה.

לֹא תֵבֹשִׁי וְלֹא תִכָּלְמִי
מַה תִּשְׁתּוֹחֲחִי וּמַה תֶּהֱמִי
בָּךְ יֶחֱסוּ עֲנִיֵּי עַמִּי
וְנִבְנְתָה עִיר עַל תִּלָּהּ.
לְכָה דוֹדִי לִקְרַאת כַּלָּה, פְּנֵי שַׁבָּת נְקַבְּלָה.

The *Tefilla* Text

The first appearance of the chorus – לְכָה דודי לקראת כלה, פני שַׁבָּת נקבלה – is highlighted in a color that depicts the setting of the sun.

The first letter of each verse is also highlighted, to draw our attention to the acrostic of the author Rabbi Shlomo HaLevi Alkabetz's name. The acrostic spells *שלמה הלוי*.

The Illustration

This illustration portrays the famous story of the kabbalists of Tzefat in the sixteenth century, who would go into the fields in the hills surrounding this holy city in Eretz Yisrael and, singing this *tefilla*, would greet and welcome Shabbat as if Shabbat was a beautiful bride entering the *ḥuppa*. We see the homes of Tzefat perched on a hillside as the sun gently sets on the hills of the Galil and the tranquility and spirituality of Shabbat is ushered in. The quote from the Gemara on the following page (from *Shabbat* 119a) was the inspiration for the manner in which the kabbalists of Tzefat would welcome the Shabbat Queen.

לכה דודי 2

pp. 152–153

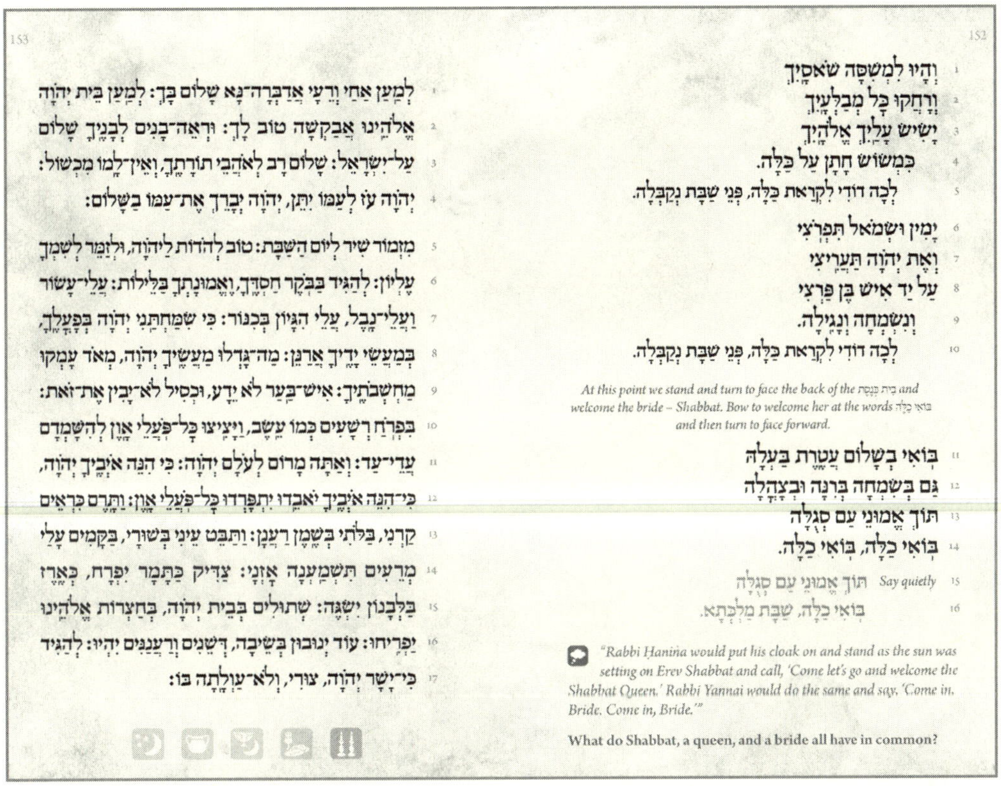

152

והיו למשסה שאסיך
ורחקו כל מבלעיך
ישיש עליך אלהיך
כמשוש חתן על כלה.
לכה דודי לקראת כלה, פני שבת נקבלה.

ימין ושמאל תפרצי
ואת יהוה תעריצי
על יד איש בן פרצי
ונשמחה ונגילה.
לכה דודי לקראת כלה, פני שבת נקבלה.

At this point we stand and turn to face the back of the בית כנסת *and welcome the bride – Shabbat. Bow to welcome her at the words* בואי כלה *and then turn to face forward.*

בואי בשלום עטרת בעלה
גם בשמחה ברנה ובצהלה
תוך אמוני עם סגלה
בואי כלה, בואי כלה.

Say quietly תוך אמוני עם סגלה
בואי כלה, שבת מלכתא.

"Rabbi Ḥanina would put his cloak on and stand as the sun was setting on Erev Shabbat and call, 'Come let's go and welcome the Shabbat Queen.' Rabbi Yannai would do the same and say, 'Come in, Bride. Come in, Bride.'"

What do Shabbat, a queen, and a bride all have in common?

153

למען אחי ורעי אדברה־נא שלום בך: למען בית יהוה
אלהינו אבקשה טוב לך: וראה־בנים לבניך שלום
על־ישראל: שלום רב לאהבי תורתך, ואין־למו מכשול:
יהוה עז לעמו יתן, יהוה יברך את־עמו בשלום:

מזמור שיר ליום השבת: טוב להדות ליהוה, ולזמר לשמך
עליון: להגיד בבקר חסדך, ואמונתך בלילות: עלי־עשור
ועלי־נבל, עלי הגיון בכנור: כי שמחתני יהוה בפעלך,
במעשי ידיך ארנן: מה־גדלו מעשיך יהוה, מאד עמקו
מחשבתיך: איש־בער לא ידע, וכסיל לא־יבין את־זאת:
בפרח רשעים כמו עשב, ויציצו כל־פעלי און להשמדם
עדי־עד: ואתה מרום לעלם יהוה: כי הנה איביך יהוה,
כי־הנה איביך יאבדו יתפרדו כל־פעלי און: ותרם כראים
קרני, בלתי בשמן רענן: ותבט עיני בשורי, בקמים עלי
מרעים תשמענה אזני: צדיק כתמר יפרח, כארז
בלבנון ישגה: שתולים בבית יהוה, בחצרות אלהינו
יפריחו: עוד ינובון בשיבה, דשנים ורעננים יהיו: להגיד
כי־ישר יהוה, צורי, ולא־עולתה בו:

The *Tefilla* Text

The last verse of the last stanza that is repeated – תוך אמוני עם סגולה, בואי כלה, בואי כלה – is highlighted in a color that depicts the setting of the sun.

The first letter of each verse is also highlighted in red-brown, to draw our attention to the acrostic of the author Rabbi Shlomo HaLevi Alkabetz's name. The acrostic spells שלמה הלוי.

The *Kavanot*

Conceptual Translation of:

לְכָה דודי לקראת כלָּה, פני שַׁבָּת נקבלָה

Thought Question:
The quote that begins this thought question, from *Shabbat* 119a, is the Talmudic source for the practice

of the sixteenth-century Tzefat kabbalists who would walk into the fields on the hills surrounding their city and welcome the Shabbat. No doubt it was an inspiration to the sixteenth-century author of this *tefilla*, Rabbi Shlomo HaLevi Alkabetz. The quote introduces us to the description of Shabbat as a queen (found at the end of this *tefilla* in the Sephardi siddur), and as a bride (as seen in *Lekha Dodi*). It also helps us to see Shabbat as something tangible, that needs respecting and observing, and not just something that happens to us (rather, we happen to Shabbat!). This is an important message for our children.

שמע 1

pp. 154–155

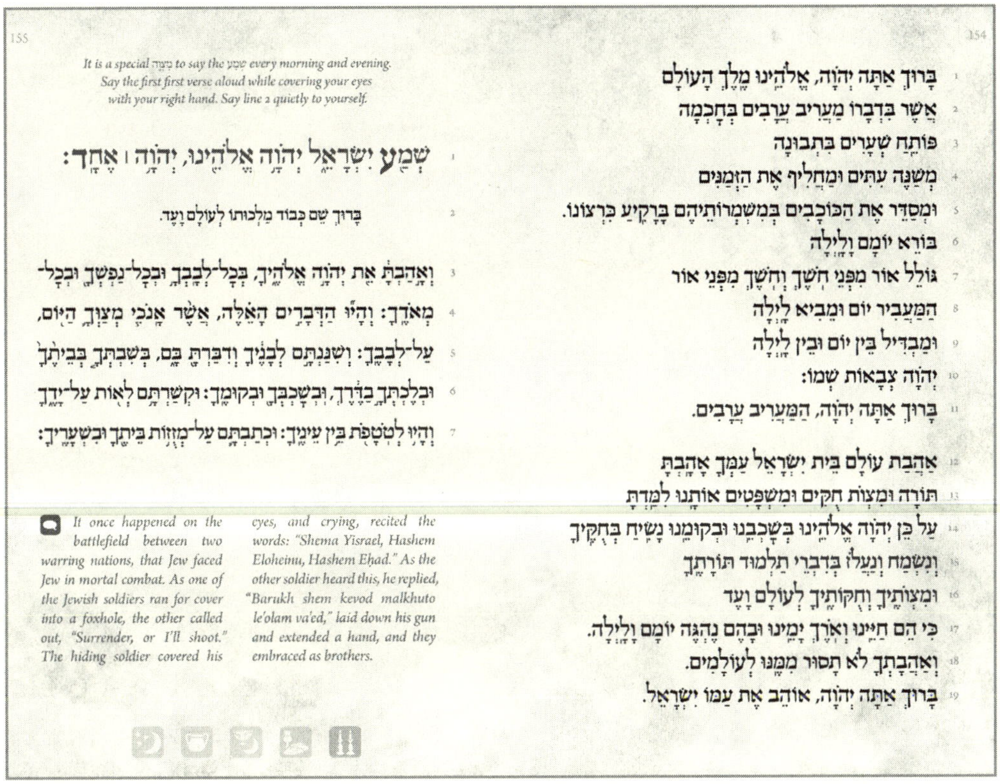

154

1 בָּרוּךְ אַתָּה יְהֹוָה, אֱלֹהֵינוּ מֶלֶךְ הָעוֹלָם
2 אֲשֶׁר בִּדְבָרוֹ מַעֲרִיב עֲרָבִים בְּחָכְמָה
3 פּוֹתֵחַ שְׁעָרִים בִּתְבוּנָה
4 מְשַׁנֶּה עִתִּים וּמַחֲלִיף אֶת הַזְּמַנִּים
5 וּמְסַדֵּר אֶת הַכּוֹכָבִים בְּמִשְׁמְרוֹתֵיהֶם בָּרָקִיעַ כִּרְצוֹנוֹ.
6 בּוֹרֵא יוֹמָם וָלָיְלָה
7 גּוֹלֵל אוֹר מִפְּנֵי חֹשֶׁךְ וְחֹשֶׁךְ מִפְּנֵי אוֹר
8 הַמַּעֲבִיר יוֹם וּמֵבִיא לָיְלָה
9 וּמַבְדִּיל בֵּין יוֹם וּבֵין לָיְלָה
10 יְהֹוָה צְבָאוֹת שְׁמוֹ:
11 בָּרוּךְ אַתָּה יְהֹוָה, הַמַּעֲרִיב עֲרָבִים.

12 אַהֲבַת עוֹלָם בֵּית יִשְׂרָאֵל עַמְּךָ אָהָבְתָּ
13 תּוֹרָה וּמִצְוֹת חֻקִּים וּמִשְׁפָּטִים אוֹתָנוּ לִמַּדְתָּ
14 עַל כֵּן יְהֹוָה אֱלֹהֵינוּ בְּשָׁכְבֵנוּ וּבְקוּמֵנוּ נָשִׂיחַ בְּחֻקֶּיךָ
15 וְנִשְׂמַח וְנַעֲלֹז בְּדִבְרֵי תַלְמוּד תּוֹרָתֶךָ
16 וּמִצְוֹתֶיךָ וְחֻקּוֹתֶיךָ לְעוֹלָם וָעֶד
17 כִּי הֵם חַיֵּינוּ וְאֹרֶךְ יָמֵינוּ וּבָהֶם נֶהְגֶּה יוֹמָם וָלָיְלָה.
18 וְאַהֲבָתְךָ לֹא תָסוּר מִמֶּנּוּ לְעוֹלָמִים.
19 בָּרוּךְ אַתָּה יְהֹוָה, אוֹהֵב אֶת עַמּוֹ יִשְׂרָאֵל.

155

It is a special מִצְוָה *to say the* שְׁמַע *every morning and evening. Say the first first verse aloud while covering your eyes with your right hand. Say line 2 quietly to yourself.*

1 שְׁמַע יִשְׂרָאֵל יְהֹוָה אֱלֹהֵינוּ, יְהֹוָה ׀ אֶחָד:
2 בָּרוּךְ שֵׁם כְּבוֹד מַלְכוּתוֹ לְעוֹלָם וָעֶד.
3 וְאָהַבְתָּ אֵת יְהֹוָה אֱלֹהֶיךָ, בְּכָל־לְבָבְךָ וּבְכָל־נַפְשְׁךָ וּבְכָל־
4 מְאֹדֶךָ: וְהָיוּ הַדְּבָרִים הָאֵלֶּה, אֲשֶׁר אָנֹכִי מְצַוְּךָ הַיּוֹם,
5 עַל־לְבָבֶךָ: וְשִׁנַּנְתָּם לְבָנֶיךָ וְדִבַּרְתָּ בָּם, בְּשִׁבְתְּךָ בְּבֵיתֶךָ
6 וּבְלֶכְתְּךָ בַדֶּרֶךְ, וּבְשָׁכְבְּךָ וּבְקוּמֶךָ: וּקְשַׁרְתָּם לְאוֹת עַל־יָדֶךָ
7 וְהָיוּ לְטֹטָפֹת בֵּין עֵינֶיךָ: וּכְתַבְתָּם עַל־מְזֻזוֹת בֵּיתֶךָ וּבִשְׁעָרֶיךָ:

It once happened on the battlefield between two warring nations, that Jew faced Jew in mortal combat. As one of the Jewish soldiers ran for cover into a foxhole, the other called out, "Surrender, or I'll shoot." The hiding soldier covered his eyes, and crying, recited the words: "Shema Yisrael, Hashem Eloheinu, Hashem Eḥad." As the other soldier heard this, he replied, "Barukh shem kevod malkhuto le'olam va'ed," laid down his gun and extended a hand, and they embraced as brothers.

The *Tefilla* Text

The first line of the *Shema* – שמע ישראל יהוה אלהינו יהוה אחד – is highlighted in the color of the story.

The *Kavanot*

Story:
This powerful story has many incarnations, from many conflicts in history where Jews were pitted against each other fighting for their host country. The best known citing is in S. Ansky's "*The Enemy at His Pleasure: A Journey through the Jewish Pale of Settlement During World War I*" in which he reports ten different versions of the same story. However, there is reason to believe that the story may have pre-dated WWI (that is not to say it didn't also happen during WWI as

well).[47] This particular version of the story is based on a telling from the Falkland's War in 1982, between Britain and Argentina.[48]

The powerful imagery of the story inspires us to realize how the *Shema* is a universal and ultimate declaration of Jewish faith and identity in the Jewish world, and while Jews may differ in their appearance and language and culture and even national allegiance at any point in Jewish history, we are all part of one people and one nation, and the *Shema* reminds us of that.

47. Research on this can be found here: http://onthemainline.blogspot.co.il/2009/11/two-soldiers-and-shema-yisrael.html
48. This has been reported here: http://www.thejc.com/node/67100

שמע 2

pp. 156–157

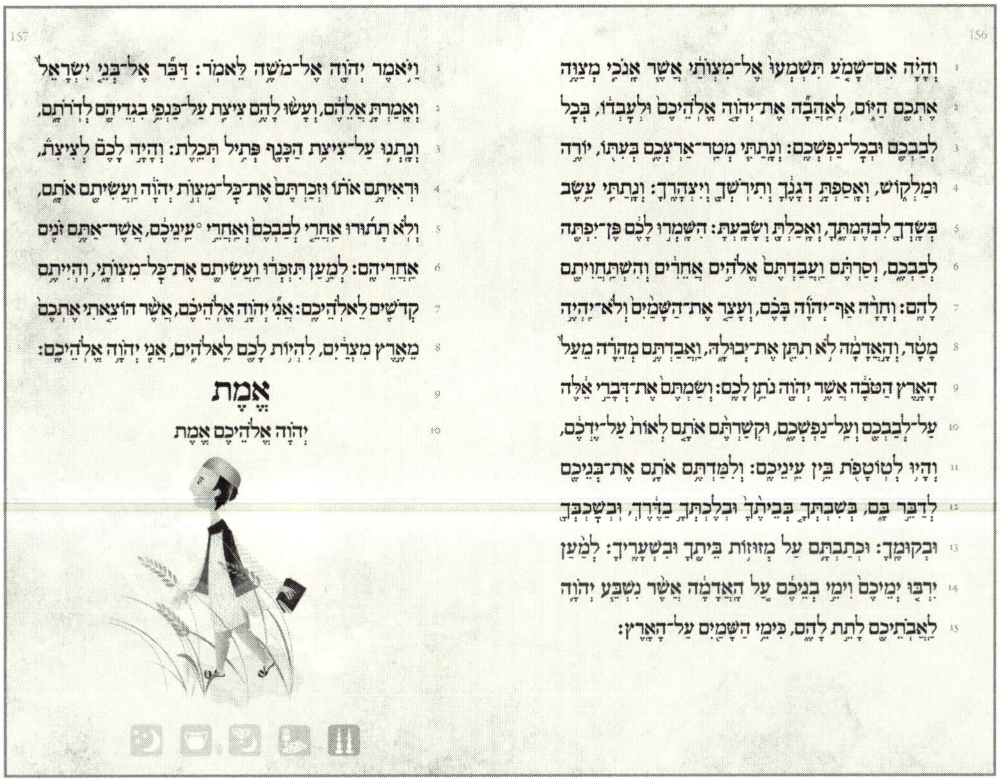

156

והיה אם־שמע תשמעו אל־מצותי אשר אנכי מצוה
אתכם היום, לאהבה את־יהוה אלהיכם ולעבדו, בכל
לבבכם ובכל־נפשכם: ונתתי מטר־ארצכם בעתו, יורה
ומלקוש, ואספת דגנך ותירשך ויצהרך: ונתתי עשב
בשדך לבהמתך, ואכלת ושבעת: השמרו לכם פן־יפתה
לבבכם, וסרתם ועבדתם אלהים אחרים והשתחויתם
להם: וחרה אף־יהוה בכם, ועצר את־השמים ולא־יהיה
מטר, והאדמה לא תתן את־יבולה, ואבדתם מהרה מעל
הארץ הטבה אשר יהוה נתן לכם: ושמתם את־דברי אלה
על־לבבכם ועל־נפשכם, וקשרתם אתם לאות על־ידכם,
והיו לטוטפת בין עיניכם: ולמדתם אתם את־בניכם
לדבר בם, בשבתך בביתך ובלכתך בדרך, ובשכבך
ובקומך: וכתבתם על מזוזות ביתך ובשעריך: למען
ירבו ימיכם וימי בניכם על האדמה אשר נשבע יהוה
לאבתיכם לתת להם, כימי השמים על־הארץ:

157

ויאמר יהוה אל־משה לאמר: דבר אל־בני ישראל
ואמרת אלהם, ועשו להם ציצת על־כנפי בגדיהם לדרתם,
ונתנו על־ציצת הכנף פתיל תכלת: והיה לכם לציצת,
וראיתם אתו וזכרתם את־כל־מצות יהוה ועשיתם אתם,
ולא תתורו אחרי לבבכם ואחרי °עיניכם, אשר־אתם זנים
אחריהם: למען תזכרו ועשיתם את־כל־מצותי, והייתם
קדשים לאלהיכם: אני יהוה אלהיכם, אשר הוצאתי אתכם
מארץ מצרים, להיות לכם לאלהים, אני יהוה אלהיכם:

אמת

יהוה אלהיכם אמת

The Illustration

In the second paragraph of the *Shema* on page 78 of the siddur in the weekday section, we find the same biblical character as this page, harvesting the ears of grain with which he has been blessed by Hashem. The second paragraph of the *Shema* focuses on the accepting of the yoke of mitzvot observance, and the text sets up a covenant between God and His people. If we keep His commandments, then He will ensure that the weather conditions are conducive to prosperity and wealth and that is what we see in the illustration there. Here, it is Shabbat, and we have the same character wearing his best Shabbat clothes, walking on his way to the *Beit Kenesset*, past the field where he spends his week toiling, ignoring the trappings and stress of that part of his life, as he becomes part of nature and the environment, and spends 25 hours at peace with the world.

ושמרו

pp. 158–159

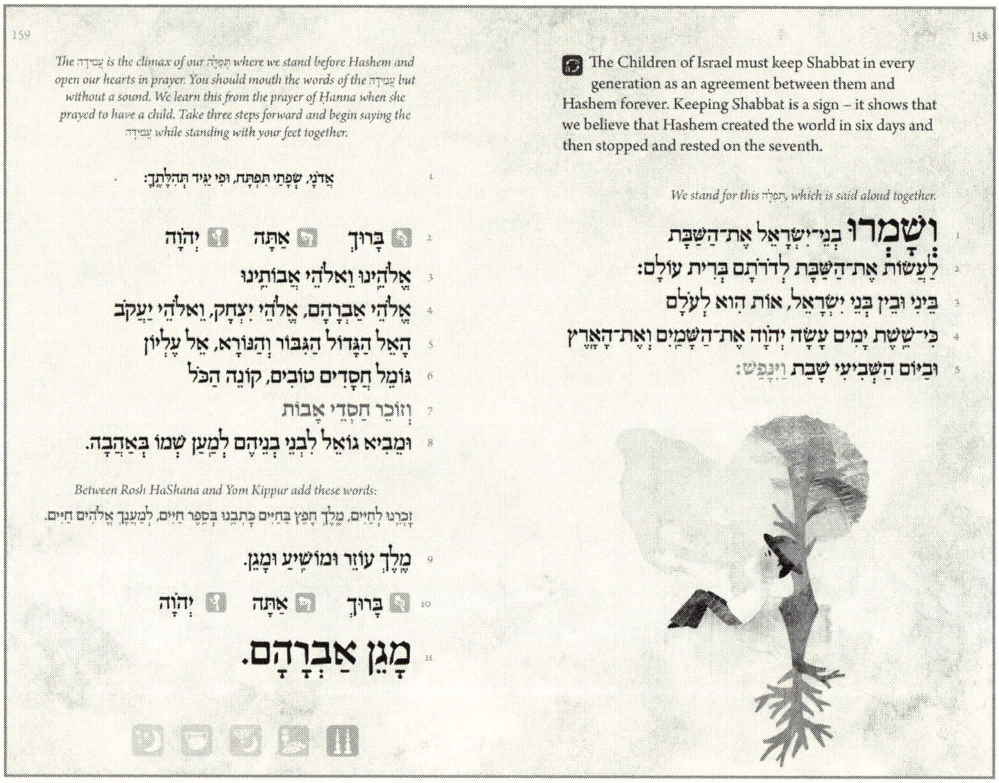

158

The Children of Israel must keep Shabbat in every generation as an agreement between them and Hashem forever. Keeping Shabbat is a sign – it shows that we believe that Hashem created the world in six days and then stopped and rested on the seventh.

We stand for this תְּפִלָּה, which is said aloud together.

1 וְשָׁמְרוּ בְנֵי־יִשְׂרָאֵל אֶת־הַשַּׁבָּת
2 לַעֲשׂוֹת אֶת־הַשַּׁבָּת לְדֹרֹתָם בְּרִית עוֹלָם:
3 בֵּינִי וּבֵין בְּנֵי יִשְׂרָאֵל, אוֹת הִוא לְעֹלָם
4 כִּי־שֵׁשֶׁת יָמִים עָשָׂה יְהוָה אֶת־הַשָּׁמַיִם וְאֶת־הָאָרֶץ
5 וּבַיּוֹם הַשְּׁבִיעִי שָׁבַת וַיִּנָּפַשׁ:

159

The עֲמִידָה is the climax of our תְּפִלָּה where we stand before Hashem and open our hearts in prayer. You should mouth the words of the עֲמִידָה but without a sound. We learn this from the prayer of Ḥanna when she prayed to have a child. Take three steps forward and begin saying the עֲמִידָה while standing with your feet together.

1 אֲדֹנָי, שְׂפָתַי תִּפְתָּח, וּפִי יַגִּיד תְּהִלָּתֶךָ:
2 בָּרוּךְ אַתָּה יְהוָה
3 אֱלֹהֵינוּ וֵאלֹהֵי אֲבוֹתֵינוּ
4 אֱלֹהֵי אַבְרָהָם, אֱלֹהֵי יִצְחָק, וֵאלֹהֵי יַעֲקֹב
5 הָאֵל הַגָּדוֹל הַגִּבּוֹר וְהַנּוֹרָא, אֵל עֶלְיוֹן
6 גּוֹמֵל חֲסָדִים טוֹבִים, קוֹנֵה הַכֹּל
7 וְזוֹכֵר חַסְדֵי אָבוֹת
8 וּמֵבִיא גוֹאֵל לִבְנֵי בְנֵיהֶם לְמַעַן שְׁמוֹ בְּאַהֲבָה.

Between Rosh HaShana and Yom Kippur add these words:

זָכְרֵנוּ לְחַיִּים, מֶלֶךְ חָפֵץ בַּחַיִּים, וְכָתְבֵנוּ בְּסֵפֶר הַחַיִּים, לְמַעַנְךָ אֱלֹהִים חַיִּים.

9 מֶלֶךְ עוֹזֵר וּמוֹשִׁיעַ וּמָגֵן.
10 בָּרוּךְ אַתָּה יְהוָה
11 מָגֵן אַבְרָהָם.

The *Tefilla* Text

The word וינפש is highlighted in the green of the tree in the illustration, and the words וזוכר חסדי אָבות are highlighted in the brown of the roots of the tree in the illustration.

The Illustration

The illustration on this page is a reappearance of the "*Avot* Tree" found on page 90, in the weekday *Amida*. The "*Avot* Tree" is a metaphor for the role of the *Avot* as the roots of the tree that is the Jewish people. For the Jewish people to thrive and be healthy, the tree must have an elaborate system of roots. Roots give the tree nutrition and sustain it, provide vital irrigation, and ensure stability for the tree, so it won't be blown over in the wind. So our ancestors, the *Avot* and *Imahot*, provide these things for us. They provide spiritual sustenance, in the form of inspiration and role modeling, and they provide stability and protection, through their meritorious acts and relationship with God (*zekhut avot*). Today, Shabbat, the tree is also providing a place of tranquil rest, and protection from the sun.

The *Kavanot*

Conceptual Translation of:

וְשָׁמְרוּ בְנֵי-יִשְׂרָאֵל, אֶת-הַשַּׁבָּת, לַעֲשׂוֹת אֶת-הַשַּׁבָּת לְדֹרֹתָם, בְּרִית עוֹלָם. בֵּינִי, וּבֵין בְּנֵי יִשְׂרָאֵל--אוֹת הִוא, לְעֹלָם: כִּי-שֵׁשֶׁת יָמִים, עָשָׂה ה' אֶת-הַשָּׁמַיִם וְאֶת-הָאָרֶץ, וּבַיּוֹם הַשְּׁבִיעִי, שָׁבַת וַיִּנָּפַשׁ.

גבורה/קדושת השם

pp. 160–161

160

1 אַתָּה גִּבּוֹר לְעוֹלָם, אֲדֹנָי

2 מְחַיֵּה מֵתִים אַתָּה, רַב לְהוֹשִׁיעַ

Between Simḥat Torah and Pesaḥ add these words:

3 מַשִּׁיב הָרְוּחַ וּמוֹרִיד הַגֶּשֶׁם

If you are in Israel between Pesaḥ and Shemini Atzeret add these words:

מוֹרִיד הַטָּל

4 מְכַלְכֵּל חַיִּים בְּחֶסֶד, מְחַיֵּה מֵתִים בְּרַחֲמִים רַבִּים

5 סוֹמֵךְ נוֹפְלִים, וְרוֹפֵא חוֹלִים, וּמַתִּיר אֲסוּרִים

6 וּמְקַיֵּם אֱמוּנָתוֹ לִישֵׁנֵי עָפָר.

7 מִי כָמְוֹךָ, בַּעַל גְּבוּרוֹת

8 וּמִי דּוֹמֶה לָּךְ

9 מֶלֶךְ, מֵמִית וּמְחַיֶּה וּמַצְמִיחַ יְשׁוּעָה.

Between Rosh HaShana and Yom Kippur add these words:

10 מִי כָמְוֹךָ אַב הָרַחֲמָן, זוֹכֵר יְצוּרָיו בְּרַחֲמִים לְחַיִּים.

11 וְנֶאֱמָן אַתָּה לְהַחֲיוֹת מֵתִים.

12 בָּרוּךְ אַתָּה יְהֹוָה

13 **מְחַיֵּה הַמֵּתִים.**

161

1 אַתָּה קָדוֹשׁ וְשִׁמְךָ קָדוֹשׁ

2 וּקְדוֹשִׁים בְּכָל יוֹם יְהַלְלְוּךָ סֶּלָה.

3 בָּרוּךְ אַתָּה יְהֹוָה

4 **הָאֵל הַקָּדוֹשׁ.**

Between Rosh HaShana and Yom Kippur change the ending of this בְּרָכָה to these words:

הַמֶּלֶךְ הַקָּדוֹשׁ.

Eliezer had a trusty cow that worked hard for him all week long. When it came to Shabbat they both rested from a hard week of work. The time came when Eliezer had to sell his cow, and he got a good price from his non-Jewish neighbor. After a few days the neighbor returned with the cow, frustrated and angry. "Your cow is hard working," said the neighbor, "but every Saturday she refuses to work. I tried everything but she only works for six days a week! I demand a refund." Eliezer then whispered something into the ear of the cow, who immediately got up and returned to her new owner's field to begin working. Shocked, the man asked Eliezer what he told the cow. Eliezer told him that he explained to the cow that she no longer belonged to a Jew and so it was now okay for her to work on Shabbat. The non-Jew was so moved by this, that he pledged to learn more about his Creator and promised that he too would allow the cow to rest every Shabbat.

The *Kavanot*

Story:
This sweet story presents the place of animals in Shabbat observance. We know from the verse said in *Kiddush* on Shabbat day (Shemot 20:9, page 230) that the injunction to rest on Shabbat includes giving our domestic animals rest too. The question is whether that is because we should not benefit from work on Shabbat, even if it is performed by an animal, or whether it is because animals deserve a day of rest too. Rambam seems to rule the latter in his *Mishneh Torah* (*Hilkhot Shabbat* 20:1) and uses the verse Shemot 23:12 as his proof text. Eliezer's anthropomorphized cow seems to understand this halakha, and refuses to work on Shabbat, until Eliezer explains to him that the halakha no longer applies to him because he is no longer owned by a Jew. The non-Jew was so moved by the cow's understanding and commitment to this (and perhaps to the humanity in the laws of Shabbat) that he decided to learn more about Judaism (and to let his cow continue to rest on Shabbat!).

קדושת היום

pp. 162–163

162

1 אַתָּה קִדַּשְׁתָּ אֶת יוֹם הַשְּׁבִיעִי לִשְׁמֶךָ
2 תַּכְלִית מַעֲשֵׂה שָׁמַיִם וָאָרֶץ
3 וּבֵרַכְתּוֹ מִכָּל הַיָּמִים, וְקִדַּשְׁתּוֹ מִכָּל הַזְּמַנִּים
4 וְכֵן כָּתוּב בְּתוֹרָתָךְ
5 וַיְכֻלּוּ הַשָּׁמַיִם
6 וְהָאָרֶץ וְכָל־צְבָאָם:
7 וַיְכַל אֱלֹהִים בַּיּוֹם הַשְּׁבִיעִי
8 מְלַאכְתּוֹ אֲשֶׁר עָשָׂה
9 וַיִּשְׁבֹּת בַּיּוֹם הַשְּׁבִיעִי
10 מִכָּל־מְלַאכְתּוֹ אֲשֶׁר עָשָׂה:
11 וַיְבָרֶךְ אֱלֹהִים אֶת־יוֹם הַשְּׁבִיעִי, וַיְקַדֵּשׁ אֹתוֹ
12 כִּי בוֹ שָׁבַת מִכָּל־מְלַאכְתּוֹ, אֲשֶׁר־בָּרָא אֱלֹהִים לַעֲשׂוֹת:

It is written in Your Torah: Hashem finished creating the heaven and the earth on the seventh day, and then rested from all the work He had done. And Hashem blessed it – He made it special.

"More than the Jews have kept Shabbat, Shabbat has kept the Jews."

What does Shabbat do for you?

"The Mashiaḥ will come if all Jews keep just one Shabbat, because Shabbat is equal to all the other mitzvot."

Why do you think Shabbat is equal to all the other mitzvot?

163

1 אֱלֹהֵינוּ וֵאלֹהֵי אֲבוֹתֵינוּ, רְצֵה נָא בִמְנוּחָתֵנוּ.
2 קַדְּשֵׁנוּ בְּמִצְוֹתֶיךָ, שִׂים חֶלְקֵנוּ בְּתוֹרָתֶךָ
3 שַׂבְּעֵנוּ מִטּוּבָךְ, שַׂמֵּחַ נַפְשֵׁנוּ בִּישׁוּעָתָךְ
4 וְטַהֵר לִבֵּנוּ לְעָבְדְּךָ בֶּאֱמֶת.
5 וְהַנְחִילֵנוּ, יְהוָה אֱלֹהֵינוּ
6 בְּאַהֲבָה וּבְרָצוֹן שַׁבַּת קָדְשֶׁךָ
7 וְיָנוּחוּ בָהּ כָּל יִשְׂרָאֵל מְקַדְּשֵׁי שְׁמֶךָ.
8 בָּרוּךְ אַתָּה יְהוָה
9 מְקַדֵּשׁ הַשַּׁבָּת.

The *Tefilla* Text

The words תכלית מַעֲשֵׂה שָׁמַיִם וָאָרֶץ are highlighted in the turquoise of the creation scene in the illustration.

The Illustration

In this illustration, we have a depiction of a creation scene, linked to the verses from the first chapter of Bereshit which describe it. We have sky and the heavens, the land and the sea, vegetation and animals. The illustration is missing man, and asks the child to place themselves in the scene and see themselves as part of the original creation story, that still continues today.

Conceptual Translation of:

ויכלו השָׁמים והָאָרץ, וכָל-צבָאָם. ויכל אלהים ביום השביעי, מלאכתו אֲשר עָשָׂה; וישבת ביום השביעי, מכָל-מלאכתו אֲשר עָשָׂה. ויבָרך אלהים את-יום השביעי, ויקדש אתו: כי בו שָׁבת מכָל-מלאכתו, אֲשר-בָרָא אלהים לעֲשׂות.

Thought Question 1:

This famous quote, from the early Zionist thinker Aḥad Ha'am (Asher Ginsberg) in *Al Parashat Derakhim* 51,[49] asks the reader to reflect on the national impact of Shabbat observance. What impact does Shabbat observance have on each of us as individuals, and on us as a people? Is Shabbat a good opportunity to recharge our physical and spiritual batteries? Has Shabbat observance prevented complete assimilation into the non-Jewish societies where Jews have been living for the past two thousand years? In what other ways can Shabbat be seen as important to the survival of the Jewish people? The thought question that follows asks the child to relate this to their own lives, on a more personal rather than national level.

Thought Question 2:

This often cited idea comes from the Midrash (*Shemot Raba* 25:121) and the Talmud (Yerushalmi, *Ta'anit* 1:10). Perhaps the message is that if everyone really experienced the tranquility and peace that Shabbat brings, then the *Tikkun Olam* necessary for the arrival of Mashiaḥ would happen naturally. The follow-up thought question pushes the reader to consider what values and experiences are inherent in observing Shabbat that led *Ḥazal* to equate Shabbat with all the other mitzvot. The answer probably lies in the verse Shemot 31:17 in which Shabbat is described as an אות – a sign that the world was created by God. By keeping Shabbat we are making a declaration that we believe that God created the world ex nihilo, and remains involved in it to this day. This is the basis of our faith and the entire Torah.

49. This idea is also quoted by Rav Waldenberg, *Tzitz Eliezer* 12:92; and a similar idea appears in the *Kuzari* 3:10.

הודאה/שלום

pp. 166–167

166

During Ḥanukka say עַל הַנִּסִּים:

עַל הַנִּסִּים וְעַל הַפֻּרְקָן וְעַל הַגְּבוּרוֹת וְעַל הַתְּשׁוּעוֹת וְעַל הַנִּפְלָאוֹת וְעַל הַנֶּחָמוֹת שֶׁעָשִׂיתָ לַאֲבוֹתֵינוּ בַּיָּמִים הָהֵם בַּזְּמַן הַזֶּה.

בִּימֵי מַתִּתְיָה בֶּן יוֹחָנָן כֹּהֵן גָּדוֹל חַשְׁמוֹנַאי וּבָנָיו, כְּשֶׁעָמְדָה מַלְכוּת יָוָן הָרְשָׁעָה עַל עַמְּךָ יִשְׂרָאֵל לְשַׁכְּחָם תּוֹרָתָךְ וּלְהַעֲבִירָם מֵחֻקֵּי רְצוֹנָךְ, וְאַתָּה בְּרַחֲמֶיךָ הָרַבִּים עָמַדְתָּ לָהֶם בְּעֵת צָרָתָם, רַבְתָּ אֶת רִיבָם, דַּנְתָּ אֶת דִּינָם, נָקַמְתָּ אֶת נִקְמָתָם, מָסַרְתָּ גִבּוֹרִים בְּיַד חַלָּשִׁים, וְרַבִּים בְּיַד מְעַטִּים, וּרְשָׁעִים בְּיַד צַדִּיקִים, וּטְמֵאִים בְּיַד טְהוֹרִים, וְזֵדִים בְּיַד עוֹסְקֵי תוֹרָתֶךָ. לְךָ עָשִׂיתָ שֵׁם גָּדוֹל וְקָדוֹשׁ בְּעוֹלָמָךְ, וּלְעַמְּךָ יִשְׂרָאֵל עָשִׂיתָ תְּשׁוּעָה גְדוֹלָה וּפֻרְקָן כְּהַיּוֹם הַזֶּה. וְאַחַר כָּךְ בָּאוּ בָנֶיךָ לִדְבִיר בֵּיתֶךָ, וּפִנּוּ אֶת הֵיכָלֶךָ, וְטִהֲרוּ אֶת מִקְדָּשֶׁךָ, וְהִדְלִיקוּ נֵרוֹת בְּחַצְרוֹת קָדְשֶׁךָ, וְקָבְעוּ שְׁמוֹנַת יְמֵי חֲנֻכָּה אֵלּוּ, בְּהַלֵּל וּבְהוֹדָאָה, וְעָשִׂיתָ עִמָּהֶם נִסִּים וְנִפְלָאוֹת, וְנוֹדֶה לְשִׁמְךָ הַגָּדוֹל, סֶלָה.

וְעַל כֻּלָּם
יִתְבָּרַךְ וְיִתְרוֹמַם וְיִתְנַשֵּׂא תָּמִיד שִׁמְךָ מַלְכֵּנוּ לְעוֹלָם וָעֶד
וְכָל הַחַיִּים יוֹדוּךָ סֶּלָה

Between Rosh HaShana and Yom Kippur add these words:

וּכְתֹב לְחַיִּים טוֹבִים כָּל בְּנֵי בְרִיתֶךָ.

וִיהַלְלוּ וִיבָרְכוּ אֶת שִׁמְךָ הַגָּדוֹל בֶּאֱמֶת לְעוֹלָם כִּי טוֹב
הָאֵל יְשׁוּעָתֵנוּ וְעֶזְרָתֵנוּ סֶלָה, הָאֵל הַטּוֹב.
בָּרוּךְ אַתָּה יְהֹוָה
הַטּוֹב שִׁמְךָ וּלְךָ נָאֶה לְהוֹדוֹת.

167

שִׂים שָׁלוֹם טוֹבָה וּבְרָכָה
חַיִּים חֵן וָחֶסֶד, צְדָקָה וְרַחֲמִים
עָלֵינוּ וְעַל כָּל יִשְׂרָאֵל עַמֶּךָ.
וּבָרְכֵנוּ אָבִינוּ כֻּלָּנוּ כְּאֶחָד בְּאוֹר פָּנֶיךָ
כִּי בְאוֹר פָּנֶיךָ נָתַתָּ לָּנוּ, יְהֹוָה אֱלֹהֵינוּ
תּוֹרָה וְחַיִּים, אַהֲבָה וָחֶסֶד, צְדָקָה וְרַחֲמִים, בְּרָכָה וְשָׁלוֹם.
וְטוֹב בְּעֵינֶיךָ לְבָרְכֵנוּ, וּלְבָרֵךְ אֶת כָּל עַמְּךָ יִשְׂרָאֵל
בְּרֹב עֹז וְשָׁלוֹם.

Between Rosh HaShana and Yom Kippur add these words:

וּבְסֵפֶר חַיִּים, בְּרָכָה וְשָׁלוֹם, וּפַרְנָסָה טוֹבָה, וִישׁוּעָה וְנֶחָמָה, וּגְזֵרוֹת טוֹבוֹת, נִזָּכֵר וְנִכָּתֵב לְפָנֶיךָ, אֲנַחְנוּ וְכָל עַמְּךָ יִשְׂרָאֵל, לְחַיִּים טוֹבִים וּלְשָׁלוֹם.

בָּרוּךְ אַתָּה יְהֹוָה
הַמְבָרֵךְ אֶת עַמּוֹ
יִשְׂרָאֵל בַּשָּׁלוֹם. אָמֵן

יִהְיוּ לְרָצוֹן אִמְרֵי־פִי וְהֶגְיוֹן לִבִּי לְפָנֶיךָ, יְהֹוָה צוּרִי וְגוֹאֲלִי:

Why do you think these two *berakhot* follow each other?
How do you think saying "thank you" can lead to peace?

The *Tefilla* Text

The concluding words of the *berakha* of *Hoda'a* – וְלָךְ נָאֶה להודות – and the concluding words of the *berakha* of *Shalom* – המְבָרֵךְ את עמו יִשְׂרָאֵל בשָׁלום – are highlighted in the color of the thought question.

The *Kavanot*

Conceptual Translation of:
שָׁלוֹם רָב עַל יִשְׂרָאֵל עַמְּךָ תָּשִׂים לְעוֹלָם כִּי אתה הוא מֶלֶךְ אָדוֹן לְכָל הַשָּׁלוֹם. וטוב בעינֶיךָ לְבָרֵךְ את עמךָ יִשְׂרָאֵל בכָל עֵת ובכָל שָׁעָה בשלומֶךָ. בָּרוּךְ אתה ה' המברך את עמו יִשְׂרָאֵל בשָׁלום.

Thought Question:
These two berakhot are found in juxtaposition in every *Amida*. While we are primarily thanking Hashem and asking Him for peace, there is a message contained

in the proximity of the two concepts. Showing gratitude leads to humility. Showing gratitude to people connects you to them and brings you closer to them. These both lead to peace between people and increase peace in our world.

אלהי נצר

pp. 168–169

168

1 אֱלֹהַי
2 נְצֹר לְשׁוֹנִי מֵרָע וּשְׂפָתַי מִדַּבֵּר מִרְמָה
3 וְלִמְקַלְלַי נַפְשִׁי תִדֹּם, וְנַפְשִׁי כֶּעָפָר לַכֹּל תִּהְיֶה.
4 פְּתַח לִבִּי בְּתוֹרָתֶךָ, וְאַחֲרֵי מִצְוֹתֶיךָ תִּרְדֹּף נַפְשִׁי.
5 וְכָל הַקָּמִים עָלַי לְרָעָה
6 מְהֵרָה הָפֵר עֲצָתָם וְקַלְקֵל מַחְשְׁבוֹתָם.
7 יִהְיוּ כְּמֹץ לִפְנֵי־רוּחַ וּמַלְאַךְ יְהוָה דּוֹחֶה:
8 עֲשֵׂה לְמַעַן שְׁמָךְ, עֲשֵׂה לְמַעַן יְמִינָךְ
9 עֲשֵׂה לְמַעַן תּוֹרָתָךְ, עֲשֵׂה לְמַעַן קְדֻשָּׁתָךְ.
10 לְמַעַן יֵחָלְצוּן יְדִידֶיךָ, הוֹשִׁיעָה יְמִינְךָ וַעֲנֵנִי:
11 יִהְיוּ לְרָצוֹן אִמְרֵי־פִי וְהֶגְיוֹן לִבִּי לְפָנֶיךָ, יְהוָה צוּרִי וְגֹאֲלִי:

"If you only have enough money to buy either Shabbat candles, or wine for *kiddush*, or Ḥanukkah candles, then you should buy Shabbat candles because they create *Shalom Bayit*."

How can the Shabbat candles provide *shalom* in your house?

How can you provide *shalom* in your house this Shabbat?

169

As you finish the עֲמִידָה *you should stop and think that you have just had the opportunity and honor to stand before Hashem. To be respectful, bow as you take three steps back. Then bow to the left, right and center as the pictures show.*

Between Rosh HaShana and Yom Kippur say הַשָּׁלוֹם *instead of* שָׁלוֹם.

12 עֹשֶׂה שָׁלוֹם / הַשָּׁלוֹם / בִּמְרוֹמָיו
13 הוּא בְּרַחֲמָיו יַעֲשֶׂה שָׁלוֹם עָלֵינוּ
14 וְעַל כָּל עַמּוֹ יִשְׂרָאֵל
15 וְאִמְרוּ אָמֵן.

The *Tefilla* Text

Each time it appears, the word שָׁלוֹם is highlighted in the color of the dove from the illustration.

The Illustration

Our familiar friend, the harbinger of peace, is with us once again. The white dove is traditionally seen as a symbol of peace. This comes from the story of Noaḥ and the flood. At the conclusion of the flood Noaḥ let a dove fly free to determine if the waters were abating. The dove returned to him with an olive branch (also a symbol of peace for the same reason) to demonstrate that the waters were in fact receding, and the world was entering a new peaceful age after the destruction of the flood. Here we have the *yona* flying to meet our character who is dressed in her finest Shabbat dress, sitting on a bench watching the peaceful Shabbat world around her. The *yona* can also be found on pages 130, 132, 209, and 256.

The *Kavanot*

Thought Question:
This quote is from the Gemara, *Shabbat*, 23b. Rambam codifies this halakhic position in his *Mishneh Torah*, where he concludes his Laws of Ḥanukka (4:14) with this quote:

> If one is confronted with the [simultaneous mitzva] to light one's household lamp [for Shabbat] and to light the Ḥanukka lamp… then the [Shabbat] household lamp takes precedence because it contributes to *shalom bayit* (domestic peace and tranquility). After all, the divine name is also to be erased [in the biblical ritual of the wife suspected of adultery – *Sota*] in order to facilitate the making of peace between man and woman. Great is *shalom* (peace)! For the whole Torah was given to make peace in the world as it says in the Bible: "Its ways are ways of pleasantness and all its paths are peace" (Mishlei 3:17).

The link between Shabbat and *shalom* is clear, and is explored on each page of this siddur where the *berakha* of *Shalom* appears in the Shabbat section (pages 208 and 225). The classic greeting of "Shabbat Shalom" can be a powerful message if we explore it. Light and warmth lead to comfort in the family home, and this will lead to the opportunity for love and togetherness. *Shalom Bayit* is a core value in Judaism, and these questions ask the child to consider how they will contribute to the *shalom* in their house this Shabbat.

עלינו

pp. 170–171

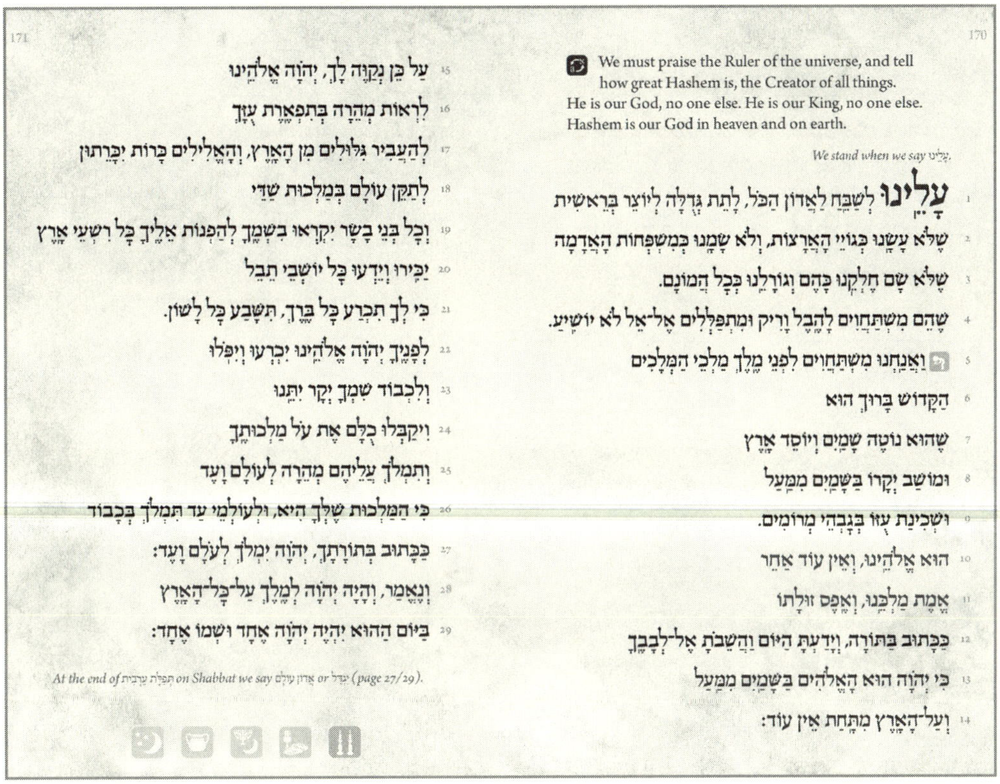

170

We must praise the Ruler of the universe, and tell how great Hashem is, the Creator of all things.
He is our God, no one else. He is our King, no one else.
Hashem is our God in heaven and on earth.

We stand when we say עָלֵינוּ.

עָלֵינוּ לְשַׁבֵּחַ לַאֲדוֹן הַכֹּל, לָתֵת גְּדֻלָּה לְיוֹצֵר בְּרֵאשִׁית
שֶׁלֹּא עָשָׂנוּ כְּגוֹיֵי הָאֲרָצוֹת, וְלֹא שָׂמָנוּ כְּמִשְׁפְּחוֹת הָאֲדָמָה
שֶׁלֹּא שָׂם חֶלְקֵנוּ כָּהֶם וְגוֹרָלֵנוּ כְּכָל הֲמוֹנָם.
שֶׁהֵם מִשְׁתַּחֲוִים לָהֶבֶל וָרִיק וּמִתְפַּלְּלִים אֶל־אֵל לֹא יוֹשִׁיעַ.
וַאֲנַחְנוּ מִשְׁתַּחֲוִים לִפְנֵי מֶלֶךְ מַלְכֵי הַמְּלָכִים
הַקָּדוֹשׁ בָּרוּךְ הוּא
שֶׁהוּא נוֹטֶה שָׁמַיִם וְיוֹסֵד אָרֶץ
וּמוֹשַׁב יְקָרוֹ בַּשָּׁמַיִם מִמַּעַל
וּשְׁכִינַת עֻזּוֹ בְּגָבְהֵי מְרוֹמִים.
הוּא אֱלֹהֵינוּ, וְאֵין עוֹד אַחֵר
אֱמֶת מַלְכֵּנוּ, וְאֶפֶס זוּלָתוֹ
כַּכָּתוּב בַּתּוֹרָה, וְיָדַעְתָּ הַיּוֹם וַהֲשֵׁבֹתָ אֶל־לְבָבֶךָ
כִּי יְהוָה הוּא הָאֱלֹהִים בַּשָּׁמַיִם מִמַּעַל
וְעַל־הָאָרֶץ מִתָּחַת אֵין עוֹד:

171

עַל כֵּן נְקַוֶּה לְךָ, יְהוָה אֱלֹהֵינוּ
לִרְאוֹת מְהֵרָה בְּתִפְאֶרֶת עֻזֶּךָ
לְהַעֲבִיר גִּלּוּלִים מִן הָאָרֶץ, וְהָאֱלִילִים כָּרוֹת יִכָּרֵתוּן
לְתַקֵּן עוֹלָם בְּמַלְכוּת שַׁדַּי
וְכָל בְּנֵי בָשָׂר יִקְרְאוּ בִשְׁמֶךָ לְהַפְנוֹת אֵלֶיךָ כָּל רִשְׁעֵי אָרֶץ
יַכִּירוּ וְיֵדְעוּ כָּל יוֹשְׁבֵי תֵבֵל
כִּי לְךָ תִּכְרַע כָּל בֶּרֶךְ, תִּשָּׁבַע כָּל לָשׁוֹן.
לְפָנֶיךָ יְהוָה אֱלֹהֵינוּ יִכְרְעוּ וְיִפֹּלוּ
וְלִכְבוֹד שִׁמְךָ יְקָר יִתֵּנוּ
וִיקַבְּלוּ כֻלָּם אֶת עֹל מַלְכוּתֶךָ
וְתִמְלֹךְ עֲלֵיהֶם מְהֵרָה לְעוֹלָם וָעֶד
כִּי הַמַּלְכוּת שֶׁלְּךָ הִיא, וּלְעוֹלְמֵי עַד תִּמְלֹךְ בְּכָבוֹד
כַּכָּתוּב בְּתוֹרָתֶךָ, יְהוָה יִמְלֹךְ לְעֹלָם וָעֶד:
וְנֶאֱמַר, וְהָיָה יְהוָה לְמֶלֶךְ עַל־כָּל־הָאָרֶץ
בַּיּוֹם הַהוּא יִהְיֶה יְהוָה אֶחָד וּשְׁמוֹ אֶחָד:

At the end of תְּפִלַּת עַרְבִית *on Shabbat we say* אֲדוֹן עוֹלָם *or* יִגְדַּל *(page 27/29).*

The *Tefilla* Text

The following lines of the *Tefilla* text are highlighted in the color of the Conceptual Translation, as they are the focus of the translation on this page:

עָלֵינוּ לשבח לאֲדון הכל, לָתת גדלָה ליוצר בראשית
הוא אלהֵינו, אין עוד.
אמת מלכנו, אפֵס זולָתו
כי ה׳ הוא הָאלהים בשָׁמַיִם ממַעל ועל־הָאָרֶץ מתָּחת, אין עוד:

ברכת הבנים

pp. 172–173

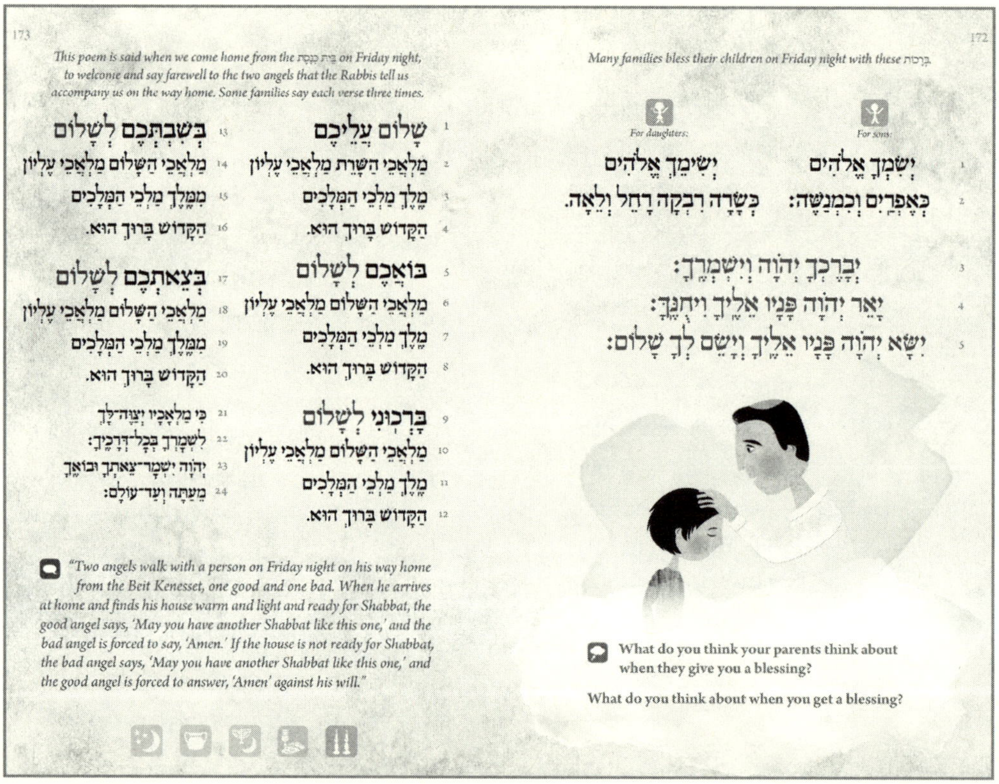

Many families bless their children on Friday night with these בְּרָכוֹת.

For sons:

יְשִׂמְךָ אֱלֹהִים
כְּאֶפְרַיִם וְכִמְנַשֶּׁה:

For daughters:

יְשִׂימֵךְ אֱלֹהִים
כְּשָׂרָה רִבְקָה רָחֵל וְלֵאָה.

יְבָרֶכְךָ יְהוָה וְיִשְׁמְרֶךָ:
יָאֵר יְהוָה פָּנָיו אֵלֶיךָ וִיחֻנֶּךָּ:
יִשָּׂא יְהוָה פָּנָיו אֵלֶיךָ וְיָשֵׂם לְךָ שָׁלוֹם:

What do you think your parents think about when they give you a blessing?

What do you think about when you get a blessing?

This poem is said when we come home from the בֵּית כְּנֶסֶת on Friday night, to welcome and say farewell to the two angels that the Rabbis tell us accompany us on the way home. Some families say each verse three times.

שָׁלוֹם עֲלֵיכֶם
מַלְאֲכֵי הַשָּׁרֵת מַלְאֲכֵי עֶלְיוֹן
מִמֶּלֶךְ מַלְכֵי הַמְּלָכִים
הַקָּדוֹשׁ בָּרוּךְ הוּא.

בּוֹאֲכֶם לְשָׁלוֹם
מַלְאֲכֵי הַשָּׁלוֹם מַלְאֲכֵי עֶלְיוֹן
מִמֶּלֶךְ מַלְכֵי הַמְּלָכִים
הַקָּדוֹשׁ בָּרוּךְ הוּא.

בָּרְכוּנִי לְשָׁלוֹם
מַלְאֲכֵי הַשָּׁלוֹם מַלְאֲכֵי עֶלְיוֹן
מִמֶּלֶךְ מַלְכֵי הַמְּלָכִים
הַקָּדוֹשׁ בָּרוּךְ הוּא.

בְּשִׁבְתְּכֶם לְשָׁלוֹם
מַלְאֲכֵי הַשָּׁלוֹם מַלְאֲכֵי עֶלְיוֹן
מִמֶּלֶךְ מַלְכֵי הַמְּלָכִים
הַקָּדוֹשׁ בָּרוּךְ הוּא.

צֵאתְכֶם לְשָׁלוֹם
מַלְאֲכֵי הַשָּׁלוֹם מַלְאֲכֵי עֶלְיוֹן
מִמֶּלֶךְ מַלְכֵי הַמְּלָכִים
הַקָּדוֹשׁ בָּרוּךְ הוּא.

כִּי מַלְאָכָיו יְצַוֶּה־לָּךְ
לִשְׁמָרְךָ בְּכָל־דְּרָכֶיךָ:
יְהוָה יִשְׁמָר־צֵאתְךָ וּבוֹאֶךָ
מֵעַתָּה וְעַד־עוֹלָם:

"Two angels walk with a person on Friday night on his way home from the Beit Kenesset, one good and one bad. When he arrives at home and finds his house warm and light and ready for Shabbat, the good angel says, 'May you have another Shabbat like this one,' and the bad angel is forced to say, 'Amen.' If the house is not ready for Shabbat, the bad angel says, 'May you have another Shabbat like this one,' and the good angel is forced to answer, 'Amen' against his will."

The *Tefilla* Text

The text of the priestly blessing is highlighted in the turquoise of the illustration:

יְבָרֶכְךָ ה׳ וְיִשְׁמְרֶךָ:
יָאֵר ה׳ פָּנָיו אֵלֶיךָ וִיחֻנֶּךָּ:
יִשָּׂא ה׳ פָּנָיו אֵלֶיךָ וְיָשֵׂם לְךָ שָׁלוֹם:

The word שָׁלוֹם each time it appears in *Shalom Aleikhem* is highlighted in the color of the story.

The Illustration

The intense love between father and daughter is obvious here in the illustration, as our character receives her weekly Shabbat *berakha* from her abba.

The *Kavanot*

Thought Question:
This beautiful and powerful thought question asks the child to consider the emotions they and their parents are both experiencing at this intimate and powerful moment. There are no right and wrong answers, but the child should be encouraged to ask their parents and to share their own emotions at this time.

Story:
This well-known story from the Gemara (*Shabbat* 119b) is the background to the Shabbat poem of *Shalom Aleikhem*. It will encourage the child to appreciate the beauty of their Shabbat home, and the hard work that was necessary to make it look and feel that way.

קידוש

pp. 174–175

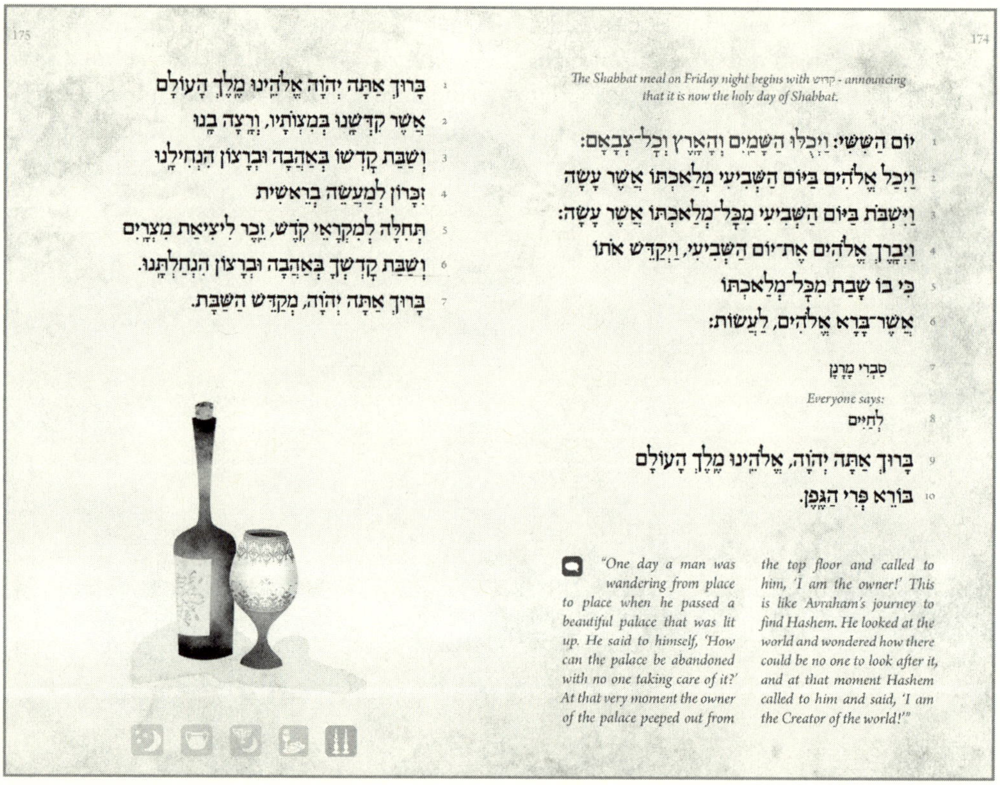

174

The Shabbat meal on Friday night begins with קידוש *- announcing that it is now the holy day of Shabbat.*

1 יוֹם הַשִּׁשִּׁי: וַיְכֻלּוּ הַשָּׁמַיִם וְהָאָרֶץ וְכָל־צְבָאָם:
2 וַיְכַל אֱלֹהִים בַּיּוֹם הַשְּׁבִיעִי מְלַאכְתּוֹ אֲשֶׁר עָשָׂה
3 וַיִּשְׁבֹּת בַּיּוֹם הַשְּׁבִיעִי מִכָּל־מְלַאכְתּוֹ אֲשֶׁר עָשָׂה:
4 וַיְבָרֶךְ אֱלֹהִים אֶת־יוֹם הַשְּׁבִיעִי, וַיְקַדֵּשׁ אֹתוֹ
5 כִּי בוֹ שָׁבַת מִכָּל־מְלַאכְתּוֹ
6 אֲשֶׁר־בָּרָא אֱלֹהִים, לַעֲשׂוֹת:

7 סַבְרִי מָרָנָן

Everyone says:

8 לְחַיִּים

9 בָּרוּךְ אַתָּה יְהוָה, אֱלֹהֵינוּ מֶלֶךְ הָעוֹלָם
10 בּוֹרֵא פְּרִי הַגָּפֶן.

"One day a man was wandering from place to place when he passed a beautiful palace that was lit up. He said to himself, 'How can the palace be abandoned with no one taking care of it?' At that very moment the owner of the palace peeped out from the top floor and called to him, 'I am the owner!' This is like Avraham's journey to find Hashem. He looked at the world and wondered how there could be no one to look after it, and at that moment Hashem called to him and said, 'I am the Creator of the world!'"

175

1 בָּרוּךְ אַתָּה יְהוָה אֱלֹהֵינוּ מֶלֶךְ הָעוֹלָם
2 אֲשֶׁר קִדְּשָׁנוּ בְּמִצְוֹתָיו, וְרָצָה בָנוּ
3 וְשַׁבַּת קָדְשׁוֹ בְּאַהֲבָה וּבְרָצוֹן הִנְחִילָנוּ
4 זִכָּרוֹן לְמַעֲשֵׂה בְרֵאשִׁית
5 תְּחִלָּה לְמִקְרָאֵי קֹדֶשׁ, זֵכֶר לִיצִיאַת מִצְרָיִם
6 וְשַׁבַּת קָדְשְׁךָ בְּאַהֲבָה וּבְרָצוֹן הִנְחַלְתָּנוּ.
7 בָּרוּךְ אַתָּה יְהוָה, מְקַדֵּשׁ הַשַּׁבָּת.

The *Tefilla* Text

The first verse of *Kiddush* – וַיְכֻלּוּ הַשָּׁמַיִם וְהָאָרֶץ וְכָל־צְבָאָם: – is highlighted in the color of the story, and the words בּוֹרֵא פְּרִי הַגָּפֶן are highlighted in the red of the wine in the *Kiddush* cup in the illustration.

The Illustration

The beautiful and ornate *Kiddush* cup, honoring Shabbat with its splendor, stands next to the bottle of wine on the Shabbat table in the illustration, ready for the start of the meal in the home.

Story:

This midrash, from *Bereshit Raba* 39:1, connects to *Kiddush* through the themes of creation and chosenness. It is one of a few midrashim that fill the gaps in the narrative of the Torah text that gives us a limited picture of Avraham's background, and why he was chosen by Hashem to be the progenitor of the Jewish People. It describes in a metaphorical way Avraham's spiritual journey (parallel to the physical journey of his *aliya* to Eretz Yisrael in response to the command of לך לך in *Bereshit* 12:1, on which this midrash is a commentary).

The original text can be read in different ways[50] and the simplest reading for young readers has been chosen for this paraphrased translation. The man who is on a (physical/spiritual) journey comes across a magnificent palace that has clearly been built by someone impressive and important. He sees that the lights are on in the palace, but it seems like no one is home. That seems strange to the traveler. Why would there be a beautiful palace, with the lights burning, yet it seems to be abandoned? In response to his rhetorical question the owner of the palace pops his head out from a window on the top floor, and informs the man that in fact the palace is not abandoned – it has an owner (who built it) and who is in fact currently living and taking care of it (despite the fact that sometimes it appears as if he is not present). The owner of the palace is God, who not only created the world, but looks after it, even if sometimes it is hard to perceive that He is in fact doing so.[51]

A second interpretation worth considering (although abstract and potentially difficult for children to relate to) is that of A.J. Heschel,[52] who interprets the meaning behind the palace being "lit up" as "full of light." Heschel believes that Avraham was seized by a mystic vision of the beauty of the universe, and found God within the light.

For more advanced readers, you may wish to share with them the original Hebrew and Rabbi Sacks' own interpretation of the midrash, which takes the midrash in a different direction. Rabbi Sacks focuses on the word דולקת which we have translated as "lit up," and asserts that a better translation is "in flames." This makes the man's question even stronger – where is the person in charge of this palace when it is on fire and needs attention? But this creates a problem when it comes to the owner's response. Why is he peeping? Why is he in the palace when it is on fire? And why does he only appear once the man looks for him? Rabbi Sacks says that the palace is the world, and the fire is chaos and evil that still exists in the world (unlike some other belief systems, Judaism does not deny the existence of evil in the world by rationalizing it away). God is in the world, and did create the world. But He refuses to put out the fire on His own. He only peeps out from the top floor, looking for a partner. And that partner is Avraham, and the Jewish people, who must partner God in *Tikkun Olam* and thereby put out the fire of evil and chaos in the world.

This is the Midrash in the original Hebrew:

א ויאמר ה׳ אל אברם לך לך מארצך וגו׳ ר׳ יצחק פתח (תהלים מה) שמעי בת וראי והטי אזנך ושכחי עמך ובית אביך אמר רבי יצחק משל לאחד שהיה עובר ממקום למקום וראה בירה אחת דולקת אמר תאמר שהבירה זו בלא מנהיג הציץ עליו בעל הבירה אמר לו אני הוא בעל הבירה כך לפי שהיה אבינו אברהם אומר תאמר שהעולם הזה בלא מנהיג הציץ עליו הקב״ה ואמר לו אני הוא בעל העולם (שם) ויתאו המלך יפיך כי הוא אדוניך ויתאו המלך יפיך ליפותיך בעולם והשתחוי לו הוי ויאמר ה׳ אל אברם:

50. See Rabbi Jonathan Sacks, *A Letter in the Scroll*, Free Press, 2004, chapter 5.
51. This is an "intelligent design" argument for the existence of God, and can also be found in the Midrash quoted on page 26 of the siddur (from *Temura* 3).
52. *God in Search of Man: A Philosophy of Judaism*, Farrar, Straus and Giroux, 1976.

מנוחה ושמחה

pp. 176–177

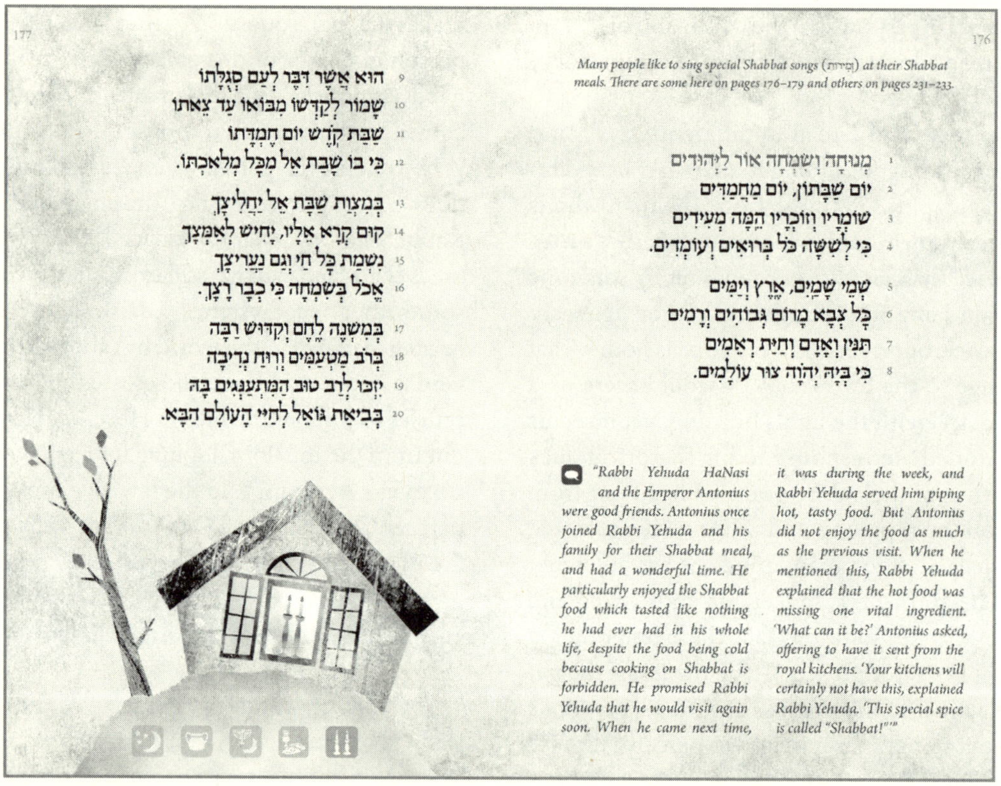

176

Many people like to sing special Shabbat songs (זְמִירוֹת) at their Shabbat meals. There are some here on pages 176–179 and others on pages 231–233.

1 מְנוּחָה וְשִׂמְחָה אוֹר לַיְּהוּדִים
2 יוֹם שַׁבָּתוֹן, יוֹם מַחֲמַדִּים
3 שׁוֹמְרָיו וְזוֹכְרָיו הֵמָּה מְעִידִים
4 כִּי לְשִׁשָּׁה כֹּל בְּרוּאִים וְעוֹמְדִים.

5 שְׁמֵי שָׁמַיִם, אֶרֶץ וְיַמִּים
6 כָּל צְבָא מָרוֹם גְּבוֹהִים וְרָמִים
7 תַּנִּין וְאָדָם וְחַיַּת רְאֵמִים
8 כִּי בְּיָהּ יְהוָה צוּר עוֹלָמִים.

"Rabbi Yehuda HaNasi and the Emperor Antonius were good friends. Antonius once joined Rabbi Yehuda and his family for their Shabbat meal, and had a wonderful time. He particularly enjoyed the Shabbat food which tasted like nothing he had ever had in his whole life, despite the food being cold because cooking on Shabbat is forbidden. He promised Rabbi Yehuda that he would visit again soon. When he came next time, it was during the week, and Rabbi Yehuda served him piping hot, tasty food. But Antonius did not enjoy the food as much as the previous visit. When he mentioned this, Rabbi Yehuda explained that the hot food was missing one vital ingredient. 'What can it be?' Antonius asked, offering to have it sent from the royal kitchens. 'Your kitchens will certainly not have this,' explained Rabbi Yehuda. 'This special spice is called "Shabbat!"'"

177

9 הוּא אֲשֶׁר דִּבֶּר לְעַם סְגֻלָּתוֹ
10 שָׁמוֹר לְקַדְּשׁוֹ מִבּוֹאוֹ עַד צֵאתוֹ
11 שַׁבַּת קֹדֶשׁ יוֹם חֶמְדָּתוֹ
12 כִּי בוֹ שָׁבַת אֵל מִכָּל מְלַאכְתּוֹ.

13 בְּמִצְוַת שַׁבָּת אֵל יַחֲלִיצָךְ
14 קוּם קְרָא אֵלָיו, יָחִישׁ לְאַמְּצָךְ
15 נִשְׁמַת כָּל חַי וְגַם נַעֲרִיצָךְ
16 אֱכֹל בְּשִׂמְחָה כִּי כְבָר רָצָךְ.

17 בְּמִשְׁנֶה לֶחֶם וְקִדּוּשׁ רַבָּה
18 בְּרֹב מַטְעַמִּים וְרוּחַ נְדִיבָה
19 יִזְכּוּ לְרַב טוּב הַמִּתְעַנְּגִים בָּהּ
20 בְּבִיאַת גּוֹאֵל לְחַיֵּי הָעוֹלָם הַבָּא.

The *Tefilla* Text

The first line of the *zemer* – מנוחה ושמחה אור ליהודים – is highlighted in the color of the light from the illustration, and the words אכל בשמחה כי כבר רָצָך are highlighted in the color of the roof in the illustration.

The Illustration

The light in Jewish homes on Shabbat mentioned in the *zemer* on this page is beautifully illustrated here. The light seems to emanate not only from the Shabbat candles, but from the home itself, from the people and the atmosphere that is contained within it. It is obvious to all who pass by that here is a house full of *Oneg Shabbat* and *Shalom Bayit*.

The *Kavanot*

Story:
This midrashic story (*Bereshit Raba* 11:4) paints a beautiful picture of Rabbi Yehuda HaNasi's home on Shabbat. The atmosphere and warmth and love that was there translated into the tangible result that even the food tasted better, despite it being cold. Sometimes the psychological and emotional state of a person will have tangible effect on their physical state. In this instance, Shabbat and the atmosphere that comes with it made this food taste better.

It is important to note that there is no halakha that requires food to be cold on Shabbat, and we do not know that Rabbi Yehuda HaNasi had only cold food on Shabbat. However, the laws of heating up food on Shabbat, making sure that no cooking takes place on Shabbat itself, are complex, and therefore sometimes food that would be eaten hot during the week is eaten cold on Shabbat. In the story this is used as a feature to make the experience even more dramatic – the cold food on Shabbat tasted better, because of the secret ingredient of Shabbat, than the same food served hot during the week.

צור משלו

pp. 178–179

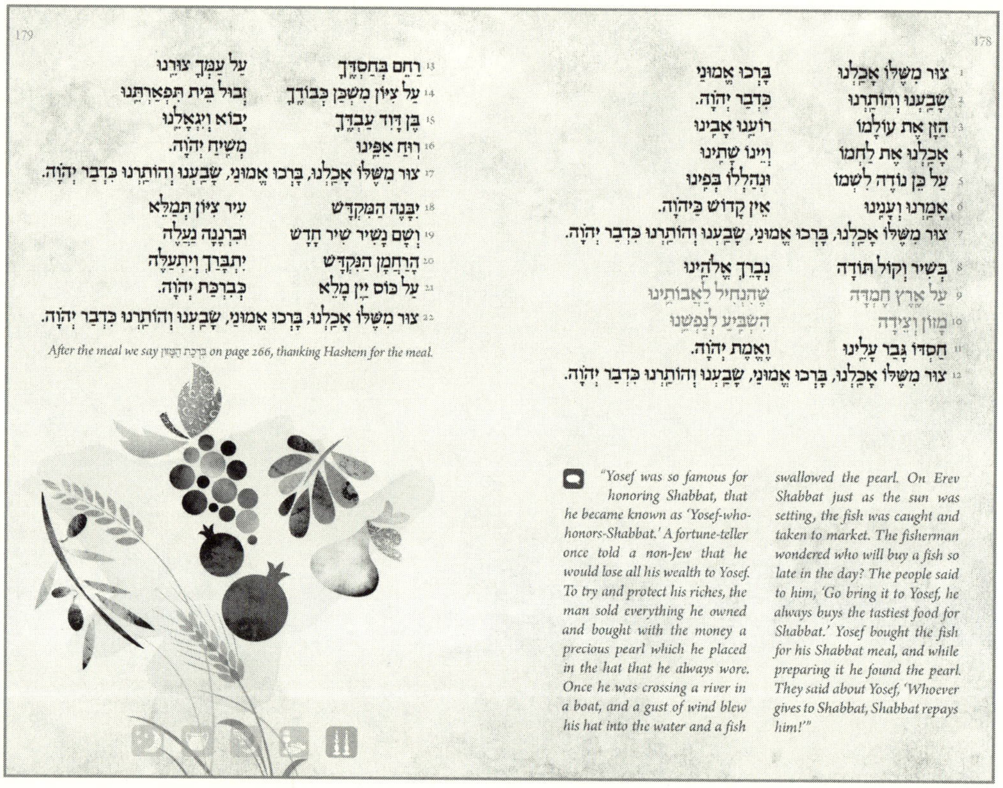
179

רַחֵם בְּחַסְדֶּךָ   עַל עַמְּךָ צוּרֵנוּ
עַל צִיּוֹן מִשְׁכַּן כְּבוֹדֶךָ   זְבוּל בֵּית תִּפְאַרְתֵּנוּ
בֶּן דָּוִד עַבְדֶּךָ   יָבוֹא וְיִגְאָלֵנוּ
רוּחַ אַפֵּינוּ   מְשִׁיחַ יְהוָה.
צוּר מִשֶּׁלּוֹ אָכַלְנוּ, בָּרְכוּ אֱמוּנַי, שָׂבַעְנוּ וְהוֹתַרְנוּ כִּדְבַר יְהוָה.

יִבָּנֶה הַמִּקְדָּשׁ   עִיר צִיּוֹן תְּמַלֵּא
וְשָׁם נָשִׁיר שִׁיר חָדָשׁ   וּבִרְנָנָה נַעֲלֶה
הָרַחֲמָן הַנִּקְדָּשׁ   יִתְבָּרַךְ וְיִתְעַלֶּה
עַל כּוֹס יַיִן מָלֵא   כְּבִרְכַּת יְהוָה.
צוּר מִשֶּׁלּוֹ אָכַלְנוּ, בָּרְכוּ אֱמוּנַי, שָׂבַעְנוּ וְהוֹתַרְנוּ כִּדְבַר יְהוָה.

After the meal we say בִּרְכַּת הַמָּזוֹן *on page 266, thanking Hashem for the meal.*

178

צוּר מִשֶּׁלּוֹ אָכַלְנוּ   בָּרְכוּ אֱמוּנַי
שָׂבַעְנוּ וְהוֹתַרְנוּ   כִּדְבַר יְהוָה.
הַזָּן אֶת עוֹלָמוֹ   רוֹעֵנוּ אָבִינוּ
אָכַלְנוּ אֶת לַחְמוֹ   וְיֵינוֹ שָׁתִינוּ
עַל כֵּן נוֹדֶה לִשְׁמוֹ   וּנְהַלְּלוֹ בְּפִינוּ
אָמַרְנוּ וְעָנִינוּ   אֵין קָדוֹשׁ כַּיהוָה.
צוּר מִשֶּׁלּוֹ אָכַלְנוּ, בָּרְכוּ אֱמוּנַי, שָׂבַעְנוּ וְהוֹתַרְנוּ כִּדְבַר יְהוָה.

בְּשִׁיר וְקוֹל תּוֹדָה   נְבָרֵךְ אֱלֹהֵינוּ
עַל אֶרֶץ חֶמְדָּה   שֶׁהִנְחִיל לַאֲבוֹתֵינוּ
מָזוֹן וְצֵידָה   הִשְׂבִּיעַ לְנַפְשֵׁנוּ
חַסְדּוֹ גָּבַר עָלֵינוּ   וֶאֱמֶת יְהוָה.
צוּר מִשֶּׁלּוֹ אָכַלְנוּ, בָּרְכוּ אֱמוּנַי, שָׂבַעְנוּ וְהוֹתַרְנוּ כִּדְבַר יְהוָה.

"Yosef was so famous for honoring Shabbat, that he became known as 'Yosef-who-honors-Shabbat.' A fortune-teller once told a non-Jew that he would lose all his wealth to Yosef. To try and protect his riches, the man sold everything he owned and bought with the money a precious pearl which he placed in the hat that he always wore. Once he was crossing a river in a boat, and a gust of wind blew his hat into the water and a fish swallowed the pearl. On Erev Shabbat just as the sun was setting, the fish was caught and taken to market. The fisherman wondered who will buy a fish so late in the day? The people said to him, 'Go bring it to Yosef, he always buys the tastiest food for Shabbat.' Yosef bought the fish for his Shabbat meal, and while preparing it he found the pearl. They said about Yosef, 'Whoever gives to Shabbat, Shabbat repays him!'"

The *Tefilla* Text

The words עַל אֶרֶץ חֶמְדָּה שֶׁהִנְחִיל לַאֲבוֹתֵינוּ מָזוֹן וְצֵידָה הִשְׂבִּיעַ לְנַפְשֵׁנוּ are highlighted in the color of the illustration, relating to the land of Israel and food, in particular the *Shivat HaMinim*.

The Illustration

The *zemer* mentions the bountiful Land of Israel, and food and provisions that satisfy body and soul. These are represented in the illustration of the *Shivat HaMinim* – the seven species native to Eretz Yisrael. They are wheat, barley, grapes, olives, pomegranates, figs and dates. They also appear in the siddur on pages 246 and 266.

The *Kavanot*

Story:

This story, taken from the Gemara (*Shabbat* 119a), introduces to us many important concepts, such as reward (and punishment), *hashgaḥa peratit* (divine providence), miracles/God acting through nature, etc. but the most important theme and the reason the story is found here in this part of the siddur, is its celebration of the Talmudic character of Yosef-who-honors-Shabbat for his commitment to honoring Shabbat. Those who honor Shabbat may not always receive a financial reward such as this, but will always be rewarded with a meaningful and special Shabbat experience – the more you put into Shabbat the more you will be able to take out.

נשמת 1

pp. 180–181

181

14 מְחַיֵּה מֵתִים, וְרוֹפֵא חוֹלִים
15 פּוֹקֵחַ עִוְרִים, וְזוֹקֵף כְּפוּפִים.
16 הַמֵּשִׂיחַ אִלְּמִים וְהַמְפַעְנֵחַ נֶעֱלָמִים
17 וּלְךָ לְבַדְּךָ אֲנַחְנוּ מוֹדִים.
18 וְאִלּוּ פִינוּ מָלֵא שִׁירָה כַּיָּם
19 וּלְשׁוֹנֵנוּ רִנָּה כַּהֲמוֹן גַּלָּיו
20 וְשִׂפְתוֹתֵינוּ שֶׁבַח כְּמֶרְחֲבֵי רָקִיעַ
21 וְעֵינֵינוּ מְאִירוֹת כַּשֶּׁמֶשׁ וְכַיָּרֵחַ
22 וְיָדֵינוּ פְרוּשׂוֹת כְּנִשְׁרֵי שָׁמָיִם
23 וְרַגְלֵינוּ קַלּוֹת כָּאַיָּלוֹת
24 אֵין אֲנַחְנוּ מַסְפִּיקִין לְהוֹדוֹת לְךָ, יְהוָה אֱלֹהֵינוּ
25 וּלְבָרֵךְ אֶת שְׁמֶךָ, מַלְכֵּנוּ
26 עַל אַחַת מֵאֶלֶף אַלְפֵי אֲלָפִים
27 וְרֹב רִבֵּי רְבָבוֹת פְּעָמִים הַטּוֹבוֹת
28 נִסִּים וְנִפְלָאוֹת שֶׁעָשִׂיתָ עִמָּנוּ וְעִם אֲבוֹתֵינוּ מִלְּפָנִים
29 מִמִּצְרַיִם גְּאַלְתָּנוּ, יְהוָה אֱלֹהֵינוּ, מִבֵּית עֲבָדִים פְּדִיתָנוּ
30 בְּרָעָב זַנְתָּנוּ, וּבְשָׂבָע כִּלְכַּלְתָּנוּ
31 מֵחֶרֶב הִצַּלְתָּנוּ, מִדֶּבֶר מִלַּטְתָּנוּ

180

For the beginning of תפלת שחרית*, turn to pages 9–61.*
Then continue here with נשמת*.*

1 נִשְׁמַת כָּל חַי
2 תְּבָרֵךְ אֶת שִׁמְךָ, יְהוָה אֱלֹהֵינוּ
3 וְרוּחַ כָּל בָּשָׂר תְּפָאֵר וּתְרוֹמֵם זִכְרְךָ מַלְכֵּנוּ תָּמִיד.
4 מִן הָעוֹלָם וְעַד הָעוֹלָם אַתָּה אֵל
5 וּמִבַּלְעָדֶיךָ אֵין לָנוּ מֶלֶךְ גּוֹאֵל וּמוֹשִׁיעַ
6 פּוֹדֶה וּמַצִּיל וְעוֹנֶה וּמְרַחֵם
7 בְּכָל עֵת צָרָה וְצוּקָה, אֵין לָנוּ מֶלֶךְ עוֹזֵר וְסוֹמֵךְ אֶלָּא אָתָּה.
8 אֱלֹהֵי הָרִאשׁוֹנִים וְהָאַחֲרוֹנִים
9 אֱלוֹהַּ כָּל בְּרִיּוֹת, אֲדוֹן כָּל תּוֹלָדוֹת
10 הַמְהֻלָּל בְּכָל הַתִּשְׁבָּחוֹת
11 הַמְנַהֵג עוֹלָמוֹ בְּחֶסֶד וּבְרִיּוֹתָיו בְּרַחֲמִים.
12 וַיהוָה אֱלֹהִים אֱמֶת, לֹא יָנוּם וְלֹא יִישָׁן
13 הַמְעוֹרֵר יְשֵׁנִים וְהַמֵּקִיץ נִרְדָּמִים

The *Tefilla* Text

The words ועינינו מאירות כשמש וכירח are highlighted in the yellow of the sun in the illustration, and the words וידינו פרושות כנשרי שמים are highlighted in the dark red of the eagle in the illustration.

The Illustration

The weekday *Pesukei DeZimra* focuses our attention on God in creation and in history, in order to inspire us and prepare us to stand before Him during the *Amida*. But we don't have the time on a weekday morning to take a step back and evaluate our personal and direct relationship with Hashem. On Shabbat we do, and we begin here with *Nishmat* focusing on our soul and its relationship with Hashem. Many of the verses here describe our soul in physical terms as a metaphor, yearning to draw close to and praise Hashem. The illustration has picked out two of these – *and if our eyes shone like the sun and the moon; if our hands were outstretched like eagles of the sky;* these images, an eagle, the sun and the moon (hiding in the form of the sun) are represented here on the page.

נשמת 2

pp. 182–183

183

כִּי כָל פֶּה לְךָ יוֹדֶה, וְכָל לָשׁוֹן לְךָ תְשַׁבֵּחַ
וְכָל עַיִן לְךָ תְצַפֶּה
וְכָל בֶּרֶךְ לְךָ תִכְרַע
וְכָל קוֹמָה לְפָנֶיךָ תִשְׁתַּחֲוֶה
וְהַלְּבָבוֹת יִירָאוּךָ
וְכָל קֶרֶב וּכְלָיוֹת יְזַמְּרוּ לִשְׁמֶךָ
כַּדָּבָר שֶׁנֶּאֱמַר
כָּל עַצְמֹתַי תֹּאמַרְנָה יְהוָה מִי כָמוֹךָ
מַצִּיל עָנִי מֵחָזָק מִמֶּנּוּ, וְעָנִי וְאֶבְיוֹן מִגֹּזְלוֹ:
שַׁוְעַת עֲנִיִּים אַתָּה תִשְׁמַע, צַעֲקַת הַדַּל תַּקְשִׁיב וְתוֹשִׁיעַ.

One Friday night Rabbi Avraham Ibn Ezra once had a dream. An angel in the form of a man stood in front of him holding out a sealed letter. As the Ibn Ezra opened the letter he realized it was from Shabbat! The letter asked that Shabbat, the eternal covenant, be observed in a way that is unique from the other days of the week. Shabbat then promised to look after the Ibn Ezra just as he had observed Shabbat from his youth. But the letter ends with criticism of the Ibn Ezra. Shaking he pleaded with the angel to explain to him his sin. The angel replied that one of his students had become careless in his Shabbat observance. From that day on the Ibn Ezra was careful to not only observe Shabbat himself, but to ensure those he could influence to do the same

182

וּמֵחֳלָאִים רָעִים וְרַבִּים דִּלִּיתָנוּ.
עַד הֵנָּה עֲזָרוּנוּ רַחֲמֶיךָ, וְלֹא עֲזָבוּנוּ חֲסָדֶיךָ
עַל כֵּן, אֵבָרִים שֶׁפִּלַּגְתָּ בָּנוּ
וְרוּחַ וּנְשָׁמָה שֶׁנָּפַחְתָּ בְּאַפֵּינוּ
וְלָשׁוֹן אֲשֶׁר שַׂמְתָּ בְּפִינוּ
הֵן הֵם יוֹדוּ וִיבָרְכוּ וִישַׁבְּחוּ וִיפָאֲרוּ
אֶת שִׁמְךָ מַלְכֵּנוּ תָּמִיד

כָּל עַצְמֹתַי תֹּאמְרְנָה יְהוָה מִי כָמוֹךָ (Tehillim 35:10)

"All of my bones will say 'Who is like You Hashem?'"

How can we use our actual bodies to pray to Hashem?

The *Tefilla* Text

The words וְרוּחַ וּנְשָׁמָה שֶׁנָּפַחְתָּ בְּאַפֵּינוּ וְלָשׁוֹן אֲשֶׁר שַׂמְתָּ בְּפִינוּ are highlighted in the turquoise of the illustration, and the words כִּי כָל פֶּה לְךָ יוֹדֶה, וְכָל לָשׁוֹן לְךָ תְשַׁבֵּחַ, וְכָל עַיִן לְךָ תְצַפֶּה, וְכָל בֶּרֶךְ לְךָ תִכְרַע, וְכָל קוֹמָה לְפָנֶיךָ תִשְׁתַּחֲוֶה, וְהַלְּבָבוֹת יִירָאוּךָ, וְכָל קֶרֶב וּכְלָיוֹת יְזַמְּרוּ לִשְׁמֶךָ are highlighted in the color of the thought question.

The Illustration

The weekday *Pesukei DeZimra* focuses our attention on God in creation and in history, in order to inspire us and prepare us to stand before Him during the *Amida*. But we don't have the time on a weekday morning to take a step back and evaluate our personal and direct relationship with Hashem. On Shabbat we do, and we begin here with *Nishmat* focusing on our soul and its relationship with Hashem. In the illustration we have our character in her Shabbat dress, blowing the seeds from a dandelion, and connecting to Hashem through nature. But this scene has an ethereal hue to it, as the girl who in her white Shabbat dress looks angelic, blows the white seeds with her breath, which emanates from inside her depths. Hasidic tradition suggests that on Shabbat we acquire a *neshama yetera* – an extra soul. On Shabbat we breathe more deeply and think more clearly. And in fact, the word for soul (נשמה) and breath (נשימה) are closely related.

The *Kavanot*

Thought Question:
Focusing on the words from the *tefilla* – כִּי כָל פֶּה לְךָ יוֹדֶה, וְכָל לָשׁוֹן לְךָ תְשַׁבֵּחַ, וְכָל עַיִן לְךָ תְצַפֶּה, וכָל בֶּרֶךְ לְךָ תִכְרַע, וְכָל קוֹמָה לְפָנֶיךָ תִשְׁתַּחֲוֶה, וְהַלְּבָבוֹת יִירָאוּךָ, וְכָל קֶרֶב וּכְלָיוֹת יְזַמְּרוּ לִשְׁמֶךָ – that describe how with every limb of our bodies we pray to God and praise and worship Him, this *kavana* provides another verse with the same idea succinctly expressed. Tehillim 35:10 describes our very bones praising God.

The thought question that follows asks the student to consider how our very bodies can serve and pray to Hashem. Possible answers could include the performing of mitzvot that entail actions, looking after one's body as a religious act and seeing this as a way to show gratitude to Hashem for it as a gift, and the movement we often make when we pray to Hashem (known as *shockeling* in Yiddish).

שוכן עד

pp. 184–185

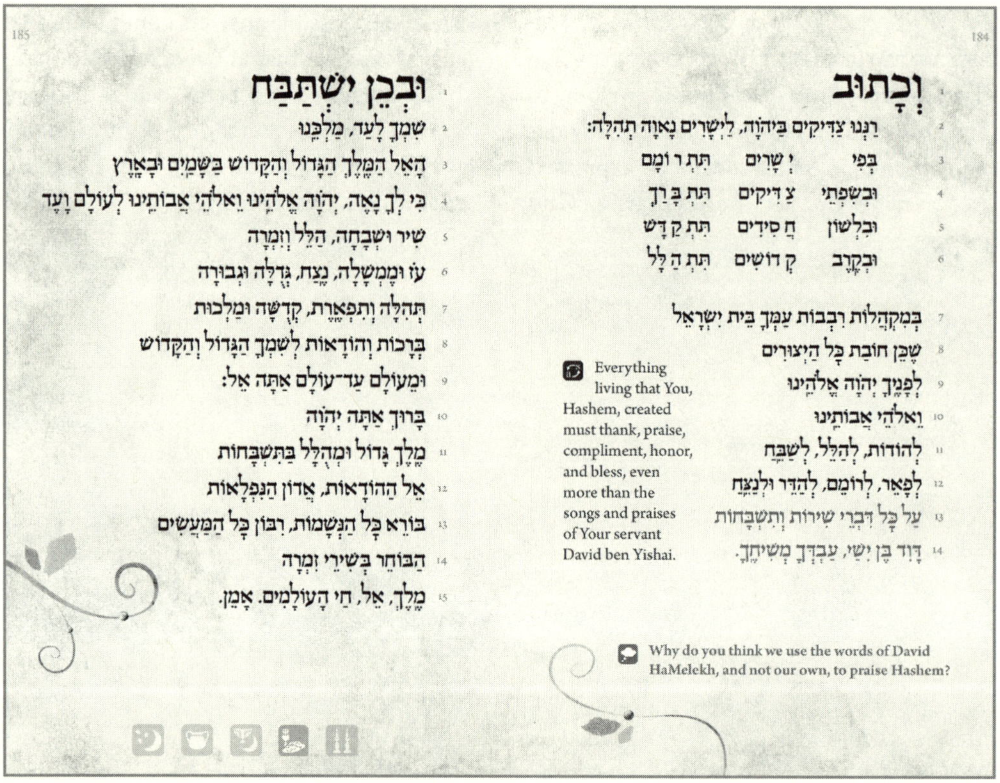

184

וְכָתוּב

רַנְּנוּ צַדִּיקִים בַּיהוָה, לַיְשָׁרִים נָאוָה תְהִלָּה:

בְּפִי יְשָׁרִים תִּתְרוֹמָם

וּבְשִׂפְתֵי צַדִּיקִים תִּתְבָּרַךְ

וּבִלְשׁוֹן חֲסִידִים תִּתְקַדָּשׁ

וּבְקֶרֶב קְדוֹשִׁים תִּתְהַלָּל

בְּמִקְהֲלוֹת רִבְבוֹת עַמְּךָ בֵּית יִשְׂרָאֵל

שֶׁכֵּן חוֹבַת כָּל הַיְצוּרִים

לְפָנֶיךָ יְהוָה אֱלֹהֵינוּ

וֵאלֹהֵי אֲבוֹתֵינוּ

לְהוֹדוֹת, לְהַלֵּל, לְשַׁבֵּחַ

לְפָאֵר, לְרוֹמֵם, לְהַדֵּר וּלְנַצֵּחַ

עַל כָּל דִּבְרֵי שִׁירוֹת וְתִשְׁבְּחוֹת

דָּוִד בֶּן יִשַׁי, עַבְדְּךָ מְשִׁיחֶךָ.

Everything living that You, Hashem, created must thank, praise, compliment, honor, and bless, even more than the songs and praises of Your servant David ben Yishai.

Why do you think we use the words of David HaMelekh, and not our own, to praise Hashem?

185

וּבְכֵן יִשְׁתַּבַּח

שִׁמְךָ לָעַד, מַלְכֵּנוּ

הָאֵל הַמֶּלֶךְ הַגָּדוֹל וְהַקָּדוֹשׁ בַּשָּׁמַיִם וּבָאָרֶץ

כִּי לְךָ נָאֶה, יְהוָה אֱלֹהֵינוּ וֵאלֹהֵי אֲבוֹתֵינוּ לְעוֹלָם וָעֶד

שִׁיר וּשְׁבָחָה, הַלֵּל וְזִמְרָה

עֹז וּמֶמְשָׁלָה, נֶצַח, גְּדֻלָּה וּגְבוּרָה

תְּהִלָּה וְתִפְאֶרֶת, קְדֻשָּׁה וּמַלְכוּת

בְּרָכוֹת וְהוֹדָאוֹת לְשִׁמְךָ הַגָּדוֹל וְהַקָּדוֹשׁ

וּמֵעוֹלָם עַד־עוֹלָם אַתָּה אֵל:

בָּרוּךְ אַתָּה יְהוָה

מֶלֶךְ גָּדוֹל וּמְהֻלָּל בַּתִּשְׁבָּחוֹת

אֵל הַהוֹדָאוֹת, אֲדוֹן הַנִּפְלָאוֹת

בּוֹרֵא כָּל הַנְּשָׁמוֹת, רִבּוֹן כָּל הַמַּעֲשִׂים

הַבּוֹחֵר בְּשִׁירֵי זִמְרָה

מֶלֶךְ, אֵל, חַי הָעוֹלָמִים. אָמֵן.

The *Tefilla* Text

The words עַל כָּל דברי שירות ותשבחות דָוד בן ישי, עבדך משיחֶךָ are highlighted in the same color as the thought question.

The Illustration

On pages 118/119, we have the *berakha* of מלכות בית דוד illustrated with David's Harp with shoots flowering from it. This is an expression of the prayer for the restoration of the Davidic monarchy, one of the accepted elements of the Messianic redemption. This illustration was chosen because of the language of צמיחה in the *berakha* – the language of flowering and gradual sprouting. This language was also the inspiration for the terminology used in the Prayer for the State of Israel (page 212) – ראשית צמיחת גאֻלָּתֵנוּ – the beginning of the flowering of our redemption. This language suggests that we believe the modern State of Israel is the initial stage of the redemptive process, but by no means the completion of it (and nor are we saying it is a process that cannot be reversed if we do not merit it). While the process has begun, it will be slow and steady, and require investment, patience, hope and faith. We are living in a generation in which we believe this has started, and we pray it will continue, ultimately leading to the national redemption God has promised us.

On this page we have the same sprouting vegetation, linked to the words from the *tefilla* –

עַל כָּל דברי שירות ותשבחות דָוד בן ישי, עבדך משיחך.

(We should praise You) even beyond all the words of song and praise of David, son of Yishai, Your servant, Your anointed.

The *Kavanot*

Thought Question:
This question refers to the line in the *tefilla* (highlighted) that describes our use of verses from Tehillim as the core text of our *tefilla* (especially in *Pesukei DeZimra,* the section that is just coming to a close here), and asks the child to think why we rely on King David's words (or in fact the words of *Ḥazal* for the rest of *tefilla*) to express our prayers rather than our own spontaneous words. There are many different approaches to be taken here, but the simplest to understand is to explore King David's talent with words and poetry. We rely on him in the same way as we rely on a musician to play music that expresses the way we feel, and the way we would play if we had the talent ourselves. We use his words, but in a way that allows us to channel our own spiritual emotions through them. The responsibility for emotional connection to the *tefillot* and to Hashem still rests on us.

אל אדון

pp. 188–189

The *Tefilla* Text

The words קָרָא לַשֶּׁמֶשׁ ויזרח אור are highlighted in the orange of the rising sun in the illustration, and the words רָאָה והתקין צורת הלבנה are highlighted in the turquoise of the moon in the illustration.

The first letter of each line of the *tefilla* is also highlighted, in brown drawing our attention to the *Alef-Beit* acrostic.

The Illustration

In the ongoing process of spiritual and mystical inspiration in the Shabbat version of *Pesukei DeZimra*, leading to a Shabbat audience with Hashem, this *tefilla* has mystical overtones that are reminiscent of the vision of the divine chariot in Yeḥezkel. The *tefilla* also explores the spiritual impact of the heavenly lights, as they dance across our skies with strength and might, splendor and beauty, radiating light and expressing joy. The illustration has these lights dancing across the page, and for only the second time in the siddur the moon makes its own appearance, separate from the sun, forcing us to consider it on its own as a giver of light and joy.

The *Kavanot*

Thought Question:

This quote from the Gemara (*Berakhot* 57b) compares Shabbat to sunshine, and states that they are both a small taste of the experience of the World to Come. The thought question asks the child to reflect on what Shabbat and sunshine may have in common, which in turn will help us to understand what the World to Come may be like. Shabbat and sunshine are both tranquil, nourishing, spiritually inspiring, and both physically and spiritually beautiful. But perhaps words are inadequate to describe either Shabbat or the World to Come, and rather they need experiencing for us to truly understand. So maybe the experience of Shabbat and sunshine is the best way we can understand the World to Come.

לאל אשר

pp. 190–191

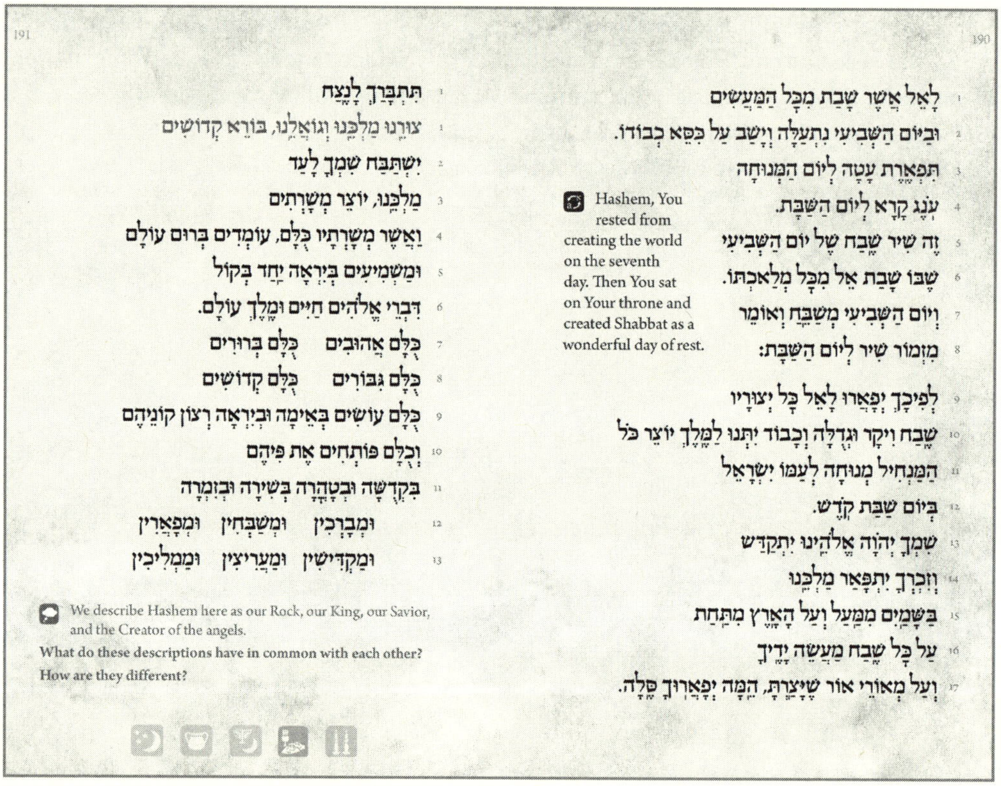

190

לָאֵל אֲשֶׁר שָׁבַת מִכָּל הַמַּעֲשִׂים
וּבַיּוֹם הַשְּׁבִיעִי נִתְעַלָּה וְיָשַׁב עַל כִּסֵּא כְבוֹדוֹ.
תִּפְאֶרֶת עָטָה לְיוֹם הַמְּנוּחָה
עֹנֶג קָרָא לְיוֹם הַשַּׁבָּת.
זֶה שִׁיר שֶׁבַח שֶׁל יוֹם הַשְּׁבִיעִי
שֶׁבּוֹ שָׁבַת אֵל מִכָּל מְלַאכְתּוֹ.
וְיוֹם הַשְּׁבִיעִי מְשַׁבֵּחַ וְאוֹמֵר
מִזְמוֹר שִׁיר לְיוֹם הַשַּׁבָּת:

לְפִיכָךְ יְפָאֲרוּ לָאֵל כָּל יְצוּרָיו
שֶׁבַח וִיקָר וּגְדֻלָּה וְכָבוֹד יִתְּנוּ לַמֶּלֶךְ יוֹצֵר כֹּל
הַמַּנְחִיל מְנוּחָה לְעַמּוֹ יִשְׂרָאֵל
בִּקְדֻשָּׁתוֹ בְּיוֹם שַׁבַּת קֹדֶשׁ.
שִׁמְךָ יְהֹוָה אֱלֹהֵינוּ יִתְקַדַּשׁ
וְזִכְרְךָ יִתְפָּאַר מַלְכֵּנוּ
בַּשָּׁמַיִם מִמַּעַל וְעַל הָאָרֶץ מִתָּחַת
עַל כָּל שֶׁבַח מַעֲשֵׂה יָדֶיךָ
וְעַל מְאוֹרֵי אוֹר שֶׁיָּצַרְתָּ, הֵמָּה יְפָאֲרוּךָ סֶּלָה.

Hashem, You rested from creating the world on the seventh day. Then You sat on Your throne and created Shabbat as a wonderful day of rest.

191

תִּתְבָּרַךְ לָנֶצַח
צוּרֵנוּ מַלְכֵּנוּ וְגוֹאֲלֵנוּ, בּוֹרֵא קְדוֹשִׁים
יִשְׁתַּבַּח שִׁמְךָ לָעַד
מַלְכֵּנוּ, יוֹצֵר מְשָׁרְתִים
וַאֲשֶׁר מְשָׁרְתָיו כֻּלָּם, עוֹמְדִים בְּרוּם עוֹלָם
וּמַשְׁמִיעִים בְּיִרְאָה יַחַד בְּקוֹל
דִּבְרֵי אֱלֹהִים חַיִּים וּמֶלֶךְ עוֹלָם.
כֻּלָּם אֲהוּבִים כֻּלָּם בְּרוּרִים
כֻּלָּם גִּבּוֹרִים כֻּלָּם קְדוֹשִׁים
כֻּלָּם עוֹשִׂים בְּאֵימָה וּבְיִרְאָה רְצוֹן קוֹנֵיהֶם
וְכֻלָּם פּוֹתְחִים אֶת פִּיהֶם
בִּקְדֻשָּׁה וּבְטָהֳרָה בְּשִׁירָה וּבְזִמְרָה
וּמְבָרְכִין וּמְשַׁבְּחִין וּמְפָאֲרִין
וּמַקְדִּישִׁין וּמַעֲרִיצִין וּמַמְלִיכִין

We describe Hashem here as our Rock, our King, our Savior, and the Creator of the angels.

What do these descriptions have in common with each other? How are they different?

The *Tefilla* Text

The words לָאֵל אֲשֶׁר שָׁבַת מִכָּל הַמַּעֲשִׂים בּיוֹם השביעי נתעלָה וישב על כסא כבודו. תפארת עָטָה ליום המנוחה עֹנג קָרָא ליום השבת. are highlighted in the color of the conceptual translation.

The words צוּרֵנוּ מלכנו וגואֲלנו, בורא קדושים are highlighted in the color of the thought question.

The *Kavanot*

Thought Question:
This *tefilla* describes God in many diverse ways: our Rock, our King, our Savior, and the Creator of the angels. This thought question explores what these have in common (and perhaps why these were chosen as the way we describe Hashem here). The first

three seem to be powerful roles that require strength to fulfill. Arguably we can say that God as Creator also takes strength, but a more creative power than the first three. A king can be a savior and a rock (protector) for his people. But only God can truly create, and create spiritual beings such as angels.

את שם

pp. 192–193

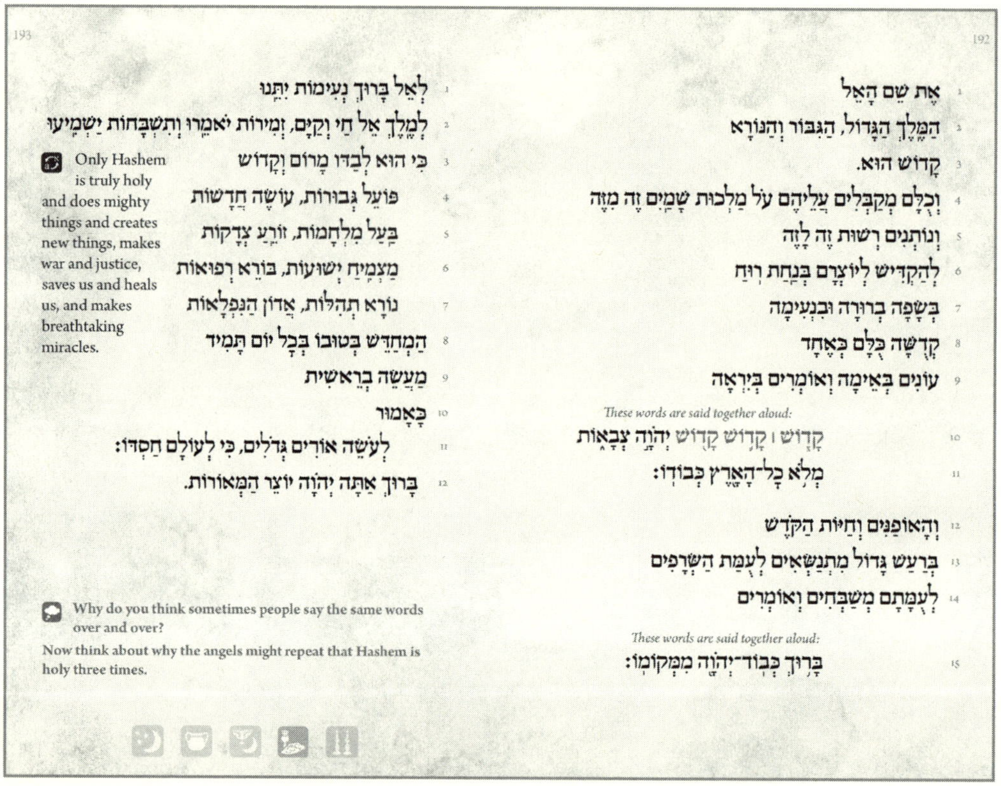

192

1 אֶת שֵׁם הָאֵל

2 הַמֶּלֶךְ הַגָּדוֹל, הַגִּבּוֹר וְהַנּוֹרָא

3 קָדוֹשׁ הוּא.

4 וְכֻלָּם מְקַבְּלִים עֲלֵיהֶם עֹל מַלְכוּת שָׁמַיִם זֶה מִזֶּה

5 וְנוֹתְנִים רְשׁוּת זֶה לָזֶה

6 לְהַקְדִּישׁ לְיוֹצְרָם בְּנַחַת רוּחַ

7 בְּשָׂפָה בְרוּרָה וּבִנְעִימָה

8 קְדֻשָּׁה כֻּלָּם כְּאֶחָד

9 עוֹנִים בְּאֵימָה וְאוֹמְרִים בְּיִרְאָה

These words are said together aloud:

10 קָדוֹשׁ ׀ קָדוֹשׁ קָדוֹשׁ יְהוָה צְבָאוֹת

11 מְלֹא כָל־הָאָרֶץ כְּבוֹדוֹ:

12 וְהָאוֹפַנִּים וְחַיּוֹת הַקֹּדֶשׁ

13 בְּרַעַשׁ גָּדוֹל מִתְנַשְּׂאִים לְעֻמַּת הַשְּׂרָפִים

14 לְעֻמָּתָם מְשַׁבְּחִים וְאוֹמְרִים

These words are said together aloud:

15 בָּרוּךְ כְּבוֹד־יְהוָה מִמְּקוֹמוֹ:

193

1 לָאֵל בָּרוּךְ נְעִימוֹת יִתֵּנוּ

2 לַמֶּלֶךְ אֵל חַי וְקַיָּם, זְמִירוֹת יֹאמֵרוּ וְתִשְׁבָּחוֹת יַשְׁמִיעוּ

3 כִּי הוּא לְבַדּוֹ מָרוֹם וְקָדוֹשׁ

4 פּוֹעֵל גְּבוּרוֹת, עוֹשֶׂה חֲדָשׁוֹת

5 בַּעַל מִלְחָמוֹת, זוֹרֵעַ צְדָקוֹת

6 מַצְמִיחַ יְשׁוּעוֹת, בּוֹרֵא רְפוּאוֹת

7 נוֹרָא תְהִלּוֹת, אֲדוֹן הַנִּפְלָאוֹת

8 הַמְחַדֵּשׁ בְּטוּבוֹ בְּכָל יוֹם תָּמִיד

9 מַעֲשֵׂה בְרֵאשִׁית

10 כָּאָמוּר

11 לְעֹשֵׂה אוֹרִים גְּדֹלִים, כִּי לְעוֹלָם חַסְדּוֹ:

12 בָּרוּךְ אַתָּה יְהוָה יוֹצֵר הַמְּאוֹרוֹת.

Only Hashem is truly holy and does mighty things and creates new things, makes war and justice, saves us and heals us, and makes breathtaking miracles.

Why do you think sometimes people say the same words over and over?

Now think about why the angels might repeat that Hashem is holy three times.

The *Tefilla* Text

The words קָדוֹשׁ, קָדוֹשׁ, קָדוֹשׁ are highlighted in the color of the thought question, and the words כי הוא לבדו מרום וקדוש פועל גבורות, עושה חֲדָשׁוֹת בַּעַל מִלְחָמוֹת, זוֹרֵעַ צְדָקוֹת מַצְמִיחַ יְשׁוּעוֹת, בורא רפואות נוֹרָא תהלות, אֲדוֹן הנפלָאות are highlighted in the color of the conceptual translation.

The *Kavanot*

Thought Question:

We often repeat things that are really important, or words we want to remember or emphasize. Here, it is impossible to find words that are adequate to describe God's holiness, so instead the angels use the word holy over and over again (perhaps in a different medium we would have them shouting them for emphasis and intensity).

אהבה רבה

pp. 194–195

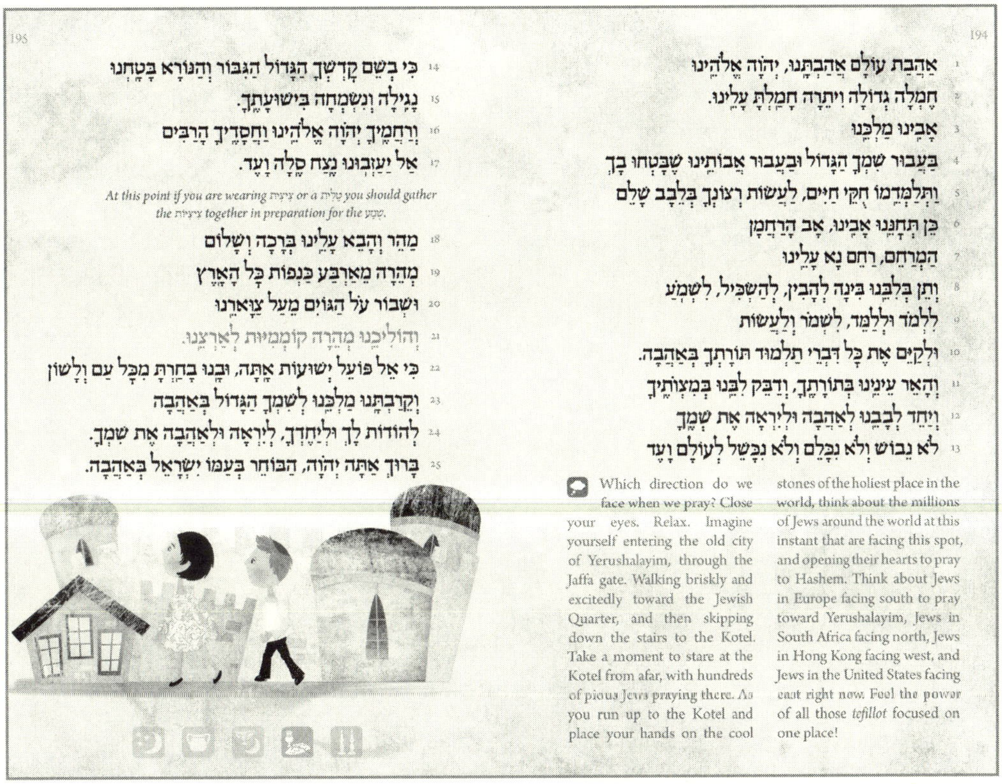

194

אַהֲבַת עוֹלָם אֲהַבְתָּנוּ, יְהֹוָה אֱלֹהֵינוּ
חֶמְלָה גְדוֹלָה וִיתֵרָה חָמַלְתָּ עָלֵינוּ.
אָבִינוּ מַלְכֵּנוּ
בַּעֲבוּר שִׁמְךָ הַגָּדוֹל וּבַעֲבוּר אֲבוֹתֵינוּ שֶׁבָּטְחוּ בָךְ
וַתְּלַמְּדֵמוֹ חֻקֵּי חַיִּים, לַעֲשׂוֹת רְצוֹנְךָ בְּלֵבָב שָׁלֵם
כֵּן תְּחָנֵּנוּ אָבִינוּ, אָב הָרַחֲמָן
הַמְרַחֵם, רַחֵם נָא עָלֵינוּ
וְתֵן בְּלִבֵּנוּ בִינָה לְהָבִין, לְהַשְׂכִּיל, לִשְׁמֹעַ
לִלְמֹד וּלְלַמֵּד, לִשְׁמֹר וְלַעֲשׂוֹת
וּלְקַיֵּם אֶת כָּל דִּבְרֵי תַלְמוּד תּוֹרָתְךָ בְּאַהֲבָה.
וְהָאֵר עֵינֵינוּ בְּתוֹרָתֶךָ, וְדַבֵּק לִבֵּנוּ בְּמִצְוֹתֶיךָ
וְיַחֵד לְבָבֵנוּ לְאַהֲבָה וּלְיִרְאָה אֶת שְׁמֶךָ
לֹא נֵבוֹשׁ וְלֹא נִכָּלֵם וְלֹא נִכָּשֵׁל לְעוֹלָם וָעֶד

Which direction do we face when we pray? Close your eyes. Relax. Imagine yourself entering the old city of Yerushalayim, through the Jaffa gate. Walking briskly and excitedly toward the Jewish Quarter, and then skipping down the stairs to the Kotel. Take a moment to stare at the Kotel from afar, with hundreds of pious Jews praying there. As you run up to the Kotel and place your hands on the cool stones of the holiest place in the world, think about the millions of Jews around the world at this instant that are facing this spot, and opening their hearts to pray to Hashem. Think about Jews in Europe facing south to pray toward Yerushalayim, Jews in South Africa facing north, Jews in Hong Kong facing west, and Jews in the United States facing east right now. Feel the power of all those *tefillot* focused on one place!

195

כִּי בְשֵׁם קָדְשְׁךָ הַגָּדוֹל הַגִּבּוֹר וְהַנּוֹרָא בָּטָחְנוּ
נָגִילָה וְנִשְׂמְחָה בִּישׁוּעָתֶךָ.
וְרַחֲמֶיךָ יְהֹוָה אֱלֹהֵינוּ וַחֲסָדֶיךָ הָרַבִּים
אַל יַעַזְבוּנוּ נֶצַח סֶלָה וָעֶד.

At this point if you are wearing ציצית *or a* טלית *you should gather the* ציצית *together in preparation for the* שמע.

מַהֵר וְהָבֵא עָלֵינוּ בְּרָכָה וְשָׁלוֹם
מְהֵרָה מֵאַרְבַּע כַּנְפוֹת כָּל הָאָרֶץ
וּשְׁבוֹר עֹל הַגּוֹיִם מֵעַל צַוָּארֵנוּ
וְהוֹלִיכֵנוּ מְהֵרָה קוֹמְמִיּוּת לְאַרְצֵנוּ.
כִּי אֵל פּוֹעֵל יְשׁוּעוֹת אָתָּה, וּבָנוּ בָחַרְתָּ מִכָּל עַם וְלָשׁוֹן
וְקֵרַבְתָּנוּ מַלְכֵּנוּ לְשִׁמְךָ הַגָּדוֹל בְּאַהֲבָה
לְהוֹדוֹת לָךְ וּלְיַחֶדְךָ, לְיִרְאָה וּלְאַהֲבָה אֶת שְׁמֶךָ.
בָּרוּךְ אַתָּה יְהֹוָה, הַבּוֹחֵר בְּעַמּוֹ יִשְׂרָאֵל בְּאַהֲבָה.

The *Tefilla* Text

The words וְהוֹלִיכֵנוּ מְהֵרָה קוֹמְמִיּוּת לְאַרְצֵנוּ. are highlighted in the color of the Jerusalem stone in the walls of Jerusalem in the illustration.

The Illustration

On page 73 where this *tefilla* is first found in the siddur in the weekday *Shaharit*, the following quote from Rabbi E.E. Dessler is found: *"Love and giving always come together."*[53] This *tefilla* talks of God's love for us,

53. "Discourse on Loving Kindness." See the explanation in this Companion there for a fuller quote and explanation of this idea.

and has two examples of "gifts" that God has given us because of His love for us. This should in turn generate love in us for Him. They are His Torah, and Eretz Yisrael – mentioned in the context of the ingathering of the exiles (on the following page of the siddur). This illustration has our characters taking a Shabbat walk in Yerushalayim. This is connected to the words in the *tefilla* that speak about the ingathering of the exiles, and indirectly refer to Eretz Yisrael and Yerushalayim as a gift of love from Hashem to us. It also reminds us of the similar illustration in the Koren Children's Siddur that has our characters walking home on Friday night from *Beit Kenesset* on pages 78/79.

The *Kavanot*

Thought Question:
This thought question asks the children to calculate in their minds in which direction they are facing when they pray. The answer is always *mizraḥ*, or towards Yerushalayim, but not always eastward. The thought question then becomes an imagination simulation, asking the children to imagine being in Yerushalayim, and at the Kotel, and experiencing the power of being in the place towards which millions of Jews are directing their prayers. This is something we should have in mind during all of our *tefillot*, as a way to connect to Hashem, our land and our people there. It is placed on this page of the siddur because of the sentence (that is highlighted in the color of the illustration – see above) that asks Hashem to bring us back to our homeland, and complete the ingathering of the exiles.

שמע 3/אבות

pp. 198–199

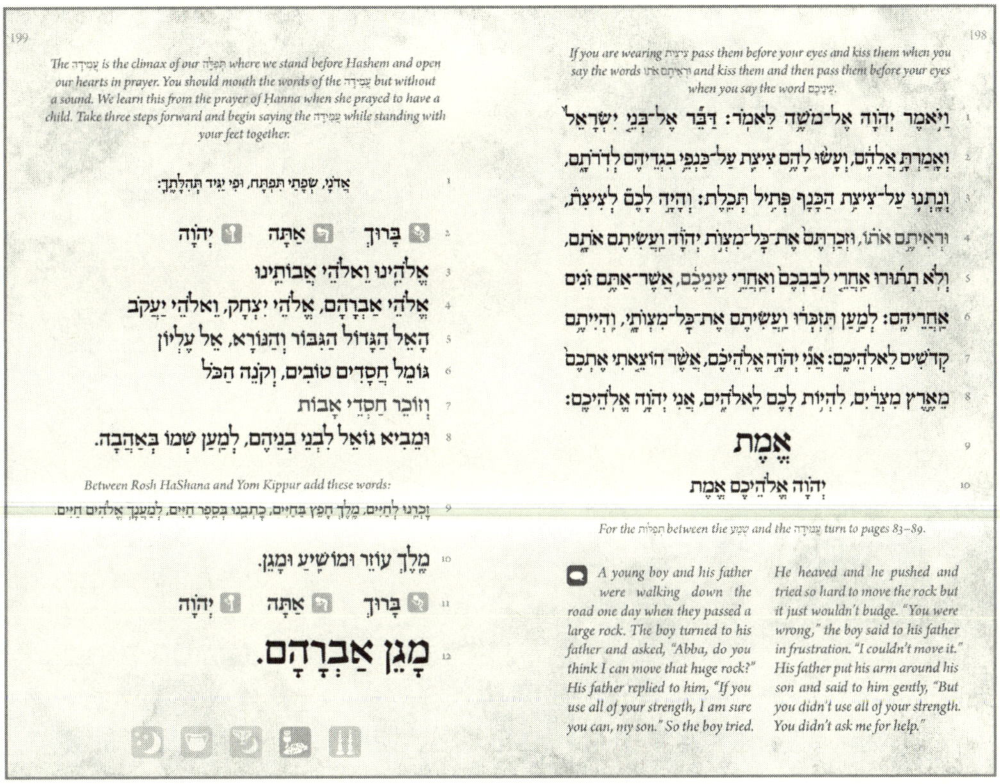

198

If you are wearing ציצית pass them before your eyes and kiss them when you say the words וראיתם אתו and kiss them and then pass them before your eyes when you say the word עיניכם.

1 ויאמר יהוה אל־משה לאמר: דבר אל־בני ישראל
2 ואמרת אלהם, ועשו להם ציצת על־כנפי בגדיהם לדרתם,
3 ונתנו על־ציצת הכנף פתיל תכלת: והיה לכם לציצת,
4 וראיתם אתו, וזכרתם את־כל־מצות יהוה ועשיתם אתם,
5 ולא תתורו אחרי לבבכם ואחרי עיניכם, אשר־אתם זנים
6 אחריהם: למען תזכרו ועשיתם את־כל־מצותי, והייתם
7 קדשים לאלהיכם: אני יהוה אלהיכם, אשר הוצאתי אתכם
8 מארץ מצרים, להיות לכם לאלהים, אני יהוה אלהיכם:
9 אמת
10 יהוה אלהיכם אמת

For the תפלות between the שמע and the עמידה turn to pages 83–89.

A young boy and his father were walking down the road one day when they passed a large rock. The boy turned to his father and asked, "Abba, do you think I can move that huge rock?" His father replied to him, "If you use all of your strength, I am sure you can, my son." So the boy tried. He heaved and he pushed and tried so hard to move the rock but it just wouldn't budge. "You were wrong," the boy said to his father in frustration. "I couldn't move it." His father put his arm around his son and said to him gently, "But you didn't use all of your strength. You didn't ask me for help."

199

The עמידה is the climax of our תפלה where we stand before Hashem and open our hearts in prayer. You should mouth the words of the עמידה but without a sound. We learn this from the prayer of Hanna when she prayed to have a child. Take three steps forward and begin saying the עמידה while standing with your feet together.

1 אדני, שפתי תפתח, ופי יגיד תהלתך:
2 ברוך אתה יהוה
3 אלהינו ואלהי אבותינו
4 אלהי אברהם, אלהי יצחק, ואלהי יעקב
5 האל הגדול הגבור והנורא, אל עליון
6 גומל חסדים טובים, וקנה הכל
7 וזוכר חסדי אבות
8 ומביא גואל לבני בניהם, למען שמו באהבה.

Between Rosh HaShana and Yom Kippur add these words:

9 זכרנו לחיים, מלך חפץ בחיים, כתבנו בספר חיים, למענך אלהים חיים.
10 מלך עוזר ומושיע ומגן.
11 ברוך אתה יהוה
12 מגן אברהם.

The *Tefilla* Text

The words וראיתם אתו and עיניכם are highlighted in the color of the rubric to remind those wearing *tzitzit* to kiss them at this point.

The words וזוכר חסדי אבות are highlighted in the color of the story.

The *Kavanot*

Story:
This story explores the role of parents as support and help in our lives. Parents, and previous generations as a whole, feel a responsibility to their children, and naturally function in this role. This is one approach to the *Avot* mentioned in the first *berakha* of each *Amida*. The *Avot* intercede on our behalf and we benefit from their merit (*Zekhut Avot*). They are our roots and our support, and carry us on their shoulders. Sometimes literally.

גבורה/קדושת השם

pp. 200–201

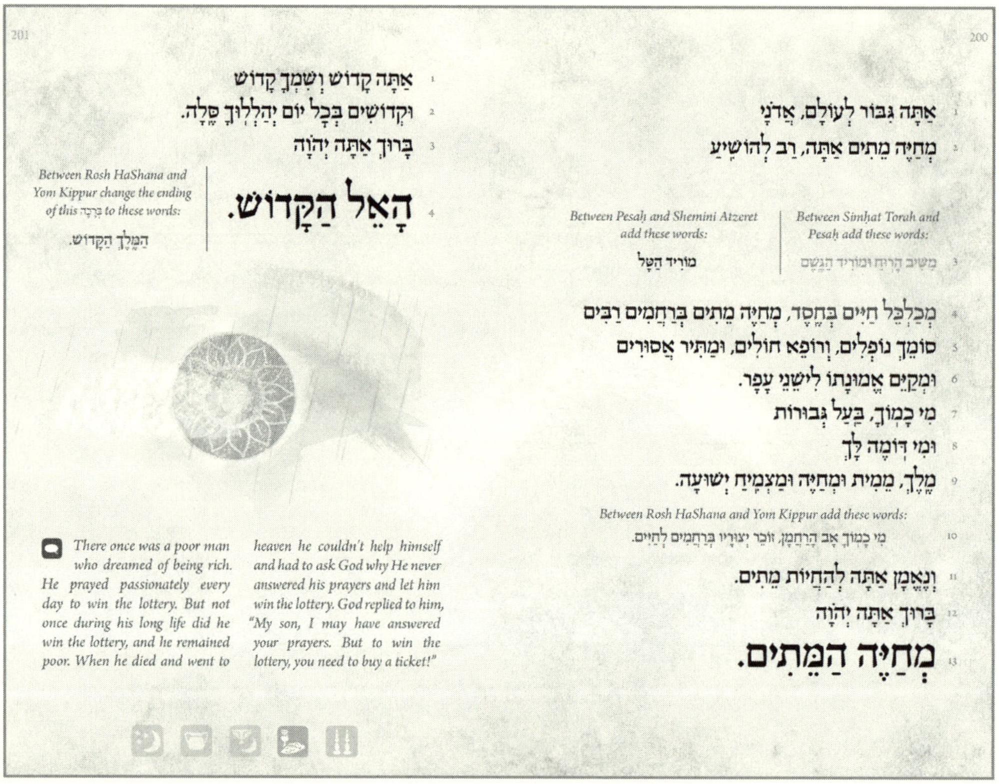

200

1 אַתָּה גִּבּוֹר לְעוֹלָם, אֲדֹנָי

2 מְחַיֵּה מֵתִים אַתָּה, רַב לְהוֹשִׁיעַ

Between Simḥat Torah and Pesaḥ add these words:

3 מַשִּׁיב הָרְוּחַ וּמוֹרִיד הַגֶּשֶׁם

Between Pesaḥ and Shemini Atzeret add these words:

מוֹרִיד הַטָּל

4 מְכַלְכֵּל חַיִּים בְּחֶסֶד, מְחַיֵּה מֵתִים בְּרַחֲמִים רַבִּים

5 סוֹמֵךְ נוֹפְלִים, וְרוֹפֵא חוֹלִים, וּמַתִּיר אֲסוּרִים

6 וּמְקַיֵּם אֱמוּנָתוֹ לִישֵׁנֵי עָפָר.

7 מִי כָמְוֹךָ, בַּעַל גְּבוּרוֹת

8 וּמִי דְּוֹמֶה לָּךְ

9 מֶלֶךְ, מֵמִית וּמְחַיֶּה וּמַצְמִיחַ יְשׁוּעָה.

Between Rosh HaShana and Yom Kippur add these words:

10 מִי כָמְוֹךָ אַב הָרַחֲמָן, זוֹכֵר יְצוּרָיו בְּרַחֲמִים לְחַיִּים.

11 וְנֶאֱמָן אַתָּה לְהַחֲיוֹת מֵתִים.

12 בָּרוּךְ אַתָּה יְהֹוָה

13 **מְחַיֵּה הַמֵּתִים.**

201

1 אַתָּה קָדוֹשׁ וְשִׁמְךָ קָדוֹשׁ

2 וּקְדוֹשִׁים בְּכָל יוֹם יְהַלְלְוּךָ סֶּלָה.

3 בָּרוּךְ אַתָּה יְהֹוָה

4 **הָאֵל הַקָּדוֹשׁ.**

Between Rosh HaShana and Yom Kippur change the ending of this בְּרָכָה *to these words:*

הַמֶּלֶךְ הַקָּדוֹשׁ.

There once was a poor man who dreamed of being rich. He prayed passionately every day to win the lottery. But not once during his long life did he win the lottery, and he remained poor. When he died and went to heaven he couldn't help himself and had to ask God why He never answered his prayers and let him win the lottery. God replied to him, "My son, I may have answered your prayers. But to win the lottery, you need to buy a ticket!"

The *Tefilla* Text

The words משיב הָרוח ומוריד הגשם are highlighted in the blue of the rain in the illustration, and the words מכלכל חיים בחסד, are highlighted in the color of the story.

The Illustration

The weather is a powerful expression of God's *gevura* – both in terms of its power and strength, and in God's life-giving and life-sustaining role in the world.

Rabbi Soloveitchik's approach to the word *gevura* is self-sacrifice.[54] In the context of God this would be contraction (*tzimtzum*) – the infinite God contracts

54. See Mesorat HaRav Siddur on *Birkkot HaShaḥar*.

Himself in order to create the world and to allow us to live. The illustration here, based on the first illustration for this *berakha* found on page 92, represents this role of God as Giver of life, through the sun and rain, essential elements necessary for life to exist on this planet. However, here a rainbow has been added, giving the scene a more tranquil and peaceful theme. The rainbow in the flood story in *Parashat Noaḥ* is the sign of the covenant between humanity and God that He will never again destroy humanity. It is therefore a peaceful sign, and an appropriate symbol to add to this *berakha* on Shabbat, a day that is synonymous with tranquility and peace.

The *Kavanot*

Story:
This story, often told in the form of a joke, contains an important message of partnership with Hashem. Placed on the page with the *berakha* of *Gevura*, where we remind ourselves that it is Hashem that provides for our needs, it is also important to remember that we cannot stand back and wait for Hashem to provide us with our needs, without making efforts to partner Him, and meet Him half way.

אלהי נצור

pp. 208–209

209

As you finish the עמידה you should stop and think that you have just had the opportunity and honor to stand before Hashem. To be respectful, bow as you take three steps back. Then bow to the left, right and center as the pictures show.

Between Rosh HaShana and Yom Kippur say השלום instead of שלום.

12 עשה שלום / השלום / במרומיו
13 הוא ברחמיו יעשה שלום עלינו
14 ועל כל עמו ישראל
15 ואמרו אמן.

208

1 אלהי
2 נצר לשוני מרע ושפתי מדבר מרמה
3 ולמקללי נפשי תדם, ונפשי כעפר לכל תהיה.
4 פתח לבי בתורתך, ואחרי מצותיך תרדף נפשי.
5 וכל הקמים עלי לרעה
6 מהרה הפר עצתם וקלקל מחשבותם.
7 יהיו כמץ לפני־רוח ומלאך יהוה דחה:
8 עשה למען שמך, עשה למען ימינך
9 עשה למען תורתך, עשה למען קדשתך.
10 למען יחלצון ידידיך, הושיעה ימינך וענני:
11 יהיו לרצון אמרי־פי והגיון לבי לפניך, יהוה צורי וגאלי:

וכתתו חרבותם לאתים וחניתותיהם למזמרות, לא־ישא גוי אל־גוי חרב ולא־ילמדו עוד מלחמה. (Yeshayahu 2:4)

Why do you think we greet people on Shabbat by saying שבת שלום?

What might be the deeper connection between שבת and שלום?

The *Tefilla* Text

Each time it appears, the word שָׁלוֹם is highlighted in the color of the thought question.

The Illustration

Our familiar friend the white dove visits us once again for this *berakha* of peace. As mentioned previously, the *yona* is traditionally seen as a symbol of peace, from its role in the story of Noaḥ and the flood. Here the *yona* is perched on a tree, and just as we are encouraged to see ourselves as part of nature on Shabbat, and refrain from manipulating, destroying, or even creating anything on this day, so the *yona* here takes her place in nature and the world. The *yona* can also be found on pages 130, 132, 169, and 256.

The *Kavanot*

Thought Question:

This famous verse from Yeshayahu describes a utopian time of universal peace in messianic times, when man will no longer need tools of war, but will rather use its resources for peaceful purposes only. The thought questions that follow ask the child to consider why "Shabbat Shalom" is the traditional greeting on Shabbat, and if there is a deeper connection between Shabbat and peace. That connection could be the utopian nature of Shabbat. On Shabbat we put materialism and hierarchies aside, and everyone, equal in the eyes of Hashem and of the community, exists in a utopian tranquility for 25 hours. This may be the meaning behind the link made between Shabbat and the World to Come (*Berakhot* 57b – page 188 of the siddur).

The link between Shabbat and *shalom* is explored on each page of this siddur where the *berakha* of *Shalom* appears in the Shabbat section (pages 168 and 225).

תפילה לשלום המדינה

pp. 212–213

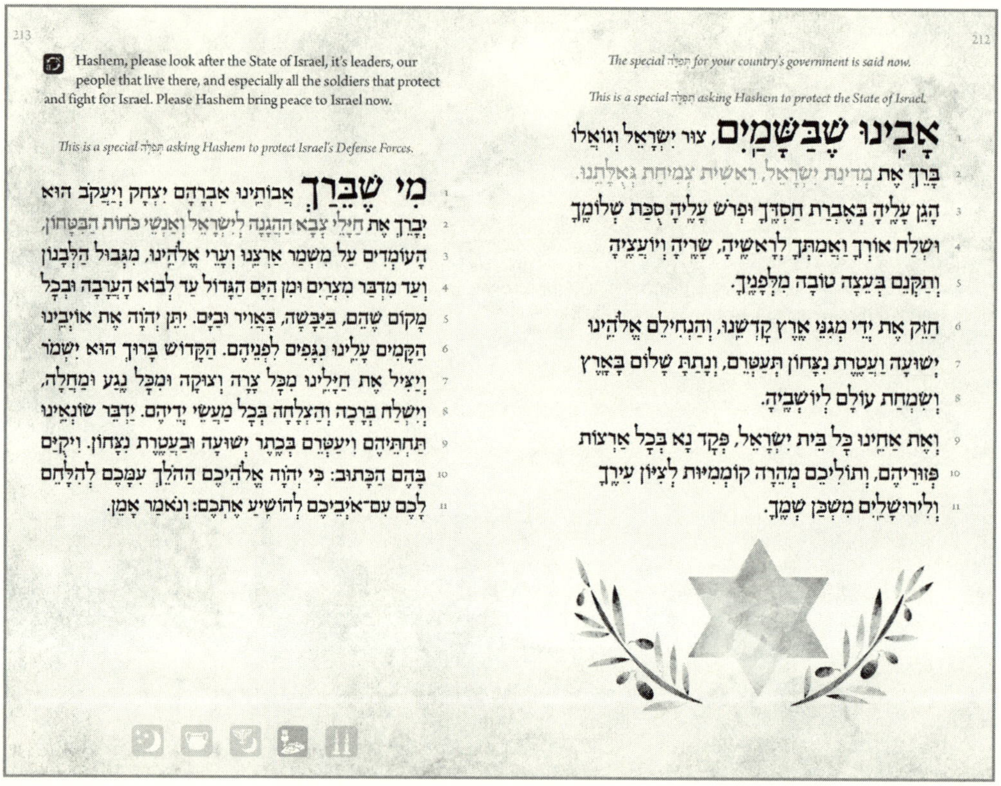
212

The special תְּפִלָּה for your country's government is said now.

This is a special תְּפִלָּה asking Hashem to protect the State of Israel.

אָבִינוּ שֶׁבַּשָּׁמַיִם, צוּר יִשְׂרָאֵל וְגוֹאֲלוֹ
בָּרֵךְ אֶת מְדִינַת יִשְׂרָאֵל, רֵאשִׁית צְמִיחַת גְּאֻלָּתֵנוּ.
הָגֵן עָלֶיהָ בְּאֶבְרַת חַסְדֶּךָ וּפְרֹשׂ עָלֶיהָ סֻכַּת שְׁלוֹמֶךָ
וּשְׁלַח אוֹרְךָ וַאֲמִתְּךָ לְרָאשֶׁיהָ, שָׂרֶיהָ וְיוֹעֲצֶיהָ
וְתַקְּנֵם בְּעֵצָה טוֹבָה מִלְּפָנֶיךָ.

חַזֵּק אֶת יְדֵי מְגִנֵּי אֶרֶץ קָדְשֵׁנוּ, וְהַנְחִילֵם אֱלֹהֵינוּ
יְשׁוּעָה וַעֲטֶרֶת נִצָּחוֹן תְּעַטְּרֵם, וְנָתַתָּ שָׁלוֹם בָּאָרֶץ
וְשִׂמְחַת עוֹלָם לְיוֹשְׁבֶיהָ.

וְאֶת אַחֵינוּ כָּל בֵּית יִשְׂרָאֵל, פְּקָד נָא בְּכָל אַרְצוֹת
פְּזוּרֵיהֶם, וְתוֹלִיכֵם מְהֵרָה קוֹמְמִיּוּת לְצִיּוֹן עִירֶךָ
וְלִירוּשָׁלַיִם מִשְׁכַּן שְׁמֶךָ.

213

Hashem, please look after the State of Israel, it's leaders, our people that live there, and especially all the soldiers that protect and fight for Israel. Please Hashem bring peace to Israel now.

This is a special תְּפִלָּה asking Hashem to protect Israel's Defense Forces.

מִי שֶׁבֵּרַךְ אֲבוֹתֵינוּ אַבְרָהָם יִצְחָק וְיַעֲקֹב הוּא
יְבָרֵךְ אֶת חַיָּלֵי צְבָא הַהֲגָנָה לְיִשְׂרָאֵל וְאַנְשֵׁי כֹּחוֹת הַבִּטָּחוֹן,
הָעוֹמְדִים עַל מִשְׁמַר אַרְצֵנוּ וְעָרֵי אֱלֹהֵינוּ, מִגְּבוּל הַלְּבָנוֹן
וְעַד מִדְבַּר מִצְרַיִם וּמִן הַיָּם הַגָּדוֹל עַד לְבוֹא הָעֲרָבָה וּבְכָל
מָקוֹם שֶׁהֵם, בַּיַּבָּשָׁה, בָּאֲוִיר וּבַיָּם. יִתֵּן יְהוָה אֶת אוֹיְבֵינוּ
הַקָּמִים עָלֵינוּ נִגָּפִים לִפְנֵיהֶם. הַקָּדוֹשׁ בָּרוּךְ הוּא יִשְׁמֹר
וְיַצִּיל אֶת חַיָּלֵינוּ מִכָּל צָרָה וְצוּקָה וּמִכָּל נֶגַע וּמַחֲלָה,
וְיִשְׁלַח בְּרָכָה וְהַצְלָחָה בְּכָל מַעֲשֵׂי יְדֵיהֶם. יַדְבֵּר שׂוֹנְאֵינוּ
תַּחְתֵּיהֶם וִיעַטְּרֵם בְּכֶתֶר יְשׁוּעָה וּבַעֲטֶרֶת נִצָּחוֹן. וִיקֻיַּם
בָּהֶם הַכָּתוּב: כִּי יְהוָה אֱלֹהֵיכֶם הַהֹלֵךְ עִמָּכֶם לְהִלָּחֵם
לָכֶם עִם־אֹיְבֵיכֶם לְהוֹשִׁיעַ אֶתְכֶם: וְנֹאמַר אָמֵן.

The *Tefilla* Text

The words מדינת ישׂרָאל, ראשית צמיחת גאֻלָּתֵנוּ are highlighted in the blue of the *Magen David* in the illustration, and the words חַיָּלֵי צְבָא הַהֲגָנָה לְיִשְׂרָאֵל וְאַנְשֵׁי כֹּחוֹת הַבִּטָּחוֹן are highlighted in the green of the olive branches in the illustration.

The Illustration

On this page, where we have the *tefilla* for the State of Israel, and for the safety of the Israel Defense Forces, we have an illustration that captures both in one image. The *Magen David* is the national symbol, and the center focus of the flag of the State of Israel, and the olive branches that are reaching out from underneath the

Magen David are found in many military insignia in the IDF. The message there (and the message of this illustration) is that while the hopes and dreams of the People of Israel are for peace, they are prepared to fight for their country and to defend their people.

ימלוך ה׳ לעולם

pp. 214–215

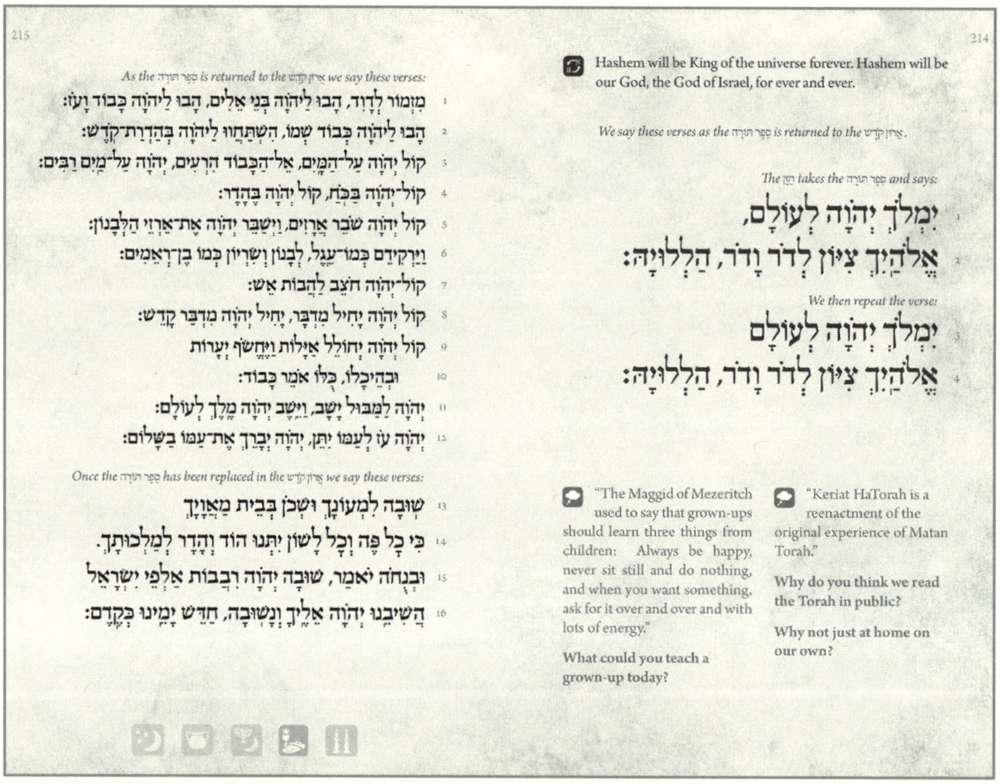

The *Tefilla* Text

The verse יִמְלֹךְ יְהוָה לְעוֹלָם אֱלֹהַיִךְ צִיּוֹן לְדֹר וָדֹר, הַלְלוּיָהּ: is highlighted in the color of the conceptual translation.

The *Kavanot*

Thought Question 1:
"*Keriat HaTorah* is reenacting the original experience of *Matan Torah*" – this is the paraphrased opinion of Rabbi J.B. Soloveitchik, and his rationale for understanding the position of the Rambam who rules that one must stand for *Keriat HaTorah*.

> *Keriat HaTorah*, the Rav claimed, is not merely the collective or communal recital of Torah text. Instead, it ***reenacts*** the pivotal moment at Har Sinai during which God's word was delivered to a human audience. As a re-dramatization of Sinai, the posture of the audience must resemble the quaking and trembling reported about the participants at Sinai. (Regarding the actual halakha, the *Shulḥan Arukh* requires that the reader stand but not the audience. The Rema cites that there are those who are "*maḥmir* to stand" during *Keriat HaTorah*. See *Oraḥ Ḥayyim* 141:1 for a discussion regarding the reader, and 146:4 regarding the audience.)"[55]

The thought question itself asks the children to consider why *Ḥazal* have ritualized the public reading of the Torah. One approach is the direction the quote encourages to go in – that it is an event of experiential value. But there could be more basic educational reasons – during periods of Jewish history where literacy was less widespread, and access to books/Torah scrolls even less common, this was the only opportunity for the average Jew to hear the words of Torah. Today we live in an age of increased literacy and book dissemination, and yet there is still a communal value to public Torah reading, bringing the community together every Shabbat to hear the Torah read.

Thought Question 2:

This wonderful quote from the Maggid of Mezeritch is placed on this page of the siddur, as many communities have the custom to ask a child to take center stage in the adult-dominated world of the main sanctuary of the synagogue and say the verses beginning with ימלוך. The Maggid knew that we can all learn from every child. These three character traits of the average child are ideals to strive for, though rarely seen as appropriate behavior for an adult. The Maggid disagrees!

The follow-up thought question gives the child a sense of empowerment and self-worth, asking him/her to consider what they have to teach the grown-ups in their life. The question does not ask if they have something to teach, but what do they have to teach!

55. Rav Moshe Taragin, http://www.vbm-torah.org/shavuot/shav69-mt.htm

תכנת שבת

pp. 218–219

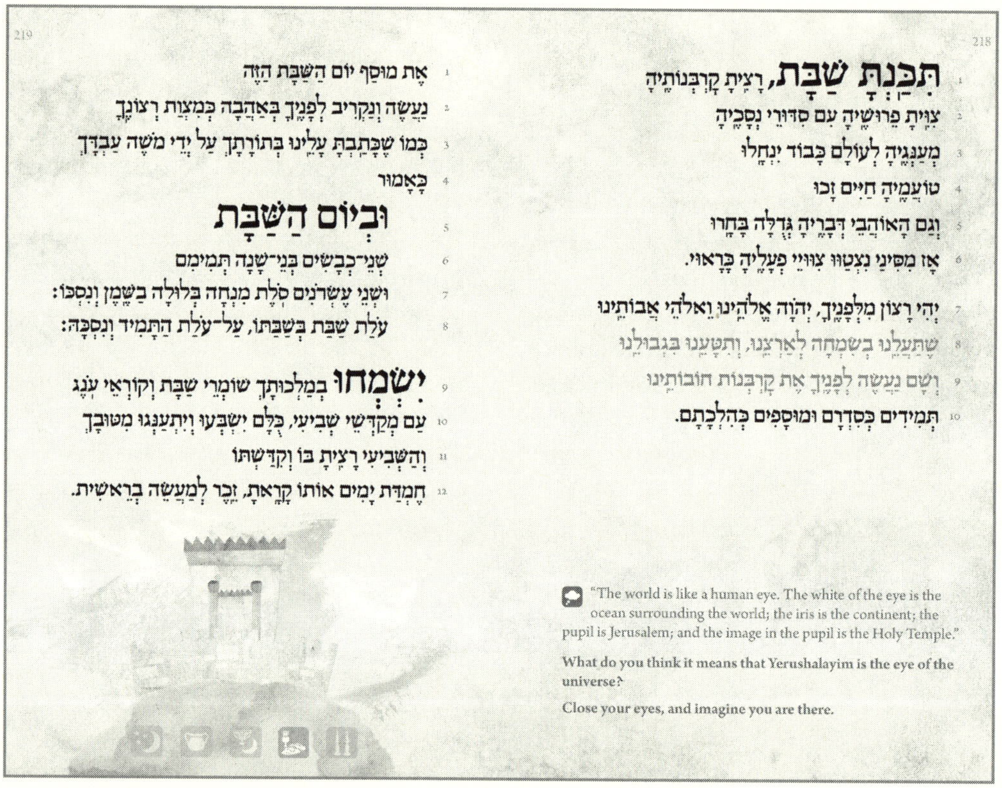

218

תִּכַּנְתָּ שַׁבָּת, רָצִיתָ קָרְבְּנוֹתֶיהָ
צִוִּיתָ פֵּרוּשֶׁיהָ עִם סִדּוּרֵי נְסָכֶיהָ
מְעַנְּגֶיהָ לְעוֹלָם כָּבוֹד יִנְחָלוּ
טוֹעֲמֶיהָ חַיִּים זָכוּ
וְגַם הָאוֹהֲבִים דְּבָרֶיהָ גְּדֻלָּה בָּחָרוּ
אָז מִסִּינַי נִצְטַוּוּ צִוּוּיֵי פְעָלֶיהָ כָּרָאוּי.

יְהִי רָצוֹן מִלְּפָנֶיךָ, יְהוָה אֱלֹהֵינוּ וֵאלֹהֵי אֲבוֹתֵינוּ
שֶׁתַּעֲלֵנוּ בְשִׂמְחָה לְאַרְצֵנוּ, וְתִטָּעֵנוּ בִּגְבוּלֵנוּ
וְשָׁם נַעֲשֶׂה לְפָנֶיךָ אֶת קָרְבְּנוֹת חוֹבוֹתֵינוּ
תְּמִידִים כְּסִדְרָם וּמוּסָפִים כְּהִלְכָתָם.

"The world is like a human eye. The white of the eye is the ocean surrounding the world; the iris is the continent; the pupil is Jerusalem; and the image in the pupil is the Holy Temple."

What do you think it means that Yerushalayim is the eye of the universe?

Close your eyes, and imagine you are there.

219

אֶת מוּסַף יוֹם הַשַּׁבָּת הַזֶּה
נַעֲשֶׂה וְנַקְרִיב לְפָנֶיךָ בְּאַהֲבָה כְּמִצְוַת רְצוֹנֶךָ
כְּמוֹ שֶׁכָּתַבְתָּ עָלֵינוּ בְּתוֹרָתֶךָ עַל יְדֵי מֹשֶׁה עַבְדֶּךָ
כָּאָמוּר

וּבְיוֹם הַשַּׁבָּת
שְׁנֵי־כְבָשִׂים בְּנֵי־שָׁנָה תְּמִימִם
וּשְׁנֵי עֶשְׂרֹנִים סֹלֶת מִנְחָה בְּלוּלָה בַשֶּׁמֶן וְנִסְכּוֹ:
עֹלַת שַׁבַּת בְּשַׁבַּתּוֹ, עַל־עֹלַת הַתָּמִיד וְנִסְכָּהּ:

יִשְׂמְחוּ בְמַלְכוּתְךָ שׁוֹמְרֵי שַׁבָּת וְקוֹרְאֵי עֹנֶג
עַם מְקַדְּשֵׁי שְׁבִיעִי, כֻּלָּם יִשְׂבְּעוּ וְיִתְעַנְּגוּ מִטּוּבֶךָ
וְהַשְּׁבִיעִי רָצִיתָ בּוֹ וְקִדַּשְׁתּוֹ
חֶמְדַּת יָמִים אוֹתוֹ קָרָאתָ, זֵכֶר לְמַעֲשֵׂה בְרֵאשִׁית.

The *Tefilla* Text

The words שתעלנו בשמחה לארצנו ותטענו בגבולנו ושם נעשה לפניך את קרבנות חובותינו are highlighted in the gold of the *Beit HaMikdash* in the illustration.

The Illustration

On this page, where we read about the *Shabbat Musaf* service in the *Beit HaMikdash*, we have an immediately recognizable illustration of the *Beit HaMikdash* in Yerushalayim. Putting the *Musaf Amida* in a more concrete physical context will help bring *Musaf* alive for the child, rather than abstract words describing a remote ritual that is hard to relate to.

The *Kavanot*

Thought Question:

This Talmudic quote (*Derekh Eretz Zuta* 9) gives us a visual physical representation of the centrality of Yerushalayim and the *Beit HaMikdash* to Judaism and Judaism's world outlook. Just like the eye is a series of concentric areas leading to the pupil in the center, so the world is a series of concentric areas of increasing holiness and importance, with the *Beit HaMikdash* in Yerushalayim at the center. When we pray we face Yerushalayim (and if we are in Yerushalayim we face towards where the Temple used to stand) and we turn our hearts towards it in a spiritual sense. This source is placed here during *Musaf* for Shabbat to enhance the experience of replicating the *Korban Musaf* with *Tefillat Musaf.* We focus on Yerushalayim during all our *tefillot*, but all the more so during *Musaf*, when we remember that if the *Beit HaMikdash* were still standing, we would be there offering the *Korban Musaf.*

אלהי נצור

pp. 224–225

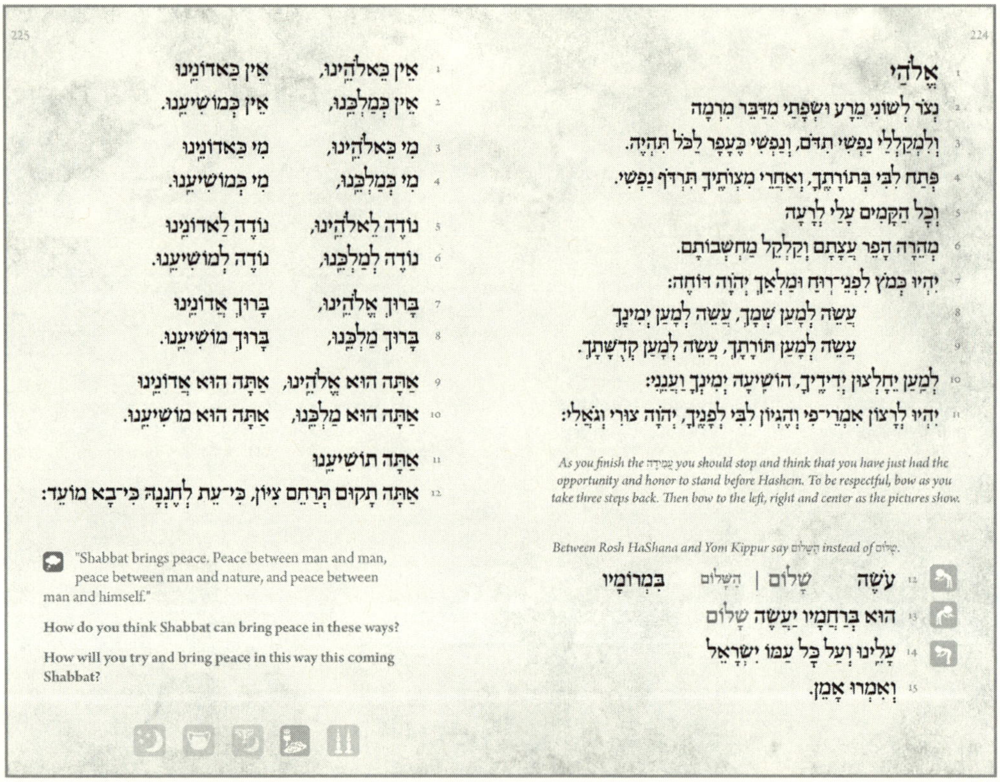

224

1 אֱלֹהַי

2 נְצֹר לְשׁוֹנִי מֵרָע וּשְׂפָתַי מִדַּבֵּר מִרְמָה

3 וְלִמְקַלְלַי נַפְשִׁי תִדֹּם, וְנַפְשִׁי כֶּעָפָר לַכֹּל תִּהְיֶה.

4 פְּתַח לִבִּי בְּתוֹרָתֶךָ, וְאַחֲרֵי מִצְוֹתֶיךָ תִּרְדֹּף נַפְשִׁי.

5 וְכָל הַקָּמִים עָלַי לְרָעָה

6 מְהֵרָה הָפֵר עֲצָתָם וְקַלְקֵל מַחְשַׁבְתָּם.

7 יִהְיוּ כְּמֹץ לִפְנֵי־רוּחַ וּמַלְאַךְ יְהֹוָה דֹּחֶה:

8 עֲשֵׂה לְמַעַן שְׁמֶךָ, עֲשֵׂה לְמַעַן יְמִינֶךָ

9 עֲשֵׂה לְמַעַן תּוֹרָתֶךָ, עֲשֵׂה לְמַעַן קְדֻשָּׁתֶךָ.

10 לְמַעַן יֵחָלְצוּן יְדִידֶיךָ, הוֹשִׁיעָה יְמִינְךָ וַעֲנֵנִי:

11 יִהְיוּ לְרָצוֹן אִמְרֵי־פִי וְהֶגְיוֹן לִבִּי לְפָנֶיךָ, יְהֹוָה צוּרִי וְגֹאֲלִי:

As you finish the עֲמִידָה you should stop and think that you have just had the opportunity and honor to stand before Hashem. To be respectful, bow as you take three steps back. Then bow to the left, right and center as the pictures show.

Between Rosh HaShana and Yom Kippur say הַשָּׁלוֹם instead of שָׁלוֹם.

12 עֹשֶׂה שָׁלוֹם | הַשָּׁלוֹם בִּמְרוֹמָיו

13 הוּא בְּרַחֲמָיו יַעֲשֶׂה שָׁלוֹם

14 עָלֵינוּ וְעַל כָּל עַמּוֹ יִשְׂרָאֵל

15 וְאִמְרוּ אָמֵן.

225

1 אֵין כֵּאלֹהֵינוּ, אֵין כַּאדוֹנֵינוּ

2 אֵין כְּמַלְכֵּנוּ, אֵין כְּמוֹשִׁיעֵנוּ.

3 מִי כֵאלֹהֵינוּ, מִי כַאדוֹנֵינוּ

4 מִי כְמַלְכֵּנוּ, מִי כְמוֹשִׁיעֵנוּ.

5 נוֹדֶה לֵאלֹהֵינוּ, נוֹדֶה לַאדוֹנֵינוּ

6 נוֹדֶה לְמַלְכֵּנוּ, נוֹדֶה לְמוֹשִׁיעֵנוּ.

7 בָּרוּךְ אֱלֹהֵינוּ, בָּרוּךְ אֲדוֹנֵינוּ

8 בָּרוּךְ מַלְכֵּנוּ, בָּרוּךְ מוֹשִׁיעֵנוּ.

9 אַתָּה הוּא אֱלֹהֵינוּ, אַתָּה הוּא אֲדוֹנֵינוּ

10 אַתָּה הוּא מַלְכֵּנוּ, אַתָּה הוּא מוֹשִׁיעֵנוּ.

11 אַתָּה תוֹשִׁיעֵנוּ

12 אַתָּה תָקוּם תְּרַחֵם צִיּוֹן, כִּי־עֵת לְחֶנְנָהּ כִּי־בָא מוֹעֵד:

"Shabbat brings peace. Peace between man and man, peace between man and nature, and peace between man and himself."

How do you think Shabbat can bring peace in these ways?

How will you try and bring peace in this way this coming Shabbat?

The *Tefilla* Text

Each time it appears, the word שָׁלוֹם is highlighted in the color of the thought question.

The *Kavanot*

Thought Question:
This quote comes from A.J. Heschel's famous and celebrated book *The Sabbath*.[56] Once again it explores the link between peace and Shabbat. The experience of Shabbat and the activities intrinsic to Shabbat lead to peace in these relationships. All the people of the community are brought together, as equals, sharing in this day together. The divisions of the week, whether

56. *The Sabbath: Its Meaning for Modern Man*, Farrar, Straus and Giroux, 2005.

they are financial or social, are put aside as everyone refocuses their attentions on their values and their God and their families. Man also takes 25 hours out from the rat race of dominating and conquering our environment. For the day of Shabbat we all become part of nature rather than its master, and refrain from manipulating or changing nature. And finally, with the removal of the stresses of life, we can all individually reconnect with our own essence, recharge our physical and spiritual batteries, and start the week again refreshed and truer to ourselves. This is how Shabbat brings peace between man and his fellow, his environment, and himself.

The link between Shabbat and *shalom* is explored on each page of this siddur where the *berakha* of *Shalom* appears in the Shabbat section (pages 168 and 208).

עלינו

pp. 226–227

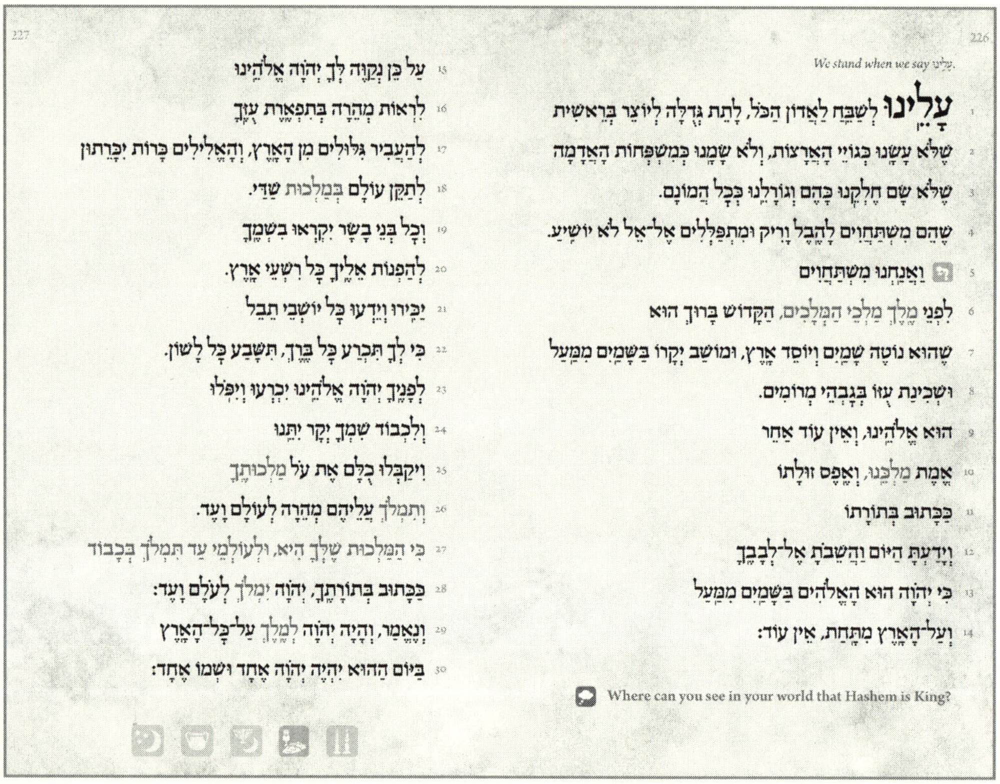
226

We stand when we say עָלֵינוּ.

עָלֵינוּ לְשַׁבֵּחַ לַאֲדוֹן הַכֹּל, לָתֵת גְּדֻלָּה לְיוֹצֵר בְּרֵאשִׁית
שֶׁלֹּא עָשָׂנוּ כְּגוֹיֵי הָאֲרָצוֹת, וְלֹא שָׂמָנוּ כְּמִשְׁפְּחוֹת הָאֲדָמָה
שֶׁלֹּא שָׂם חֶלְקֵנוּ כָּהֶם וְגוֹרָלֵנוּ כְּכָל הֲמוֹנָם.
שֶׁהֵם מִשְׁתַּחֲוִים לְהֶבֶל וָרִיק וּמִתְפַּלְלִים אֶל־אֵל לֹא יוֹשִׁיעַ.
וַאֲנַחְנוּ מִשְׁתַּחֲוִים
לִפְנֵי מֶלֶךְ מַלְכֵי הַמְּלָכִים, הַקָּדוֹשׁ בָּרוּךְ הוּא
שֶׁהוּא נוֹטֶה שָׁמַיִם וְיוֹסֵד אָרֶץ, וּמוֹשַׁב יְקָרוֹ בַּשָּׁמַיִם מִמַּעַל
וּשְׁכִינַת עֻזּוֹ בְּגָבְהֵי מְרוֹמִים.
הוּא אֱלֹהֵינוּ, וְאֵין עוֹד אַחֵר
אֱמֶת מַלְכֵּנוּ, וְאֶפֶס זוּלָתוֹ
כַּכָּתוּב בְּתוֹרָתוֹ
וְיָדַעְתָּ הַיּוֹם וַהֲשֵׁבֹתָ אֶל־לְבָבֶךָ
כִּי יְהוָה הוּא הָאֱלֹהִים בַּשָּׁמַיִם מִמַּעַל
וְעַל־הָאָרֶץ מִתָּחַת, אֵין עוֹד:

Where can you see in your world that Hashem is King?

227

עַל כֵּן נְקַוֶּה לְּךָ יְהוָה אֱלֹהֵינוּ
לִרְאוֹת מְהֵרָה בְּתִפְאֶרֶת עֻזֶּךָ
לְהַעֲבִיר גִּלּוּלִים מִן הָאָרֶץ, וְהָאֱלִילִים כָּרוֹת יִכָּרֵתוּן
לְתַקֵּן עוֹלָם בְּמַלְכוּת שַׁדַּי.
וְכָל בְּנֵי בָשָׂר יִקְרְאוּ בִשְׁמֶךָ
לְהַפְנוֹת אֵלֶיךָ כָּל רִשְׁעֵי אָרֶץ.
יַכִּירוּ וְיֵדְעוּ כָּל יוֹשְׁבֵי תֵבֵל
כִּי לְךָ תִּכְרַע כָּל בֶּרֶךְ, תִּשָּׁבַע כָּל לָשׁוֹן.
לְפָנֶיךָ יְהוָה אֱלֹהֵינוּ יִכְרְעוּ וְיִפֹּלוּ
וְלִכְבוֹד שִׁמְךָ יְקָר יִתֵּנוּ
וִיקַבְּלוּ כֻלָּם אֶת עֹל מַלְכוּתֶךָ
וְתִמְלֹךְ עֲלֵיהֶם מְהֵרָה לְעוֹלָם וָעֶד.
כִּי הַמַּלְכוּת שֶׁלְּךָ הִיא, וּלְעוֹלְמֵי עַד תִּמְלֹךְ בְּכָבוֹד
כַּכָּתוּב בְּתוֹרָתֶךָ, יְהוָה יִמְלֹךְ לְעֹלָם וָעֶד:
וְנֶאֱמַר, וְהָיָה יְהוָה לְמֶלֶךְ עַל־כָּל־הָאָרֶץ
בַּיּוֹם הַהוּא יִהְיֶה יְהוָה אֶחָד וּשְׁמוֹ אֶחָד:

The *Tefilla* Text

Every appearance of the root word מלך is highlighted in the color of the thought question.

The *Kavanot*

Thought Question:
At various other places in the siddur we have explored what is meant by God as King (for example pages 98, 134, and 142). This is a core theme of this *tefilla* (which itself features three times in the siddur). This thought question asks the child to look for examples of God's

kingship in the world. While abstract, if the concept of kingship is understood, then examples of it in the world are possible to explore. Such as God's role in history (*Hashgaḥa*), nature as proof that he created the world (and owns it like a king has sovereignty over a country), and most importantly examples of His people crowning Him as King (such as saying *Aleinu*, doing mitzvot, etc.).

שיר של יום/אדון עולם

pp. 228–229

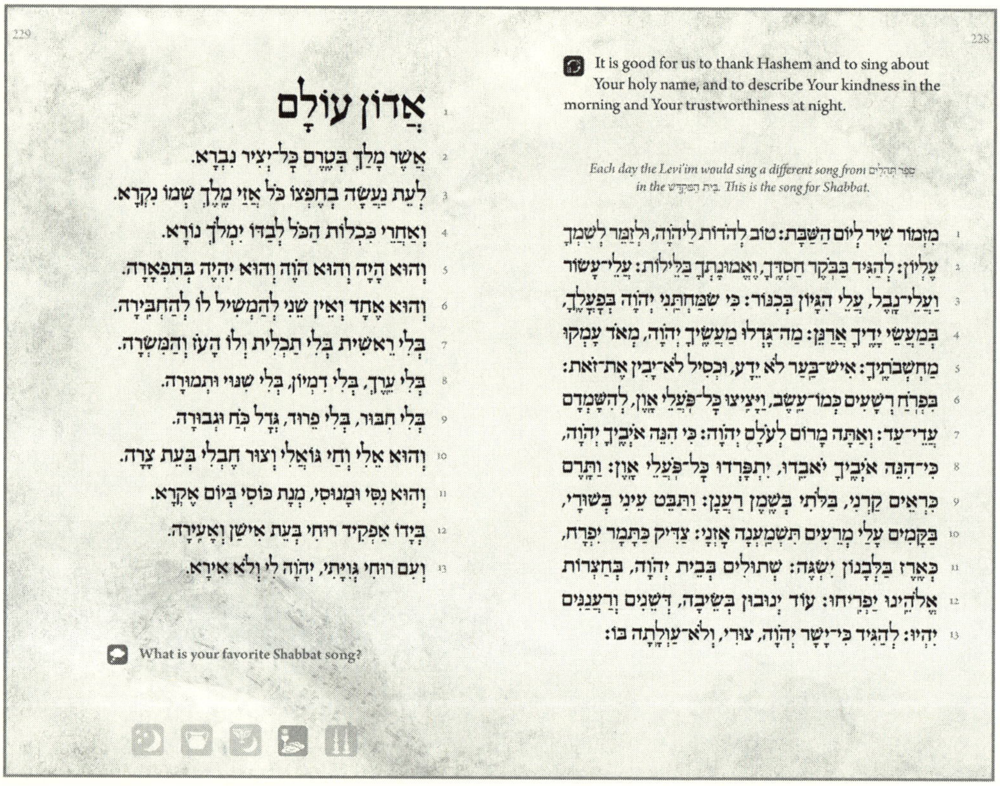

228

It is good for us to thank Hashem and to sing about Your holy name, and to describe Your kindness in the morning and Your trustworthiness at night.

Each day the Levi'im would sing a different song from ספר תהלים *in the* בית המקדש*. This is the song for Shabbat.*

מזמור שיר ליום השבת: טוב להדות ליהוה, ולזמר לשמך
עליון: להגיד בבקר חסדך, ואמונתך בלילות: עלי־עשור
ועלי־נבל, עלי הגיון בכנור: כי שמחתני יהוה בפעלך,
במעשי ידיך ארנן: מה־גדלו מעשיך יהוה, מאד עמקו
מחשבתיך: איש־בער לא ידע, וכסיל לא־יבין את־זאת:
בפרח רשעים כמו־עשב, ויציצו כל־פעלי און, להשמדם
עדי־עד: ואתה מרום לעלם יהוה: כי הנה איביך יהוה,
כי־הנה איביך יאבדו, יתפרדו כל־פעלי און: ותרם
כראים קרני, בלתי בשמן רענן: ותבט עיני בשורי,
בקמים עלי מרעים תשמענה אזני: צדיק כתמר יפרח,
כארז בלבנון ישגה: שתולים בבית יהוה, בחצרות
אלהינו יפריחו: עוד ינובון בשיבה, דשנים ורעננים
יהיו: להגיד כי־ישר יהוה, צורי, ולא־עולתה בו:

229

אדון עולם
אשר מלך בטרם כל־יציר נברא.
לעת נעשה בחפצו כל אזי מלך שמו נקרא.
ואחרי ככלות הכל לבדו ימלך נורא.
והוא היה והוא הוה והוא יהיה בתפארה.
והוא אחד ואין שני להמשיל לו להחבירה.
בלי ראשית בלי תכלית ולו העז והמשרה.
בלי ערך, בלי דמיון, בלי שנוי ותמורה.
בלי חבור, בלי פרוד, גדל כח וגבורה.
והוא אלי וחי גואלי וצור חבלי בעת צרה.
והוא נסי ומנוסי, מנת כוסי ביום אקרא.
בידו אפקיד רוחי בעת אישן ואעירה.
ועם רוחי גויתי, יהוה לי ולא אירא.

What is your favorite Shabbat song?

The *Tefilla* Text

The verses, טוב להדות לה׳, ולזמר לשמך עליון: להגיד בבקר חסדך, ואמונתך בלילות: are highlighted in the color of the conceptual translation.

The *Kavanot*

Thought Question:
Adon Olam is more than likely not the answer to this question, but Shabbat and singing go hand in hand as a way to enhance the physical and spiritual enjoyment of Shabbat. What is your favorite Shabbat song?

There are other music related questions and stories in the siddur found on pages 39, 50, 52, 148, 184, and 229.

קידוש/יום שבתון

pp. 230–231

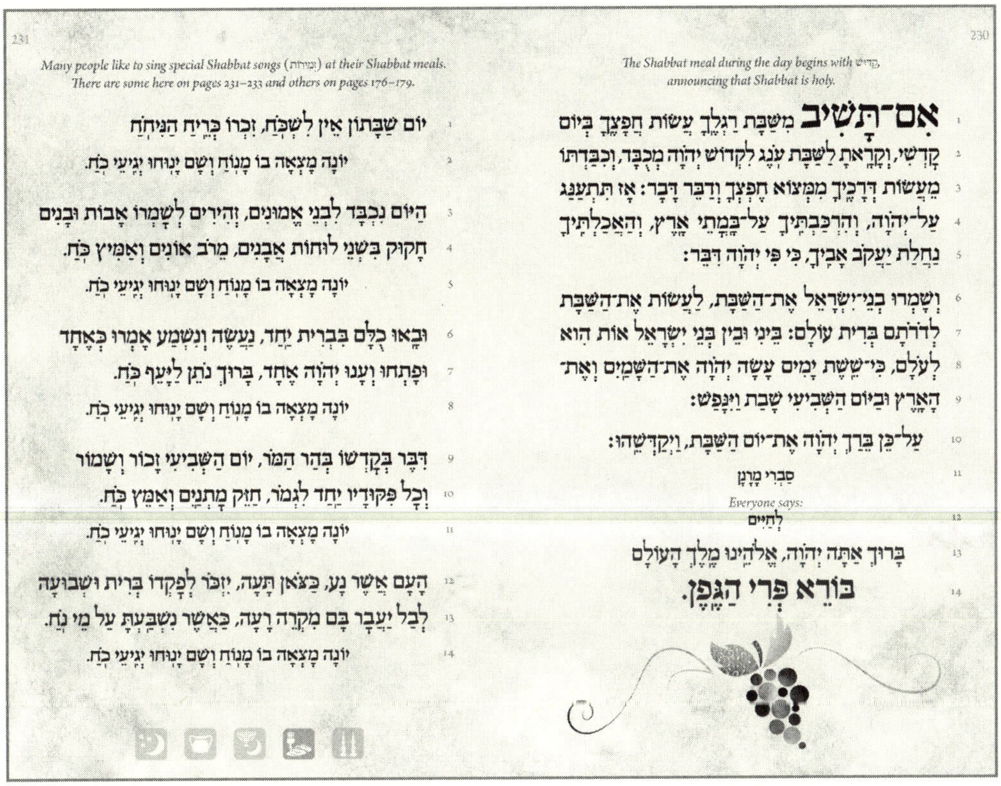

230

The Shabbat meal during the day begins with קידוש, *announcing that Shabbat is holy.*

אִם־תָּשִׁיב מִשַּׁבָּת רַגְלֶךָ עֲשׂוֹת חֲפָצֶךָ בְּיוֹם קָדְשִׁי, וְקָרָאתָ לַשַּׁבָּת עֹנֶג לִקְדוֹשׁ יְהֹוָה מְכֻבָּד, וְכִבַּדְתּוֹ מֵעֲשׂוֹת דְּרָכֶיךָ מִמְּצוֹא חֶפְצְךָ וְדַבֵּר דָּבָר: אָז תִּתְעַנַּג עַל־יְהֹוָה, וְהִרְכַּבְתִּיךָ עַל־בָּמֳתֵי אָרֶץ, וְהַאֲכַלְתִּיךָ נַחֲלַת יַעֲקֹב אָבִיךָ, כִּי פִּי יְהֹוָה דִּבֵּר:

וְשָׁמְרוּ בְנֵי־יִשְׂרָאֵל אֶת־הַשַּׁבָּת, לַעֲשׂוֹת אֶת־הַשַּׁבָּת לְדֹרֹתָם בְּרִית עוֹלָם: בֵּינִי וּבֵין בְּנֵי יִשְׂרָאֵל אוֹת הִוא לְעֹלָם, כִּי־שֵׁשֶׁת יָמִים עָשָׂה יְהֹוָה אֶת־הַשָּׁמַיִם וְאֶת־הָאָרֶץ וּבַיּוֹם הַשְּׁבִיעִי שָׁבַת וַיִּנָּפַשׁ:

עַל־כֵּן בֵּרַךְ יְהֹוָה אֶת־יוֹם הַשַּׁבָּת, וַיְקַדְּשֵׁהוּ:

סַבְרִי מָרָנָן

Everyone says:

לְחַיִּים

בָּרוּךְ אַתָּה יְהֹוָה, אֱלֹהֵינוּ מֶלֶךְ הָעוֹלָם

בּוֹרֵא פְּרִי הַגָּפֶן.

231

Many people like to sing special Shabbat songs (זמירות) *at their Shabbat meals. There are some here on pages 231–233 and others on pages 176–179.*

יוֹם שַׁבָּתוֹן אֵין לִשְׁכֹּחַ, זִכְרוֹ כְּרֵיחַ הַנִּיחֹחַ
יוֹנָה מָצְאָה בוֹ מָנוֹחַ וְשָׁם יָנוּחוּ יְגִיעֵי כֹחַ.

הַיּוֹם נִכְבָּד לִבְנֵי אֱמוּנִים, זְהִירִים לְשָׁמְרוֹ אָבוֹת וּבָנִים
חָקוּק בִּשְׁנֵי לוּחוֹת אֲבָנִים, מֵרֹב אוֹנִים וְאַמִּיץ כֹּחַ.
יוֹנָה מָצְאָה בוֹ מָנוֹחַ וְשָׁם יָנוּחוּ יְגִיעֵי כֹחַ.

וּבָאוּ כֻלָּם בִּבְרִית יַחַד, נַעֲשֶׂה וְנִשְׁמַע אָמְרוּ כְּאֶחָד
וּפָתְחוּ וְעָנוּ יְהֹוָה אֶחָד, בָּרוּךְ נֹתֵן לַיָּעֵף כֹּחַ.
יוֹנָה מָצְאָה בוֹ מָנוֹחַ וְשָׁם יָנוּחוּ יְגִיעֵי כֹחַ.

דִּבֶּר בְּקָדְשׁוֹ בְּהַר הַמֹּר, יוֹם הַשְּׁבִיעִי זָכוֹר וְשָׁמוֹר
וְכָל פִּקּוּדָיו יַחַד לִגְמֹר, חַזֵּק מָתְנַיִם וְאַמֵּץ כֹּחַ.
יוֹנָה מָצְאָה בוֹ מָנוֹחַ וְשָׁם יָנוּחוּ יְגִיעֵי כֹחַ.

הָעָם אֲשֶׁר נָע, כַּצֹּאן תָּעָה, יִזְכֹּר לְפָקְדוֹ בְּרִית וּשְׁבוּעָה
לְבַל יַעֲבָר בָּם מִקְרֵה רָעָה, כַּאֲשֶׁר נִשְׁבַּעְתָּ עַל מֵי נֹחַ.
יוֹנָה מָצְאָה בוֹ מָנוֹחַ וְשָׁם יָנוּחוּ יְגִיעֵי כֹחַ.

The *Tefilla* Text

All words with the root of קדש and the conclusion to the berakha בורא פרי הגפן are highlighted in the color of the cluster of grapes in the illustration.

The first letters of each verse in the song יום שבתון are highlighted in red calling attention to the acrostic of the author Rabbi Yehuda HaLevi's name. The acrostic spells יהודה.

יום זה מכבד

pp. 232–233

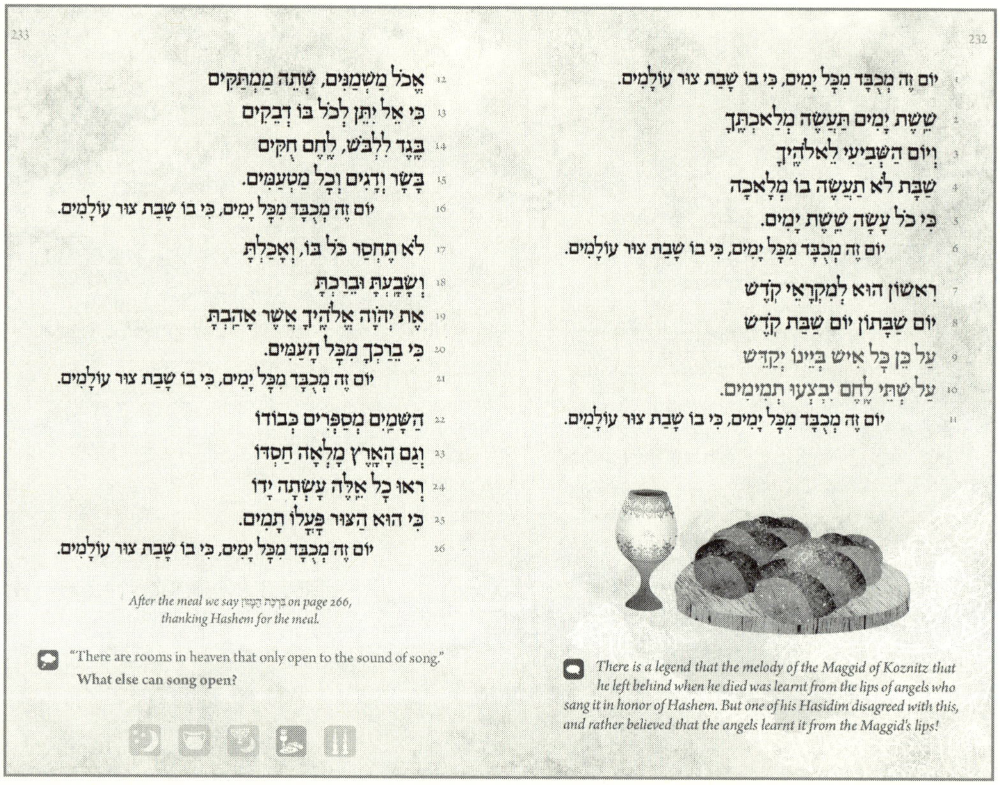

232

יום זה מכבד מכל ימים, כי בו שבת צור עולמים.

ששת ימים תעשה מלאכתך
ויום השביעי לאלהיך
שבת לא תעשה בו מלאכה
כי כל עשה ששת ימים.
יום זה מכבד מכל ימים, כי בו שבת צור עולמים.

ראשון הוא למקראי קדש
יום שבתון יום שבת קדש
על כן כל איש ביינו יקדש
על שתי לחם יבצעו תמימים.
יום זה מכבד מכל ימים, כי בו שבת צור עולמים.

There is a legend that the melody of the Maggid of Koznitz that he left behind when he died was learnt from the lips of angels who sang it in honor of Hashem. But one of his Hasidim disagreed with this, and rather believed that the angels learnt it from the Maggid's lips!

233

אכל משמנים, שתה ממתקים
כי אל יתן לכל בו דבקים
בגד ללבש, לחם חקים
בשר ודגים וכל מטעמים.
יום זה מכבד מכל ימים, כי בו שבת צור עולמים.

לא תחסר כל בו, ואכלת
ושבעת וברכת
את יהוה אלהיך אשר אהבת
כי ברכך מכל העמים.
יום זה מכבד מכל ימים, כי בו שבת צור עולמים.

השמים מספרים כבודו
וגם הארץ מלאה חסדו
ראו כל אלה עשתה ידו
כי הוא הצור פעלו תמים.
יום זה מכבד מכל ימים, כי בו שבת צור עולמים.

After the meal we say ברכת המזון on page 266, thanking Hashem for the meal.

"There are rooms in heaven that only open to the sound of song."
What else can song open?

The *Tefilla* Text

The words על כן כל איש ביינו יקדש and על שתי לחם יבצעו תמימים are highlighted in the color of the *Kiddush* cup and the *ḥallot* in the illustration.

The Illustration

On the page where the *zemer* mentions the wine of *Kiddush* and the two *ḥallot* of the *seuda* that we are obligated to have in honor of Shabbat, we have our ornate *Kiddush* cup (that also appears with Friday night *Kiddush* and *havdala*) and two *ḥallot.*

The *Kavanot*

Thought Question:
"There are rooms in heaven that only open to the sound of song" is a quote from the kabbalistic work the *Zohar*. Song can also open rooms in people's hearts, including the one singing!

Story:
The Hasidim take their *niggunim* (melodies) very seriously, and if we agree that music has the power to open hearts and help souls to soar, then we should be open to the possibility that we can receive them from the angels, and teach them in return.

The role of music and song in our *tefillot* is explored on pages 39, 52, 119, and 184 of the siddur.

הבדלה

pp. 234–235

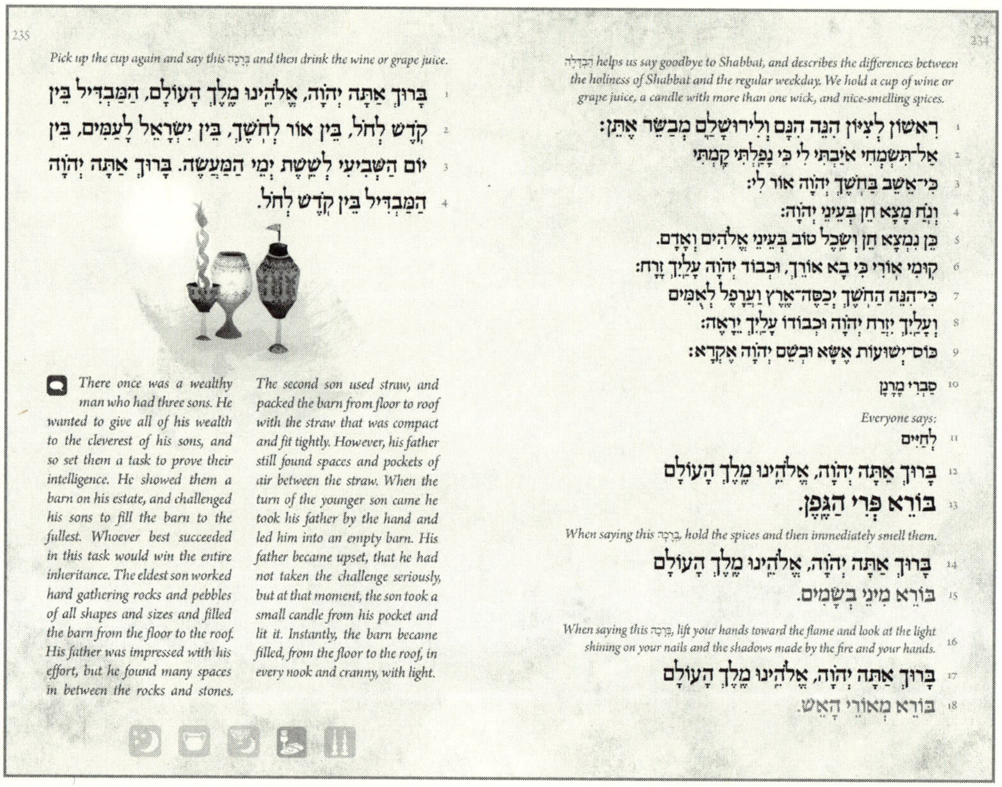

234

הַבְדָּלָה helps us say goodbye to Shabbat, and describes the differences between the holiness of Shabbat and the regular weekday. We hold a cup of wine or grape juice, a candle with more than one wick, and nice-smelling spices.

רִאשׁוֹן לְצִיּוֹן הִנֵּה הִנָּם וְלִירוּשָׁלַםִ מְבַשֵּׂר אֶתֵּן:
אַל־תִּשְׂמְחִי אֹיַבְתִּי לִי כִּי נָפַלְתִּי קָמְתִּי
כִּי־אֵשֵׁב בַּחֹשֶׁךְ יְהוָה אוֹר לִי:
וְנֹחַ מָצָא חֵן בְּעֵינֵי יְהוָה:
בֵּן נִמְצָא חֵן וְשֵׂכֶל טוֹב בְּעֵינֵי אֱלֹהִים וְאָדָם.
קוּמִי אוֹרִי כִּי בָא אוֹרֵךְ, וּכְבוֹד יְהוָה עָלַיִךְ זָרָח:
כִּי־הִנֵּה הַחֹשֶׁךְ יְכַסֶּה־אֶרֶץ וַעֲרָפֶל לְאֻמִּים
וְעָלַיִךְ יִזְרַח יְהוָה וּכְבוֹדוֹ עָלַיִךְ יֵרָאֶה:
כּוֹס־יְשׁוּעוֹת אֶשָּׂא וּבְשֵׁם יְהוָה אֶקְרָא:

סַבְרִי מָרָנָן

Everyone says:

לְחַיִּים

בָּרוּךְ אַתָּה יְהוָה, אֱלֹהֵינוּ מֶלֶךְ הָעוֹלָם
בּוֹרֵא פְּרִי הַגָּפֶן.

When saying this בְּרָכָה*, hold the spices and then immediately smell them.*

בָּרוּךְ אַתָּה יְהוָה, אֱלֹהֵינוּ מֶלֶךְ הָעוֹלָם
בּוֹרֵא מִינֵי בְשָׂמִים.

When saying this בְּרָכָה*, lift your hands toward the flame and look at the light shining on your nails and the shadows made by the fire and your hands.*

בָּרוּךְ אַתָּה יְהוָה, אֱלֹהֵינוּ מֶלֶךְ הָעוֹלָם
בּוֹרֵא מְאוֹרֵי הָאֵשׁ.

235

Pick up the cup again and say this בְּרָכָה *and then drink the wine or grape juice.*

בָּרוּךְ אַתָּה יְהוָה, אֱלֹהֵינוּ מֶלֶךְ הָעוֹלָם, הַמַּבְדִּיל בֵּין
קֹדֶשׁ לְחֹל, בֵּין אוֹר לְחֹשֶׁךְ, בֵּין יִשְׂרָאֵל לָעַמִּים, בֵּין
יוֹם הַשְּׁבִיעִי לְשֵׁשֶׁת יְמֵי הַמַּעֲשֶׂה. בָּרוּךְ אַתָּה יְהוָה
הַמַּבְדִּיל בֵּין קֹדֶשׁ לְחֹל.

There once was a wealthy man who had three sons. He wanted to give all of his wealth to the cleverest of his sons, and so set them a task to prove their intelligence. He showed them a barn on his estate, and challenged his sons to fill the barn to the fullest. Whoever best succeeded in this task would win the entire inheritance. The eldest son worked hard gathering rocks and pebbles of all shapes and sizes and filled the barn from the floor to the roof. His father was impressed with his effort, but he found many spaces in between the rocks and stones. The second son used straw, and packed the barn from floor to roof with the straw that was compact and fit tightly. However, his father still found spaces and pockets of air between the straw. When the turn of the younger son came he took his father by the hand and led him into an empty barn. His father became upset, that he had not taken the challenge seriously, but at that moment, the son took a small candle from his pocket and lit it. Instantly, the barn became filled, from the floor to the roof, in every nook and cranny, with light.

The *Tefilla* Text

The words בורא מאורי האש are highlighted in the color of the *havdala* flame in the illustration. The words בורא פרי הגפן. are highlighted in the red of the wine in the cup in the illustration. The words בורא מיני בשמים are highlighted in the brown color of the spice box in the illustration.

The Illustration

The required ritual objects for *havdala* are found here in the illustration – the multi-wick *havdala* candle, the spice box, and the same *Kiddush* cup that we used to sanctify Shabbat will now be used to separate between the holiness of Shabbat and the profane nature of the weekday.

The *Kavanot*

Conceptual Translation of:

המבדיל בין קֹדש לחל, בין אור לחֹשך, בין ישׂרָאל לָעמים, בין יום השביעי לשֵׁשת ימי המעֲשׂה.

Story:
This clever story explores the phenomenon of light and the far-reaching impact it can have on us. It asks the children to reflect on the impact of the *havdala* candle's flame, in the same way as we consider the impact of the light generated by the Shabbat candles. Light of course can refer to a physical light and a spiritual light, and the flame of the *havdala* candle can also represent the light of Torah that should fill every nook and cranny of our coming week.

הלל 1

pp. 238–239

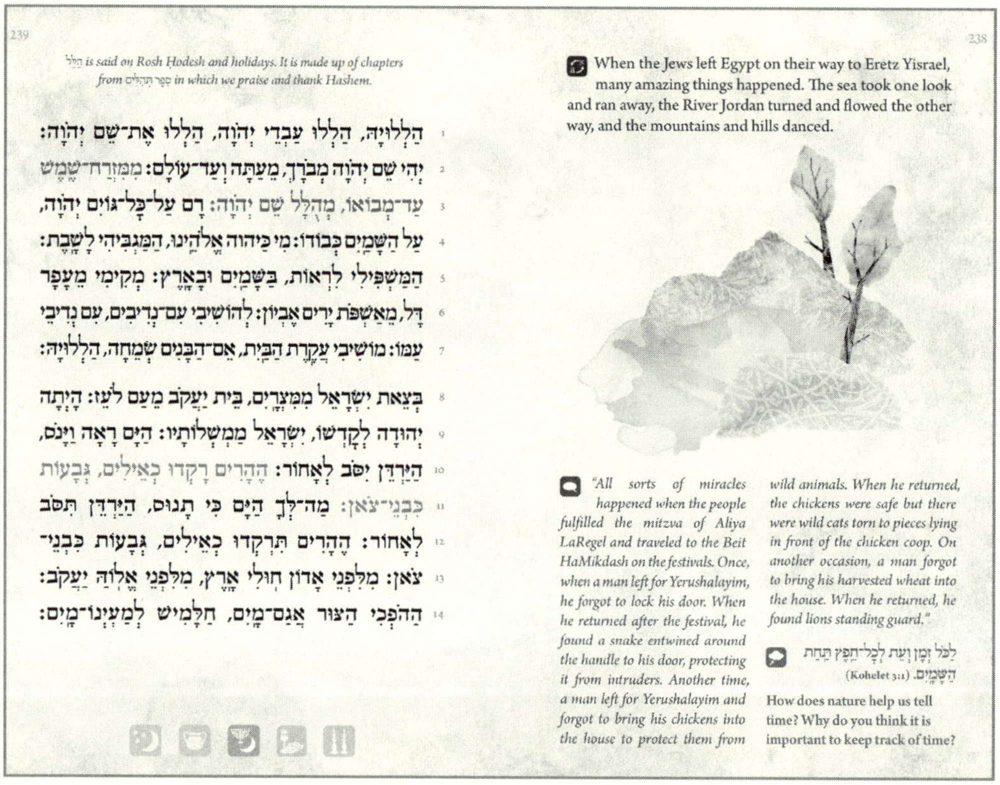
239

הלל is said on Rosh Hodesh and holidays. It is made up of chapters from ספר תהלים in which we praise and thank Hashem.

הללויה, הללו עבדי יהוה, הללו את־שם יהוה: יהי שם יהוה מברך, מעתה ועד־עולם: ממזרח־שמש עד־מבואו, מהלל שם יהוה: רם על־כל־גוים יהוה, על השמים כבודו: מי כיהוה אלהינו, המגביהי לשבת: המשפילי לראות, בשמים ובארץ: מקימי מעפר דל, מאשפת ירים אביון: להושיבי עם־נדיבים, עם נדיבי עמו: מושיבי עקרת הבית, אם־הבנים שמחה, הללויה:

בצאת ישראל ממצרים, בית יעקב מעם לעז: היתה יהודה לקדשו, ישראל ממשלותיו: הים ראה וינס, הירדן יסב לאחור: ההרים רקדו כאילים, גבעות כבני־צאן: מה־לך הים כי תנוס, הירדן תסב לאחור: ההרים תרקדו כאילים, גבעות כבני־צאן: מלפני אדון חולי ארץ, מלפני אלוה יעקב: ההפכי הצור אגם־מים, חלמיש למעינו־מים:

238

When the Jews left Egypt on their way to Eretz Yisrael, many amazing things happened. The sea took one look and ran away, the River Jordan turned and flowed the other way, and the mountains and hills danced.

"All sorts of miracles happened when the people fulfilled the mitzva of Aliya LaRegel and traveled to the Beit HaMikdash on the festivals. Once, when a man left for Yerushalayim, he forgot to lock his door. When he returned after the festival, he found a snake entwined around the handle to his door, protecting it from intruders. Another time, a man left for Yerushalayim and forgot to bring his chickens into the house to protect them from wild animals. When he returned, the chickens were safe but there were wild cats torn to pieces lying in front of the chicken coop. On another occasion, a man forgot to bring his harvested wheat into the house. When he returned, he found lions standing guard."

לכל זמן ועת לכל־חפץ תחת השמים. (Kohelet 3:1)

How does nature help us tell time? Why do you think it is important to keep track of time?

The *Tefilla* Text

Translation:

Halleluya! Servants of the Lord, give praise; praise the name of the Lord. Blessed be the name of the Lord now and for evermore. From the rising of the sun to its setting, may the Lord's name be praised. High is the Lord above all nations; His glory is above the heavens. Who is like the Lord our God, who sits enthroned so high, yet turns so low to see the heavens and the earth? He raises the poor from the dust and the needy from the refuse heap, giving them a place alongside princes, the princes of His people. He makes the woman in a childless house a happy mother of children. Halleluya!

When Israel came out of Egypt, the house of Jacob from a people of foreign tongue, Judah became His sanctuary, Israel His dominion. The sea saw and fled; the Jordan turned back. The mountains skipped like rams, the hills like lambs. Why was it, sea, that you fled? Jordan, why did you turn back? Why, mountains, did you skip like rams, and you, hills, like lambs? It was at the presence of the Lord, Creator of the earth, at the presence of the God of Jacob, who turned the rock into a pool of water, flint into a flowing spring.

Highlighted Text:
The verses ממזרח-שמש עד-מבואו מהֻלָּל, שם ה׳ and הֶהָרִים, תרקדו כאילים; גבָעות, כבני-צאן are highlighted in colors from the illustration.

Educational Themes contained in the text:

- Sunrise/set (daily cycle of time)
- God of history (involved in the world)
- The joy of childbirth/child rearing
- *Yetziat Mitzrayim*
- Natural miracles (first paragraph) vs. supernatural miracles (second paragraph)
- Images from *betzet Yisrael* (splitting of Reed Sea/Jordan; skipping mountains; water from the rock)
- Nature itself trembles at the power of God

The Illustration

In *Hallel* in general we are giving testimony and paying homage to Hashem as master of nature and human history. In the first paragraph on this page God acts through nature, but in the second paragraph we find God changing nature in order to perform supernatural miracles to influence human history. The illustration presents the images of some of these miracles, with a body of water, and mountains and hills. However, it is unclear from the illustration whether they are obeying the laws of nature or not. The message in this is twofold. Firstly, even when nature operates according to its laws, it is no less miraculous or divine, and still reason enough to say *Hallel*. Secondly, theories can be put forward to explain the supernatural miracles from Jewish history in natural scientific ways (such as explaining the splitting of the Yam Suf by mans of a tsunami or earthquake of some sort). This does not minimize their miraculous nature, and in fact it may inspire us further to see the way God manipulates nature in order to influence history.

The *Kavanot*

Conceptual Translation of:

בצאת ישְׂרָאל, ממצרָים; בית יעֲקב, מעם לעז.
היָם רָאָה, וינָס; הירדן, יסב לאָחור.
ההָרים, רָקדו כאילים; גבָעות, כבני-צאן.

Story:
This colorful story describes miracles that took place to encourage people to feel safe to travel to Yerushalayim to fulfill the mitzva of *Aliya LaRegel* on *Ḥagim*. *Hallel* is said on *Ḥagim*, and also describes miracles, both natural and supernatural, here on this page.

Thought Question:
This quote from Kohelet presents time in its widest sense, while the time-keeping from the daily solar cycle depicted in the chapter of Tehillim on our page is time in its more micro-sense. The Jewish calendar and the festivals therein also help give our lives a rhythm of time and perspective on life. There is comfort knowing that at the end of a difficult day there will be a new dawn and a fresh start just around the corner, just as there is comfort in the cycle of the seasons, knowing that even in the depths of winter the spring awaits us with a rebirth. Similarly, the annual rhythm of the Jewish calendar, with its focus on God's role in history, also gives us comfort and faith.

Activity ideas:

- Build a sundial with your class
- Artwork project expressing the themes of each season
- Time games – such as get your class to estimate a minute without looking at the clock/watch. Closest to it gets a prize (or points).
- Find time-lapse videos on YouTube for daily or yearly cycles

הלל 2

pp. 240–241

241

יהוה זְכָרָנוּ יְבָרֵךְ, יְבָרֵךְ אֶת־בֵּית יִשְׂרָאֵל, יְבָרֵךְ אֶת־בֵּית אַהֲרֹן: יְבָרֵךְ יִרְאֵי יְהוָה, הַקְּטַנִּים עִם־הַגְּדֹלִים: יֹסֵף יְהוָה עֲלֵיכֶם, עֲלֵיכֶם וְעַל־בְּנֵיכֶם: בְּרוּכִים אַתֶּם לַיהוָה, עֹשֵׂה שָׁמַיִם וָאָרֶץ: הַשָּׁמַיִם שָׁמַיִם לַיהוָה, וְהָאָרֶץ נָתַן לִבְנֵי־אָדָם: לֹא הַמֵּתִים יְהַלְלוּ־יָהּ, וְלֹא כָּל יֹרְדֵי דוּמָה: וַאֲנַחְנוּ נְבָרֵךְ יָהּ, מֵעַתָּה וְעַד־עוֹלָם, הַלְלוּיָהּ:

מָה־אָשִׁיב לַיהוָה, כָּל־תַּגְמוּלוֹהִי עָלָי: כּוֹס יְשׁוּעוֹת אֶשָּׂא, וּבְשֵׁם יְהוָה אֶקְרָא: נְדָרַי לַיהוָה אֲשַׁלֵּם, נֶגְדָה־נָּא לְכָל־עַמּוֹ: יָקָר בְּעֵינֵי יְהוָה, הַמָּוְתָה לַחֲסִידָיו: אָנָּה יְהוָה כִּי־אֲנִי עַבְדֶּךָ, אֲנִי־עַבְדְּךָ בֶּן־אֲמָתֶךָ, פִּתַּחְתָּ לְמוֹסֵרָי: לְךָ־אֶזְבַּח זֶבַח תּוֹדָה, וּבְשֵׁם יְהוָה אֶקְרָא: נְדָרַי לַיהוָה אֲשַׁלֵּם, נֶגְדָה־נָּא לְכָל־עַמּוֹ: בְּחַצְרוֹת בֵּית יְהוָה, בְּתוֹכֵכִי יְרוּשָׁלָםִ, הַלְלוּיָהּ:

הַלְלוּ אֶת־יְהוָה כָּל־גּוֹיִם, שַׁבְּחוּהוּ כָּל־הָאֻמִּים:
כִּי גָבַר עָלֵינוּ חַסְדּוֹ, וֶאֱמֶת־יְהוָה לְעוֹלָם
הַלְלוּיָהּ:

240

Hashem remembers us and will bless us. The heavens are Hashem's but He gave the earth to humans. We will bless Hashem, now and forever. Halleluya!

Once a small mouse accidently woke a mighty lion who was dozing in the sunshine. Just as the lion was about to eat him the mouse pleaded, "Please don't! One day I might be of help to you." The lion laughed until he almost cried. "What could you possibly help me with?" he sniggered. But he admired the mouse's bravery and let him go. Not long afterwards, the lion became caught in a hunters trap. He struggled to free himself but the ropes were too strong. As he roared loudly in frustration the mouse came running and called out, "Don't worry, I can set you free!" He gnawed through the ropes and the lion went free. As the lion thanked him he said to him, "Who would have thought that someone as tiny as a mouse could save a mighty lion!"

"Hashem said to Adam: 'Look at My beautiful world. Everything I have created I have created for you. But be careful not to spoil and destroy My world. If you do, no one will fix it.'"

How can we care for the world that Hashem created for us?

What will you do today to care for your world?

The *Tefilla* Text

Translation:

The Lord remembers us and will bless us. He will bless the house of Israel. He will bless the house of Aaron. He will bless those who fear the Lord, small and great alike. May the Lord give you increase: you and your children. May you be blessed by the Lord, Maker of heaven and earth. The heavens are the Lord's, but the earth He has given over to mankind. It is not the dead who praise the Lord, nor those who go down to the silent grave. But we will bless the Lord, now and for ever. Halleluya!

How can I repay the Lord for all His goodness to me? I will lift the cup of salvation and call on the name of the Lord. I will fulfill my vows to the Lord in the presence of all His people. Grievous in the Lord's sight is the death of His devoted ones. Truly, Lord, I am Your servant; I am Your servant, the son of Your maidservant. You set me free from my chains. To You I shall bring a thanksgiving-offering and call on the Lord by name. I will fulfill my vows to the Lord in the presence of all His people, in the courts of the House of the Lord, in your midst, Jerusalem. Halleluya.

Praise the Lord, all nations; acclaim Him, all you peoples; for His loving-kindness to us is strong, and the Lord's faithfulness is everlasting. Halleluya.

Highlighted Text:
The following verses are highlighted in the color of the story:

יְבָרֵךְ, יִרְאֵי ה׳ הַקְּטַנִּים, עִם-הַגְּדֹלִים.
יֹסֵף ה׳ עֲלֵיכֶם; עֲלֵיכֶם, וְעַל בְּנֵיכֶם.

The following verse is highlighted in the color of the thought question:

הַשָּׁמַיִם שָׁמַיִם, לַה׳; וְהָאָרֶץ, נָתַן לִבְנֵי-אָדָם.

Educational Themes contained in the text:

- Partnership between us and Hashem (השמים שמים לה׳ והארץ נתן לבני אדם)
- Hashem cares for the small and great alike (הקטנים עם הגדולים)
- He gave the earth to mankind to look after – environmental ethics
- How can I thank Hashem for everything I have? I cannot – an impossible task
- Cup of salvation (wine libation, or wine drunk at a *mesibat hodaya*)
- Yerushalayim
- *Beit HaMikdash*
- All the nations of the world coming together to praise Hashem

The Illustration

The illustration is a visual depiction of the story found below it, and explained below here. The story and illustration were inspired by the verse יְבָרֵךְ, יראי ה׳ הקטנים, עם-הגדלים, and the message implied there – Hashem connects to great and small alike, each one equal in His eyes as His creations.

The *Kavanot*

Conceptual Translation of:

ה׳, זְכָרָנוּ יְבָרֵךְ:
יְבָרֵךְ, אֶת-בֵּית יִשְׂרָאֵל יְבָרֵךְ, אֶת-בֵּית אַהֲרֹן.
הַשָּׁמַיִם שָׁמַיִם, לַה׳; וְהָאָרֶץ, נָתַן לִבְנֵי-אָדָם.
וַאֲנַחְנוּ, נְבָרֵךְ יָהּ מֵעַתָּה וְעַד-עוֹלָם הַלְלוּ-יָהּ.

Story:
This well-known story from Aesop's Fables is anchored to the verse יְבָרֵךְ, יראי ה׳ הקטנים, עם-הגדלים, declaring that small and large alike will praise Hashem, relate to Hashem, and connect to Hashem. Because Hashem doesn't value His creations based on external appearances or stature, so these things never present a barrier to relationship with Hashem. The story explores this equality between creatures of different sizes, and encourages us not to judge value and worth based on these criteria, just as God does not. The lion cannot imagine a situation where he will need the mouse, and rely on the mouse for his own safety, but that time comes, and the lesson is learned.

Thought Question:
The verse הַשָּׁמַיִם שָׁמַיִם, לַה׳; וְהָאָרֶץ, נָתַן לִבְנֵי-אָדָם suggests that Hashem gives over the world He created to us His creations, to do with it whatever we wish. He has dominion of the heavens and we have dominion over the earth. However, this is not without limitations and responsibility, and this midrash, from *Kohelet Raba* (7:13), clarifies this. The world is here for us to use, but only responsibly and ethically. The follow-up thought questions make this concept real and personal for the child, asking them to consider what they can do to look after the world, and not in an abstract sense, but in a practical way, this very day.

Activity ideas:
Organize your class to create a school-wide environmental awareness project, such as recycling in the school, or a compost heap, or community garden.

הלל 3

pp. 242–243

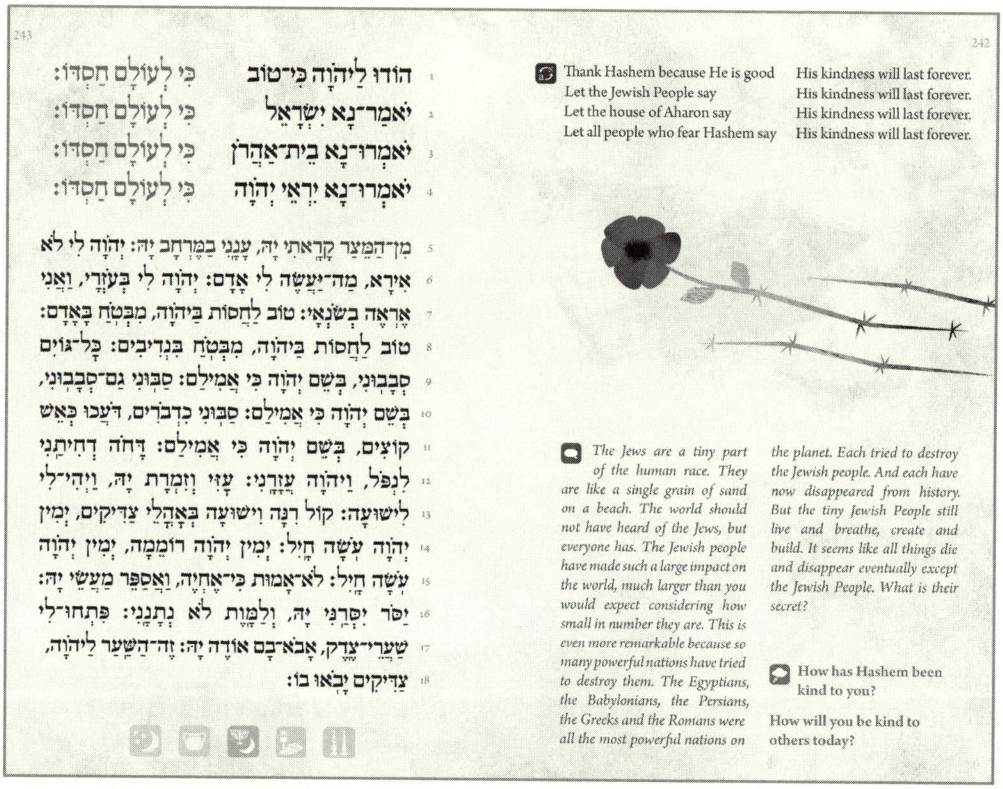

242

Thank Hashem because He is good — His kindness will last forever.
Let the Jewish People say — His kindness will last forever.
Let the house of Aharon say — His kindness will last forever.
Let all people who fear Hashem say — His kindness will last forever.

The Jews are a tiny part of the human race. They are like a single grain of sand on a beach. The world should not have heard of the Jews, but everyone has. The Jewish people have made such a large impact on the world, much larger than you would expect considering how small in number they are. This is even more remarkable because so many powerful nations have tried to destroy them. The Egyptians, the Babylonians, the Persians, the Greeks and the Romans were all the most powerful nations on the planet. Each tried to destroy the Jewish people. And each have now disappeared from history. But the tiny Jewish People still live and breathe, create and build. It seems like all things die and disappear eventually except the Jewish People. What is their secret?

How has Hashem been kind to you?

How will you be kind to others today?

243

1 הוֹדוּ לַיהוָה כִּי־טוֹב — כִּי לְעוֹלָם חַסְדּוֹ:
2 יֹאמַר־נָא יִשְׂרָאֵל — כִּי לְעוֹלָם חַסְדּוֹ:
3 יֹאמְרוּ־נָא בֵית־אַהֲרֹן — כִּי לְעוֹלָם חַסְדּוֹ:
4 יֹאמְרוּ־נָא יִרְאֵי יְהוָה — כִּי לְעוֹלָם חַסְדּוֹ:

5 מִן־הַמֵּצַר קָרָאתִי יָּהּ, עָנָנִי בַמֶּרְחָב יָהּ: יְהוָה לִי לֹא
6 אִירָא, מַה־יַּעֲשֶׂה לִי אָדָם: יְהוָה לִי בְּעֹזְרָי, וַאֲנִי
7 אֶרְאֶה בְשֹׂנְאָי: טוֹב לַחֲסוֹת בַּיהוָה, מִבְּטֹחַ בָּאָדָם:
8 טוֹב לַחֲסוֹת בַּיהוָה, מִבְּטֹחַ בִּנְדִיבִים: כָּל־גּוֹיִם
9 סְבָבוּנִי, בְּשֵׁם יְהוָה כִּי אֲמִילַם: סַבּוּנִי גַם־סְבָבוּנִי,
10 בְּשֵׁם יְהוָה כִּי אֲמִילַם: סַבּוּנִי כִדְבֹרִים, דֹּעֲכוּ כְּאֵשׁ
11 קוֹצִים, בְּשֵׁם יְהוָה כִּי אֲמִילַם: דַּחֹה דְחִיתַנִי
12 לִנְפֹּל, וַיהוָה עֲזָרָנִי: עָזִּי וְזִמְרָת יָהּ, וַיְהִי־לִי
13 לִישׁוּעָה: קוֹל רִנָּה וִישׁוּעָה בְּאָהֳלֵי צַדִּיקִים, יְמִין
14 יְהוָה עֹשָׂה חָיִל: יְמִין יְהוָה רוֹמֵמָה, יְמִין יְהוָה
15 עֹשָׂה חָיִל: לֹא־אָמוּת כִּי־אֶחְיֶה, וַאֲסַפֵּר מַעֲשֵׂי יָהּ:
16 יַסֹּר יִסְּרַנִּי יָּהּ, וְלַמָּוֶת לֹא נְתָנָנִי: פִּתְחוּ־לִי
17 שַׁעֲרֵי־צֶדֶק, אָבֹא־בָם אוֹדֶה יָהּ: זֶה־הַשַּׁעַר לַיהוָה,
18 צַדִּיקִים יָבֹאוּ בוֹ:

The *Tefilla* Text

Translation:

Thank the Lord for He is good, His loving-kindness is for ever.
Let Israel say His loving-kindness is for ever.
Let the house of Aaron say His loving-kindness is for ever.
Let those who fear the Lord say His loving-kindness is for ever.

In my distress I called on the Lord. The Lord answered me and set me free. The Lord is with me; I will not be afraid. What can man do to me? The Lord is with me. He is my Helper. I will see the downfall of my enemies. It is better to take refuge in the Lord than to trust in man. It is better to take refuge in the Lord than to trust in princes. The nations all surrounded me, but in the Lord's name I drove them off. They surrounded me on every side, but in the Lord's name I drove them off. They surrounded me like bees, they attacked me as fire attacks brushwood, but in the Lord's name I drove them off. They thrust so hard against me, I nearly fell, but the Lord came to my help. The Lord is my strength and my song; He has become my salvation. Sounds of song and salvation resound in the tents of the righteous: "The Lord's right hand has done mighty deeds. The Lord's right hand is lifted high. The Lord's right hand has done mighty deeds." I will not die but live, and tell what the Lord has done. The Lord has chastened me severely, but He has not given me over to death. Open for me the gates of righteousness that I may enter them and thank the Lord. This is the gateway to the Lord; through it, the righteous shall enter.

Highlighted Text:
The words כי לעולם חסדו, each time they appear, are highlighted in the color of the thought question.

The verse מִן-המצר, קָרָאתִי יָּהּ; עָנָנִי במרחב יָהּ is highlighted in the color of the anemone in the illustration.

Educational Themes contained in the text:

- *Hodu* = *Yehuda* = *Yehudi* = the definition of a Jew is one who thanks Hashem
- Four groups here:
- Mankind
- Israel
- *Levi'im*
- Those closest to Hashem
- Calling out to Hashem in times of distress – national distress in Jewish history
- Better to trust in Hashem than in man

The Illustration

The verse highlighted in the color of the anemone in the illustration is מִן-המצר, קָרָאתִי יָּהּ; עָנָנִי במרחב יָהּ, which Rabbi Sacks has translated: *"In my distress I called on the Lord. The Lord answered me and set me free."* However, the word המצר, translated as distress, more literally means straits or narrow place – a location, either geographic or conceptual, of pressure and stress. And the word מרחָב, translated as freedom, more literally means expanse or wideness – a location, either geographic or conceptual, of freedom and comfort. This verse could be an emotive description of twentieth-century Jewish history. From the darkest hour of Jewish history, the straits and narrowest of places, the Shoah, God's people called out to Him. And He answered from the plains and expanses of Eretz Yisrael, and created a safe-haven and refuge for them in their ancient homeland. The illustration poignantly captures this with the anemone (*kalanit* in Hebrew, Israel's national flower) growing from the barbed wire of the concentration camps. In what seemed to be an impossible feat – the growth of beauty and salvation from darkness and destruction (just as the sprouting of a flower from barbed wire seems impossible) – the State of Israel was born just three years following the end of the Second World War. When considered together with the excerpt from Mark Twain's essay on the Jews, found below the illustration, it is clear that this is the overarching narrative of Jewish history. For this we thank God, and from it find deep faith and inspiration.

The *Kavanot*

Conceptual Translation of:

הודו לה׳ כי-טוב: כי לעולם חסדו.
יאמר-נָא ישׂראל: כי לעולם חסדו.
יאמרו-נָא בית-אהרן: כי לעולם חסדו.
יאמרו-נָא יראי ה׳: כי לעולם חסדו.

Story:
This is an adaptation of the famous "Concerning the Jews" by Mark Twain. In it, Twain beautifully describes the themes of Jewish history – all the most powerful empires in world history have tried to destroy the Jews, a tiny and insignificant people. Not only did they fail, and the Jews continue to exist, but we have thrived and contributed to the world in a profoundly disproportionate way to our tiny number. This piece complements the illustration, and is also linked to the verse מִן-המצר, קָרָאתִי יָּהּ; עָנָנִי במרחב יָהּ – despite the trying times in our history, God has answered us, and brought us

to a time that is broad and not narrow, safe and secure, so that we can thrive and prosper.

The original text of the Twain excerpt is as follows:

> If the statistics are right, the Jews constitute but one per cent of the human race. It suggests a nebulous dim puff of star-dust lost in the blaze of the Milky Way. Properly the Jew ought hardly to be heard of; but he is heard of, has always been heard of. He is as prominent on the planet as any other people, and his commercial importance is extravagantly out of proportion to the smallness of his bulk. His contributions to the worlds list of great names in literature, science, art, music, finance, medicine and abstruse learning are also way out of proportion to the weakness of his numbers.
>
> He has made a marvelous fight in the world, in all the ages; and has done it with his hands tied behind him. He could be vain of himself, and be excused for it. The Egyptian, the Babylonian, and the Persian arose, filled the planet with sound and splendor, then faded to dream-stuff and passed away; the Greek and Roman followed, and made a vast noise, and they are gone; other peoples have sprung up and held their torch high for a time, but it burned out, and they sit in twilight now, or have vanished.
>
> The Jew saw them all, beat them all, and is now what he always was, exhibiting no decadence, no infirmities of age, no weakening of his parts, no slowing of his energies, no dulling of his alert and aggressive mind. All things are mortal but the Jew; all other forces pass, but he remains. What is the secret of his immortality?[57]

Thought Questions:
These thought questions reflect on the verses in *Hallel* that thank Hashem for His kindness to us. The questions refuse to allow this to be glossed over or taken for granted, and encourage us to explore what this might mean in a real and practical way in our lives. It asks the child to think carefully where in their life they have experienced God's kindness. The second question pushes the child to grow from that awareness, and become a better person for it. Learning from the kindness received from Hashem, the questions ask them to consider when they will be kind today, showing Hashem that they try to emulate Him, and that they deserve His kindness.

Activity ideas:
Form a roaming band of *Ḥesed* Agents – roam the school campus looking for acts of kindness to do (possibly arrange opportunities ahead of time).

57. Mark Twain, "Concerning The Jews," Harper's Magazine, March, 1898.

הלל 4

pp. 244–245

245

1 אוֹדְךָ כִּי עֲנִיתָנִי, וַתְּהִי־לִי לִישׁוּעָה:

2 אוֹדְךָ כִּי עֲנִיתָנִי, וַתְּהִי־לִי לִישׁוּעָה:

3 אֶבֶן מָאֲסוּ הַבּוֹנִים, הָיְתָה לְרֹאשׁ פִּנָּה:

4 אֶבֶן מָאֲסוּ הַבּוֹנִים, הָיְתָה לְרֹאשׁ פִּנָּה:

5 מֵאֵת יְהֹוָה הָיְתָה זֹּאת, הִיא נִפְלָאת בְּעֵינֵינוּ:

6 מֵאֵת יְהֹוָה הָיְתָה זֹּאת, הִיא נִפְלָאת בְּעֵינֵינוּ:

7 זֶה־הַיּוֹם עָשָׂה יְהֹוָה, נָגִילָה וְנִשְׂמְחָה בוֹ:

8 זֶה־הַיּוֹם עָשָׂה יְהֹוָה, נָגִילָה וְנִשְׂמְחָה בוֹ:

9 אָנָּא יְהֹוָה הוֹשִׁיעָה נָּא:

10 אָנָּא יְהֹוָה הוֹשִׁיעָה נָּא:

11 אָנָּא יְהֹוָה הַצְלִיחָה נָּא:

12 אָנָּא יְהֹוָה הַצְלִיחָה נָּא:

244

Hashem please save us!
Hashem help us succeed!

Hashem please save us!
Hashem help us succeed!

In 1878, before there was a State of Israel, 18 young yeshiva students left Tzefat to build a farming community where they could work the land and study Torah. Although they were inexperienced farmers, they made up for that with their enthusiasm and love of Eretz Yisrael. They bought a small piece of land in the north of Israel that would later be named Rosh Pina and began to build and farm. Their first year there, they planted potatoes in the spring, but were disappointed to see that the potatoes had not grown. So they turned the soil to choose a different crop only to find the potatoes hiding beneath the soil! Many of the original settlers left because life was so hard, but with the help of new waves of Aliya, Rosh Pina grew and today almost 3,000 people live there. The name means "cornerstone." The verse says the stone that was rejected has become the cornerstone. After years of neglect, Rosh Pina was one of the first Zionist settlements and became one of the cornerstones on which the future State of Israel was built.

The *Tefilla* Text

Translation:

I will thank You, for You answered me, and became my salvation.
The stone the builders rejected has become the main cornerstone.
This is the Lord's doing. It is wondrous in our eyes.
This is the day the Lord has made. Let us rejoice and be glad in it.
Lord, please, save us. Lord, please, save us.
Lord, please, grant us success. Lord, please, grant us success.

Highlighted Text:

The verse אבן, מָאֲסוּ הבונים הָיְתָה, לראש פִּנָּה is highlighted in the color of the story.

The verse אָנָּא ה׳, הוֹשִׁיעָה נָּא; אָנָּא ה׳, הצליחָה נָא is highlighted in the color of the conceptual translation.

Educational Themes contained in the text:

- Thanks for salvation already received – seeing the salvation in our lives

- *Rosh Pina* = link to the first *aliya* settlement
- The stone rejected (by the world) = the Jewish people, rejected by the world, is Hashem's cornerstone for His plans in the world

- Or the stone rejected is David, misunderstood by his family, later to become the cornerstone of Jewish sovereignty – from shepherd to king
- Or the stone rejected is Eretz Yisrael, neglected for 2000 years, which then became the cornerstone of the third Jewish Commonwealth
- *Hoshea* is help from Hashem. *Hatzlaḥa* is our achievements. We ask Hashem for help helping ourselves.

The Illustration

In this illustration we have two residents from Rosh Pina, celebrating and singing *Hallel* to Hashem (with joyous music and song) for the first crops produced there. The story of Rosh Pina is found on the page of the siddur, and its connection to the verse אבן, מָאֲסו הבונים הָיתָה, לראש פִּנָּה is found below. A successful crop is always a source of immense joy and gratitude to Hashem, in any year and in any place, and the illustration on the following page is another resident of Rosh Pina bringing the first fruits – the *Bikkurim* – in gratitude to Hashem. But the joy from the very first successful produce from the new settlement, one that proved initially tremendously challenging to farm, is proof that the settler's hopes and dreams are being fulfilled, and is without compare.

The *Kavanot*

Conceptual Translation of:

אָנָּא ה׳, הושיעָה נָּא; אָנָּא ה׳, הצליחָה נָּא

Story:

The verse אבן, מָאֲסו הבונים הָיתָה, לראש פִּנָּה, speaks of a stone that was rejected by the builders, but ultimately became the cornerstone of a great building project. The story of Rosh Pina (the meaning of which is "cornerstone"), one of the first modern-day Zionist settlements in Eretz Yisrael, is parallel to this idea. The land of Israel was barren and neglected for hundreds of years. And then, in the late nineteenth century, Jews began to return to their ancient homeland, and to farm and build and tend to the land. And ultimately Rosh Pina became one of the settlements that formed the foundation (cornerstone!) of the future State of Israel.

הלל 5

pp. 246–247

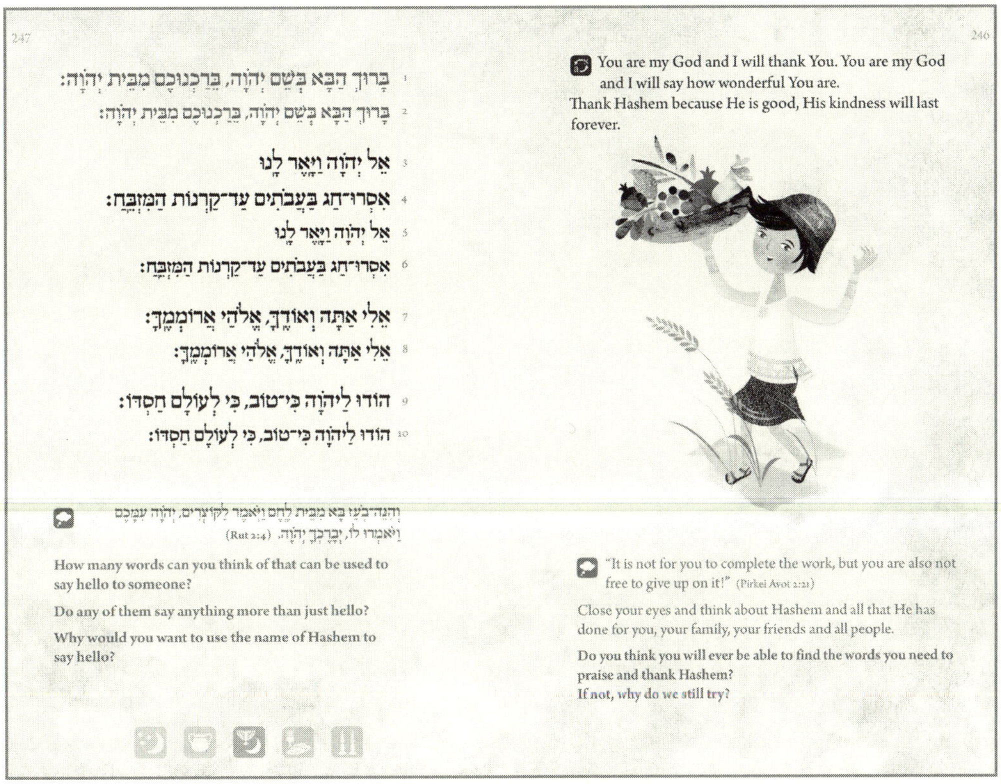
246

You are my God and I will thank You. You are my God and I will say how wonderful You are.
Thank Hashem because He is good, His kindness will last forever.

"It is not for you to complete the work, but you are also not free to give up on it!" (Pirkei Avot 2:21)

Close your eyes and think about Hashem and all that He has done for you, your family, your friends and all people.

Do you think you will ever be able to find the words you need to praise and thank Hashem?
If not, why do we still try?

247

1 בָּרוּךְ הַבָּא בְּשֵׁם יְהֹוָה, בֵּרַכְנוּכֶם מִבֵּית יְהֹוָה:
2 בָּרוּךְ הַבָּא בְּשֵׁם יְהֹוָה, בֵּרַכְנוּכֶם מִבֵּית יְהֹוָה:
3 אֵל יְהֹוָה וַיָּאֶר לָנוּ
4 אִסְרוּ־חַג בַּעֲבֹתִים עַד־קַרְנוֹת הַמִּזְבֵּחַ:
5 אֵל יְהֹוָה וַיָּאֶר לָנוּ
6 אִסְרוּ־חַג בַּעֲבֹתִים עַד־קַרְנוֹת הַמִּזְבֵּחַ:
7 אֵלִי אַתָּה וְאוֹדֶךָּ, אֱלֹהַי אֲרוֹמְמֶךָּ:
8 אֵלִי אַתָּה וְאוֹדֶךָּ, אֱלֹהַי אֲרוֹמְמֶךָּ:
9 הוֹדוּ לַיהֹוָה כִּי־טוֹב, כִּי לְעוֹלָם חַסְדּוֹ:
10 הוֹדוּ לַיהֹוָה כִּי־טוֹב, כִּי לְעוֹלָם חַסְדּוֹ:

וְהִנֵּה־בֹעַז בָּא מִבֵּית לֶחֶם וַיֹּאמֶר לַקּוֹצְרִים, יְהֹוָה עִמָּכֶם
וַיֹּאמְרוּ לוֹ, יְבָרֶכְךָ יְהֹוָה. (Rut 2:4)

How many words can you think of that can be used to say hello to someone?

Do any of them say anything more than just hello?

Why would you want to use the name of Hashem to say hello?

The *Tefilla* Text

Translation:
Blessed is one who comes in the name of the Lord; we bless you from the House of the Lord.
The Lord is God; He has given us light. Bind the festival offering with thick cords [and bring it] to the horns of the altar.
You are my God and I will thank You; You are my God, I will exalt You.
Thank the Lord for He is good, His loving-kindness is for ever.

Highlighted Text:
The verse בָּרוּךְ הַבָּא, בשם ה׳ ברכנוכם, מבית ה׳ is highlighted in the color of the thought question.

Educational Themes contained in the text:

- Showing up in the name of Hashem
- Showing up in the House of Hashem (blessing made by priests to those that come to the Temple)
- God has given us light

- *Korbanot*
- All God's creations praising/thanking (linking back to *Ashrei* and *Pesukei DeZimra*)

The Illustration

Here we have another resident of Rosh Pina joyously bringing the *Bikkurim* from the community – the first fruits that were brought to the *Beit HaMikdash* as an offering of gratitude (Devarim 26:1–11). Her platter includes each of the *Shivat HaMinim* – the seven species native to Eretz Yisrael. They are wheat, barley, grapes, olives, pomegranates, figs and dates. They represent the bountiful promise of prosperity from Eretz Yisrael. The *Bikkurim* represent for us quintessential themes for the *Hallel* section of our *tefilla*, each of which we must say praise for – the calendar and its agricultural festivals; modern Jewish history and God's role therein; Eretz Yisrael and Yerushalayim as God's gifts to us; and God's role as sustainer of life. The *Shivat HaMinim* also appear in the siddur on pages 179 and 266.

The *Kavanot*

Conceptual Translation of:

אלי אתָה ואודךָ; אלהי, אֲרוממךָ.
הודו לה׳ כי-טוב: כי לעולָם חסדו.

Thought Question 1:
Expanding on the verse at the top of this page – בָרוך הבָא, בשם ה׳ ברכנוכם, מבית ה׳ – this verse from *Megilat Rut* describes how Boaz would greet his workers in the fields by using the name of Hashem. The reflection question asks the student to consider what message one is sending if one says hello using the name of Hashem (the same question could be asked of the Modern Hebrew greeting "*shalom*"). The message you are saying when you use the name of God to greet a person is that God is always on your mind and on your lips. You are giving the person you are greeting a blessing that God should be with them, and saying so much more than just hello.

Activity ideas:
Going around the class, see how many languages (or different types of English greetings) we can find to say hello.

Thought Question 2:
The objective of *Hallel* is to praise God for all He has done in our lives, and especially for those events commemorated annually in the Jewish calendar. However, the task is immense and impossible – to sufficiently praise God for all He does for us nationally and personally. The mishna in *Avot* reassures us that despite the importance of the task, we are not responsible to complete it. But also, despite the impossible nature of the task, we are not free to give up. We must simply do our best. We try because we have to. Because we need to praise God, even if our efforts are insufficient. Our praise is not for God, but for us, to generate gratitude in us.

Activity ideas:

- Take a random object and place it in the middle of the room. Everyone takes a turn to say something praiseful about it.
- *Shevaḥ* tennis – Two opponents play back and forth saying nice things about each other. The first to hesitate or fail to think of one within five seconds, loses.
- Compliment bang-bang – Bang-bang is a game when everyone stands in a circle, and the teacher calls out the name of one student. The student must duck to avoid being shot, as the person on either side of him turns and "shoots" (with their fingers, making the sound bang-bang) the person in between. In this version, instead of shooting, they must compliment them. Whoever is out (the student whose name is called if they didn't duck in time, or the student who was second to the compliment) leaves the circle and calls the next person's name. When there are only

two players left they stand back-to-back. The teacher begins to count and on each count the students take a step away from each other, until the teacher misses a number, when they must each turn and draw their guns and compliment the other. The winner is the first to do that.

ראשי חדשים

pp. 250–251

250

1 רָאשֵׁי חֳדָשִׁים לְעַמְּךָ נָתַתָּ
2 זְמַן כַּפָּרָה לְכָל תּוֹלְדוֹתָם
3 בִּהְיוֹתָם מַקְרִיבִים לְפָנֶיךָ זִבְחֵי רָצוֹן
4 שְׂעִירֵי חַטָּאת לְכַפֵּר בַּעֲדָם.
5 זִכָּרוֹן לְכֻלָּם יִהְיֶה, תְּשׁוּעַת נַפְשָׁם מִיַּד שׂוֹנֵא.
6 מִזְבֵּחַ חָדָשׁ בְּצִיּוֹן תָּכִין
7 וְעוֹלַת רֹאשׁ חֹדֶשׁ נַעֲלֶה עָלָיו
8 וּשְׂעִירֵי עִזִּים נַעֲשֶׂה בְרָצוֹן
9 וּבַעֲבוֹדַת בֵּית הַמִּקְדָּשׁ נִשְׂמַח כֻּלָּנוּ
10 וּבְשִׁירֵי דָוִד עַבְדֶּךָ נִשְׁמַע בְּעִירֶךָ
11 הָאֲמוּרִים לִפְנֵי מִזְבְּחֶךָ.
12 אַהֲבַת עוֹלָם תָּבִיא לָהֶם
13 וּבְרִית אָבוֹת לַבָּנִים תִּזְכֹּר.

251

1 יְהִי רָצוֹן מִלְּפָנֶיךָ, יְהוָה אֱלֹהֵינוּ וֵאלֹהֵי אֲבוֹתֵינוּ
2 שֶׁתַּעֲלֵנוּ בְשִׂמְחָה לְאַרְצֵנוּ, וְתִטָּעֵנוּ בִּגְבוּלֵנוּ
3 וְשָׁם נַעֲשֶׂה לְפָנֶיךָ אֶת קָרְבְּנוֹת חוֹבוֹתֵינוּ
4 תְּמִידִים כְּסִדְרָם וּמוּסָפִים כְּהִלְכָתָם.
5 אֶת מוּסַף יוֹם רֹאשׁ הַחֹדֶשׁ הַזֶּה
6 נַעֲשֶׂה וְנַקְרִיב לְפָנֶיךָ בְּאַהֲבָה כְּמִצְוַת רְצוֹנֶךָ
7 כְּמוֹ שֶׁכָּתַבְתָּ עָלֵינוּ בְּתוֹרָתֶךָ
8 עַל יְדֵי מֹשֶׁה עַבְדֶּךָ מִפִּי כְבוֹדֶךָ
9 כָּאָמוּר
10 וּבְרָאשֵׁי חָדְשֵׁיכֶם תַּקְרִיבוּ עֹלָה לַיהוָה
11 פָּרִים בְּנֵי־בָקָר שְׁנַיִם וְאַיִל אֶחָד
12 כְּבָשִׂים בְּנֵי־שָׁנָה שִׁבְעָה, תְּמִימִם:

"When witnesses came to the court to say they had spotted the new moon, the judges had to let the Jewish communities outside of Israel know it was Rosh Ḥodesh. They lit a torch on top of the Mount of Olives in Jerusalem, and waved the torch until the Jews on the next mountain did the same, and then the Jews on a third mountain would do the same, and so on, until it looked as if the whole diaspora was one large bonfire!"

The *Tefilla* Text

Translation:

You have given New Moons to Your people as a time of atonement for all their offspring. They would bring You offerings of goodwill, and goats as sin-offerings for atonement. May it serve as a remembrance for them all, and a deliverance of their lives from the hand of the enemy. May You establish a new altar in Zion, and may we offer on it the New Moon burnt-offering, and prepare goats in favor. May we all rejoice in the Temple service, and may the songs of David Your servant, be heard in Your city, chanted before Your altar. Bestow on them everlasting love, and remember the covenant of the fathers for their children.

May it be Your will, o lord *our God and God of our fathers, to bring us up to our land with joy and to plant us within our borders, and there we will prepare for You our obligatory offerings: the regular daily offerings in their order, and the additional offerings according to their law. The additional offering of this New Moon day we will prepare and offer to You with love according to Your will's commandment, as You have written for us in Your Torah by Your own word, through Your servant Moses, as it is said:*

"On your new moons, present as a burnt-offering to the Lord, two young bulls, one ram, and seven yearling lambs without blemish."

Highlighted Text:
The words רָאשֵׁי חָדְשִׁים לְעַמְּךָ נָתַתָּ are highlighted in the color of the flames in the illustration.

Educational Themes contained in the text:

- Rosh Ḥodesh bonfires
- Renewal
- Cycles
- We fix the calendar not God!
- Atonement
- *Korbanot*

The Illustration

This *tefilla* is the *Musaf* that is said on Rosh Ḥodesh in place of the *Musaf* sacrifice that was offered on Rosh Ḥodesh. In the time of the *Beit HaMikdash*, Rosh Ḥodesh was declared by the court on the basis of testimony from two witnesses who saw the first appearance of the first sliver of the new moon. This illustration depicts the process of informing the Diaspora communities of the fixing of the new month. The story from the Gemara (*Rosh HaShana* 22b) that describes this also appears on the page.

The *Kavanot*

Story:
This story from the Gemara (*Rosh HaShana* 22b) tells of the process of fixing Rosh Ḥodesh and therefore the calendar, and of the informing of this to the Diaspora communities. This process highlights the power given to us by the halakhic system to set the calendar for ourselves. The calendar is the source of national identity, and ensures national cohesiveness and unity; the power to fix it has been placed in the hands of the people.

ומנחתם/רצה

pp. 252–253

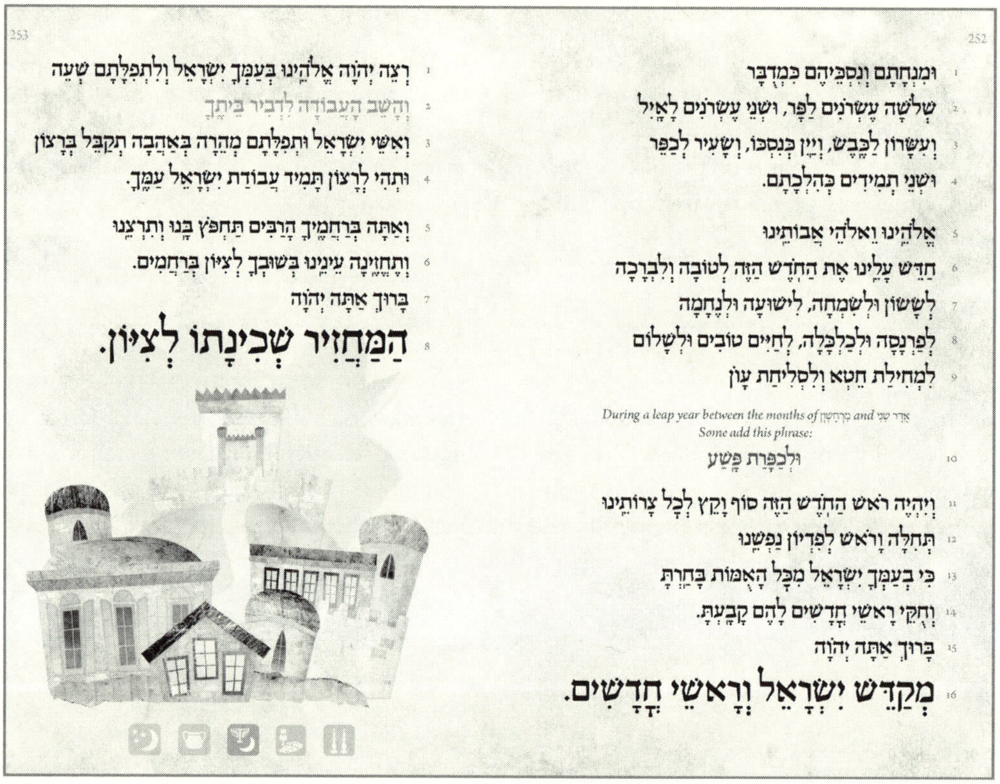
252

1 וּמִנְחָתָם וְנִסְכֵּיהֶם כִּמְדֻבָּר
2 שְׁלֹשָׁה עֶשְׂרֹנִים לַפָּר, וּשְׁנֵי עֶשְׂרֹנִים לָאָיִל
3 וְעִשָּׂרוֹן לַכֶּבֶשׂ, וְיַיִן כְּנִסְכּוֹ, וְשָׂעִיר לְכַפֵּר
4 וּשְׁנֵי תְמִידִים כְּהִלְכָתָם.

5 אֱלֹהֵינוּ וֵאלֹהֵי אֲבוֹתֵינוּ
6 חַדֵּשׁ עָלֵינוּ אֶת הַחֹדֶשׁ הַזֶּה לְטוֹבָה וְלִבְרָכָה
7 לְשָׂשׂוֹן וּלְשִׂמְחָה, לִישׁוּעָה וּלְנֶחָמָה
8 לְפַרְנָסָה וּלְכַלְכָּלָה, לְחַיִּים טוֹבִים וּלְשָׁלוֹם
9 לִמְחִילַת חֵטְא וְלִסְלִיחַת עָוֹן

During a leap year between the months of מַרְחֶשְׁוָן *and* אֲדָר שֵׁנִי
Some add this phrase:

10 וּלְכַפָּרַת פָּשַׁע

11 וִיהִי רֹאשׁ הַחֹדֶשׁ הַזֶּה סוֹף וָקֵץ לְכָל צָרוֹתֵינוּ
12 תְּחִלָּה וָרֹאשׁ לְפִדְיוֹן נַפְשֵׁנוּ
13 כִּי בְעַמְּךָ יִשְׂרָאֵל מִכָּל הָאֻמּוֹת בָּחַרְתָּ
14 וְחֻקֵּי רָאשֵׁי חֳדָשִׁים לָהֶם קָבָעְתָּ.
15 בָּרוּךְ אַתָּה יְהֹוָה
16 **מְקַדֵּשׁ יִשְׂרָאֵל וְרָאשֵׁי חֳדָשִׁים.**

253

1 רְצֵה יְהֹוָה אֱלֹהֵינוּ בְּעַמְּךָ יִשְׂרָאֵל וְלִתְפִלָּתָם שְׁעֵה
2 וְהָשֵׁב הָעֲבוֹדָה לִדְבִיר בֵּיתֶךָ
3 וְאִשֵּׁי יִשְׂרָאֵל וּתְפִלָּתָם מְהֵרָה בְּאַהֲבָה תְקַבֵּל בְּרָצוֹן
4 וּתְהִי לְרָצוֹן תָּמִיד עֲבוֹדַת יִשְׂרָאֵל עַמֶּךָ.

5 וְאַתָּה בְּרַחֲמֶיךָ הָרַבִּים תַּחְפֹּץ בָּנוּ וְתִרְצֵנוּ
6 וְתֶחֱזֶינָה עֵינֵינוּ בְּשׁוּבְךָ לְצִיּוֹן בְּרַחֲמִים.
7 בָּרוּךְ אַתָּה יְהֹוָה
8 **הַמַּחֲזִיר שְׁכִינָתוֹ לְצִיּוֹן.**

The *Tefilla* Text

Translation:

And their meal-offerings and wine-libations as ordained: three-tenths of an ephah for each bull, two-tenths of an ephah for the ram, one-tenth of an ephah for each lamb, wine for the libations, a male goat for atonement, and two regular daily offerings according to their law.

O God and God of our ancestors, renew for us the coming month for good and blessing, joy and gladness, deliverance and consolation, sustenance and support, good life and peace, pardon of sin and forgiveness of iniquity. May this New Moon day constitute the final end of all our troubles, and the start and beginning of the redemption of our souls. For You have chosen Your people Israel from all nations, and have instituted for them rules for the New Moon. Blessed are You, Lord, who sanctifies Israel and the New Moons.

Find favor, Lord our God, in Your people Israel and their prayer. Restore the service to Your most holy House, and accept in love and favor the fire-offerings of Israel and their prayer. May the service of Your people Israel always find favor with You.

And may You, with Your abundant compassion, desire us and be pleased with us. And may our eyes witness Your return to Zion in compassion. Blessed are You, Lord, who restores His Presence to Zion.

Highlighted Text:
The words והָשב את הָעֲבוֹדָה לדביר ביתְךָ are highlighted in the gold of the *Beit HaMikdash* in the illustration.

Educational Themes contained in the text:

- Meal offerings/wine libations
- *Korbanot*
- Renewal
- Cycles
- Chosen people
- Yerushalayim/*geula*
- We fix the calendar not God (He sanctifies us, then we sanctify the new moon)
- Time

The Illustration

As *Musaf* for Rosh Ḥodesh continues in our siddur, and begins to conclude with the standard final three berakhot of every *Amida*, we turn our attention to Yerushalayim and the *Beit HaMikdash*. We pray in every *Amida* that Hashem returns to Yerushalayim and reestablishes the Temple service, including the *Musaf* service on Rosh Ḥodesh. The illustration helps return our focus there, with a depiction of the *Beit HaMikdash* in all its splendor, and the houses of Yerushalayim that we have become familiar with on several pages of the siddur (for example, pages 54, 177, and 195). Note that there is a path from these houses to the *Beit HaMikdash* that sits perched upon Har Moriya at the top of the illustration. The path represents our ancient yearning and hopes and dreams to return to a rebuilt Yerushalayim. While the beautiful houses of Yerushalayim exist today in a vibrant and bustling Yerushalayim, there is no full redemption and no *Beit HaMikdash*, and so the path is still an important presence in our life – our prayers are still needed for the final redemption.

הודאה

pp. 254–255

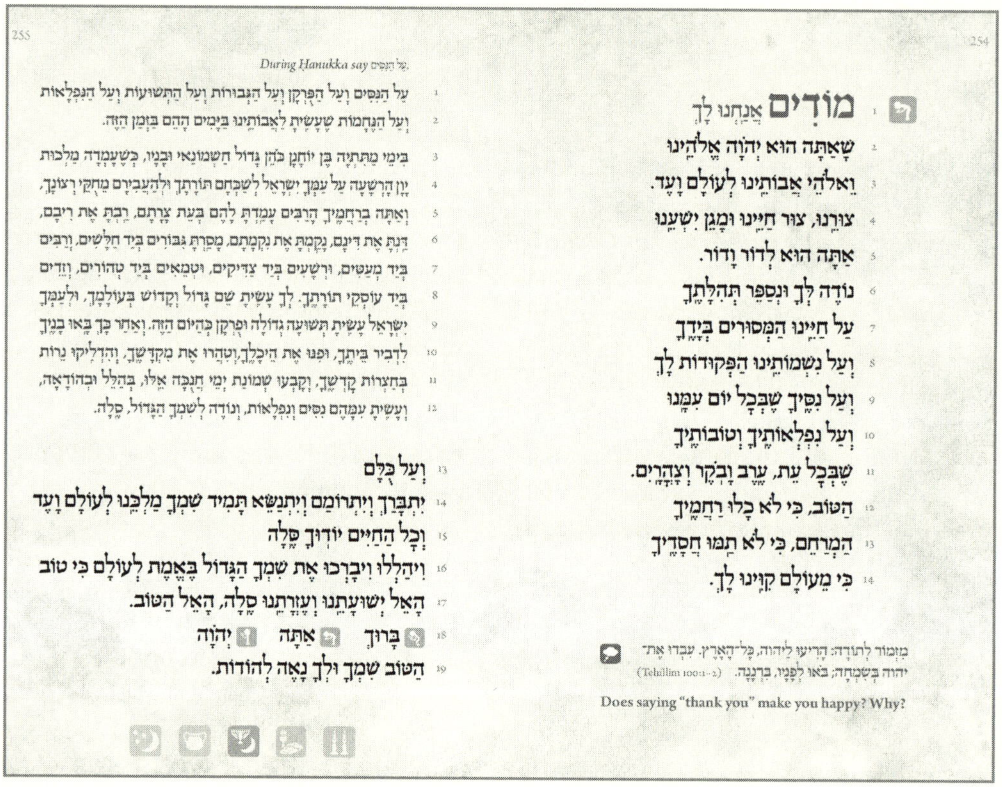

254

מודים אנחנו לך
שאתה הוא יהוה אלהינו
ואלהי אבותינו לעולם ועד.
צורנו, צור חיינו ומגן ישענו
אתה הוא לדור ודור.
נודה לך ונספר תהלתך
על חיינו המסורים בידך
ועל נשמותינו הפקודות לך
ועל נסיך שבכל יום עמנו
ועל נפלאותיך וטובותיך
שבכל עת, ערב ובקר וצהרים.
הטוב, כי לא כלו רחמיך
המרחם, כי לא תמו חסדיך
כי מעולם קוינו לך.

מזמור לתודה: הריעו ליהוה, כל־הארץ. עבדו את־
יהוה בשמחה; באו לפניו, ברננה. (Tehillim 100:1–2)

Does saying "thank you" make you happy? Why?

255

During Ḥanukka say על הנסים.

על הנסים ועל הפרקן ועל הגבורות ועל התשועות ועל הנפלאות
ועל המלחמות שעשית לאבותינו בימים ההם בזמן הזה.

בימי מתתיה בן יוחנן כהן גדול חשמונאי ובניו, כשעמדה מלכות
יון הרשעה על עמך ישראל לשכחם תורתך ולהעבירם מחקי רצונך,
ואתה ברחמיך הרבים עמדת להם בעת צרתם, רבת את ריבם,
דנת את דינם, נקמת את נקמתם, מסרת גבורים ביד חלשים, ורבים
ביד מעטים, ורשעים ביד צדיקים, וטמאים ביד טהורים, וזדים
ביד עוסקי תורתך. לך עשית שם גדול וקדוש בעולמך, ולעמך
ישראל עשית תשועה גדולה ופרקן כהיום הזה. ואחר כך באו בניך
לדביר ביתך, ופנו את היכלך, וטהרו את מקדשך, והדליקו נרות
בחצרות קדשך, וקבעו שמונת ימי חנכה אלו, בהלל ובהודאה,
ועשית עמהם נסים ונפלאות, ונודה לשמך הגדול, סלה.

ועל כלם
יתברך ויתרומם ויתנשא תמיד שמך מלכנו לעולם ועד
וכל החיים יודוך סלה
ויהללו ויברכו את שמך הגדול באמת לעולם כי טוב
האל ישועתנו ועזרתנו סלה, האל הטוב.
ברוך אתה יהוה
הטוב שמך ולך נאה להודות.

The *Tefilla* Text

Highlighted Text:
The words מודים אֲנַחְנוּ לָךְ are highlighted in the color of the thought question.

The *Kavanot*

Thought Question:
This verse from *Sefer Tehillim* is from chapter 100 and is said as part of *Pesukei DeZimra* every day. The chapter is titled a "song of thanks," and then goes on to describe service of Hashem with joy and happiness. The thought question asks the student to consider why giving thanks would lead to happiness. Perhaps giving thanks leads to gratitude and awareness of how much we have and have to be thankful for, and this can lead to joy. This thought question is placed here on the page where the *berakha* of thanksgiving is found once again.

שים שלום/אלהי נצר

pp. 256–257

256

שִׂים שָׁלוֹם טוֹבָה וּבְרָכָה
חַיִּים חֵן וָחֶסֶד, צְדָקָה וְרַחֲמִים
עָלֵינוּ וְעַל כָּל יִשְׂרָאֵל עַמֶּךָ.
וּבָרְכֵנוּ אָבִינוּ כֻּלָּנוּ כְּאֶחָד בְּאוֹר פָּנֶיךָ
כִּי בְאוֹר פָּנֶיךָ נָתַתָּ לָּנוּ יְהֹוָה אֱלֹהֵינוּ תּוֹרָה וְחַיִּים
אַהֲבָה וָחֶסֶד, צְדָקָה וְרַחֲמִים, בְּרָכָה וְשָׁלוֹם
וְטוֹב בְּעֵינֶיךָ לְבָרְכֵנוּ וּלְבָרֵךְ אֶת כָּל עַמְּךָ יִשְׂרָאֵל
בְּרֹב עֹז וְשָׁלוֹם.
בָּרוּךְ אַתָּה יְהֹוָה
הַמְבָרֵךְ אֶת עַמּוֹ יִשְׂרָאֵל בַּשָּׁלוֹם.
אָמֵן.

257

יִהְיוּ לְרָצוֹן אִמְרֵי־פִי וְהֶגְיוֹן לִבִּי לְפָנֶיךָ, יְהֹוָה צוּרִי וְגֹאֲלִי:
אֱלֹהַי
נְצֹר לְשׁוֹנִי מֵרָע וּשְׂפָתַי מִדַּבֵּר מִרְמָה
וְלִמְקַלְלַי נַפְשִׁי תִדֹּם, וְנַפְשִׁי כֶּעָפָר לַכֹּל תִּהְיֶה.
פְּתַח לִבִּי בְּתוֹרָתֶךָ, וְאַחֲרֵי מִצְוֹתֶיךָ תִּרְדֹּף נַפְשִׁי.
וְכָל הַקָּמִים עָלַי לְרָעָה
מְהֵרָה הָפֵר עֲצָתָם וְקַלְקֵל מַחְשְׁבוֹתָם.
יִהְיוּ כְּמֹץ לִפְנֵי־רוּחַ וּמַלְאַךְ יְהֹוָה דּוֹחֶה:
עֲשֵׂה לְמַעַן שְׁמֶךָ, עֲשֵׂה לְמַעַן יְמִינֶךָ
עֲשֵׂה לְמַעַן תּוֹרָתֶךָ, עֲשֵׂה לְמַעַן קְדֻשָּׁתֶךָ.
לְמַעַן יֵחָלְצוּן יְדִידֶיךָ, הוֹשִׁיעָה יְמִינְךָ וַעֲנֵנִי:
יִהְיוּ לְרָצוֹן אִמְרֵי־פִי וְהֶגְיוֹן לִבִּי לְפָנֶיךָ, יְהֹוָה צוּרִי וְגֹאֲלִי:

As you finish the עֲמִידָה you should stop and think that you have just had the opportunity and honor to stand before Hashem. To be respectful, bow as you take three steps back. Then bow to the left, right and center as the pictures show.

עֹשֶׂה שָׁלוֹם בִּמְרוֹמָיו
הוּא בְּרַחֲמָיו יַעֲשֶׂה שָׁלוֹם עָלֵינוּ
וְעַל כָּל עַמּוֹ יִשְׂרָאֵל
וְאִמְרוּ אָמֵן.

The *Tefilla* Text

Highlighted Text:
The words שָׁלוֹם are highlighted in the color of the dove from the illustration.

The Illustration

For the final time in our siddur, our old friend the *yona* visits us for this, the final *berakha* of peace in the final *Amida* in the siddur. As mentioned previously, the *yona* is traditionally seen as a symbol of peace, from its role in the story of Noaḥ and the flood. Here the *yona* is perched on a branch, with the sliver of moon appearing behind him signifying that the new month has recently begun. As we start a new month, we hope and pray it will be a peaceful one for us and the whole world. The *yona* can also be found on pages 130, 132, 169, and 209.

סוכות

pp. 262–263

263

On Sukkot there is a mitzva to take the אַרְבָּעָה מִינִים. On days other than Shabbat, hold the לוּלָב with the הֲדַסִּים and the עֲרָבוֹת in your right hand. Hold the אֶתְרוֹג upside down in your left hand, while you say the בְּרָכָה. Then turn the אֶתְרוֹג the right way up and shake the אַרְבָּעָה מִינִים.

1 בָּרוּךְ אַתָּה יְהֹוָה, אֱלֹהֵינוּ מֶלֶךְ הָעוֹלָם
2 אֲשֶׁר קִדְּשָׁנוּ בְּמִצְוֹתָיו, וְצִוָּנוּ עַל נְטִילַת לוּלָב.

Say this בְּרָכָה before shaking the אַרְבָּעָה מִינִים the first time you do this mitzva this year.

3 בָּרוּךְ אַתָּה יְהֹוָה, אֱלֹהֵינוּ מֶלֶךְ הָעוֹלָם
4 שֶׁהֶחֱיָנוּ וְקִיְּמָנוּ וְהִגִּיעָנוּ לַזְּמַן הַזֶּה.

Say this בְּרָכָה on Sukkot before you sit in the sukka for a meal.

5 בָּרוּךְ אַתָּה יְהֹוָה, אֱלֹהֵינוּ מֶלֶךְ הָעוֹלָם
6 אֲשֶׁר קִדְּשָׁנוּ בְּמִצְוֹתָיו, וְצִוָּנוּ לֵישֵׁב בַּסֻּכָּה.

262

It was the first day of Sukkot and Reb Elimelekh of Lizhensk was standing before the community with his lulav and etrog, about to begin singing Hallel, when he stopped dead, and started to sniff the air. "I can smell Gan Eden," he said, as he began to walk around the shul from person to person, sniffing at every etrog he could see. Finally he stopped in front of a poor, modest-looking man at the back of the shul. "Tell me, Reb Yid, from where did you get your etrog?" the rebbe asked. "Well, that is some story," the man replied. "The mitzva of lulav and etrog is particularly dear to me, and I save half my earnings every year just so I can buy the best etrog available. But this year, on my way to buy it, I came across a poor wagon-driver who barely earned enough money to feed his wife and children. He was weeping and so I asked him what the matter was. He explained that his horse had suddenly died, and he was desperate and didn't know what to do. So I used almost all my money to buy this poor fellow a horse, only leaving me a few rubles to buy this very plain etrog." "This is no plain etrog," Reb Elimelekh exclaimed. "With those few rubles you bought an etrog from the Garden of Eden itself."

The *Tefilla* Text

Highlighted Text:
The words על נטילת לולָב are highlighted in the color of the *lulav* from the illustration, and the words לישב בסכָה are highlighted in the color of the *sukka* that the boy is building in the illustration.

The Illustration

On this page our characters are preparing to fulfill the two mitzvot found on the page – sitting in a *sukka* and taking the *Arba'at HaMinim.* The boy is getting a bit muddled trying to remember from the previous year how the beams of wood fit together to become the *sukka* in which he and his family will sit for the duration of Sukkot. On the facing page both characters are taking their *Arba'at HaMinim* and are about to say the *berakha*. Notice how they are holding the *etrog* upside down with the *pitom* facing downwards while saying the berakha, so that they will not have fulfilled the mitzva already by the time they come to say the *berakha*. Once they have said it, they will turn the *etrog* the right way up, and follow the instructions in the siddur for waving of the *Arba'at HaMinim*.

The *Kavanot*

Story:
This beautiful Hasidic story has many appropriate themes to discuss on Sukkot. The main focus is the man who put this mitzva above all others in the year, and above his financial welfare too. He was rewarded with a special mystical *etrog* which cost little money but was very dear in value because it was earned with kindness and love. While this man placed the mitzva of taking an *etrog* above all other mitzvot and his own welfare, he put kindness to his fellow above that, and for that he was rewarded.

ברכת המזון 1

pp. 266–267

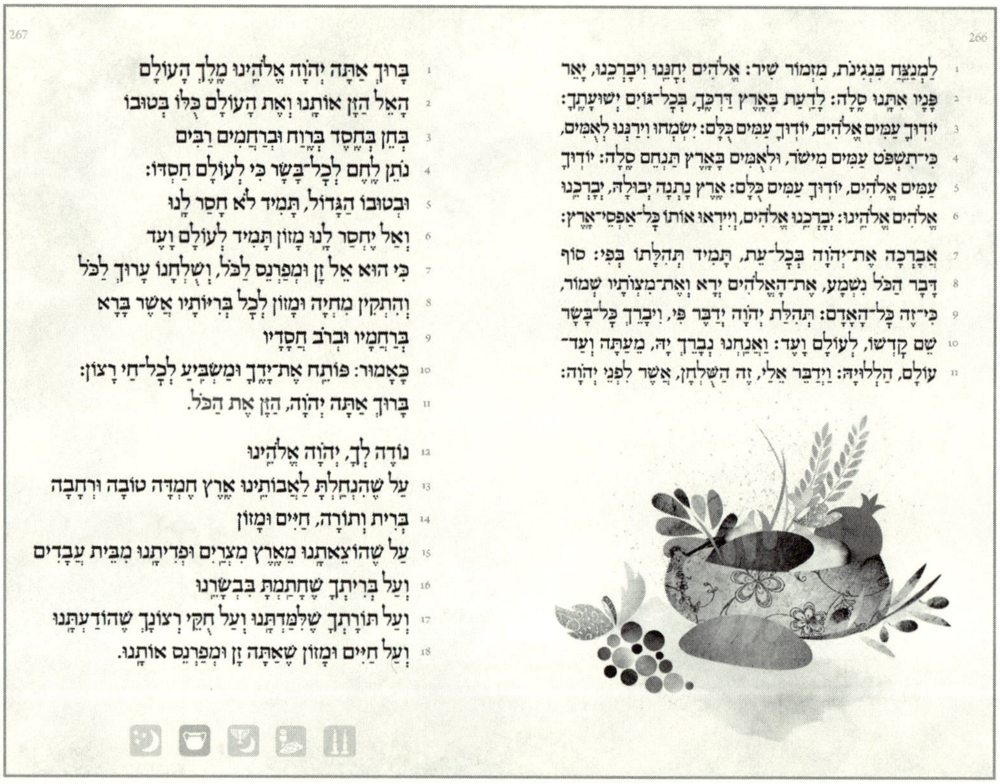

266

לַמְנַצֵּחַ בִּנְגִינֹת, מִזְמוֹר שִׁיר: אֱלֹהִים יְחָנֵּנוּ וִיבָרְכֵנוּ, יָאֵר פָּנָיו אִתָּנוּ סֶלָה: לָדַעַת בָּאָרֶץ דַּרְכֶּךָ, בְּכָל־גּוֹיִם יְשׁוּעָתֶךָ: יוֹדוּךָ עַמִּים אֱלֹהִים, יוֹדוּךָ עַמִּים כֻּלָּם: יִשְׂמְחוּ וִירַנְּנוּ לְאֻמִּים, כִּי־תִשְׁפֹּט עַמִּים מִישֹׁר, וּלְאֻמִּים בָּאָרֶץ תַּנְחֵם סֶלָה: יוֹדוּךָ עַמִּים אֱלֹהִים, יוֹדוּךָ עַמִּים כֻּלָּם: אֶרֶץ נָתְנָה יְבוּלָהּ, יְבָרְכֵנוּ אֱלֹהִים אֱלֹהֵינוּ: יְבָרְכֵנוּ אֱלֹהִים, וְיִירְאוּ אוֹתוֹ כָּל־אַפְסֵי־אָרֶץ:

אֲבָרְכָה אֶת־יְהוָה בְּכָל־עֵת, תָּמִיד תְּהִלָּתוֹ בְּפִי: סוֹף דָּבָר הַכֹּל נִשְׁמָע, אֶת־הָאֱלֹהִים יְרָא וְאֶת־מִצְוֹתָיו שְׁמוֹר, כִּי־זֶה כָּל־הָאָדָם: תְּהִלַּת יְהוָה יְדַבֶּר פִּי, וִיבָרֵךְ כָּל־בָּשָׂר שֵׁם קָדְשׁוֹ, לְעוֹלָם וָעֶד: וַאֲנַחְנוּ נְבָרֵךְ יָהּ, מֵעַתָּה וְעַד־עוֹלָם, הַלְלוּיָהּ: וַיְדַבֵּר אֵלַי, זֶה הַשֻּׁלְחָן, אֲשֶׁר לִפְנֵי יְהוָה:

267

בָּרוּךְ אַתָּה יְהוָה אֱלֹהֵינוּ מֶלֶךְ הָעוֹלָם
הָאֵל הַזָּן אוֹתָנוּ וְאֶת הָעוֹלָם כֻּלּוֹ בְּטוּבוֹ
בְּחֵן בְּחֶסֶד בְּרֶוַח וּבְרַחֲמִים רַבִּים
נֹתֵן לֶחֶם לְכָל־בָּשָׂר כִּי לְעוֹלָם חַסְדּוֹ:
וּבְטוּבוֹ הַגָּדוֹל, תָּמִיד לֹא חָסַר לָנוּ
וְאַל יֶחְסַר לָנוּ מָזוֹן תָּמִיד לְעוֹלָם וָעֶד
כִּי הוּא אֵל זָן וּמְפַרְנֵס לַכֹּל, וְשֻׁלְחָנוֹ עָרוּךְ לַכֹּל
וְהִתְקִין מִחְיָה וּמָזוֹן לְכָל בְּרִיּוֹתָיו אֲשֶׁר בָּרָא
בְּרַחֲמָיו וּבְרֹב חֲסָדָיו
כָּאָמוּר: פּוֹתֵחַ אֶת־יָדֶךָ וּמַשְׂבִּיעַ לְכָל־חַי רָצוֹן:
בָּרוּךְ אַתָּה יְהוָה, הַזָּן אֶת הַכֹּל.

נוֹדֶה לְּךָ, יְהוָה אֱלֹהֵינוּ
עַל שֶׁהִנְחַלְתָּ לַאֲבוֹתֵינוּ אֶרֶץ חֶמְדָּה טוֹבָה וּרְחָבָה
בְּרִית וְתוֹרָה, חַיִּים וּמָזוֹן
עַל שֶׁהוֹצֵאתָנוּ מֵאֶרֶץ מִצְרַיִם וּפְדִיתָנוּ מִבֵּית עֲבָדִים
וְעַל בְּרִיתְךָ שֶׁחָתַמְתָּ בִּבְשָׂרֵנוּ
וְעַל תּוֹרָתְךָ שֶׁלִּמַּדְתָּנוּ וְעַל חֻקֵּי רְצוֹנְךָ שֶׁהוֹדַעְתָּנוּ
וְעַל חַיִּים וּמָזוֹן שֶׁאַתָּה זָן וּמְפַרְנֵס אוֹתָנוּ.

The *Tefilla* Text

Highlighted Text:
The conclusion to each of the four *berakhot* of *Birkat HaMazon* are highlighted in brown.

The Illustration

Once again we have the appearance of the *Shivat HaMinim* – the seven species native to Eretz Yisrael – in this illustration. They represent God's sustaining and feeding us, and also connect us to the second and third *berakhot* of *Birkat HaMazon* which speak about Eretz Yisrael and Yerushalayim. The species are wheat, barley, grapes, olives, pomegranates, figs and dates. They also appear in the siddur on pages 179 and 246.